Doctor John Remembers

Doctor John Remembers

The Spiritual Journey and Ministry of a Christian Physician

DR. JOHN HENRY MOORE

Foreword by
MARK COPPENGER

RESOURCE *Publications* · Eugene, Oregon

DOCTOR JOHN REMEMBERS
The Spiritual Journey and Ministry of a Christian Physician

Resource Publications
An Imprint of Wipf and Stock Publishers
199 W. 8th Ave., Suite 3
Eugene, OR 97401

www.wipfandstock.com

PAPERBACK ISBN: 978-1-6667-6244-0
HARDCOVER ISBN: 978-1-6667-6245-7
EBOOK ISBN: 978-1-6667-6246-4

Table of Contents

II. FAMILY STORIES ALONG THE JOURNEY

III. FRIENDS ALONG THE JOURNEY

IV. SPIRITUAL LESSONS ALONG THE JOURNEY

Foreword

I hesitate to submit a foreword to this book since I still feel the sting of a rebuke Dr. Moore visited upon us as a team of two when I was his pastor back in 1984. I know it's been nearly four decades since that event, but a wound that deep is not easily forgotten. I grant you that I'm grateful for his willingness to be my first volunteer for weeknight, evangelistic visitation, using the SBC's Continuing Witness Training material. And, yes, we'd been blessed by the opportunities to present the gospel, whatever the response. But on this particular evening, I was frustrated. We'd been following the pattern of calling ahead to see if this was a good time for us to come by, and we'd gotten a "No" for the second or third time. Hanging up the phone, I said something dismissive, essentially writing off this lost man as a waste of our time. Then John Henry asked rhetorically, "Aren't you glad the Lord is more patient with us than we are with him?"

Ouch! Didn't he know how tough it was to be a pastor and that I was giving the task my all? The last thing I needed was some deacon judging and thus discouraging me in the midst of my noble strivings. But, of course, it was the just what I needed to hear that evening, and he had the wisdom, grace, courage and standing to provide it. And sure enough, in the weeks that followed, we found our way into that house and did, indeed, witness to the man and his wife. Alas, he was not open to our biblical presentation and invitation, but that's not the end of the story.

A year or so later, the man's wife died in a single-car accident on narrow, winding road between El Dorado and Monroe, Louisiana. Out of the blue, he called to ask if I'd do the funeral, and, of course, I said "Yes." As I recall, there were about fifty in attendance at a little church in a neighboring town. And they heard me say that the last time I saw his wife, I gave her the basics of the gospel, and I believed she'd like me to repeat it for them. So I did, thanks to the faithfulness of Dr. John Henry Moore in pressing me to be scripturally and spiritually diligent in evangelism.

Yes, the wounds of a friend are faithful (Prov 27:6), but, I'll hasten to say that the righteous hits from my friend John are outnumbered a thousand times by the pleasant and, indeed, exhilarating blessings he and Cathy have passed along to Sharon and me, beginning with those challenging and gratifying days in South Arkansas. And it is such a privilege to commend these "Dr. John" memoirs to readers.

One of my favorite passages, one I love to preach from, is Paul's "Farewell to the Ephesian Elders" (Acts 20:17–38). I go with the title, "Spiritual Heroes," and I track through Paul's account of his life and ministry, commending it to the congregants. It being Paul, the standard is high, and I preach with a heavy dose of embarrassed self-consciousness. But I don't preach it as a pipe dream, for there are laymen in those congregations who could fill the bill. Many of them I've come to know, but none, in my experience, surpasses John Henry Moore in fitting the Pauline template.

This past Christmas, Sharon and I visited an overseas family member, and the day before we left, I sent John Henry an update on the book. He got right back to me with troubling news, that he had been admitted to the hospital with "Covid pneumonia," complicated by an underlying heart condition (which he addresses in these memoirs). He observed, "I don't believe I am in danger of meeting Jesus before completion of the book, but I am looking forward to what He has for me." And in a follow-up message the same day, "[W]e are all at peace. Pray for Cathy and our family. . . And if I soon meet Him what a glorious story it will make!!"

We had another brief, email exchange the next day as he helped me with a detail in the book. (I was on a short layover in an airport along the way.) And then I heard nothing till the evening before Christmas Eve, when his daughter, Mary Kay, texted me with news of his death. So yes, John Henry is now enjoying what he was looking forward to—"what He [Jesus] has for me." And those of us who knew him understand that a good deal of what Jesus has for us has come already in the person of John Henry, who lived Christ in so many ways, to our great blessing and spiritual advantage.

Providentially, John Henry left us these memoirs, and those of us he left behind are confident that their spiritual impact will reverberate across the years, stirring, edifying, and, yes, entertaining those who knew him and loved his Savior. There's an old hymn, "Must I Go and Empty-Handed?" that pictures the plight of the person who makes it to heaven by the grace and mercy of God, but who has no "trophy" (in the form of another won to Christ through earthly witness) to lay at his feet. It concludes with the admonition, "Ere the night of death o'ertake thee, strive for souls while still you may." This book makes it clear that John Henry Moore's entry to heaven was not empty-handed. And I pray and trust that, through the ministry of this book, yet more souls will be saved, and that more soul-winners will be birthed, to the glory of God.

In one of our SBC training courses at FBC El Dorado, we were asked to consider not only how many apples were on the tree, but also how many trees were in the apple. That is to say, while it's important to consider how much fruit we might bear, we also need to consider how many fruit-bearers might come from the fruit our faithful discipleship. John Henry will surely recognize in heaven at least some of those he led to the Lord on earth, but he may well be puzzled when meeting a Brazilian, Czech, or South Arkansas saint claiming to be a debtor to his witness—not to his direct witness, but rather a debtor to a debtor to his face-to-face presentation of the gospel. Or, perhaps, to the testimony of his memoirs.

Mark Coppenger
Retired Professor of Christian Philosophy and Ethics
Southern Baptist Theological Seminary

Acknowledgements

Remembering and recounting these stories of my life has been a real joy despite taking more than ten years to complete. I'm thankful to so many who have challenged and encouraged me along the journey. My Savior, the Lord Jesus Christ, is at the heart of all I have purposed to accomplish. The day I married my beautiful wife, Cathy, was second in significance only to our salvation together in Dallas on August 6, 1977. She has been at my side for fifty-seven years to faithfully love, challenge, and encourage me, and none of this would have been possible apart from her.

Our three children, John Aaron and wife Gina, Mary Kay and husband Dave, and Ginny and husband John, along with our eight wonderful grandchildren and a great-grandchild, have been the sources of great love, joy, and delight with only a very few challenges. Each one has inspired me to write this small account of the life God has given me.

Mary Kay was the first to encourage me to begin writing these stories after she set up the blog account. Upon retiring from medical practice ten years ago, I had the time necessary to begin. Initially I began writing to leave the stories for our children and grandchildren to pass on to their families. They have heard most of them at least once, and many of them multiple times. I had no thought initially of putting them in book form.

I love stories and developed the desire to be a story-teller like my Pop. As a young man I would sit for hours and listen to him tell one story after another about his life and the people who influenced him. I heard each of his stories multiple times but never tired of hearing them. I believe he would have loved these stories just like I loved his.

When I was five years old, Pop married Athie, who became our step-mother for the next sixty years. She loved us as her own, and I cherish her sacrifice and memory. The stories she generated in our family are legendary.

My brother Berry Lee, whom I called Bubba, was much older and wiser and was always my hero. He was the greatest Christian I've ever known, and his influence on me was huge. After Cathy and I had been married twelve years, it was his challenge and persistence which led to our salvation. The impact of his life and witness has been felt in my family now down through four generations. I miss him greatly.

My sister Marilyn, who is slightly older, cared for me as a baby when our mother Lydia, who was called Mimi by her children, died unexpectedly of breast cancer. I have always looked up to her and even now ask for her advice and wisdom. She and her late husband George made many overseas mission trips with Cathy and me, and the spiritual bonds between the four of us are cherished.

Over the past year, my former pastor and beloved friend, Mark Coppenger, has encouraged me to publish these stories. He has the knowledge and expertise in writing and publishing, and he and his wife Sharon have spent countless hours on this project. Their work for me is a labor of love, and Cathy and I love them and are grateful for them on many levels.

The men who commented on the book are beloved pastors who helped shape and encourage the spiritual lives of Cathy, our children and me. The two exceptions are Dr. Smart who was a trusted medical colleague during our years in El Dorado, and Tim Huddleston, whom I met in Branson, and who has become a great and valued friend.

It is not possible in this limited space to thank the countless people whom Cathy and I love, and who have helped lead us into a closer walk with Jesus. The Lord himself will reward them with much greater praise and honor than we ever could.

Dr. John Henry Moore

I. The Spiritual Journey with Cathy

The journey with Cathy began during my medical-internship year in Atlanta in 1964, and our courtship resulted in marriage the following year. Our life together for fifty-seven years has been a continuing love story of two lives united in Christ becoming one.

1. "THEE I LOVE," PART 1

The Beginning of a Love Story Which Has Lasted and Thrived for Fifty-Seven Years

Bride and Groom, August 7, 1965

As a young man having just received his MD degree from the University of Arkansas in June, 1964 I set out for Atlanta, Georgia for my internship at Grady Memorial Hospital. I had no idea the events over the next 12 months would alter my life forever.

The University of Arkansas Medical School in Little Rock is a good school but has relatively small in patient numbers, and I was looking for a larger training facility with many more thousand patient visits annually. One of my top choices was Cook County Hospital in Chicago, but fortunately my visit there was in December. I immediately knew I couldn't tolerate the extreme winter weather conditions, so I opted for the more moderate climate of Atlanta. In a few months following my arrival in Atlanta on July 1, 1964, I would discover the wisdom of my choice.

One of my best friends throughout college and medical school was Dan Moore, and he also decided to train at Grady (the hospital known locally as "the Gradies") in Atlanta. Dan had been married for several years, and his wife Marsha got a job teaching at an elementary school in DeKalb

County. After a month or so she began telling me about "a beautiful girl with whom she taught school," trying to convince me she would be a good match. Marsha was always trying to find a date for me, so I put off pursuing her latest prospect. After about a month of prodding with no response from me, she said she was giving up on me and recommending this individual as a date for my pediatrician roommate. I reluctantly agreed to go on a double date with the Moores. When I went to her apartment door to meet her, and she identified herself as "Cathy Young," I was immediately taken by her beauty and charm. I also was amazed she had agreed to go out on a date with me! Marsha had been telling her nice things about me which probably weren't all true. Our first date in August, 1964, was to a well-known pub for young people, which I soon discovered was not to her liking. Our second date was to church! I was doing all I could to impress her. We continued dating over the next month, and I became more and more convinced Cathy was the perfect one for me. In November, 1964, I proposed marriage to her, and she accepted!

There were two major obstacles for our setting an exact wedding date. At the completion of my internship in July, 1965, I had to be accepted into a four-year surgical training program and then get a deferment for four years from active duty in the Air Force. The war in Vietnam was escalating in 1965, and the military was commissioning all doctors into service unless they were in an advanced specialty training program. Fortunately, I was accepted into the LSU Surgical program at Charity Hospital in New Orleans, and within a month I received a Berry Plan Deferment for four years. We set the wedding date for August 7, 1965, which was one month after I was to begin my surgical training in New Orleans.

Our wedding was beautiful and especially meaningful because Cathy's dad, George Young, who was a premier building contractor in Fort Lauderdale, had just completely remodeled Park Temple Methodist Church. Our wedding was the first event in this gorgeous church. I was in such a groom's state of mind I don't remember much of the actual ceremony. I do know I had the words "Thee I Love" inscribed in her wedding band, and I promised to love her unconditionally until death separated us. Our honeymoon was simply a two-day's driving trip to our new apartment in New Orleans, with a few scheduled stops along the way. On my Intern's salary of $175 per month, we didn't have any surplus cash for a more elaborate trip.

Out first home was in the Bissonet Plaza Apartments in Metairie, which was a twenty-five-minute drive from Charity Hospital. Cathy got a job teaching fifth graders in an elementary school in nearby Kenner, and her income was our primary financial source since my salary at Charity Hospital was so meager. On our one-month anniversary, Hurricane Betsy hit New Orleans, a harrowing event on which I'll write more down the way.

We had many memorable experiences from our four New Orleans years, but none surpasses the birth of our first child, John Aaron, born on July 7, 1967. At the time, we lived in a subdivision called Delmont Village on the West Bank in Algiers, and two of our neighbors and close friends were John and Jean Boyd. They were a retired couple in their sixties from upstate New York, and they became surrogate parents for us in addition to being wonderful friends.

Our next move was in 1969 when I went on active duty in the Medical Corps of the Air Force, and we were stationed at Moody Air Force Base in Valdosta, Georgia. I was the only surgeon assigned to the hospital, which gave me the freedom to set my own schedule and have an independence very close to that of a private practice physician. During those two years, the most significant event was the birth of our second child, Mary Katharine (Mary Kay) on February 10, 1970. I have written an account of her birth ("A Birthing at Moody Air Force Base Hospital"). We lived in town rather than on the Air Force base, and our neighborhood was filled with lots of kids and playmates for our children. We decided early on when we began having children that Cathy would stop teaching school and stay at home with them. The additional income I received as an Air Force major allowed us such a luxury.

While in South Georgia, we enjoyed an additional family benefit— the freedom to travel the six hours down Interstate 75 to Cathy's family home in Fort Lauderdale, Florida. It was such a blessing for all of us during those years to spend time with all of Cathy's family, including her dad and mom, her brother George, his wife Dawn, and their two children Jenifer and George. Cathy's sister Nancy and son Clay lived in central Florida, and we were able to spend some time with them also. I was fortunate to have been permanently stationed at Moody the entire two years of active duty while the Vietnam War was in full force. Many of my friends and medical colleagues were sent to the front lines to provide care for the wounded.

When I was discharged from active duty in the Air Force in August, 1971, Cathy and I made the decision to move to El Dorado, Arkansas, to establish our home. We decided I should begin my surgical practice in partnership with my brother Berry Lee, who had been a family doctor in El Dorado since 1957. I would like to say we had spent many hours in prayer trying to decide our next steps, but we were only occasional church attenders and not believers in the Lord Jesus Christ. We had spent many hours discussing the pros and cons of life in El Dorado, but prayer was not the central focus of our decision-making process at the time. It was seven years later in El Dorado when we found new life and purpose when the Lord Jesus Christ changed us.

2. A LIFE-CHANGING LETTER

Unexpected Help from a Prominent Politician Allows Us to Set a Wedding Date

OREN HARRIS
4TH DIST., ARKANSAS

HOME ADDRESS:
EL DORADO, ARKANSAS

CHAIRMAN:
COMMITTEE ON
INTERSTATE AND FOREIGN
COMMERCE

Congress of the United States
House of Representatives
Washington, D. C.

September 25, 1964

Dr. John Henry Moore
Box 25338
Grady Memorial Hospital
Atlanta, Georgia 30303

Dear John:

Thank you for your letter of September 21, advising me that you plan to continue your medical training in general surgery and asking for my assistance in obtaining a military deferment so that you may complete your training.

It is good to hear from you. I am proud of your progress and I know your father and the family must also be proud of you.

I have taken this matter up with Dr. Fish, to whom you referred in your letter, and have notified him of my interest in your application for deferment. He has advised me that you have a very good chance of being selected for deferment under the Berry Plan. If, for some reason, you are not selected under this plan he has several alternative suggestions which I will take up with you at the proper time.

If I can be of any further assistance to you on this or any other matter, please do not hesitate to let me know.

With kindest personal regards,

Sincerely yours,

OREN HARRIS, M. C.

OH:p

Oren Harris Letter

I HAVE RECEIVED A number of official letters in my professional life, but few have altered the direction of my life as much as the one I received from my congressional representative in 1964. It came in response to the only letter I have ever written to a congressman.

In 1964, I graduated from the University of Arkansas Medical School and moved to Atlanta, Georgia to begin a one-year rotating internship at Grady Memorial Hospital. A rotating internship meant I was not specializing during that year, but was to spend three months in training as a new physician in each of the four medical fields—internal medicine, pediatrics, obstetrics & gynecology, and surgery. During that eventful year, I met and began a courtship with Cathy Young of Fort Lauderdale, Florida, who was the most beautiful woman I had ever met. After dating for several months, we were both convinced that we were meant to spend a lifetime together in marriage, and we began making plans for our future. I was certain I wanted to pursue a career in general surgery, which required four additional years of surgical training. The salaries for a surgical resident in those days was very low and not enough to support a husband and wife, but Cathy was an elementary school teacher and, with our combined salaries, we were certain we could make it. The major obstacle we faced was the war raging in Vietnam. Every able-bodied physician completing his internship was immediately commissioned into active duty in one of the branches of the armed forces. I had already enlisted in the Air Force as a medical student and was certain to enter active duty as a captain following my internship.

There was an option which allowed physicians enough time to complete their training, a federal deferment called the Berry Plan. One had to apply through a federal agency in Washington and then just wait. No one knew the criteria used for that selection, and there were no contact numbers to call to determine one's status in the process. Cathy and I didn't want to marry one month and then have me ship out to Vietnam the next, so our anxieties were high. In addition, a residency program would not accept me unless I had already secured the proper deferment for the full length of their training.

I called Pop and Mom one day to let them know how Cathy and I were doing and that I had not "heard anything from Washington." Pop asked casually, "Why don't you write my friend, Congressman Oren Harris to see if he can help you? He's a pretty powerful man in Washington." I didn't know much about Congressman Harris except that he was from El Dorado and had been our representative from the Fourth Congressional District of Arkansas for many years. What I didn't know was that he was chairman of the Committee on Interstate and Foreign Commerce and was one of the best known and respected men on Capitol Hill. I immediately sat down and crafted a lengthy, hand-written letter to the congressman explaining my situation and asking for his help. Within a week I received the letter you see above, and I knew I would be hearing very soon from the proper authorities. Within just a few days, I received a telegram from the agency handling deferments stating I had been selected to receive a four-year deferment allowing me to continue my surgical training!

Cathy and I were ecstatic! Now I could apply for the LSU Surgical Program at Charity Hospital in New Orleans, and we could make definite plans for our marriage in the fall of 1965. Within a month of receiving the deferment, I was accepted into the LSU Program which was to begin on July 1, 1965. Cathy and I set the wedding date for August 7, 1965, in her home town of Fort Lauderdale. When all those plans were finalized, I wrote Congressman Harris a thank you letter telling him how grateful I was for his help and all about our future plans. Again, I received a wonderful personal letter from him, which I have also saved.

As an interesting footnote, I never had a personal meeting with Congressman Harris until 1971, when Cathy and I moved back to El Dorado and joined the First Baptist Church where Judge and Mrs. Harris were members. He had been appointed a federal district judge by President Lyndon Johnson in 1965 and took his seat on the bench in El Dorado on August 11, 1965, four days after our marriage.

In the early 1980s, I accepted a teaching position at First Baptist Church to co-teach the Men's Theater Bible Class along with Bob Watson, Bob Merkle, and Judge Harris. It was a wonderful class with a long, illustrious history dating back to the oil boom days of the 1920s, and the class had been meeting for many of those years in the Rialto Theater. I had the joy and privilege of getting to personally know Judge Harris and learning from his storehouse of wisdom. On more than one occasion, I was able to recount what a major influence he had been to Cathy and me and had shown him the letter he wrote so long before that had changed the direction of our lives. We both agreed that God is so good in leading us in the right paths, even though at the time we may not have been fully trusting in him.

3. "BERRY, GET THAT BOY A NEW PAIR OF SHOES!"

A Wedding Gift of the Most Expensive Shoes in New Orleans

Cathy and I met in 1964 in Atlanta during my internship year at Grady Memorial Hospital. This was my first employment following medical school, and, in those days, internship and residency salaries were below poverty levels. Interns at Grady were paid $175 per month, and after taxes and Social Security were deducted, I received a whopping check from the hospital for $79 every two weeks! Needless to say, I was not financially able to lavish expensive dinners and gifts on Cathy during our courtship. We usually had one nice dinner out together every two weeks, followed by lots of burgers and hot dogs on most other dinner dates, which were few. The hospital did provide free meals for me as part of my compensation package, but I don't recall taking Cathy to the hospital for a romantic hospital meal.

I proposed marriage to Cathy in the spring of 1965, and we set a wedding date for August 7, 1965, at Park Temple Methodist Church, her home church in Fort Lauderdale. We had awaited two significant events which had to occur prior to setting the wedding date. I had to get a four-year military deferment from active duty in the Air Force. The war in Vietnam was in full swing, and the Air Force was taking doctors right out of internship into the military. Then I had to secure a four-year residency assignment, which I did in the LSU Surgery Department in New Orleans. The deferment was secured and my residency was to begin on July 1, 1965. The wedding date was set, and I scheduled a one-month vacation in August after the first month of employment.

Cathy's dad, George Young, was one of the premier building contractors in South Florida, and during the early months of 1965, his company began a major renovation of Park Temple Church. We were given assurance the renovations would be completed in time for our wedding, and Cathy was especially excited our wedding would be the first major event in the renovated sanctuary. I'm confident her dad was receiving extra pressure from his wife, Virginia, to make certain the work was completed on time!

Those days of summer in 1965 were extremely busy for both Cathy and me. She was in Fort Lauderdale making all her preparations for the big event while attending wedding showers given by her family and friends. The letters and phone calls I received from her were filled with excited anticipation and joy, and I loved reading and hearing all of the details. I completed my work at Grady Hospital and packed my few belongings for the move to New Orleans.

Following the move and the month of transitional work in New Orleans, I packed my clothes into my red Corvair Monza convertible and drove to Fort Lauderdale. To say I had some pre-wedding anxiety would be a huge understatement. I knew I loved Cathy and wanted to spend the rest of my life with her, but I didn't know her family very well, and the culture of South Florida was completely foreign to this South Arkansan. I wanted to make as good an impression as possible, and I purposed to dress as nicely as I could afford. As part of my wedding wardrobe, I noticed my dress shoes, which were at least seven years old, were showing significant wear. I found a good cobbler in New Orleans and had the shoes refurbished including a half-sole. I thought they looked almost new.

My Mom and Pop were able to make the wedding trip, along with Bubba and his oldest child Lydia, who was eleven years old. My Aunt Lillie Mae accompanied Bubba and Lydia on their flight to Fort Lauderdale, and their experiences on the trip were memorable.

The wedding was beautiful and the newly finished sanctuary was stunning in its elegant detail. Cathy was by far the central figure of the wedding, and she was absolutely gorgeous! I was very nervous and prayed I would not make any blunders like falling down or fainting or doing anything which would draw attention to me or detract from Cathy. As we knelt at the altar at one point for a commitment prayer by the senior pastor of the church, I couldn't hear it but was told that my mom gasped when she saw my newly half-soled shoes. I had not thought when I had the cobbler work done that people would be looking at my shoe soles during the wedding. Besides, I had gotten the hole patched and considered this more than sufficient.

During the reception Mom asked me when I had gotten my shoes fixed, and I told her just prior to the wedding. She turned to Pop and said to him, "Berry, you need to get this boy a new pair of shoes for his wedding present." He thought that was a good idea and said when we returned to New Orleans, I should go to the Imperial Shoe Store on Canal Street to purchase a good pair and "send him the bill." I don't recall his ever making such an offer to me. He apparently had prior experiences with the Imperial Shoe Store.

When Cathy and I returned to New Orleans during our honeymoon month we discovered the Imperial Shoe Store was downtown near the beginning of Canal Street. The store had been in business for many years and was indeed the premier shoe store of New Orleans, catering to the wealthy clients of the city. When a well-dressed salesman approached us, I said something to him I had never said to any salesman before: "I would like the most expensive pair of shoes you have in the store!" His eyes brightened, and he said he assumed I wanted a pair of dress and not casual shoes. He brought me a pair of wingtip, cordovan, Johnston & Murphy shoes which were beautiful. They fit perfectly, and I purchased them without asking the price. He agreed to send Pop the bill when he discovered I was a resident physician at Charity Hospital living on poverty-level wages. It was then the salesman told me the shoes were $125 plus tax.

I wish I could have been present when Pop received the bill for the wedding gift Mom had urged him to give. To Pop's credit, he never complained about the cost of the best shoes I ever owned. I wore them regularly to church and special events for the next fifteen years, and they always looked nice and felt great!

PS: The comparable value of $125 in 1965 in today's economy is almost $950. What a wedding gift!

4. THE WEDDING GIFT WE DIDN'T WANT

Within a Month of Our Wedding, We Faced a Life-Threatening Hurricane Named Betsy

Hurricane Katrina was the deadliest and most destructive Atlantic hurricane of the 2005 hurricane season. It struck New Orleans on August 28 resulting in flooding of about 80 percent of the city and causing untold millions of dollars in damage with loss of more than eighteen hundred lives. The other major hurricane which hit New Orleans with severe destructive force was Hurricane Betsy, and this one occurred on September 9, 1965. I remember the date and the event well because Cathy and I lived through it, and it occurred one month and two days following our wedding. I began my surgical training at Charity Hospital in New Orleans on July 1, 1965, following a year of internship in Atlanta. There I had met and fallen in love with Cathy Young from Fort Lauderdale. She had come to Atlanta in the fall of 1964 to begin her elementary school teaching career and had only been there a few months before a mutual friend introduced us. Following a courtship during our one year in Atlanta we decided to join our lives together in marriage.

The war in Vietnam was raging, and I had an obligation to fulfill in the US Air Force. I had been commissioned as an officer in the medical corps during medical school, and unless I could get a four-year deferment, I could not be accepted into the surgical training program I desired. I applied for the deferment and waited four long months before getting good news from the Pentagon; then I was accepted into the surgical training program at Charity Hospital, and we set a wedding date for one month after my residency began. It was as simple as that. Or so we thought!!

Charity Hospital was a massive twenty story hospital which had been the training center for tens of thousands of doctors and nurses for nearly two hundred and fifty years. The surgical training was second to none in the country, and I was thrilled to finally begin the four-year program on the LSU Surgical Service. My residency chief allowed me to work the month of July and take my month-long vacation in August for our wedding and honeymoon. Cathy and I married on August 7, 1965 in Fort Lauderdale, where her family lived and where she grew up. Our wedding was perfect in a perfect setting, and we began our life together so full of big plans for the future.

The honeymoon was certainly not fancy, because we were living within our budget, which at best was very meager. We drove toward Arkansas where we visited my family, and then we drove around to see some sights in a state in which she had never travelled. When the month ended, we returned to New Orleans where she began her elementary teaching position in Kenner, Louisiana, a suburb of New Orleans, and I returned to my work at Charity. We lived in a beautiful new apartment near her school in Kenner, but it was a twenty-five-minute drive to the hospital.

In the first week of September, there were advanced warnings about Hurricane Betsy which had formed in the Atlantic Ocean, and it was tracking toward the Gulf coasts of Louisiana and Texas. Cathy had prior experience with hurricanes from her life in South Florida, but this was all new to me, and I was very nervous. My unrest bordered on fear when I learned I was on call at the hospital on the night of September 9, when the hurricane was to make landfall and strike New Orleans.

Cathy had made advanced preparations by filling our bathtub with water which we might need if the water supply became contaminated. She had all the windows taped to avoid flying glass, and she seemed very secure in our apartment on the second floor. As the evening progressed, I called her every hour to make sure she was safe, and she reassured me she was fine. When I called her at 8 p.m. and the winds were up to sixty miles per hour, I told her I had to be in the operating room for two hours, but I would call as soon as the surgery was over. When I did call at 10 p.m. the winds were now at eighty plus miles per hour. Cathy's voice had changed and her confidence had waned. She said the Mayor of Kenner had ordered the evacuation of low-lying areas because of the prospect of severe flooding, and she was now scared and alone. She asked, "Would you please come and get me?" and I told myself, "Live or die, I've got to go for my new bride, so no matter what happens, she won't be alone!" I told her I would be coming right away and not to worry!

When I ran out to the parking lot I could hardly stand upright because the winds were so strong. My car was a small convertible, which is the worst possible vehicle to be driving in these conditions. In fact, there was no one else in New Orleans I could see who was driving in these dreadful conditions. This was the most frightened I have ever been. Trees were being bent and snapping, power lines were falling and electric sparks were jumping across the highways. Flying debris had to be dodged as much as possible, and when I would cross an overpass, the winds would catch under the top of my convertible and literally move me over one full lane. I never stopped for any of the red lights which happened to still be working. I was not a Christian then, but I was so scared I was praying out loud.

When I finally made it to the apartment, I ran up the stairs, hugged Cathy quickly, grabbed her overnight case. As we began the trip, I told Cathy, "I'll drive but we both can pray." At least there were two of us praying out loud in the car, and I was not quite as frightened because we were now together. I know we made the return trip in record time. In all of the trips I made to Charity Hospital over the next four years, I don't recall ever seeing it as a place of personal safety and peace like it did that night in 1965 on our one-month (and two day) wedding anniversary.

5. THE WEDDING GIFT WHICH KEPT ON GIVING

An Irritant for Two Years

When Cathy and I were married fifty-six years ago in Fort Lauderdale, I was overwhelmed. I'd just completed an internship at Grady Memorial Hospital in Atlanta, was in the first month of training as a general surgeon at Charity Hospital in New Orleans, and I had met and married the most beautiful woman I had ever known, amazed she had even consented to an initial date with me. Her family was prominent and well-known in south Florida. They'd been pioneer settlers in Fort Lauderdale, and her grandfather and father had built hotels, office buildings, and homes throughout the county. My family was well-known in south Arkansas, primarily because my grandfather and father had provided medical care in the area for the previous sixth years. When our wedding was announced in the newspapers of our respective towns, the wedding gifts began pouring in. Because the volume was so high it took Cathy almost a year to respond with thank you notes. Our apartment in New Orleans was so small, we had to store many of the gifts in our parents' homes for several years. All of the gifts were beautiful, thoughtful and useful, and we loved and needed all but one. This particular gift was not on the bride's wish list, but was given none the less. It became a source a great irritation, but more about this later.

When Cathy and I began dating she had the nicest car she had purchased just before moving to Atlanta. It was a 1964 white Oldsmobile Cutlass with a red interior. She kept it spotless on the outside and clean on the inside, and it was tight and fun to drive.

The Car

I owned a 1964 Chevy Corvair Monza convertible, which was red with a white interior so we were a pretty sporty couple, at least car-wise even before we met!

For our honeymoon trip we chose Cathy's car because it was a little roomier with more luggage space, and it offered a bit more comfortable ride. I had a month's vacation from Charity Hospital, so we could take our time driving from Fort Lauderdale back to Arkansas for me to introduce my new bride to the Land of Opportunity. She had not been introduced to the majority of my family and none of my friends in El Dorado, and I was anxious for all of them to meet and know my beautiful wife. In addition to our time in El Dorado, we drove into north Arkansas for her to see the beauty of the Ozarks and see my alma mater, The University of Arkansas at Fayetteville. We had no idea then that exactly thirty-five years later we would move there.

After establishing our residence in New Orleans, we lived in two locations; an apartment in Kenner, in which we lived the first year, and a duplex apartment in Algiers on the west bank of the Mississippi, where we lived for the final three years. We kept both cars because Cathy had to drive to the two different elementary schools in which she taught, and for me, it was at least a fifteen-minute drive one-way to the hospital.

Cathy and I began noticing an irritating rattle in her Cutlass shortly after moving to New Orleans. It was not a constant noise, and we could only hear it when we hit a moderate sized bump in the road. It seemed to be coming from the passenger side, so I checked the right-side door and fenders frequently. Occasionally when we thought of it, we would ask the local Oldsmobile dealer's service department to check the tires and axles for rattles on the right side, but nothing was found. The one constant rattle occurred when we drove onto our driveway in Algiers because there was an irregular bump in the concrete there.

After nearly two years of our four-year stay in New Orleans, we took the car to a service station for an oil change, and they put it on a rack to drain the oil and check the under surface thoroughly. The technician asked, "Do you want to leave this cowbell under here?" Thinking he was telling some kind of joke, I said, "What are you talking about?" He answered, "Look here," and there it was—a cowbell attached tightly by a chain to the drive shaft. Everything suddenly came to light. Before our wedding, Cathy's brother George had said he would watch our car and make certain no pranksters would write on it or pull any tricks on us. Right! He had carefully engineered the attachment of that cowbell so it would not draw too much attention, but it would be a constant irritation like a tiny rock in your shoe. It worked for almost two years! When we called to tell him we'd finally found it, he'd almost forgotten about it and couldn't believe we had put up with it for so long. His wedding "gift" had been giving to us far more than any other gift we received—almost daily, and without any signs of deterioration. Thanks, Brother George, for your well-thought-out gift!

PS: You can read about our return gift to George in "The Visiting Doctor Has a Bad Day."

6. THE ELEVATOR OPERATOR

An Unplanned Obstacle to Our Safety from the Horrors of a Hurricane

Cathy and I endured a harrowing experience on the night Hurricane Betsy struck New Orleans. Of all the close-call experiences I had in driving for fifty-eight years, there is not one which even comes close to the forty-five-minute round trip from Charity Hospital to home and back on September 9, 1965. In a small convertible in eighty-miles-per-hour winds, I was fighting every second just to stay on the road. It was definitely not a trip for the faint-hearted.

I had no choice in making the trip. My sweet new bride Cathy was alone in our apartment and scared for her life. When I called from the hospital to check on her, she begged me to come rescue her. I had to be in the hospital that night, because I was on surgical call, and we anticipated multiple traumatic injuries from the hurricane. I told my chief resident I had to get Cathy and bring her back to the hospital for her safety, and any emergencies which came in would just have to wait for my return.

The initial leg was scary enough, because I wasn't sure at any moment whether the wind might blow me off the road or some flying object might crash through my windshield killing me instantly. There was no one else driving in the storm, so I didn't consider stopping for any stoplight which might still be working. I'm not sure how high my pulse rate reached during the trip, but I wouldn't have been shocked to get a twice-normal reading. And once I arrived at the apartment, I was almost surprised I'd made it.

I ran up the flight of stairs and hugged Cathy, while grabbing her overnight case, and told her to get into the car quickly. The phone rang, and I don't know why I stopped to answer, but I did. It was Cathy's Mom from Fort Lauderdale, and she asked, "How are you and Cathy doing with the hurricane?" I quickly responded, "Mom, I can't talk; I've got to take Cathy to the hospital – good bye," and I hung up. That was the very worst response I could have given, because shortly thereafter the phone service to

New Orleans went out, and Cathy's parents had no idea of the reason for my taking her to the hospital, nor of her present condition. It took me a long time to repair that damage to their trust of me.

Our return trip to Charity Hospital was equally frightening, but I was calmer, because we were together, and I felt we had a chance to make it back. I do remember we were praying out loud with great fervor. Neither Cathy nor I were believers at the time, but I'm confident this experience helped us understand in a dramatic way, our fragile condition and our need for a comforting Savior. We made it back to the hospital without injury, but there was still another hurdle I didn't anticipate.

Charity Hospital was twenty stories tall, and the first twelve stories comprised the hospital portion, while the next eight floors were the on-call rooms for the doctors. These were the days of an increased sense of morality, and there was an irrevocable rule by which no women were allowed above the thirteenth floor. This included woman doctors, whose rooms were on the thirteenth. The elevators were not self-service, but were the old fashioned type with a hand lever requiring an operator. The operators who were hired by the state of Louisiana were all handicapped in some way, and most of them were mentally challenged. As we got on the elevator in our rain-drenched clothes, I told the operator to take us to floor eighteen where my on-call room was located. Without even looking at us, the operator said, "No women above floor thirteen." I said, "It's okay, we're married." Perhaps he had heard that excuse before, so he again said, "No women above floor thirteen." I had him look at our wedding rings to prove our marriage to each other while I said in a very agitated manner, "Look, we've risked our lives driving from Kenner to get here so my wife can spend the night during the hurricane. Please punch floor eighteen!" For the last time he said, "I'm not taking her to floor eighteen." I looked the man in the eye and said to him in a tone he could not misunderstand, "If you don't push eighteen right now, I'm going to kill you!!" We immediately were taken there with no more discussion. I had never made such a threat in my life, but was reacting to the whole life-threatening event we had just experienced. Cathy was beginning to wonder just what kind of man she had recently married.

Cathy spent a restless night in the room while I spent most of the night working on trauma victims from the hurricane. She was safe from the storm which raged outside, and this was my goal for her for the night.

The next morning before the shift change, I found our elevator operator and apologized to him for my angry behavior, assuring him I would not have harmed him in any way. For the next four years I worked at Charity Hospital I would frequently encounter this same operator and joke with him to try to establish a trust and a friendship. I'm convinced he never did trust me and was never quite sure whether I could ever get mad enough to kill him! At least we never had to go through another hurricane to test my resolve.

7. TRAPPED ON BOURBON STREET

A Pregnant Wife and Terrified Husband are Rescued by an Angel in the French Quarter

Mardi Gras is an annual festival in New Orleans, one which attracts hundreds of thousands of people for a week or more of parades, parties, and merry-making. Although the basis for the celebration heralds the coming of Lent in anticipation of Easter, the festival has no resemblance to a spiritual event. In fact, just the opposite.

The four years Cathy and I lived in New Orleans while I was taking my surgical training at Charity Hospital, we were not believers in Jesus Christ, and our commitment to even regular church attendance was marginal. Our first year of life in the city we did attend some of the parades and even went down to Canal Street on Fat Tuesday (Mardi Gras) to observe what a huge crowd looks like. We were generally turned off by the drunkenness of the revelers and the overall rowdy behavior, which was overlooked and tolerated by the New Orleans police officers.

The second year we decided to go to the French Quarter one night with neighbors with whom we shared a duplex apartment on the West Bank in Gretna. Jerri and Bob Herold were a couple originally from St. Louis and about our same age. They did have three small children with whom we quickly bonded. We were newlyweds and had no children. This particular night we wanted to go to Pat O'Brien's, a very famous and popular piano bar. This entertainment venue featured group singing, Dixieland jazz music, and, of course lots of liquid refreshment which was not too objectionable to Cathy and me in those days. We seldom ever went to such a place, but this was a special occasion with our neighbors.

The crowds on the back streets of the Quarter that night were not oppressive, but as we neared Pat O'Brien's, we noticed that a large crowd had gathered outside the door and that a large mass of people had found their way inside. A horse-mounted New Orleans policeman approached us, looked directly at me, and said, "You folks look like nice people, and my advice is for you to turn around and go home!" At the same time, we watched as two mounted policemen rode their horses up into Pat O'Brien's in an effort to break up the crowd inside, which had become rowdy and dangerous. As frightened people began spilling outside, the four of us made a hasty retreat and headed for home! That was our last visit ever to Pat O'Brien's.

Cathy and I had still not learned our lesson concerning the French Quarter, because the following year in 1967 when Cathy was pregnant with our first child John Aaron, we made another Mardi Gras foray into the Quarter to experience the crowds. In looking back the only explanation for our getting on Bourbon Street was my immaturity and stupidity!

As we began attempting to move forward, I quickly realized we were trapped in this massive crowd which had to move in unison or couldn't move at all. There were people in the mob ahead of us who wanted to move toward us, and this stopped any movement whatsoever. It was at this moment I knew if one of us happened to stumble and fall, we would be trampled to death, because it would have been impossible to stand back up. I had never experienced such anxiety bordering on terror as at that moment.

Standing directly in front of us were three men whose faces we could not see, but we knew they were members of the notorious motorcycle gang Hell's Angels. Their black leather jackets had the logo of the organization on the back. The one immediately in front of me was huge, weighing at least 275 pounds and had a shaved head long before that style became popular. He was an intimidating man even from the rear. Fortunately, I could raise my hand enough to tap him on the shoulder, and when he turned around, he gave me the worst scowling face I had ever seen and blurted out, "What do you want?!" In as polite a tone as I could muster, I said, "Sir, will you please help us? My wife is five months pregnant with our first child, and we are very scared she might fall and be killed. Can you please get us out of this crowd?" It seemed like an eternity while he looked at the two of us, looked down at Cathy's enlarged tummy, and finally said, "Stay right behind me." He put both his fists on his chest and extended his elbows outward so as to appear like a giant battering ram while shouting the words, "Get out of my way!" He repeated the words several more times. He was wide enough for Cathy and me to move directly behind him.

I don't know how it was possible, but that enormous crowd parted just wide enough for the three of us to move forward for about fifty feet until we reached a side street, probably St. Peter's, which intersects Bourbon. There were lots of people on that street also but enough space so we could quickly exit to safety. We made our way back to Canal Street, having never been able to thank our new Hell's Angels friend.

The Bible speaks of angels being large, fierce creations with supernatural strength, and whose only purpose is doing the will of God, which includes protecting His children. Cathy and I are firmly convinced we encountered one of "Heaven's Angels" that afternoon in the French Quarter, and he saved our lives. I never again looked on the organization as an enemy of mine. Also, Cathy and I learned our lesson well, and resolved to never go again to the French Quarter during Mardi Gras. In fact, since becoming believers ten years later, we have no desire at all to see the French Quarter at any time.

PS: Cathy and I believe God spared our lives by his mercy that day even when we did not know him nor acknowledge him as Savior (Rom 5:8).

8. "YOUR BROTHER HAS GONE OFF THE DEEP END"

Our First Indication of a Spiritual Change in My Hero Brother

I have always had the highest esteem for my older brother Berry Lee (Bubba). From earliest remembrance he was my hero on many levels. He was an outstanding student throughout all his academic years; he was an excellent athlete in football, even playing for the Arkansas Razorbacks; he had a sterling character, and best of all he spent lots of time teaching me many sporting skills and talking to me about character. If I ever thought he had a fault, it was he was too meticulous with details, and he always insisted I mind our parents without questions.

When Bubba completed his internship year and then served two years of active duty in the Air Force, he and his wife LaNell decided to return to our hometown in El Dorado, Arkansas, where he would practice general medicine with our Pop. Most people thought Bubba would go into some type of academic medicine because he was so brilliant throughout medical school, graduating at the top of his class. While he worked hard to build a successful medical practice, he also became involved in numerous civic projects. He was one of the more prominent members of the Republican Party of Union County when it was very unpopular to be a Republican in a predominately Democratic state. He led the fight locally to get Barry Goldwater elected President, but Goldwater was soundly defeated. Everything Bubba put his hand to he did with great zeal and fervor. Pop would occasionally ask him, "What are you crusading for these days?"

Bubba and Pop practiced medicine together for eight years, while Pop's health gradually deteriorated. Pop departed this life in January, 1966 and Bubba continued in a solo practice. Cathy and I had already moved to New Orleans where I was in training as a general surgeon, and while there, we kept in touch with my mom and Bubba. We knew most of the important things which were occurring at home. What we had not heard, however, was that in mid-1967, Bubba had experienced a spiritual conversion as a result of the witness of several friends. His life was transformed, and we knew nothing about it.

Several months following his conversion I received a phone call from a prominent businessman in my hometown. I only knew him by his reputation as a respected man in the community. He said to me, "I've got some bad news to tell you about your brother." My first thought was Bubba had been seriously injured or had died, but it would have been strange for this man to call me instead of a family member. He said, "I believe your brother has gone off the deep end." "What in the world are you talking about?" I asked. He explained that Berry Lee had had "some type of religious experience," and was at the hospital talking to his patients daily "about God, church, and religious things! To make matters even worse, he was praying out loud with his patients and making an embarrassing scene for everyone else in the hospital."

It made me mad that this man was accusing my hero of being an embarrassment, and I said to him in a firm voice, "Well, just what do you want me to do, have him committed to an insane asylum?" "No, he replied politely, I just wanted to make you aware of what was happening, so you perhaps could convince him to tone it down." "Thanks for the call and the information," I said as I hung up. This occurred during a time when it was very unusual for a physician to pray with patients and to witness Christ to them. I had never experienced anything similar in my training, and I wasn't sure what to make of the accusation. Neither Cathy nor I were believers, so we weren't able to rejoice in Bubba's love for the Lord Jesus and his bravery to withstand some of the silent and now vocal accusations of insanity.

It was almost ten years to the day following this call when both Cathy and I had a spiritual conversion, and our lives changed as well. Since that day in 1977, I hadn't heard anyone accuse me of being crazy, until about three years ago, just before Bubba died. We were laughing about the impact of the phone call back in 1967 and what many people thought and said about him in those days. He then paid me one of the greatest compliments I'd ever heard from him when he said, "As crazy as people thought I was in those days, you and Cathy became a lot crazier than I ever was!" As I hugged him goodbye, I said, "Isn't it wonderful to be crazy for Jesus?"

9. THE PRAYER AT COMMANDER'S PALACE

Our First Experience of Prayer in a Restaurant

One of the best-known restaurants in New Orleans is Commander's Palace located in the historic Garden District. It's been serving delicious French and Creole cuisine in that location since the turn of the twentieth century. When Cathy and I moved to New Orleans in 1965 to begin my training in surgery at Charity Hospital, we could only dream about dining in a restaurant as elegant as the Commander's Palace, because we could not afford such luxuries. My salary during those four years never exceeded five hundred dollars per month, so Cathy's salary as an elementary school teacher was our primary source of income. Our few dining-out experiences were limited to small cafes known only to locals, and much less expensive than the well-known restaurants like Commander's Palace, Antoine's, Brennan's, and The Court of Two Sisters.

We were always thrilled when Cathy's parents from Florida or members of my family came to New Orleans for a visit. In addition to having fun and getting caught up on all family news, it usually meant going to a restaurant or two which Cathy and I could not ordinarily afford. Most of the time we still avoided the very high-end restaurants, because they were too fancy for our tastes despite the lure of exquisite food.

Cathy and I were very pleased but shocked when one evening we received a phone call from my brother Berry Lee (Bubba) asking how we were doing, and saying he would like to come for a visit very soon. He was coming alone because LaNell had to stay home and care for their four children. We told him he could come as soon as he could arrange his work schedule and could stay as long as he wanted. We were somewhat surprised since Bubba was such a home-body and seldom if ever paid a social visit with anyone, especially without LaNell. We were elated at his sudden change.

What we did not know was that Bubba had recently experienced a spiritual conversion, and that he was concerned about our spiritual condition. He was coming to visit for the purpose of witnessing Christ to his little brother and new sister-in-law! Had we known what was about to happen, we might not have been so eager to have him visit.

Earlier, I had received a phone call from an El Dorado business man telling me my brother had recently had some type of spiritual conversion and was acting very strangely at the hospital. Within the first fifteen minutes of Bubba's presence in our small apartment, both Cathy and I agreed he was different. All of his conversation was colored with remarks about his spiritual conversion and how the Holy Spirit now had control of his life.

Bubba had spoken with me in the past about character and clean, moral living, but I had never heard him use terms like "Savior, the Lord Jesus, and the Holy Spirit." These overt changes in his attitudes and conversation made us very uncomfortable. Neither of us had been spiritually converted, and whenever possible we changed the subject from religion to something less intimidating.

Bubba suggested we go out for supper that evening, and he wanted to take us to Commander's Palace. He had been there once and said he could still remember how delicious the food had been. We heartily agreed this was a good choice knowing he would pay for a meal we couldn't afford. When we arrived, I was surprised how nice it was and what a variety of wonderful sounding food was on the menu. We continued with the conversation that had begun at our apartment, but with as little focus as possible on spiritual things. We were getting caught up on everyone at home, and what it was now like for him in a solo medical practice without Pop, who had died earlier the same year.

When our food was brought to the table, it looked and smelled wonderful. When everyone was served, I politely began eating when Bubba said, "Wait, we haven't done something important. We haven't prayed." Up until this time in my immediate family, we would recite a simple memorized prayer before a meal, but it was always at home. I was twenty-seven years old and had never been in a restaurant when a prayer was said out loud, either at my table or at any other table for that matter. When Bubba started praying, seemingly too loud, I was certain everyone in Commander's Palace was staring at us. In addition, what was later typical of Bubba and his prayers, he followed the biblical mandate of praying without ceasing (or so it seemed)! This was one of the most embarrassing moments of my life and also for Cathy as she later told me. I was convinced without a doubt Bubba had gone crazy at least in the spiritual realm!

I don't remember a thing I had to eat that evening, but I do remember his long prayer. I am ashamed of my attitude toward Bubba's witness. He was simply being obedient to the command of the Holy Spirit, and I was thinking he had lost his good sense and judgment. We have not been back to Commander's Palace, but if we ever get to dine there again, we will definitely pray before we eat and won't mind if heads are turned because of our praying out loud. Since this embarrassing event Cathy and I have been redeemed and now sing from experience the words to the wonderful hymn, "*We once were lost but now are found; were blind but now we see!*"

10. A BIRTHING AT MOODY AIR FORCE BASE HOSPITAL

An Unplanned Twist with the Birth of Our First Daughter

February 10, 1970, was an exciting day for Cathy and me. We had been anticipating the birth of our second child for nine months and seemingly were better prepared than we were for our first—John Aaron, who was born in 1967 in New Orleans during my second year of surgical training. I was very busy with my work and had very poor skills as a husband and expectant father. This was during the era prior to birthing rooms and fathers were isolated from the delivery process. As a doctor I could have been present in the delivery room, but my attitude was that I didn't want to place added tension to the obstetrician Dr. Sistrunk. In reality I was more concerned about my own anxiety. So, Cathy was pretty much without my physical presence and support during her labor and delivery. I purposed to do better with our second.

I completed my surgical training in 1969, and Cathy and I moved to Valdosta, Georgia where I was assigned duty in the U.S. Air Force as a Major in the medical corps at Moody Air Force Base. The base hospital was small by Air Force standards, and I was the only surgeon, a situation which suited me well. There was only one obstetrician, Major (Dr.) Henry Schilowitz, who was from New York City and had been trained there. We had a very good professional relationship, and I assisted him on all of his major surgical procedures.

One of Cathy's best friends, Flonnie McKoy, was also pregnant with her second child and due to deliver in early February of 1970. Flonnie's husband, Pete was the base veterinarian, and he also was one of my good friends. Cathy went into labor in the early morning hours of February 10, and I drove her to the hospital about ten miles from our home in town. We discovered when we got to the hospital, Flonnie had checked in ahead of us, and she was a little further along in her labor than Cathy.

By mid-morning, Flonnie was taken into the delivery room where Dr. Schilowitz managed her delivery process. By this time Cathy was far along in her labor and requiring significant pain medication for relief. There were two delivery rooms in the operating suite, and Cathy's nurse was telling us that they were going to have to move her very soon to that second room. I called Dr. Schilowitz on the intercom and anxiously asked him if he was almost finished with Flonnie's delivery. He said the baby was delivered with no complications, but Flonnie's placenta had not separated, and he could not leave her. He said, "I guess you will have to deliver your own baby!" I told him there was no way I was going to do that except in case of a dire emergency. I had lots of experience delivering babies when I was an intern, so that was not a concern, but I was not up to the emotional stress of delivering our little girl. I said, "Henry, you let me come in there and deliver that placenta, and you get over to Room 2 to deliver Cathy's baby." He laughed and said, "If that is what you want me to do!"

We moved Cathy into Room 2 and I scrubbed my hands to assist Flonnie in the completion of her delivery. I was greatly relieved when Dr. Schilowitz scrubbed his hands and entered Room 2 minutes before Cathy delivered our baby. I was still in the process of removing the retained placenta when word came from a nurse, "You and Cathy now have a beautiful and healthy little girl!" If I were in a place where crying was appropriate, I would have shed a few tears of relief and joy.

Flonnie and Pete had their second boy, whom they named Brodie, and we our first girl, whom we named Mary Katharine. John Aaron said he was excited to have a sibling, but he had wanted a brother all along. Later I took him to the hospital to see his little sister, and after he poked at her a few times and she didn't poke back, he thought she would be all right, at least for the time being.

Cathy was kept in the hospital for three days, which helped her recovery process, and I was a lot more attentive to her, before, during, and after the delivery. At least I was learning to be a better husband and father but was still a major work in progress. The hospital sent us a bill for Cathy's hospital stay, and the total was $7.68, which we were able to pay in full! Years later when Mary Kay was a teenager and causing some stress in the family which is common to all with teens, I jokingly said to her, "I guess you get what you pay for."

Happy forty-fifth birthday Mary Kay! It's fun for us to remember and tell of your birthing at Moody Field, although you don't remember any of it. Despite your bargain basement cost to us in the beginning, you are an absolute priceless treasure to your mom and me. But you sure caused some major stress to your dad at the time of your arrival!

John Aaron, Proud Daddy, Mary Kay. Easter, 1970

11. "THEE I LOVE," PART 2

The Transition from the Air Force to a New Life in El Dorado

Cathy and I moved from Valdosta, Georgia, to El Dorado, Arkansas, in August, 1971 to begin a new phase in our journey. Our two young children, John Aaron, age four, and Mary Kay, age two, were excited about this new adventure, but Cathy and I were just a little apprehensive with lots of unanswered questions about our future. Could I make a living doing surgery in the town I grew up in? Would we be able to make the right kind of friends for ourselves and our kids? Would we fit into the culture of this small Southern town which still had many prejudiced people who had come through the tumultuous, racially-charged 1960s?

Cathy had the greatest adjustment to make, because she was separated by many miles from the culture in which she was raised and from all of her family members. In those years I was not the supportive husband I should have been in understanding Cathy's plight and the sacrifices she was making. I just assumed in time she would be able to settle into our new lifestyle and would find her place, her purpose, and accomplish her own goals. My thoughts and goals then were professional in terms of becoming the best surgeon possible and providing the most resources for our family.

Those were not bad goals but just not centered on Cathy and our children as they should have been.

The next great event in our life together was the birth of our second daughter, Ginny on November 3, 1972. By this time Cathy and I had purchased from my mom the Moore family home in which I was raised. She moved into the rental home on East 7th Street where we had been living. Our new home was large with a very large yard in which our kids could play. Our across-the-street neighbors were the Clydes and their children, Elizabeth and older brother Andrew, would play a large role in our lives, then and at a much later time.

We became members of First Baptist Church upon moving to town and immersed ourselves in the ministry of this long-established downtown church. We provided leadership, and I was a teacher of a young couples Sunday school class. I was even selected to serve as a deacon. We were fully vested as church members, but both of us felt a certain emptiness in our hearts and in our life together. We didn't fully understand our dilemma or our need until we attended a Bill Gothard seminar in Dallas, Texas in August, 1977. In "A Shopping Trip to Dallas," I've written about our salvation and life-change which occurred at that seminar on August 6, 1977, and from that day forward we were different individually and toward each other.

I began understanding on a deeper level my primary responsibilities were to love Jesus Christ with all my heart and to love and cherish Cathy as Christ loves his church (Eph 5:25–27). I acknowledged that my professional life was important, but it paled in significance to the importance of my investments into the lives of Cathy and our children. There was a definite change in our marriage relationship, but changes of that magnitude come slowly.

Our involvement into the ministry at First Baptist Church deepened, and reached its peak during the pastorate of Dr. Mark Coppenger from 1983 to 1988. Those years marked our greatest spiritual growth up to that point. We also became involved in the ministry of The International Congress on Revival (ICR) under Evangelist Bill Stafford's leadership and together made many overseas mission trips to Brazil, Western and Eastern Europe, and Ireland. We were extremely blessed to have my sister Marilyn and husband George Berry from Austin, Texas involved also in the ICR ministry, and we made many of the overseas mission trips together with them. Our love for them and the relationship with them, their children, and grandchildren deepened during those years of ministry.

In 1989 Cathy and I moved our church membership from the First Baptist Church to Immanuel Baptist Church in El Dorado, and for the next ten years were immersed into our ministry there. The most exciting times there were during the pastorate of Dr. David Uth in the mid-1990s when Immanuel Baptist had its greatest growth period. David's wife Rachel is the daughter of brother Berry Lee and his wife LaNell, so our connection to Brother David and Rachel was even closer and sweeter. We were honored to have Brother David officiate the weddings of each of our children; John Aaron to Gina Ratcliff in 1990; Mary Kay to Dave Janke in 1992; and Ginny to John Luther in 1995.

One of the more difficult times for us occurred in 1999 when we felt called to move to Largo, Florida and the First Baptist Church of Indian Rocks, where I served as the initial medical director of the church's medical clinic. (I've written extensively on this period in "God Will Make a Way"— Our Ministry in Florida.") The stress of being so far away from our children and grandchildren during that eight-month period drew Cathy and me closer together, causing each of us to depend upon the other more and to cherish our life more together.

We were thrilled to make our next move in May, 2000, to Fayette-ville, Arkansas, where our Ginny and husband John Luther lived and to become more fully vested in their family. It was there I began serving as a wound care specialist at Washington Regional Medical Center and was able to spend much more time at home with Cathy. I no longer had night calls or weekend calls, and the physical and emotional stresses of a busy surgical practice were lifted.

Our home was a beautiful energy-efficient home, which was a model all-electric home built by Ozarks Electric Company. We were told we were getting a "Cadillac home" at a "Chevrolet price," which was certainly the case. For the first time in our marriage, Cathy had a new home which she could decorate exactly according to her taste, and I loved our Fayetteville home more than all the others. It was located in a new subdivision west of town, a short 5–8 minute drive to Ginny and John's home in Savoy.

A huge highlight of our time in Fayetteville was the birth of Ginny and John's first child and their only daughter, Claire, on August 19, 2001. It was so fun watching her grow and develop and for us to have the opportunity and time to be part of her early years. Fayetteville is a short, two-hour drive to Branson, Missouri, where daughter Mary Kay, husband Dave Janke and their two daughters, Rebecca and Sara Beth, lived. We frequently made the drive there for weekend visits.

Cathy and I were well-settled in Fayetteville and wonderfully happy with our life, but an unusual turn of events directed our hearts toward an-other move, this time to Branson, Missouri. (See "The Free Medical Clinic of the Ozarks.") Friends and even some family members wondered if Cathy and I would ever settle down in one place. A church member and friend in

El Dorado at Immanuel Baptist Church once asked our son John the question, "Where are your parents living *now*?!"

With considerable prayer and some agonizing, Cathy and I believed it was God's will to move in November, 2005, to Branson, where I would be the sole Director of the Wound Care Clinic of Skaggs Memorial Hospital. More importantly we would be near our kids and grandkids, who were living there. Our plans were to spend a "few years" in Branson, retire from medical practice, and return to Fayetteville for the final days of our journey. At the time of our decision, I told Ginny through tears, "Mom and I will return—this move is not permanent—I promise!"

12. OUR FAMILY HOME IN EL DORADO

Our Journey to 1800

1800 North Madison

Growing up in a relatively small town in South Arkansas, I didn't give much thought to the home my parents had provided. I was aware it was a beautiful, two-story, colonial style house on North Madison and had a large front yard, very conducive to football games with neighborhood buddies. The yard could also be used as a scaled down baseball field, but it didn't take a very long hit to travel into a neighbor's yard. From a baseball standpoint, it was mostly useful for games of pitch and catch. I wasn't aware of most of the details of how and when the house was built, except I knew it was constructed in the mid-1930s before I was born. Pop always said it was a dream home for him and for Mimi, my birth mother, and it had taken them about five years to plan and build. He said the lumber was a "special cut" from Anthony-Williams Lumber Company, a local, well-known firm. The home was completed in 1939, and they moved into it in the spring of that year. I was born in October. The following year, Mimi was diagnosed with far-advanced breast cancer, and, despite the best treatment options available, she died in April, 1941. Pop married Athelene West in 1944, and we began adjusting to a different life style with our new mom.

Our home was distinctive and larger than the homes of all of my friends, but that was not a barrier to any of those friendships. In addition to the advantages of having a large yard for ball games, there were special hiding places in the attic and basement where we could gather and plan whatever things seemed important to us. Occasionally the basement was used for overnight campouts because of the presence of a large fireplace.

When Pop died of heart trouble in 1966, Mom remained in the home and maintained it as well as she could. At the time Cathy and I were living in New Orleans, where I was in my residency training as a general surgeon. I completed training in 1969 but had a two-year obligation to the Air Force. It was during our stint at Moody Air Force Base in Valdosta, Georgia that I learned more details about the building of our family home.

I was the only surgeon on the base which provided medical care for active duty personnel as well as a large population of retired military families living in the area. Alex Skoropat was a retired Air Force colonel whom I got to know fairly well because he developed a malignant colon cancer requiring an extensive operation. During the course of his six-to-eight-weeks treatment and recovery, I discovered that during his retirement years, he was employed by a large lumber company in South Georgia, one with connections to similar companies in other states. When he discovered I was originally from El Dorado, Arkansas, he told me he had become good friends with Aubrey Anthony, one of the brothers who owned Anthony-Williams Lumber Company in El Dorado. During the course of one conversation regarding his relationship with the Anthony family, he told me the following: "Aubrey said there was a doctor in El Dorado who got all the lumber for his home in an interesting fashion. During the depression years of the 1930s, this doctor was the 'company doctor' for Anthony-Williams, and the arrangement provided him a fixed fee each month for providing medical care for every company family. He asked us to keep a record of his account, and when he was ready to build a home, he would take his fees in lumber. When he finally decided to build, we custom-cut all the lumber for his home and treated every piece with creosote, which gave life-time termite protection." After listening to this story, I told Alex the doctor in the story was my dad, and the home he described was the one in which I grew up. What a divine appointment to learn about my home from a surgical patient who lived over eight hundred miles away!

Upon completion of my service time, Cathy and I moved to El Dorado to establish a private practice and build our lives there. We had no thoughts at the time to ever move into the family home. When Mom finally decided in 1972 that she could no longer maintain such a large home, she placed it on the market to be sold. Cathy and I were living in a very nice rental home but were expecting our third child and were thinking about buying a larger home with a larger yard. After six months there had only been one offer on the home, so with much consideration and consultation with all the family members, Cathy and I decided to purchase the home at the same price as the only offer. Shortly before the birth of Ginny, our third and final child, we took possession of our new home.

Over the next twenty years, we used and loved our home much more than I ever did as a child. Cathy and I determined early on, despite the fact that the house was large and beautiful, we wanted it to be child-friendly and not a show place of fashion elegance. After living in it for several years, one of our son John's friends innocently said to Cathy, "Mrs. Moore, your home is sure fancy on the outside, and when you and Dr. Moore can afford it, I know you will fix up the inside too!" We slowly began re-modeling each room to reflect our individual personalities and tastes. We also added a swimming pool in the backyard, which was a huge attraction, particularly for our children's friends. During the summer months it was well used.

One of my favorite poems is "Home" by Edgar Guest. It begins, "It takes a heap o' livin' in a house t' make it home," and I believe that we, indeed, did a heap of livin' and lovin' at 1800. When the children were grown and gone from home, Cathy and I sold the house to move to a more convenient home on West Elm Street. There was some sadness and nostalgia in our hearts when the sale was finalized, but I firmly believe Pops and Mimi's dream house had accomplished its purpose in providing a wonderful home for three generations of Moores!

13. THE ACCIDENT WHICH CHANGED OUR LIVES

What Was a Near-Tragedy Became a Life-Saver

Mom Young, Mary Kay, John Aaron, and Cathy—November 1971

Our two years of active duty in the US Air Force in many ways were good ones. Because I was the sole surgeon at the base hospital, I had been able to work pretty much independently with only a few of the usual military restrictions. I had avoided duty in Viet Nam, and our country's military involvement there was beginning to wind down. Our family had increased by one with the birth of Mary Katharine on February 10, 1970. Our son John Aaron was almost four years old at the time of her birth. We lived fairly close to Cathy's parents in Fort Lauderdale, Florida, which allowed us the freedom to visit and enjoy her family every few months. We loved the small-town life of Valdosta, Georgia, and, although there was an abundance of good churches, there was no spiritual hunger in either one of us. We occasionally attended First Methodist Church and had Mary Kay baptized there when she was several months old.

By the middle of 1971, we made the final decision to move our family to El Dorado, Arkansas, to begin my surgical practice. Cathy's family wanted us to move to South Florida, and it was very tempting on many levels. My family's medical ties in El Dorado and the relatively quiet and peaceful atmosphere were huge deciding factors. We certainly did not pray about our decision but relied on our best judgments. Our moving date was August 17, 1971, when I was released from active military duty.

Cathy and I moved into a very nice three-bedroom rental home on East Ninth Street in El Dorado, which was about four blocks away from my Mom's home on North Madison. It was owned by our friends, Henry and Venie Craig, who lived two doors west of us. They had maintained the home very well and had it freshly painted inside and out just before we arrived. Our rental payments were very reasonable, and we were happy with our arrangement and new friendship with the Craigs. Our plan was to rent for a year or two until we could save enough money to either build or purchase a permanent home.

On the fateful day of Cathy's accident, November 11, both she and I had been recovering from upper respiratory tract infections. As I left the house very early, my last words to her were, "Why don't you open our bedroom window and air out the room for a couple of hours." My attitude that particular morning was not the best, and my statement was more on the order of a command rather than a suggestion. I had one surgical case scheduled morning, a gall bladder removal, which usually took from one to two hours.

As I finished the procedure, I was in the recovery room writing post-operative orders when the hospital telephone operator notified me that I had an urgent call from my wife. (This was long before cell phones.) Upon answering, Cathy was almost screaming, "You need to come home right now. I've cut my foot!" I thought perhaps she had dropped a glass and cut the sole of her foot, because she usually walked around the house in bare feet. I didn't delay, however, but dressed quickly and drove home in about ten minutes.

Upon arrival there were three cars in the driveway, which increased my anxiety. As I opened the door to the kitchen, Cathy was sitting on the floor in a huge pool of blood with a thick towel wrapped around her right ankle. I estimated there was a half pint of blood on the floor. Mary Kay was standing behind her holding her security blanket and with her eyes widened in fright. My mom was standing in the kitchen in almost a state of shock, but said she had called an ambulance. As I applied more pressure to the wound, I told Mom to get me a sheet for a tourniquet, and because of her shocked state of mind, she said, "But they are brand new sheets." After applying the tourniquet, I could examine the wound more carefully. Cathy had calmed a bit, and said she told me the story. She had tried to open the bedroom window, and, because of the new paint, the window was stuck.

She lay on her back on the bed and with her right foot she kicked against the window sill. Her foot glanced off the sill, broke through the glass, and when she reflexively pulled back her foot, she deeply lacerated her ankle. The Achilles tendon was severed as well as the main vein to her foot. Fortunately, the artery was not severed, or she might have bled to death before she could get help. We got her to the hospital quickly, and I had already alerted my surgeon friends, Drs. Yocum and Tommey, who met us in the ER.

Following the successful repair, Cathy had to remain in the hospital overnight and was discharged the next day on crutches with a long leg cast on her right leg. I hired a full-time care giver for the children because I had to continue in my new medical practice, which was very small. Managing crutches and the discomfort of an ungainly cast was initially difficult for Cathy. Her pain was significant but controllable, but not being able to do her usual household tasks and care for our two small, active children was very difficult for her.

The woman we initially hired to care for the children seemed ideal. She had children of her own and was skilled in child care. In addition, she was an excellent cook and prepared wonderful meals for our family. However, after about three weeks, I received a phone call one morning at my office from the police department saying there was a problem with our care giver. She was caught in a grocery store stealing items for her own use. The embarrassing thing was that she had our one-and-a-half-year-old daughter Mary Kay with her. Someone recognized our daughter prior to their being transported to the jail, and this prompted the call to me. I drove to the jail to get Mary Kay, and found they were releasing the lady without bail while charging her with petty theft. I fired her immediately, and we began searching for her replacement.

So many people in El Dorado offered various kinds of assistance, which showed us a depth of love we had not previously experienced. Neither Cathy nor I were Christians, and we saw the love of Christ poured out on us in kind acts and also in healing words. We began to deeply examine with each other and with our children our life goals and our lack of any spiritual hunger. We wanted to raise our children in a good environment, which included church involvement. Early on we had joined First Baptist Church because that was where our family had been members for many years. We learned later that church membership and faithful attendance were not the only indicators of Christianity.

There were some wonderful Christians who ministered to us during those weeks of recovery, including Dave Dawson, who lived in Greenville, Texas, and was a Navigator friend of my brother Berry Lee. The Shepperson sisters and others along with Mrs. Garland Murphy Sr., who was eighty years old, visited us and prepared meals for us often. Cathy's mom came from Fort Lauderdale to stay for a week to assist us in so many ways but especially with our children. There were others, but these made the largest impact. They not only served us food and kindness but also cared for us with healing words of what Jesus Christ was doing in both of us. All of these experiences were impactful at a time when we were young, inexperienced, and vulnerable.

We learned, among other great truths, that the Lord Jesus comes to the weak, the sick, and the helpless with healing, with hope, and with salvation. Cathy's painful ordeal and the experiences of physical and emotional healing led us finally to surrender our lives to the salvation of Christ in 1977. What initially was a tragic accident was used by God to totally transform us. To him be all the glory!

14. A SHOPPING TRIP TO DALLAS

An Initial Challenge Leads to Our Reformation

When Cathy and I left our home in Valdosta, Georgia, where we lived for two years, we moved to my hometown of El Dorado, Arkansas. I had just completed my required time of active duty in the US Air Force. We were excited to begin this new phase of starting a private practice in general surgery and continuing to raise our family. At the time of our move, our older child John Aaron was four years old, and our daughter Mary Kay was not quite two. Our third child, Ginny, would be born within a year of our move.

There was a distinct advantage for our move to El Dorado. I was the third of three generations of Dr. Moores who practiced medicine there. My older brother Berry Lee (Bubba) had a very active general medical practice which he began with our dad (Pop) fourteen years earlier. My grandfather Dr. John Aaron had practiced for forty years in the community and was still remembered by many, although he had been dead for almost thirty years. My Pop, Dr. Berry Sr., also a general practitioner and greatly beloved in the community had died five years earlier. I knew my brother would be an immediate referral resource for my surgical practice.

There were also some disadvantages. Cathy was born and raised in south Florida, and all of her family lived there. She had no sense of personal identity in south Arkansas, and culturally this would be a huge change for her. There was a problem in our religious beliefs. Cathy was raised a Methodist, and I was baptized as a youth at the First Baptist Church in El Dorado. During our early years together, we had vacillated between Methodist and Baptist churches, but were never very faithful in attendance and never committed in faith. We were spiritually intimidated by Bubba, because he was a strong and zealous in his faith. When we were with him in private conversation, it was obvious he thought we were not saved and did not have a personal relationship with Christ. His discussions on faith with us did not seem judgmental, because we understood he was concerned about our future. But, because of our discomfort, we avoided discussions on faith with him as much as possible.

After joining First Baptist, we decided to be faithful in attendance for our children's sake. It wasn't long before I was asked to teach an adult couple's Sunday school class because of my love for teaching. My Bible knowledge was limited, so the preparation time for teaching was lengthy. Within a couple of years, I was invited to become a deacon, which I considered a high honor, and I accepted their invitation.

Despite the fact we were deeply committed to church work, I kept a clear separation of my church life from my professional life. If someone asked to discuss a particular Bible truth, I was happy to relate my own interpretation, but deep inside I knew I did not live by faith. I could see a difference in my brother's life and a few other men I knew and respected, and I knew I didn't think and live as they did.

In our sixth year in El Dorado, Bubba asked if Cathy and I would like to go to Dallas to attend a week-long seminar designed to teach couples how to raise teenagers to love and obey God. He and his wife LaNell, along with all of their children, were attending the Bill Gothard seminar, and each one assured us of its value. Bubba also added, "If you don't leave the conference believing it was of great value, I will pay all of your expenses!" That was the final motivation I needed. Cathy's attitude was more skeptical but was glad she would have the opportunity to spend the week shopping in Dallas.

The conference was huge, with more than ten thousand people packing the Dallas Convention Center to hear Bill Gothard teach his principles on the family and living the Christ life. He was not a physically impressive man, and his voice was soft and at times monotone. His teaching, however, was interesting and filled with many personal illustrations. The fact he had never married made me skeptical that he would know anything about marriage and raising children. At first, I thought, "I'm not sure I can listen to this man five hours a day for the next six days, but we'll stay so Bubba will have to foot the bill!"

On the second day his teaching so intrigued us we moved nearer the stage to see him up close rather than on the large, over-head screen. By the fifth day, we were within a few rows of the platform, and God was working greatly in our hearts. I was hearing and understanding my need for a personal relationship with Jesus Christ, and being a Christian was so much more than attending church, teaching Bible truths, or serving as a deacon. By the end of the session Bill asked if anyone in the audience had come to the point where they felt the need to surrender their life to receive the Lord's free gift of salvation. He had everyone bow their head, and those who needed salvation could pray a simple prayer of surrender to Christ. He said, "With everyone still bowing, it would be a great encouragement to me for those who asked for salvation to quickly raise their hand." I raised my hand and quickly lowered it. "Yes, thank you. What a beautiful sight of people all around this convention center raising their hands," I heard him say.

As Cathy and I walked back to our hotel, she quietly said, "I have something to tell you. I raised my hand at the invitation." I told her I had also raised mine. Neither of us knew what the other had done. When we got to our hotel room we knelt at the bed and asked the Lord to save us and give us a new heart, a new marriage and a new home. It was a very tender moment of surrender, the first time in our twelve years of marriage we had prayed together.

What was initially thought to be a shopping trip to Dallas became a life-changing experience for us as we received the greatest gift of all—the life of Christ within our hearts. Our lives were bought and paid for by Jesus Christ at Calvary two thousand years ago. He paid a debt he didn't owe, and we owed a debt we couldn't pay. What amazing grace and what a gift!

PS: We didn't ask Bubba to pay for our trip to Dallas. We should have paid for his!

15. A SPECIAL LETTER FROM GOD

The Confirmation God Gave to Cathy and Me

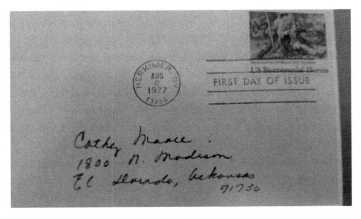

Envelope from Cathy's Mom

Cathy and I were saved and born again on August 6, 1977, at a Bill Gothard seminar in Dallas, Texas. I wrote about the experience in "A Shopping Trip to Dallas," and both Cathy and I have told the account to numerous people in various situations since. The transformation of our hearts and in our home was immediate, and although we looked the same, we didn't act the same. There are some who have an emotional experience at such a Christian conference and later are left with the nagging question, "Was my experience with the Lord Jesus really real?"

Bill Gothard spoke to that question on the last day of the conference and challenged all who prayed for salvation to ask the Lord to give them a sign of the reality of their life change. Both Cathy and I prayed that very prayer. This type of praying was a new and different experience for us, because we never prayed together for specific requests despite being married twelve years. My brother Berry Lee (Bubba) and his wife LaNell along with most of their children were present at the conference, and they were the first in our family to know about our prayer of surrender.

Following the close of the conference on Saturday, we left Dallas to return to our home in El Dorado, eager to share what had occurred. Our children—John Aaron age ten, Mary Kay age seven, and Ginny age four—were the first to hear. They couldn't fully comprehend what had happened, because we looked and sounded the same. They would soon know we were definitely different.

We had not given much thought to our prayer for confirmation from the Lord until the mail arrived the following week. Within a few days of our return home, Cathy received a letter from her mom who lived in Fort Lauderdale, Florida. Mom Young wrote letters and notes to us on a regular basis, so this letter itself caused no immediate excitement. When Cathy opened it, there was a folded, addressed, and stamped envelope inside along with an explanation. Mom was always in search of commemorative stamps and coins, and this particular stamp was a special one concerning the Young family. It had been issued to honor General Herkimer.

General Nicholas Herkimer was a brigadier general in the New York state militia during the War for Independence in the 1770s. He was a distant relative of the Young family, and she had told us of this relationship years before. But we were not aware of the fact that on August 6, 1777, General Herkimer along with his troops were ambushed by British regulars assisted by Mohawk Indians in what was known as The Battle of Oriskany. General Herkimer was mortally wounded in the leg and died ten days later. The stamp on her empty envelope commemorated the 200th anniversary of the general's brave sacrifice to free our nation. He has been memorialized in the state of New York by a town and a county named in his honor.

What caught Cathy's and my attention was what was imprinted on the envelope. On the stamp was a painting of General Herkimer leaning against a tree encouraging his troops to continue fighting at Oriskany. The post mark was from Herkimer, New York, dated August 6, 1977, two hundred years from the date of the heroic battle. The date corresponded to the day of our spiritual conversion in Dallas. Cathy's name as a Herkimer family member and her address were written by her mom, and under the stamp were the words, "First Day of Issue." After studying the envelope for a few moments Cathy exclaimed, "This is our confirmation from the Lord of what took place on that very day in Dallas. This is our letter from God!"

Was the envelope a mere coincidence, or did it have a divine purpose? Both Cathy and I are confident God answered our prayers by transforming us in Dallas, and he was responsible for her Mom's sending us a confirming letter of the event. Cathy had the envelope framed, and it hangs on our bedroom wall opposite our bed. It is a daily reminder of God's love for us and his power to transform and encourage us in our prayer life and faith walk.

16. THE VALUE OF PRAYING BEFORE MEALS

One Simple Act of Devotion Affects Many Lives

Cathy and I recently watched an episode on television of the series *Blue Bloods*, and at the conclusion of the program, the New York City Police Commissioner was seated at the table with his family preparing to have a meal. As was frequently depicted, he voiced a prayer before the meal and made the sign of the cross. It was a touching scene of his family's giving thanks before enjoying their meal and family time. Cathy and I agreed that we wished more families would follow their example and not only pray before meals but in family devotions as well.

Such was not the case for Cathy and me prior to marriage, and it was not part of our lifestyle for several years after marriage. Our families individually prayed before meals usually on Sunday, but this was the extent of our family prayer life. My family never had a family devotion and seldom talked with each other about spiritual things. Cathy's experience at home was similar.

I have previously written about the spiritual impact my brother Berry Lee (Bubba) had on us, and it began soon after we were married in 1965. During his visit with us in New Orleans several months after our wedding, he began witnessing the love of Christ to us, and one of the highlights of his visit was a special meal at Commanders Palace. I have recounted (in "The

Prayer at Commander's Palace") the shock both Cathy and I experienced when, prior to our meal, Bubba prayed what seemed like the longest prayer ever voiced. We had never been a part of anything similar.

Following our spiritual conversion twelve years later, Cathy and I understood more clearly the necessity of prayer. We believe prayer whether at home or in a restaurant is a personal matter and should never be done to impress others or make them believe we are spiritually superior. It is simply a matter of showing gratitude and praise to the One who has given us all we have.

Soon after our conversion we began praying before every meal while holding hands. In the beginning we felt self-conscious but continued because we knew this was the right thing to do. The first confirmation of our belief occurred while attending an advanced Bill Gothard seminar in Denton, Texas, in 1978, one year following our conversion.

Bubba tried to convince us the best place to stay for the seminar was on campus at North Texas State University. The conference was being held in their large gymnasium, and they were offering couples lodging in their dormitory suites at a considerable cost savings. This especially appealed to Bubba. Cathy and I discussed the options and decided to stay at a Holiday Inn, which would provide us more privacy and luxury than a dorm room. The big disadvantage was it was a fifteen-minute drive from the NTSU gym.

The morning of the start of the conference, we were in the coffee shop having breakfast and noted the restaurant was full. We remarked there must be some other event in town to have so many people in the motel, including lots of children whom we knew were not attending the Bill Gothard meeting. A couple approached our table and asked if we were attending the seminar, and we were surprised they would even suspect it, for we were not wearing our name badges. They asked if they might ride with us because they had flown to Denton from Charlotte, North Carolina, and did not have a vehicle. We got to know Gary and Virginia Cooper well over the next several days of riding back and forth together, and then having some meals together. We asked how they picked us out of a large crowded restaurant, and their response was, "We saw you praying together before the meal and suspected you might be attending the seminar!"

God used that "chance meeting" of the Coopers two years later when a couple who were well-known to us from El Dorado but living in Charlotte called me one morning. The husband tearfully told me he and his wife were having serious marital problems and were on the verge of divorce. He asked in a desperate tone, "Is there anything you can possibly do to help us?" I told him Cathy and I knew a couple in Charlotte who might be able to help. I called the Coopers, and they responded quickly by connecting with our friends and becoming a critical source for reconciliation. The marriage relationship of our friends was slowly stabilized with the aid of the Coopers, and they are still together now over thirty years later.

The Coopers were also instrumental in encouraging another set of friends who lived in a town neighboring Charlotte. He was a physician classmate, and he and his wife needed encouragement in attending the Bill Gothard seminar in Charlotte. Their experience with the Coopers and the lessons taught at the seminar strengthened their marriage and changed the dynamics of their home.

Over the years we have had people who were strangers come to our table in a restaurant and quietly say, "I saw you two praying together before your meal, and it meant a lot to me." We have never had anyone say, "I wish you wouldn't make a public display of your religion." God uses our witness for him in so many ways unknown to us, but occasionally he sends someone like the Coopers to reinforce his words: "In all your ways acknowledge Me, and I will direct your path" (Prov 3:6).

PS: Following the conference, Bubba and LaNell never stayed in another college dormitory suite. Their experience according to Bubba was not worth the cost savings.

17. REVIVAL AT FIRST BAPTIST EL DORADO

A Historic Revival Led by a Man Named Kelly Green

First Baptist Church, El Dorado, Arkansas

Cathy and I have had the privilege of serving in six different Southern Baptist churches. We have had wonderful experiences in each of the churches and have had made life-long friendships in each one.

When we moved to El Dorado in 1971 to establish my surgical practice, we immediately joined the First Baptist Church without visiting any other church. I was raised in this church and had made a profession of faith at age ten on an Easter Sunday. Many of my friends had done the same at that age, and it seemed to be the right thing. I had no understanding of grace and salvation and was simply joining the church, which I believed assured me of eternal life and a right standing with the Lord. In 1971, Pop had already departed, but Mom was still living, and her membership was at First Baptist along with Bubba and his family. We were impressed with the excellent sermons by the pastor, Dr. Don Harbuck, and his winsome personality made us immediately feel welcomed.

During our early days in El Dorado, Cathy and I were nominal church members, but then we jointly decided to become more active in church to set a better example for our two young children at the time, John Aaron and Mary Kay. Within a year we were attending a couple's Sunday school class taught by Robert Wike and slowly developing strong relationships in the class. We were exposed to Biblical principles which had previously escaped us because we had not been searching for them. We became so active in the class by 1975 that Robert asked me to co-teach it with him. I began studying the Bible in earnest and utilizing the awakening skills of teaching that God had given me. It was definitely a growing process because, in the beginning, I was a mediocre teacher at best.

As a result of a number of events and circumstances, Cathy and I attended a Bill Gothard seminar in Dallas, Texas in August, 1977, where we were transformed. For the first time the gospel promises became personal, and we were changed by the saving power of the Lord Jesus.

Dr. Harbuck continued as pastor of First Baptist until June, 1983, when he resigned to become pastor of the First Baptist Church of Chattanooga, Tennessee. I was fortunate to have been on the Pastor Search Committee, and the church eventually called Dr. Mark Coppenger as pastor in December, 1983. He had never pastored a church and had only recently graduated from seminary, but his giftedness and zeal for the Lord confirmed he was God's man for our church at this time. Over the next five years the church took a new direction in theology and ministry under Dr. Coppenger's leadership, and I believe we became the leading church in the area. There was a new emphasis on soul-winning, discipleship, local and overseas missions, and the church grew both numerically and spiritually. It was an exciting and vibrant church in which to serve.

In the spring of 1987, Dr. Coppenger announced he had scheduled a four-day, church-wide revival in August with Kelly Green, an evangelist from Mobile, Alabama. I had never heard of him and initially thought with the name "Kelly Green," he must surely have some other gimmicks to accompany his unusual name. My attitude toward him changed when he scheduled a decision-counsellor training session one month prior to the revival.

Our church began planning and praying well in advance of the August start date. Sixty-six people met at the church for a two-day training session. We used the Billy Graham Christian Life and Witnessing Course taught by two men from Oklahoma who were on Kelly's board. In addition, cottage prayer meetings were scheduled and attended by one hundred and eighty-five members. One week prior to the revival, home visits were made to personally invite people to attend. We were told by the revival team to expect two to three public decisions for every counsellor trained prior to the revival. I was skeptical of those statistics, although to my knowledge there had never been such extensive preparation prior to any revival.

The revival team included Kelly Green and his youth associate, Todd Roberts, along with gifted musicians, Mike and Faye Speck. From the outset on Sunday morning, there was an unusual sense of expectation and brokenness. Responding to altar-call invitations at the close of each service were thirty to forty people. The decisions ranged from salvation, to rededication, to request for special prayer for reconciliation over broken relationships.

At the Tuesday evening meeting, Kelly announced he sensed a special presence of the power of the Holy Spirit and was not going to preach. He quoted John 3:16 and invited all who were convicted to come to the altar. There were more than fifty public decisions this one evening and Kelly decided to extend the revival two more days. By the close of the meeting on Friday there were one hundred and ninety-eight people who had made decisions to follow Christ.

I had never before or since been part of such a revival. There were some members who attended and said what occurred was emotionalism and not a true moving of the Holy Spirit. The proof of any spiritual transformation is demonstrated by what the people are like going forward. I can name at least twenty people who are now walking with God as a direct result of what took place at that revival meeting many years ago. I am grateful God allowed Cathy and me to be there to experience the miraculous and see the invisible. God confirms in His Word "the things which are seen are temporal while the things which are not seen are eternal" (2 Cor 4:18).

PS: As an outward sign of revival, our church gave the largest love offering ever received up till then. We were able and pleased to give as much as four times our regular amount to Kelly and the Specks. To God be the glory!

18. LESSONS IN MASTERLIFE

Discipleship Training Following a Revival

MasterLife Group, 1987

During the five-year pastorate of Dr. Mark Coppenger in the mid-1980s at First Baptist Church El Dorado, there was a renewed emphasis in personal evangelism and discipleship. Our evangelistic efforts were fueled by the Southern Baptist program called Continuing Witness Training (CWT), and those trained in this method of evangelism met once weekly at the church. We would go into the community in teams of two in a door-to-door fashion to introduce the gospel to those who had never received Christ as Savior.

As we improved and perfected this outreach, the Arkansas Baptist State Convention scheduled a state-wide training session for CWT at our church. Pastors and leaders from all over the state came to First Baptist to be trained in evangelism, and leaders from our church became their teachers. It was both refreshing and a little intimidating for us to be training pastors who were seminary trained and some of whom had years of experience in vocational ministry. On the final evening of the training, we went into the community in teams to witness. I don't remember how many people received Christ as Savior that evening, but as I recall eight people were saved.

In addition to evangelism, the church began a discipleship program called MasterLife. There were training sessions in various home groups of ten to twelve people using the material designed by Dr. Avery T. Willis. Dr. Willis and his wife served as missionaries for fourteen years with the International Mission Board in Indonesia. They returned in the late 1970s to work for the Sunday School Board (now LifeWay Christian Resources). He developed the MasterLife material which was translated into fifty languages and used in a hundred countries. The same material is being used today for the glory of God.

In 1987 Cathy and I had a MasterLife group which met for two hours in our home every Sunday night for twelve weeks. The photo above was made one night when all the members of our group were present. Joe and DeAnne Hegi were in their twenties and were the youngest members of the group. There were three couples who were in their late sixties and seventies and are now in glory. Tommy and Cleo Reeves, Ed and Lorene Rogers, and Jim and Lila Johnston added so much wisdom and maturity, and we were all blessed by their testimonies and faithfulness to the Lord. Bob and Sarah Merkle are still active at First Baptist and remain wonderful friends to Cathy and me.

As we studied God's Word and prayed together each week, God knitted our hearts together in special ways and gave us insights into ourselves and into each other. Tommy and Cleo lived on Madison about two blocks from our home, and we had known them for years. I had bought many suits and shirts from Tommy, who owned and managed B. W. Reeves Clothing Store. By the time of our meetings, Tommy had been a deacon at First Baptist for over fifty years. During one of our sessions Tommy was bemoaning the fact he was growing progressively blind as a result of a medical problem. He voiced his frustrations and anger at God for allowing this affliction to occur since he had been so faithful. Seated next to him was Lorene Rogers who had lost most of her vision several years earlier, and when Tommy finished speaking, she quietly but firmly rebuked him for his self-pity. She reminded him that God was not finished with him, and he could serve the Lord in different and even greater ways if he would submit to His power and enablement. It was a very touching moment, and months later Tommy would confess her rebuke that evening was a major turning point for his acceptance of the blindness.

One Sunday afternoon I was preparing to teach a lesson in the evening on personal witnessing to people who were lost. I was reminded by the Holy Spirit that I had a patient in the hospital who had just undergone a major operation for a malignancy, and I wasn't sure of her salvation. I had known Mildred Bell since early childhood, because she and her husband lived next door to my favorite aunt, Lilly Mae Smith. Mildred was also the mother of my good friend W.I. Bell. W.I. was an excellent photographer in El Dorado and had a very popular studio. He taken some of the most treasured photos we have of our children and family. I was so convicted that I left my study and drove to the hospital to witness to Mrs. Bell. She was alone in her room and had recovered enough from the operation to be able to understand the things from God's Word. As I pulled my chair to her bedside, W. I. arrived for his afternoon visit and stood behind my chair. As I was telling Mildred how much God loved her and wanted to enter into her heart, W.I. was saying, "That's right Mother. Listen to John Henry and do what he tells you." It was as if he were cheering for her and praying at the same time. Finally, in a very tender moment with tears in her eyes, Mildred bowed her head and asked the Lord Jesus to save her and become the Lord of her life. There was rejoicing with tears in her hospital room, and the Word says there was also a great celebration in heaven.

Later in the evening I was able to give testimony at our MasterLife group when the Master takes control of your life, the results will bring glory to him alone. He will bring life to those who are spiritually dead and light into the lives of all who are in darkness.

19. THE FIRST MISSION TRIP TO BRAZIL

The Church Develops a Heart for Overseas Missions

Brazil mission team, 1986

45

Dr. Mark Coppenger became the pastor of First Baptist Church in El Dorado in 1983, and as a young and enthusiastic pastor, he brought changes to the church. The former pastor Dr. Don Harbuck had faithfully served the church for twenty-nine years, but in his last few years, the church had become complacent and lost its earlier zeal for soul winning and missions. One of Dr. Coppenger's priorities was a refocus on evangelism, and a few members began training in door- to-door witnessing using the Continuing Witness Training (CWT) program. It took almost a year before the training bore fruit, but those involved remained faithful. Along with other changes there was a greater hunger for short-term overseas mission trips. At the time, the Arkansas Baptist Convention was in a cooperative effort with the Baptists of Brazil in a linkage called the Amazon-Arkansas Partnership Mission. Our church made plans for its first mission trip to Brazil in August, 1986.

Cathy and I had never been on a mission trip and were convinced this was the Lord's will for us. Our children were old enough for us to be away from them for the ten days required to make the trip. Our church was combining forces with members of Three Creeks Baptist Church to go deep into the Amazon region to a small town named Redenção (Hay' den saw) in the state of Pará. We began the planning meetings in April, and soon a total of thirty people were committed to make the trip. The purpose of our mission was to begin the building of two churches in Redenção and to send teams doing door to door evangelism. In addition to Cathy and me, my brother Berry Lee (Bubba) and his youngest daughter Becky made plans to go. (Years before Bubba had made a mission trip to Panama where he provided medical care to the Kuna tribe on the San Blas Island.) The photo above shows our entire team and includes Pastor Lowell Snow of Three Creeks Baptist and four of his members.

As part of our preparation, each of us wrote our personal salvation testimony. This was translated into Portuguese and printed on a single sheet with English on the front and Portuguese on the back. Each missionary had multiple testimony sheets for distributing in airports, shops, on the streets, and in the homes we were to visit. In our planning sessions, we had people with Brazilian backgrounds tutor us in the language, customs, and cultural differences. The meetings helped in bonding our team and gave us opportunities to commit ourselves in prayer for the work ahead.

Cathy and I wanted a few days of rest with her family in Florida before leaving for Brazil, so we drove to Fort Lauderdale with Mary Kay and Ginny. On the trip we stopped in Kissimmee, Florida, to briefly visit Cathy's sister Nancy and husband Norman to see their new law office which Norman had designed. John Aaron was already in Fort Lauderdale having spent several weeks working with his Uncle George (Cathy's brother). Those days of being together at Gram Young's ocean-front apartment were both fun and relaxing.

The plane trip from Miami to Belem, Brazil, was particularly memorable. I had flown overseas once years before, but because I don't particularly enjoy flying, I had more anxiety than necessary. Cathy said that during the six-hour flight, I just sat there looking straight ahead without talking much and having a white-knuckled grip on the arm rests. I couldn't close my eyes for very long because my inner ear would give me the sensation the plane was in a slow climbing bank to the left.

The large Boeing 767 was packed with returning Brazilian tourists, and the cabin was hot and loud with excited Brazilian children having been to Disney World. I kept thinking that if we had an in-flight emergency, we would be surrounded with people with whom we couldn't communicate. It was not a fun experience for me, but we finally touched down in Brazil. I think I was actually surprised we made it.

On arrival in Belem at 3:00 a.m., we were met by a Mission Board missionary who assisted us in getting boarding passes for the next leg of our trip. At 7:00 a.m., we boarded a much smaller, twin-engine plane for the trip which took another three hours. As we flew south down through the Amazon region, with nothing in sight but the rain forest, I asked the flight attendant what we would do if we developed engine trouble. He said we could not land in the trees because they were as tall as two hundred feet, and it would not be wise to try to ditch in the Amazon because of the piranhas. He left the solution to my imagination. By then I was too tired to imagine.

The landing strip at the Redenção airport was a dirt runway, but we landed safely in a massive cloud of dust. The Magnum Hotel was clean and new, and the thirty members of our team completely filled it. We were the first guests in this new hotel, and were told our safety was assured since the owner was the local Chief of Police.

Our first meal was in a well-known barbeque which Brazilians call a churrascaria (shoe has' ca rea). They bring to your table a large, sword-like device holding barbecued beef, chicken, sausage and a meat called *picanha*, which is the hump of a Brahma bull. We cautiously ate the meat and rice and found it to be delicious. We had already been made aware of the risks of developing gastroenteritis ("touristas"). After a much-needed nap, we dressed for our first encounter with our Brazilian hosts when we went to the evening church service at the Temple Baptist Church.

Cathy and Bubba at Temple Baptist Church

The name of the town in Brazil which the thirty missionaries from First Baptist Church, El Dorado chose to serve in 1986 is Redenção which means "redemption." The purpose of our mission was to lead as many as possible to Christ so they might be redeemed. Our secondary purpose was to begin the building of two new churches for the work of Christ in the area.

Redenção building team (partial)

On our first evening in the city, we attended a worship service with our host congregation, Temple Baptist Church led by Pastor Rosemar (Hose' amar). He had visited and given testimony in our church in El Dorado months earlier, so we already knew him. Also in attendance were our SBC missionary hosts, Johnny and Barbara Burnett, who lived in Belem. Their son Brett accompanied them and served as one of our interpreters. The church held about one hundred and fifty people and was full of members and seekers each evening that we had worship services. At each meeting, there were fresh decisions to follow Christ.

Morning devotion, Magnum Hotel lobby

We began each morning around 6:30 with a devotion and prayer together. It was a good time to reflect on the previous day and commit ourselves to the work ahead. On at least four occasions and prior to our prayer time, Bubba, Pastor Mark, Youth Pastor Hess Hester, and I would go onto the streets of Redenção for a two to three mile jog. The locals who happened to be out those mornings, particularly the children, would look at us with amazement. The sight of Americans was rare, but to see a group of them huffing and puffing while jogging must have seemed extraordinary.

All of us would typically go to the building sites in the mornings while the temperatures were bearable and would work together until the noon break for lunch. The evangelist teams would take a short rest in the afternoon and then meet the translators at 3:00 for our door-to-door visits. Cathy and I were on a team with another couple, and we had two translators working with us. Our primary translator was Lorenz, a pharmacist with a very limited understanding of English. He would translate our testimonies to the ones we visited and continue with his own conversation inviting them to repent and receive Christ as Savior.

An unusual Brazilian custom is when one approaches a home, he claps his hands instead of knocking on the door. It is considered impolite to knock on a door. On one particular visit, an elderly gentleman came to the door without a shirt. He stepped outside and then following our conversation, he suddenly ran around to the back of the house. I thought perhaps he had been offended. In a minute or two he returned with his wife and two children. He had put on his nicest shirt. All of them bowed their heads and repented to receive the gift of Christ for salvation. He said he didn't want to make such a prayer without having on his best clothes.

On one particular afternoon of visitation, Cathy and I accompanied Lorenz to six houses and were able to present our stories. We then stopped at a bar and pool hall in which seven very rough looking characters were noisily playing pool. As we entered, their conversations suddenly stopped, and we weren't sure what would happen next. The owner got two crates which Cathy and I used as chairs, and we presented our testimonies while seated. The pool players were quiet and respectful, and, before we left, we wrote all of their names on the list of all the people who had heard the gospel this day. Down the street from the bar was a grove of trees which was providing a shady spot for a family. Cathy witnessed to them about the love of Jesus for all and especially his love for children.

Cathy sharing The Way with some children

Cathy, Bubba, Becky, and I were invited one afternoon to visit a hospital owned by a physician, Dr. Gerson, and his wife Barbara, who was also a physician. He gave us a tour of the hospital and their adjacent home while Barbara prepared some very delicious refreshments. Bubba witnessed to Dr. Gerson through our translator Alberto, a Brazilian exchange student who attended Ouachita Baptist University. Dr. Gerson had never become a Christian although his wife professed a faith in Christ. In a very tender moment, he repented and prayed for Christ to enter his heart and life. He told us through tears, "This is a moment I will never forget as long as I live!" He invited us to return on another trip to work with him in their hospital, which I was able to do in 1988.

Dr. Gerson receiving the Word through Bubba and Alberto, 1986

A highlight of our witness in Redenção was a showing of the *Jesus Film* produced in association with Campus Crusade for Christ. It had been translated into Portuguese and was brought to Redenção by Alberto. We had chosen to show the film in the town square on Saturday night, which is traditionally a gathering time for the locals. Earlier that day, we had a sound truck driving around the area announcing the showing of the film that evening. Since there was very little electrical power available, we had a gasoline-operated generator to power the projector plus a speaker system connected to Pastor Rosemar's car battery. The screen was a big bed sheet attached to a wooden frame we had built. A phenomenon I wasn't aware of is that when one projects a film on such a screen, the movie can be viewed on both sides, thus doubling the number of people who can view it. Approximately five hundred people saw the movie and heard the message of salvation in their native tongue. I believe this was the first movie ever seen by many in attendance.

When our time in Redenção was completed, each of us believed we had been faithful to go where the Lord had invited and experienced Him in a new and fresh way. Upon return home and reflecting back, we believe at least two hundred salvation decisions were made by the people in Redenção to follow Christ by faith. Cathy and I were grateful to have been part of this team of believers and are confident we will again meet our Brazilian brothers and sisters when Christ returns.

Bubba, Becky, and team thanking God for the spiritual fruit

20. AN ABORTED MEDICAL MISSION TRIP

Success in Missions Is Never Guaranteed

Volume XLI   Thursday, August 2, 1984

A DOOR SLAMMED SHUT

The family of Dr. John Henry Moore has returned to us from a frustrating attempt at ministry. It was their aim to join with a team in medical service and Bible distribution to impoverished Mexicans. The DALLAS MORNING NEWS article fused with the kind permission of that paper) explains what happened. Although Arkansans and the Moores are not named, they were indeed part of this team. It's hard to see why God would permit this callous behavior. Might it underscore an evil, provoking officials to reform? Could it have protected the team from some unseen danger? Will it force the team into a new, more effective strategy or arrangement? Who can say how God works here? But let us not doubt that He is at work. Romans 8:28 is a good beginning point in understanding this.

The Dallas Morning News

Mexico turns away medical caravan

In 1984 Cathy and I were very excited to prepare for and take our family on a medical mission trip to the southern tip of Mexico. We were not prepared for the events which followed. Brother Tommy Freeman, a wonderful pastor friend had been telling us for years about a medical mission team from Shreveport, Louisiana, who had been doing missions in Oaxaca for the previous fifteen years. We made the decision to join them this particular year.

Dr. Charles Black, a well-known and respected surgeon in Shreveport, was the trip coordinator. He and his wife Mercedes had hearts of love for the people of Oaxaca and had been making the two-thousand-mile trip to Niltepec with their team since 1969. Brother Tommy had earlier served in a Shreveport church, and he and his wife Joyce had a close relationship with the Blacks. As a result of their friendship, they made several trips to Oaxaca with them. One of my surgical associates Dr. Bill Scurlock and his wife Barbara also decided to join the team. In preparation, the Scurlocks and Cathy and I attended an organizational meeting at the Black's home in Shreveport, where we got to meet most of the team members. Present were surgeons, anesthetists, nurses, and other volunteers. The excitement was building for the trip which included not only surgical procedures for a hundred patients, but also Bible studies for adults and children along with distribution of Bibles and tracts to people in the area.

Our family prepared months in advance for the trip, and, since we had no experience in what to take, we probably took too much. Our son John was seventeen years old and was planning to assist in the surgical area without actually having to be at the operating table. He had been in the OR once to observe an appendectomy, and it was not a good experience for him. He was also going to be available to Brother Tommy to help wherever needed. Mary Kay was fourteen while Ginny was twelve, and they would be assisting Cathy and Joyce in doing backyard Bible studies with the children of the town. We rented a van large enough to transport all the Bibles and supplies for their part of the ministry, and when we finally departed El Dorado, the van was completely full.

We followed the Freemans and the Scurlocks down to Brownsville, Texas, where we connected with the remainder of the team and spent our first night there. There were five other vehicles including a large trailer which contained the surgical equipment for the scheduled procedures. Dr. Scurlock and I would be doing hernia repairs and some gynecological procedures. A surgeon skilled in cleft-palate repair was making his fourth trip, and Dr. Black was skilled in club-foot repair. We were also prepared for emergency procedures addressing appendecitis and unexpected trauma.

The next morning, Friday, the team drove across the border to the customs office at Matamoros. We thought the crossing would be routine and would take about an hour or so for clearance. Dr. Black had all the documentation and letters of need from the proper officials in Oaxaca, which stated they had been well served for all those prior fifteen years. Mercedes and several other team members were fluent in Spanish, so there was no problem with communication with the border officials. As time lagged on and we all waited in the huge parking lot, we suspected something was amiss. After about three and a half hours, Mercedes came out and told us, "Unfortunately, they are not going to let us into Mexico." The excuses ranged from the fact we did not have the proper documentation, to a border war in progress in Nicaragua, which made it too risky to allow us to enter. They said since it was Friday, we could wait until Monday and communicate with officials in Mexico City. Perhaps they would grant us clearance. We knew this was simply a delaying tactic, and we would not be allowed to cross the border at all.

We were crushed and heart-broken. We joined together in prayer for the people of Niltepec, some of whom had traveled miles on foot to have the needed operations and would now have to wait at least another year. We cried and called out to God, "Why this disappointment?" and "Why now?"

One member of the team was a reporter from the *Dallas Morning News,* and he planned to document and publish a day-by-day account of this mission in his newspaper. Instead, he wrote of the refusal of the customs officials to allow us to enter Mexico, thus thwarting the humanitarian effort for their own people. The article was printed on the front page the following day and was picked up by the Associated Press. It then appeared nationwide. Above is a partial reprint of our church bulletin and the headlines of the *Dallas Morning News* article.

We know God is sovereign and could have changed the border official's ruling which kept us from our planned mission. I believe he protected us from dangers ahead of which we were unaware and ultimately accomplished his purposes in us and in the people in Niltepec. Thanks be to God who daily fills us with his riches and leads us in his paths of righteousness!

21. THE ICR CLOTHING MINISTRY

God Opens a New Door for International Ministry

When Cathy and I began our ministry with The International Congress on Revival (ICR) in 1989, it was a result of our friendship with Brother Bill Stafford. He had taken over the leadership of the organization from the founder Manley Beasley. Brother Manley had recently died at a relatively young age from the effects of several devastating medical illnesses. Brother Bill invited me to join the reorganized board of ICR, and I agreed, although I knew very little about the history and ministry of the organization. I did know Brother Bill and was confident of his zeal for evangelism and missions.

During my first year on the board, Cathy and I did not attend the annual European conference. Each year these conferences were held in various European cities, including Vienna and Salzburg in Austria and even one year in Les Diablerets, Switzerland. The meetings were held for the benefit of Western and Eastern European pastors and their wives. Reservations were made in a very nice hotel for four days, and the conferences consisted of outstanding preaching, anointed music, and a general air of rest and renewal. All the European expenses including travel were covered by ICR. Each of these pastors worked extremely hard in their respective churches with very little compensation, and they had no extra money for leisure and travel. A few of the men served as pastors of multiple churches. And they came from a range of countries, including France, Germany, and Austria in Western Europe; and Romania, Hungary, Poland, the Czech Republic, Bulgaria, Ukraine, and Russia in Eastern Europe.

During my second year on the board, Brother Bill convinced us that our presence at the conference would be invaluable for the love and encouragement we would bring to the pastors and wives. I had no thoughts about preaching, but Cathy and I both considered leading breakout sessions in which we could share ministry ideas concerning marriage and family. We were still uncertain about the value of our attendance when we agreed to go for the first time. There were to be eighteen other Americans making the trip, and we were taking our older daughter Mary Kay, her husband Dave Janke, and our younger daughter Ginny. The conference was in Salzburg, Austria, with a side trip to Innsbruck for three days prior to the meeting. During those conference days we had many memorable experiences with our children and the new friends we met among the Americans and the European pastors. We also discovered that we did have a ministry role in attending future conferences.

Cathy noted that most of the European pastors and wives, although neatly dressed, seemed to wear the same clothes each day. She purposed in her heart she would bring at least one extra outfit the following year to give to a pastor's wife. Thus began the idea of an ICR clothing ministry.

Months in advance of each conference, Cathy began formulating ideas for obtaining clothes for the pastors' wives and asked several of our friends if they would consider giving at least one nice outfit. The response was encouraging, and she also asked if I would carry an extra suit or sports coat for a pastor. We were not taking old and worn-out suits and dresses, but clothes currently being worn which were essentially new.

Our couples Sunday school class caught the vision of this new phase of ministry, and they began bringing nice and attractive clothing for us to distribute. We had some concern that the volume and weight of the clothing would exceed the seventy-five-pound limit of the airline and thus become very expensive. We placed the clothes in large duffel bags, and, when weighed at check in, the weight did, indeed, exceed the limit. We explained to the airlines clerk the purpose for the large number of clothes, and she graciously waived all extra charges.

In addition to bringing extra clothes, Cathy called the wives of other conference attendees, and they brought extra clothing for the first time. The initial effort made for this new ministry did not produce an extremely large initial response, but when we saw the joy and delight of the recipients, we knew the ministry must continue and be enlarged going forward.

The distribution of the clothes took place in our hotel room, and, when it was announced we were giving away suits and dresses, our room filled quickly with seekers. Cathy has the unique ability to look at an individual and know the size clothing they wear, so she became known as having the spiritual gift of "sizing." She also has a great heart of generosity, which meant when the clothing we brought specifically for giving was depleted and some were still waiting, she began giving our own personal clothing. On one occasion I had brought my favorite sports coat, which was tailor-made and very expensive. When I came to the room that afternoon, I immediately spotted a tall Romanian pastor with my coat on and noted it fit him perfectly. Cathy saw me shaking his hand and said, "Doesn't that coat look perfect on Pastor Mickael?" I responded it did, but inside I didn't want to part with my coat. Cathy was teaching me to have a more generous and giving spirit.

On the first trip, we brought a new three-piece suit owned by El Dorado's Fire Chief, who was a member of our Sunday school class along with his wife. He was a very large man, and I didn't think there would be a man in attendance who could wear such a large suit. Most of the European pastors were medium to small in size. Cathy immediately spotted a Ukrainian pastor who was far above average in size. When he tried on the suit, it appeared to have been tailor-made for him. He began weeping as he told us in his marked accent that he had never in his life owned such a fine suit of clothes. We all wept and rejoiced with him. He wore the suit to every meeting for the next three days as an expression of his gratitude. When we returned home and told Chief Ben the story, he could not keep back his tears.

In the following years, the clothing ministry greatly expanded as other American wives including my sister Marilyn Berry brought increasingly greater numbers of beautiful and expensive garments to distribute. The hotels in which we stayed provided a separate room for the clothes, and the room eventually looked like a well-stocked clothing store. These tangible expressions of love and encouragement from the Lord Jesus through the wives to those European pastors and wives made the ICR ministry very special. Cathy would not acknowledge her role in this vital ministry, but it was her vision and initial planning which set all of it in motion. All glory for the fruit belongs to the Lord Jesus Christ who made it all possible.

22. "GOD WILL MAKE A WAY"

Our Ministry in Florida

Moving to Florida in October, 1999

There are thousands of excited folks moving to Florida every year and tens of thousands more who would love to move to the Sunshine State. Cathy and I were very excited to move to Largo, Florida, in October, 1999, with visions of beginning a new health care ministry there.

The First Baptist Church of Indian Rocks had been working for over a year on plans for a church-based health clinic when they contacted me in the spring of 1999 to consider becoming their first medical director. Initially I was intrigued with the concept and fully believed health care and healing should be part of the ministry of the church. However, I didn't think a clinic like this would be a good fit for a surgeon. The organizers at the church had proposed the clinic to be a minor emergency room clinic with walk-in patients needing treatment for various acute and sub-acute problems. It was not planned to be a family practice clinic for treating chronic illnesses such as hypertension, diabetes, heart disease, or chronic pediatric problems. I felt confident in my medical abilities to manage such a walk-in clinic.

In addition, the physician would function as the sports medicine doctor for the large Christian school which was part of the church, and he would have the privilege of lecturing in the school on health-related issues. I was also told that the church wanted to ordain me as a minister with full ministerial duties such as preaching, hospital visitation, and baptism along with marrying and burying privileges. This would authenticate to the church body that the clinic was a ministry of the church and not simply a free-standing medical service.

In my early discussions with Pastor Charlie Martin, I told him there were two major obstacles to our coming; the care of my aged Mom who was eighty-nine, and the requirement in Florida for taking and passing the state's medical exam. When I graduated from medical school thirty-three years earlier, I considered taking the Florida exam, but reports of its difficulty made me wonder if I could pass it. To my relief, a physician member of the FBCIR (First Baptist Church of Indian Rocks) clinic board reviewed the requirements for physician licensing and reported to Pastor Martin that a board-certified physician in surgery could receive a Florida medical license by reciprocity and was not required to take the exam. (I did not fact check for myself the state medical laws of Florida, which was a serious mistake.) In the meantime, Cathy had found a wonderful, sweet Christian named Minnie Springer who agreed to be the full-time care giver for Mom. It seemed the obstacles for us to make the move had been removed.

Following a visit to Largo and interviewing with the people associated with the clinic, we accepted their offer and planned our move in the fall of 1999. Cathy and I had spent hours together in discussion and prayer before coming to such a life-altering decision. We would be leaving home, family, church family, and countless friends we had made during the previous twenty-nine years in El Dorado. I was convinced this was the will of God, and, although Cathy was not as convinced, she chose to go willingly while honoring my decision.

No sooner had we settled into the home we purchased in Clearwater (a few miles away from the clinic) in October of 1999, I discovered that the information I was given concerning the Florida Medical Board was only partially true. A board-certified physician requesting a reciprocity license must have taken a re-certification exam in his specialty within the previous ten years. I had never been required to take such an exam in general surgery. My only option at this point was to begin studying for the exam which was to be given in Tampa in early December.

I immediately began spending six to eight hours daily studying for the exam. I tried not to think of the consequences of failing to make a passing score. In the meantime, Cathy and I immersed ourselves into the ministry of the church by agreeing to teach a senior adult Bible class. On our first Sunday, five people attended, and only two of those sweet folks were able to walk without the use of a cane or walker. One required a wheelchair. We began loving on our class members by having fellowships and dinner meetings, and within six months the class attendance increased to over seventy. The rapid growth of the class was one of the highlights of our time in Florida.

I began my additional ministries to the church family by attending weekly church staff meetings and becoming acquainted with the twenty-plus staff members. I made hospital visits, baptized at least six new believers, and even preached the sermon one Sunday evening. Pastor Martin scheduled my ordination into the gospel ministry for the last week in November. The process required sitting for two hours before an ordination council of fifteen ministers and answering all their questions concerning my understanding of biblical theology and Baptist church doctrine. They also asked me to describe my spiritual journey to this point.

The ordination service was a spiritual high for Cathy and me. All of our children and grandchildren were able to be present, which was especially wonderful. My sister Marilyn and husband George Berry from Austin, Texas, were able to attend. Cathy's brother George and wife Dawn came from Fort Lauderdale along with her nephew Clay Selfridge from Kissimmee, Florida. My brother Berry Lee (Bubba) and one of his daughters, Rachel Uth from West Monroe, Louisiana, also attended. Our good friend and evangelist Bill Stafford from Chattanooga, Tennessee, came, and both he and Bubba delivered the ordination sermons. The ordination was held on the Sunday following Thanksgiving, which was helpful in allowing so many of our family members to travel to Florida. The weekend was a definite highlight of our Florida experience, but the dreaded medical board test lay ahead the next week.

The first week in December I drove to Tampa and took the eight-hour computerized test, which was another first for me. In the previous fifty-five years of test-taking, I had never used a computer to take an examination. For the next three weeks, our anxiety level was extremely high as we awaited the test results, but I finally received written notification that I had passed!! The final requirement for licensure was an interview with the full Florida Medical Board in Orlando one month later.

An Exciting Ministry Seems to Fail

The pressure and the fear of failure was lifted from both Cathy and me when I was notified that I had successfully passed the Florida Medical Board exam. The personal interview with the full board in Orlando in January, 2000, was a formality but still was quite an experience. I had to await the arrival of the license before the Indian Rocks Medical Clinic could begin operations, so the official opening date was set for the first week in February.

Once the clinic opened, we began treating a few patients each day. We anticipated a slow start until there was a general awareness of the clinic, and we anticipated this would take several months. One piece of medical equipment I was learning to use was the x-ray machine. We had a reasonably good machine donated along with a film developer but did not have a volunteer technician to take and develop the film. Within a few weeks, I was able to take satisfactory films, and this made me appreciate more fully the value of x-ray techs. I was glad to finally be doing the health care ministry to which I believed God had called me. It was certainly different from the surgical practice of the previous thirty-one years.

After two months of clinic operation, I began having serious doubts about my future at The Indian Rocks Medical Clinic. There were two significant events which greatly affected my continuation as medical director. One was already in place when I arrived, and early on I had missed its significance. In the by-laws of the clinic structure, the medical director had no board vote on the clinic's operational matters, and I lacked final authority on these things. In effect, I was simply an employee of the board, whose chairman had no prior medical experience, yet was adamant on how the clinic was to be operated. The second event was the decision made by the board following my arrival to transition from a strictly minor emergency clinic to a general medical clinic as well. This meant we would accept church members for medical care, which might include treatment of diabetes, hypertension, and heart trouble. These primary care problems were outside of my professional skill levels, and the medical liability risks in Florida were much too great for me to go on without taking additional training.

I appealed to the pastor to intercede by having the clinic bylaws changed to give me the control of the clinic, and to make me chairman of the board. It had become evident I was not able to work harmoniously with the current chairman. He said he was not able or willing to make those changes. I told him my only option was to resign. I felt badly about leaving after such a short tenure, and I had desperately wanted the clinic to succeed. There was great sadness in Cathy and me over what seemed to be a misreading of God's call for our lives. We prayed and decided our next move should be to Fayetteville, Arkansas, where our daughter Ginny and husband John Luther lived. Our sorrow was turned to joy when we made the phone call to Ginny to tell her our decision. Her first comment was, "You are not kidding me, are you?" When we assured her we were moving there, she put the phone down and began whooping, hollering, and dancing, which we could hear through our phone. Her dog Scout joined in the celebration with loud barking. Amidst all the initial excitement of the start-up of the ministry in

Florida, Cathy and I had greatly missed our children and grandchildren in Arkansas.

The next big step involved selling our Florida home, a task which unfortunately fell on the shoulders of Cathy. I had to move to Arkansas as quickly as possible to find a job. Cathy had become skilled in marketing and selling homes, and we prayed for a fast sale. She alone began the arduous task of once more packing all our household items. Ginny and John found an apartment for us in a good location, just a few miles from the hospital. We decided I should load a U-Haul trailer with enough furniture for temporary living and proceed to Fayetteville to interview for a possible job in the wound-care field. I hated leaving Cathy alone in Florida, but financially we had only enough savings to live for two to three months without some source of income.

The morning I drove alone away from our Clearwater home was one of the saddest days of my life. I felt like not only a failure in my profession, but a spiritual failure as well. I believed I had missed the call of God and was now a sixty-year-old physician without a job. Without Cathy to encourage me on the trip, I had a huge pity party and didn't invite anyone to attend. It continued for many miles and for at least six to eight hours. It "just happened" that I had the radio tuned to a Christian station in the Memphis area. A song began playing which got my full attention: "God will make a way where there seems to be no way. He works in ways we cannot see—God will make a way for me. He will be my guide, hold me closely to his side. With love and strength for each new day, he will make a way—God will make a way." As I listened to all the verses of the song, tears of thanksgiving and repentance ran down my face. I had to stop driving for ten to fifteen minutes because it was such a powerful, emotional experience. I asked God to forgive me for not trusting his sovereignty, and I would purpose to follow wherever he led me and not look back.

My entire attitude changed that morning while driving outside Memphis, and just about the time I got into the traffic of the city, I got a telephone call from Cathy. She excitedly told me she had just sold the house for our asking price. I got so excited I took a wrong turn, got lost in Memphis, and it took an extra fifteen minutes to locate the correct road. I didn't fuss or fume one minute as I usually would have, because I was continuing the song in my heart, "God will make a way . . ."

23. THE FREE MEDICAL CLINIC OF THE OZARKS

This re-location process represented two major moves within an eight month period, but Cathy is very resilient, and we were excited to move back closer to family. It was very disappointing and a little intimidating for a sixty-year-old unemployed physician who had never experienced a major professional life failure to begin looking for a job. I could not have made such an emotional transition in life without the love, prayers and support of Cathy. I assumed that a faith-based medical clinic was not to be in my future and I stopped praying about such an idea.

Our move to Fayetteville was exciting because we were moving to a city where our daughter Ginny and her husband John Luther lived. With John's parents and grandparents living there, we already knew more people in Northwest Arkansas than we knew when we moved to Florida. Finding a home was very easy because we knew Ozarks Electric Company was building an energy-efficient home located in the outskirts of town not far from our kid's home. We had first option to purchase it. When we saw the plans and the location, we immediately bought the home, and it turned out to be our favorite home of all. The first week in town, I interviewed with a surgical group responsible for managing the Wound Care Clinic at Washington Regional Medical Center. They hired me that day to begin work as soon as possible. We began attending University Baptist Church where my good friend, Dr. H. D. McCarty, had been pastor for thirty-seven years, and we joined without visiting any other church. It seemed everything was falling in place, and we were confident we had made the correct decision to move back to Arkansas.

Adjusting to our new life in Northwest Arkansas was much easier than our Florida experience, because we had family there and an immediate sense of belonging. We quickly made friends through the church and immersed ourselves into an active role of leadership and teaching. We loved the setting of the University of Arkansas, especially the athletics, and were able to attend an increasing number of Razorback sporting events.

My work at the Wound Clinic involved a major new learning experience on my part, but with the help of the doctors and an outstanding nursing staff, I was up to speed within six months. I was working only thirty-two hours per week and earning considerably more than I earned in Florida, so financially we were more secure.

Apart from some significant problems in church, which were related to the retirement of Pastor McCarty, our life in Fayetteville was good, and Cathy and I fully intended to end our journey there. Professionally I had no immediate plans for retirement as I neared age sixty-five. My health was good, and, despite the fact I was one of four medical directors, I was doing the majority of the work. The other directors had full-time surgical practices and were happy for me to work as often as I desired. At least I was not taking night calls nor emergency room calls, and Cathy and I were able to enjoy uninterrupted nights and weekends together. Our phone seldom rang at night unless it was one of our kids calling.

Cathy and I had more time to travel and were able to visit our other children more frequently. Our son John and wife Gina lived in El Dorado, which is a five hour drive from Fayetteville, and we loved watching our three grandsons—Drew, Brady and Landon—as they grew and matured. Our daughter Mary Kay, her husband Dave and granddaughter Rebecca lived in Branson, Missouri, a short, two-hour drive away, and we made the trip there often. We grew to love Branson and the area of southwest Missouri, although Cathy and I were not big fans of the entertainment shows there. Ginny became pregnant with her first child not long after we moved to Fayetteville, so we were able to experience the excitement of our first Fayetteville grandchild. Claire was born in August, 2001, and any doubts of the wisdom of our move to Fayetteville vanished.

Early into our fifth year in Fayetteville, I got a phone call from Mary Kay in Branson concerning a close friend of hers whom we knew well. She had a serious wound problem following an operation and needed advice concerning her further care. The solution was not complicated but required a wound specialist to manage on a weekly basis for at least three months. She asked if the woman could come to Fayetteville, and I consented, but told her there was no need to make the long drive since there was a good wound clinic in Branson. She had called the clinic and was told it had closed. I called the Branson the same day to determine the reason for closure and spoke with the clinic's nurse manager. Their doctor had moved because her husband was transferred to another city, and the clinic was searching for a replacement. The nurse said, "Did you say you were a wound-care doctor?" I responded that I was, and she said, "Would you like a job here?" I said I was not looking for a job, but would be glad to talk with their recruiter to help him find a medical director.

Cathy and I were very happy with our life in Northwest Arkansas, and were not seeking another move. The attraction of a move to Branson was the opportunity to spend quality time with our kids living there. The recruiter began calling me weekly and assured me if I came to Branson, I would be the sole medical director of the clinic and could structure the clinic to my specifications. Medically this was very appealing since I did not have the same luxury in Fayetteville. Our decision for a move was brought to a head by the administration at Washington Regional Medical Center, when I was given a preliminary offer to assume the sole directorship of the clinic. The vice president in charge of all medical clinics said he would have to clear the change with administration, and I would know their decision within two weeks. I notified the physician recruiter in Branson I would likely decline their offer but would let him know soon. When I met with the official in Fayetteville, he said they had decided to "leave things as they are," to which I responded that "things would certainly not remain the same." This was a clear word to Cathy and me that a move to Branson was the correct decision.

The Fulfillment of the Vision

Cathy and I learned over the years to never make the statement, "We will never make another move!" We are fully convinced God desires we keep everything in an open hand including our place of residence. The Bible teaches we are strangers and sojourners on this earth, and our responsibility is to go where he leads. A pastor friend once said he kept his tent pegs loosely driven, so they could be pulled-up easily and his tent quickly moved when the Master called. True discernment is knowing it is the Master calling.

The desire to move from Fayetteville grew stronger as we considered the opportunities in Branson. The most painful reality was moving away from Ginny and her family, whom we dearly loved. In a very tearful exchange one evening, I told Ginny her mom (and, I believed, God) was calling us to make this move, but it would only be for a short while. Our plans were to spend three or four years in Branson and return to Fayetteville following my retirement. I have not forgotten the promise made years ago nor will Ginny allow me to forget!

The decision was finalized, and we moved to Branson in November, 2005, for me to begin the directorship of the Wound Care Clinic at Skaggs Regional Medical Center. We bought a large, beautiful home which was an easy five-minute drive to the hospital. This allowed me to come home for lunch, a luxury we had not previously enjoyed. The house was large enough to accommodate all of our kids and grandkids when they were able to visit. The Wound Clinic was staffed with outstanding nurses, all of whom had a heart for God, and we received permission from the hospital administration to witness the love of Christ to all of our patients as it was appropriate. The clinic facilities were adequate but cramped for space, particularly the area with three hyperbaric oxygen chambers. I advised the administration early on that if they were serious about clinic growth, the facilities needed to be remodeled and expanded. Initially there was reluctance to invest the necessary capital until they were more certain that I was was going to stay and work hard. I was sixty-six years old, but told them I would work four or five more years as long as my health allowed. Within the third year the hospital completed a major remodeling project, and the Wound Clinic became a beautiful, large facility capable of continued growth.

Late into my second year, I met a man named Don Rhoads who had an uncomplicated but annoying wound problem. He and his wife were planning a relatively long mission trip to Budapest, Hungary, and he didn't want a continuing wound issue since he didn't know the quality of medical care there. As we talked about Budapest, I told him Cathy and I had been there several times on mission trips. I also told him a little about our Florida experience with the faith-based medical clinic. I saw him in the clinic on one more occasion for follow-up, and his problem was quickly resolving. They were planning to leave for Budapest in January, 2008, and I received a phone call from him in early December, 2007, asking if I would meet with him and a chaplain friend for lunch. The purpose of the meeting was to discuss a faith-based medical clinic in Branson. To ask if I was excited about the possibility of such a clinic would be like asking if there are any entertainment shows in Branson.

I met with Don and Richard McCool from Lake Eufala, Oklahoma, at Bob Evans Restaurant for a meeting which was about to change our future life ministry in Branson. Richard was a chaplain with an organization called Christian Resort Ministries whose goals are to place chaplains in RV parks across the country, and to assist in the start-up of faith-based medical clinics for the medically uninsured. The purpose of each clinic was to provide quality medical care and medicines free of charge, and for each patient to have a face-to-face meeting with a trained chaplain who would present the gospel and pray with them. His organization (CRM) had started and was helping manage two other medical clinics. God had impressed them that Branson was an ideal place for a such a clinic since there was a very large population of uninsured people. The entertainment industry work was seasonal and most of the shows do not provide medical insurance. Richard said CRM was looking for a Christian physician with a heart for ministry who would be willing to take the lead for such a work. The preliminary organizational work had begun six months prior and included several area pastors and church leaders from different denominations. The clinic was not to be tied to a specific church or denomination. Richard asked if I would consider praying about becoming the director to which I replied, "No, I don't need to pray about it. God had given me the vision of such a clinic fifteen years ago." Within a week of our initial meeting, I met with Chaplain Dennis Maloney, president of CRM, and our hearts immediately connected. I saw the passion he had for such a medical and spiritual work in Branson, and I was thrilled to get started.

Many hours of hard work were done by some faithful people over the next ten months, and the Free Medical Clinic of the Ozarks opened on November 8, 2008. The board for the clinic consisted of seven people including me, a physician staff of fourteen, a nursing staff of twenty, a chaplain staff of sixteen, and at least thirty ancillary staff. All of the staff were volunteers as there were to be no paid positions. The physician, physician assistants, and nurses agreed to volunteer for at least one shift per month.

FMCO (Free Medical Clinic of the Ozarks) has been a work of God from its inception, and I have been privileged to experience his mighty hand through it. Many people have referred to the clinic as belonging to me, but I have assured them the clinic is definitely not mine. I was given the privilege of joining a large number of Christians who heard from God and responded with "Yes" when invited to join in his work. For me FMCO was the fulfillment of a vision from a faithful God.

The Work Continues

The opening of the Free Medical Clinic of the Ozarks (FMCO) on November 8, 2008, was the fulfillment of a vision God had given me at least fifteen years earlier, and He had placed the same vision in the hearts of others. One of the miraculous stories concerning the opening involved the position of executive director. In June, 2008, the clinic board discussed the immediate need for an individual experienced in the legal and administrative steps necessary to establish the clinic. The board asked me to find the person! I had no idea where to start looking but began praying with the board members and with Cathy. One week later on Sunday our Sunday school class was preparing for the monthly lunch we held in the Fellowship Hall. Standing near the kitchen door and waiting for his wife was Ed Williams, a fellow choir member and good friend. Ed and Jackie had recently moved to Branson, and had told me they were not certain why they chose this town. They had been married for seventeen years, and this was the second marriage for both. Jackie's husband died in an auto accident many years earlier. Ed's wife Dixie was from El Dorado, and I knew her well, since we both graduated from high school in the class of 1957. Dixie had died from a malignancy twenty years earlier.

In a brief conversation with Ed that Sunday morning, he said, "Did you know Dixie and I had a foster home in Russellville, Arkansas, and we had eight foster children we raised?" "I had no idea," I responded. "That had to take lots of administrative skill to establish a foster home. Would you sit down for five minutes and let me tell you what God is doing regarding a free medical clinic in Branson?" I explained the clinic concept to Ed and told him I believed he had the administrative skills and the heart to be our Executive Director. He thought for a moment and said, "John, you sure know how to ruin a man's Sunday afternoon." Ed called the next morning and reported God had spoken to him, and he would accept the responsibility. He further said he was terrified and needed our prayers and assistance. Within the next four months all the pieces were in place and the clinic opened.

There were other amazing stories regarding the clinic's beginning, but the fact it was organized and opened in such a short time confirms God's sovereign hand in it. Early in the planning phase I was hopeful the clinic could be open one evening every other week and later expand to have a clinic two nights a week. As I began recruiting doctors, one after another agreed to help, and soon there were sixteen who volunteered for one night each month. A larger number of nurses volunteered, and an equally large number of other volunteers signed up. There were also sixteen saints who agreed to be trained and serve as chaplains. We were astounded by the responses, and when the clinic opened, we were scheduled to see patients by appointment on Monday, Tuesday, and Thursday evenings from 6:00 to 9:00 p.m.

The servant work of the Free Clinic could not have been accomplished without the full support of Skaggs Regional Medical Center. Not only does the hospital provide free lab tests and X Rays, but has provided computer hardware and software. In addition, they allowed us to use their patient information website. The dietary department provides box meals for the volunteers of each evening's clinic. In July, 2012 Skaggs leased to the Free Clinic a beautiful office complex at a reasonable price.

Within the first year of the clinic operation Ed Williams believed God had used him to complete his administrative work at the clinic, and the job of executive director was assumed by Jerry Lilley on a "temporary" basis. Jerry and his wife Carolyn were founding owners of Lilley's Landing, a lakeside fishing resort on Lake Taneycomo. His background was that of CEO of Labette County Medical Center in Parsons, Kansas, for thirty years before his retirement and their move to Branson. Jerry's expertise and wisdom in managing the clinic was profound, and I told him on more than one occasion he needed to remain the "temporary director" until Jesus returned. In the latter part of 2011, Jerry was diagnosed with liver cancer and underwent multiple therapies throughout 2012, but his condition gradually worsened. Many days he came to the clinic and worked until he was almost too weak to stand. Jerry's service for the Lord was completed, and he departed this life on September 26, 2012. Tragically, one week prior to Jerry's death, Ed Williams suffered a massive stroke and remained in a coma in Mercy Hospital in Springfield, where he departed this life on the day of Jerry's burial, September 29, 2012. Two of the men God used to start and maintain the Free Clinic were called home to their Savior within a few days of each other.

In the second year of operation, we received a call from a retired physician from Effingham, Illinois, who said he and his wife had a condominium in Branson and that they lived there for two or three months each year. He requested volunteering for two morning clinics, on Tuesdays and Thursdays. We joyfully included Dr. Del Huelskoetter and his wife Ann into our FMCO family, and within one or two clinics, he became one of our most beloved doctors. His name was a bit of a challenge for most of us to pronounce, so he said, "Just call me, "Dr. Hulls!" Not long after he began his service with us, Ann was diagnosed with a head and neck malignancy, and he had to greatly reduce his time of service because of her continuing treatment regimen. When he finally had to stop his volunteer service, God raised up another retired physician, Dr. Bill Lauderdale, who was able to maintain the Tuesday and Thursday morning clinics.

God never begins a work that he does not sustain and make successful according to his sovereign purposes. I never dreamed our move to Branson would result in so many benefits for both Cathy and me. Having the joys of living near our Branson kids for these past seven years have exceeded our expectations, and this was our primary reason for the move. The seven years of work at the Wound Care Clinic was a wonderful climax to my surgical career as I retired from that work in November, 2011. The privilege of seeing the birth and growth of the faith-based Free Medical Clinic has been a highlight of my ministry life for the Lord Jesus. As the work is ongoing and the times are changing rapidly, the plans of Cathy and me are to continue our service for Him as long as He leads, and we serve with great joy and peace in our hearts (Prov 3:4, 5).

24. "THEE I LOVE," PART 3

Completing the Journey

50th Anniversary, 2015

Our move to Branson, Missouri, occurred in November, 2005, and Cathy and I bought a new home in the Branson North subdivision, a short five-minute drive from the hospital. For the first time in our marriage, I was able to regularly have lunch at home with her. Our home was large enough to accommodate all of our family for weekend visits and special holidays. We were anticipating lots of visits to such a fun town.

The Wound Care Clinic position was ideal for me at this stage in my professional life, and fortunately all the nurses working there were believers. With the administration's permission, we had a ten-minute daily devotion and prayer time for our patients at the beginning of each clinic, and we were able to pray with many of our patients. Some were led to a faith in Christ while being treated there.

Within two years of living in Branson, God opened the door in 2008 for founding of a new ministry, the Free Medical Clinic of the Ozarks. Cathy and I believe the clinic was the supernatural fulfillment of a vision God had given me years before. It was exciting for Cathy and me to be involved in such a ministry, and we began working together as chaplains praying with and encouraging people coming to the clinic for their medical care.

Because our children were members of First Baptist Church Branson, we didn't visit another church but sank our roots into the ministry there. This was a great fit in what we found to be an outstanding church. We were able to start a younger couples Sunday school class, which grew in numbers very quickly. I was fortunate to begin a teaching ministry there and quickly added two other Godly men, Hebo Hall and Dr. Marvin Schoenecke, as co-teachers. Under the pastorate of Neil Franks, FBC Branson grew into the largest Baptist church in Taney County. At my retirement from medical practice in November, 2011, Pastor Franks invited me to join the ministerial staff in charge of new member outreach and marriage mentoring. Cathy and I continued our mentoring of young married couples along with twelve other couples who had been trained as mentors for the ministry.

One of the highlights of our life in Branson occurred in July, 2015, when Cathy and others organized a second Moore Family Reunion, this time in Branson. The other reunion of our branch of the Moore Family occurred in El Dorado in 1972. Our reunion in Branson was over the Fourth of July weekend and was a wonderful success. In attendance were all of our children and grandchildren, most of brother Berry Lee and LaNell's children and grandchildren, and sister Marilyn and husband George. Two of their children and one grandchild were also able to come. It was so much fun being all together, and everyone agreed to not wait another forty-three years before having the third reunion!

The year 2016 became a physically difficult one for me because of increasing problems with coronary artery disease. Despite years of weight control and a regular exercise program, the genetic factor of heart disease in the Moore family began taking a toll on me. Seeking care in Fayetteville with cardiologist Dr. David Churchill, I found the pathway led to an open-heart procedure and a triple-bypass operation on December 1, 2016, in Fayetteville. The operation was successful with no post-operative complications, but the recovery was slower than expected and marked with persistent problems with atrial fibrillation. In the following two years, I had multiple outpatient procedures to correct the problem, but it has persisted and caused me to become more sedentary.

Throughout the years following my retirement in 2011, Cathy and I have drawn closer and more dependent upon each other. During the initial recovery phase of my heart procedure, when I was severely disabled, Cathy provided countless hours of care and support without complaint and with a cheerful spirit. She has shown me over and again what it means to be selfless and poured-out in loving one's spouse, and our journey has been instructional for us in the encouragement of married couples in our church. We believe the life lessons God continues teaching us can become life-changing for other couples.

When I had the words "Thee I Love" inscribed in Cathy's wedding band fifty-six years ago, I had no idea how those words would be lived out. At the time of our marriage, I knew I was committed to her for life, and she was committed to me. We have had a few rough spots in the journey, but there never was a time either of us believed our union was not made in heaven. When we surrendered ourselves to the lordship of Jesus Christ in Dallas in August, 1977, we didn't know how the Lord was going to use us but were confident he had a plan for us.

Over the years, Cathy and I have accumulated some earthly treasures, but they pale in light of our real treasures—our children and grandchildren. What a joy to know they are saved and living lives pleasing to our Lord. Our son John Aaron and wife Gina live in El Dorado, Arkansas, along with their youngest son Landon. He is a senior in high school and planning a career in the field of physics. Their oldest son Drew works for a mechanical engineering firm in Ruston, Louisiana. He and his wife Emily were married by me in June, 2018, and are expecting their first child in September, 2022. John and Gina's middle son Brady is currently working as a technician for Dish Network in Fayetteville, Arkansas.

Our older daughter Mary Kay and husband Dave Janke live in Branson, Missouri, with their younger daughter Sara Beth, who is a junior in high school. Their older daughter Rebecca just graduated from Ouachita Baptist University and will soon be deciding on her life's work.

Our younger daughter Ginny and husband John Luther live in Fayetteville, Arkansas, with their two children, Claire and Nathan. Claire just completed her second year at the University of Arkansas, and Nathan is in the eighth grade in a Farmington public school. They all are the delights of our hearts, and Cathy and I are so blessed to have watched them grow and mature.

I love the place God has us in for now and probably for the remainder of our journey. I echo (and supplement) the words of one of my baseball heroes Lou Gehrig, which he spoke at his retirement: "Today I consider myself the luckiest (most blessed) man on the face of the earth" (because of the Lord Jesus and Cathy).

II. Family Stories Along the Journey

Early in life, I was made aware of the critical importance of family. Seeing the love of God uniquely expressed in each one's life kept me grounded in faith. Following our marriage and the growth of our children and their subsequent marriages, the volume of family stories greatly increased. Each story has at its foundation an eternal spiritual value.

25. THE LEGACY OF DR. JOHN AARON MOORE

The Family Medical Patriarch

Dr. J. A. Moore, 1936

My grandfather, Dr. John Aaron Moore was the first of four generations of medical doctors from the Moore family. Three generations practiced medicine in El Dorado over a span of one hundred and three years, and the fourth generation who are still actively practicing are two sons of my sister Marilyn and her husband, Dr. George Berry. Their oldest son, Dr. James Berry, is a professor of anesthesiology at Vanderbilt University in Nashville, Tennessee, while the youngest of their four sons, Dr. David Berry, is a maternal-fetal specialist in Austin, Texas.

I have little remembrance of Granddad Moore because he died of heart disease in 1943 when I was only four years old. I heard many stories about him from Pop who idolized his father, from Bubba who remembered much more about him than I, and from many of my former patients when I practiced medicine in El Dorado.

The following is an article which appeared in the *El Dorado Sunday News* on September 21, 1930. Some of the words used are unusual and the format is typical of the news reporting in that day. This article is framed and hanging in our daughter Mary Kay's home in Branson, Missouri.

BELIEVERS IN EL DORADO
By Clinton Sanders

When a man builds something he believes in it.

Dr. J.A. Moore, 57, distinguished physician and organizer deluxe, has contributed materially to the building of El Dorado—and he believes in it.

Theoretically it may be said that Dr. Moore was destined to find his way to prominence in the scheme of things in El Dorado.

His father was a "booster and believer" in this community years ago. His grandfather, W.B. Gresham was a commissioner who conceived the physical layout of this thriving metropolis in the days when horse-drawn carts were regarded as the luxurious mode of travel.

Any old-timer might ejaculate, "It sorta run in the blood and Doc Moore got a double-dose of it."

The doctor is a man of uninterrupted thinking and an habitual doer. His life has been one of organization. In 28 years of successive residence here he has modestly erected to himself unseen monuments by following that program.

Dr. Moore is one of the organizers of the National Bank of Commerce; a charter member and director. He has been a stockholder in the First National Bank since its birth.

A profound Mason, Dr. Moore was instrumental in the erection of the $120,000 Masonic Temple here in 1925. He was trustee during the construction of the beautiful three-story building. He was worshipful master of the Mt. Moriah Lodge No. 18 F.A.M. at Lisbon, Ark. 1909 and 1910, and the past master of the El Dorado Lodge No. 13.

It was not that he bought his home on moving here in 1912 and of necessity make good because of the precious investment, that Dr. Moore wished to assist in the up-building of El Dorado.

This section was "home" to the young doctor. He was born May 9, 1873 on a farm near Three Creeks, Union County. He was educated in the common schools of the county and pursued a literary course at the State University, Fayetteville. Pride in, as well as obligation to a progressive community motivated the desire to make his a better town in which to live.

Even as he worked and planned to acquire an education, Dr. Moore labored for the city's betterment. He kept laboratory books and swept dormitory floors to defray expenses of a literary course in Fayetteville. Before attending his first session at the Memphis, Tenn. Hospital Medical College, the then youthful Moore retraced his steps to the farm to raise a crop and get his "stake." Successful with agriculture, he gained enough money to study a year.

He returned again to the farm and made his second crop, then back to school. In his third and last year at Memphis, he worked as a doctor's assistant and borrowed money on an 80-acre tract of land back home in order to complete his curriculum.

Following his graduation in 1898, Dr. Moore located in Lisbon, Union County where he practiced for twelve years. Removing to Dexter, N.M. for a year, he felt the urge to "come home." The year 1912 found him in El Dorado with his family.

He had married the former Miss Daisy May Graham of Lisbon, Union County in June, 1900. A conscientiously loving wife, Mrs. Moore fought for the principles of her husband. Their happy married life is happier today with three children. Walter, 29, the oldest is well-known and regarded here. He is an aviator and electrician; Berry, 27, is beginning a study of medicine, Little Rock; Lillie Mae, the only daughter, 20, is a graduate of Ouachita College, Arkadelphia.

A successful, lucrative practice has signaled Dr. Moore as a leader in his profession. He gained immeasurable respect for his untiring work in the establishment of the Warner-Brown hospital here. His time and money was for one cause—the alleviation of human suffering.

Since that memorial accomplishment, Dr. Moore has twice served as president of the hospital staff and today is its secretary. He is a charter member of the Union County Medical Society and has served as president and secretary of that body on numerous occasions. In addition, Dr. Moore is a member of the state, Southern and American Medical Societies.

In between those countless duties, he found time to do postgraduate work in Chicago in 1901; in New Orleans, 1912, 1915; in New York City, 1916, 1919 and again in 1923.

His spirit of accomplishment; however, reflects in those wee, dreary hours of a winter morning when he rode horseback for 20 miles to answer the call of patients. With the traditional "pillbox" slung about the saddle of the horse, "Doc" Moore swam chilly streams, traversed choppy fields and trudged homeward to shed a water-soaked overcoat in weather so cold the garment would stand unsupported in the hallway.

Dr. Moore prides his mustache. It's there because "I graduated and entered the practice of medicine before 26 years of age, and I wanted to look like a man."

Yes sir, the doctor still keeps his mustache- looks the part of and is a man. El Dorado is proud of him.

Granddad Moore still has a namesake legacy in El Dorado; our son John Aaron, whom we named for his great-grandfather. He and his wife Gina have lived in El Dorado since 1993 and are raising their three sons, Drew (19), Brady (17), and Landon (10). John is an attorney and Senior Vice-President of Murphy USA. The legacy in El Dorado continues.

26. DEEJI AND THE HORSELESS CARRIAGE

Deeji Gets a Driving Lesson

Deeji with Lydia, 1954

It was unfortunate for me I did not know my grandparents very well. My maternal grandfather, Henry Schmuck, had died before my birth, and my paternal grandfather, Dr. John Aaron Moore, died when I was only four years old. My parents named me for my grandfathers, thus John Henry. The only grandparent with whom I was able to have any relationship at all was my paternal grandmother, Daisy Graham Moore, who was affectionately known by everyone in the family as Deeji. She is shown above holding her first great-grandchild, Lydia (Caraway), who is Berry Lee (Bubba) and LaNell's first-born.

Deeji was in her late sixties in age when I was born in 1939, so at my earliest recollection of her, she was in her mid-seventies. She was very thin and petite in appearance and never seemed to me to have much energy or strength. I don't remember any specific illnesses she had, but I can recall only a few instances that I was in her presence apart from her home. Her bachelor son, Uncle Walter, lived with her, and up until the last year or two of her life, she prepared all the meals for them, which I think were meager. Uncle Walter was not very neat, and his bedroom always looked cluttered and disorganized. In asking Pop why Uncle Walter had such a messy room, he would say, "You know your uncle is a brilliant man and just doesn't think about things like that." Deeji kept the rest of the house neat and spotless. Her daughter Aunt Mae, who was married to Uncle Dick Smith, was her primary care-giver and was at her home daily making sure she was well-cared for and the groceries and other things needed for housekeeping were on hand. What I didn't know was that Deeji never learned to drive an automobile.

In 1910, Granddad Moore moved his family to New Mexico from Lisbon, Arkansas, which is a small community outside of El Dorado. He had contracted tuberculosis and was advised by his physicians to move to a warmer climate. Over the next two years he practiced medicine there on a much reduced scale, and the disease was cured with medications. He and Deeji and their three children moved back to El Dorado in 1912, and he began his long and very successful medical practice.

Sometime shortly after their move Pop said that Granddad bought the first gasoline-engine automobile in El Dorado and could be seen chugging around the mostly un-paved streets of town. I believe the car to be a Ford Model T, which was just becoming popular nationwide. In 1913, the Touring model sold for a whopping six hundred dollars, but offered Granddad a faster mode of transportation to make the many house calls he routinely made. Pop said that earlier Granddad drove a horse-drawn buggy pulled by his faithful horse Dolly. While he was living in Lisbon, it was said that "on many a night Dolly could be seen pulling ole' Doc Moore's buggy back home while the Doc caught up on a little, much-needed sleep."

At some point after the car was purchased, Granddad attempted to teach Deeji to drive their new and what must have seemed to her complicated machine. The levers and pedals in this automobile required a greater amount of eye-to-hand coordination than was required to drive a buggy, especially one pulled by Dolly, who knew her way around town. Granddad had a garage built to house the car, and it was located near the rear of their residence and at the end of a relatively long driveway. Following several training sessions, Granddad must have felt comfortable with Deeji's driving skills, so he allowed her to drive alone. I have a visual in my mind of the experience for both Deeji and Granddad. I can just hear Granddad's final instructions, "Now Daisy, don't forget the lever on the steering wheel to make the car move forward, and remember that the brake to stop the machine is located on the floor board on the right." She must have said, "It just doesn't feel natural holding onto a wheel instead of holding Dolly's reins!"

The first part of the trip must have gone well, and she probably went around the block at a snail's pace. I imagine that when she finally saw their driveway and was almost home, she gave the machine a little extra speed to prove her daring. As she sped down the driveway, she must have thought about Dolly needing no instructions to stop and so assumed that the carriage in which she was riding would also stop on its own. It was told by her neighbors that you could hear Miss Daisy's high-pitched voice screaming "Whoa, Dolly" as the gas-powered machine crashed through the back of the garage. It landed safely on the grass in the backyard without overturning. Fortunately, it was only Deeji's pride which suffered any serious injury, and despite Granddad's persistent and loving encouragement, Deeji never drove again her entire life. Some experiences are just too painful to risk recurrence. As far as I know, Dolly was retired to a leisure life in the pastures of Three Creeks where the family land was located and many friends of the Moore's lived. I imagine that Deeji much preferred Dolly over that fancy Model T and longed to have her back in service more than Granddad did.

27. "THE DEVIL IS LOOSE IN NEW ORLEANS!"

A Father Visits His Son

My grandfather, Dr. John Aaron Moore, was affectionately known in South Arkansas as "Dr. J. A." He was a pioneer practitioner in family medicine and was also involved in many civic and spiritual endeavors in a rapidly growing town which was fueled by the oil boom of the 1920s. When the Busey Well # 1 was completed in January, 1921, it marked the beginning of a population and financial boom for the area. Almost overnight El Dorado grew from a small agricultural town of four thousand to over forty thousand residents.

Granddad and Deeji had moved to El Dorado from Dexter, New Mexico, in 1912. They had formerly lived in South Arkansas, where he practiced medicine in Lisbon, a small community west of El Dorado. While living in Lisbon for twelve years, they had three children—John Walter (Uncle Walter), Lilly Mae (Aunt Mae), and Berry Lee (Pop). In 1910, he contracted tuberculosis and was advised to move to a warmer climate, so they moved to New Mexico where he was able to recover. When they moved to El Dorado to begin his new medical practice, they built their home at 317 N. Jackson, which was four blocks from the downtown square. At the time of their move Pop, was ten years old.

As an early settler in El Dorado Granddad was a major stockholder in two banks, the National Bank of Commerce and the First National Bank. He was one of the founders and staff members of Warner Brown Hospital, which opened in 1921, and he later served as the chief of staff for several terms. He was very active in the Masonic Order when they lived in Lisbon and was chairman of the board which built the Masonic Temple in El Dorado in 1924. Granddad's office was in the Masonic Temple building on the second floor, and that remained the office site for three generations of Moore physicians until Dr. Berry Lee Jr. (Bubba) built his office on Grove Street in 1967. By this time both Granddad and Pop had departed this life.

Granddad and Deeji were very active members of First Baptist Church, where he served as a deacon from 1912 until his death in 1943. All of their children were baptized there and received their early spiritual training through the Sunday school and the Baptist Young People's Union (BYPU), which was the name given to the Sunday evening training organization. Pop told me behind the scenes that all the boys in the church referred to BYPU as "Button Your Pants Up." As the largest and most highly visible church in downtown El Dorado, First Baptist was a spiritual leader in the rapidly growing boom town. Important decisions affecting the spiritual lives and growth of many were being made regularly. Years, later one of the long-time members and deacons at First Baptist told me that when he was a young man and a fledgling member and deacon, whenever there was a business meeting and an important vote taken on any particular issue, he would "look to see how old Dr. J. A. voted and vote exactly as he did." Granddad's wisdom and spiritual discernment were well-recognized.

Granddad's personality and demeanor were that of a dignified professional. Although friendly, he did not have an out-going personality and was never heard telling a joke or a funny story from his life experiences. Whenever seen in public and even while making house calls late at night, Granddad was fully and immaculately dressed in coat and tie and had his gold pocket watch in his vest pocket with the gold chain openly displayed. His older son (Uncle Walter) had a similar personality, but his younger son (Pop) was just the opposite. Pop was outgoing, openly friendly, talkative, and ever ready with a funny story or joke to tell. Pop was usually the life of every party, and he loved both life and parties.

When Pop graduated from the University of Arkansas Medical School in 1932, he decided Charity Hospital in New Orleans was the best place to continue training as an intern, and the city of New Orleans, known as "The Big Easy," suited his personality well. When not on duty at the hospital, he and our mother (Mimi) frequented a place in the French Quarters known as The Fireman's Band. It was partly owned by a fellow intern at Charity Hospital, and the typical customers were married couples who enjoyed the atmosphere of Dixieland music, jokes, laughter, and the serving of adult beverages. It was not a place of which Granddad approved, but he accepted the fact he and his physician son had differing views on entertainment and drinking alcoholic beverages. I'm certain my Pop never drank an alcoholic beverage in front of his dad.

After Pop and Mimi had lived in New Orleans for about six months, Granddad decided he needed to visit them to determine for himself the quality of training his son was receiving at Charity Hospital. He was also interested in seeing his only grandchild, Berry Lee Jr. (Bubba), who was five years old. Granddad rode the train because Deeji was not able to accompany him, and the drive from El Dorado by auto in those days took over ten hours.

Pop took Granddad on a grand tour of the hospital, and was able to introduce him to many of the distinguished faculty responsible for intern training. Granddad told him he was very impressed with the level of training he was receiving and gave his hearty approval. Pop thought the visit would not be complete without a tour of the French Quarter and also The Fireman's Band. Pop said his dad was very quiet during this portion of his visit and had very few comments and no questions

Upon Granddad's return to El Dorado, he was speaking with his pastor at First Baptist, Dr. John Buchanan, and was asked, "Dr. J. A., how did you find New Orleans?" According to Pop, Granddad never cracked a smile when he responded to the question: "Dr. Buchanan the devil is loose in New Orleans!" Despite the fact Pop loved living there and receiving such excellent training in Charity Hospital, I am confident Granddad was greatly relieved when two years later Pop finally delivered Mimi and Bubba from the influence of the devil in New Orleans. He brought them to a much safer El Dorado to begin their life and medical practice there. Granddad did return to New Orleans once more for a post-graduate medical course, but I know he never once set foot in the French Quarter!

28. IN REMEMBRANCE OF ME

A Mistaken View of the Communion Table

I was recently walking past the construction taking place in the foyer of our church and noticed some of the pews and other pieces of furniture were out of place. The large communion table normally at the front of the church was now sitting in the hallway, and when I saw it, I laughed out loud. It was not the table itself that was funny, but reading the inscription on the front brought back the memory of an episode years ago concerning a similar table. As a result of the table from my past, I was able to correct some faulty theology.

As a young boy about six years old, I was fairly regular in attendance at First Baptist Church in El Dorado, Arkansas. My grandfather, Dr. J. A. Moore had been one of the important lay leaders of this large downtown church. I was told he served as a deacon for many years, and I could also read his name on some of the plaques commemorating the illustrious past accomplishments of the church. My father, Dr. Berry Moore, didn't meet the qualifications to serve as a deacon and was sporadic in attendance, but he made sure that Mom had my sister and me in church on a regular basis.

The church was large and impressive in the architecture and the expense of all of the furnishings. In the front of the auditorium was a beautiful, carved communion table which must have weighed several hundred pounds. Inscribed on the front edge of the table in very ornate letters were the words, "In Remembrance of Me." I was impressed with the size and beauty of the table but was especially impressed when someone told me the table had been a gift to the church from my grandfather. By this time, he had died, so I couldn't ask him questions which a young boy might ordinarily not understand about such a table. I just accepted what I had been told and believed he had given a generous sum of money to purchase this expensive table. For me it was always a matter of familial pride when I was in church and saw that table right up front.

A few years later as a pre-teen, I walked into the sanctuary with one of my buddies, and he asked me what the words on the table meant. I was prideful, and I usually had answers to the questions which were asked in

Sunday school concerning things about church and the Bible. I told him that it had been a gift from my grandfather years ago, and it was in remembrance of him. My buddy only said, "OK." A deacon standing nearby who had heard my response said, "Yes, that table was a gift from your grandfather. However, the inscription is not referring to your grandfather but rather to Jesus. He is the reason for having the table, the church, and everything else." I was embarrassed I had to be corrected in my theology.

Following my spiritual conversion years later, God began opening my eyes to truths which have helped me worship him with more reverence and devotion. I am grateful for the heritage of faith from my grandfather and others, and I still have familial pride over his love gifts to that church. But when I read those words inscribed on any communion table, I know they are reminders for me and others to remember the Lord Jesus Christ. He is the only one worthy of remembrance, because he gave his life so we might have life and have it more abundantly (John 10:10).

29. THE FIREMAN'S BAND

A Place of Entertainment Causes Embarrassment

One of Pop's favorite stories concerning his two years of training at the world-famous Charity Hospital in New Orleans in the mid 1930s concerned a bar in the French Quarter called The Fireman's Band. This favorite hang-out for many of the doctors and nurses at "The Charity" was partially owned by one of Pop's friends, who was also an intern at the hospital.

At the time Pop and our mother Mimi had only one child, Berry Lee, who was five years old. They lived in a small apartment a few blocks off St. Charles Avenue near the downtown. Pop said the two years of their life in New Orleans were very happy, because he had finally settled into his career path in medicine. He had spent eight years in failing business ventures before deciding to follow in his father's footsteps into medicine. It wasn't easy to go back to finish college and then medical school at a later age and stage in life, but he had finally made it this far.

There wasn't much time for recreation, but occasionally they would join several of their married friends for an evening of relaxation at The Fireman's Band. This was not the typical boisterous and bawdy type of establishment often found in the French Quarter. Alcoholic beverages were served, and there was always a Dixieland band playing. The atmosphere was light, the customers were mostly married couples, and there was even a back room for their children to play with their toys. Pop said Berry Lee was always excited to go with them to The Fireman's Band.

Shortly after moving to New Orleans, they began attending St. Charles Avenue Baptist Church and found a perfect church home for them to attend. Mimi had never been baptized by immersion, and it was decided she should be properly baptized as part of their membership. It was scheduled for after an evening worship service. Following the baptism at the conclusion of the service, the pastor had Mimi, Pop, and Berry Lee stand at the front of the church so the members could come by and congratulate her and welcome them into their fellowship. One particular lady in the long line of members leaned over to shake Berry Lee's hand, and she asked him, "Young man, how are you going to celebrate your mother's baptism tonight?" He stood up straight and proudly said, "We're going to go to The Fireman's Band." Pop was speechless at Berry Lee's answer, because there were no such plans for the evening. Pop said that if he could have gotten under a pew or hidden from the view of those around, he would have done so. To make things even worse the lady asked Berry Lee, "Well, young man, just what do you plan to do at The Fireman's Band?" Thinking perhaps he might entice her to join them, he proudly said, "We sing songs, we tell jokes, and we drink Coke and Clear!" Pop said he doubted the lady knew "Clear" was a slang term used during Prohibition for a type of gin. He was absolutely certain Berry Lee had no idea what he had just said. He probably had heard someone at The Fireman's Band use the word, and he added it to the Coke which he loved drinking with the other kids in the back room.

This story has been retold many times in our family whenever Berry Lee was present, and he would always smile and sometimes chuckle. He had no recollection of the conversation. The rest of the story is what everyone in the family knew about Berry Lee. Not once in his lifetime did he ever taste "Clear" or any beverage alcohol. The only time he visited Cathy and me when we lived in New Orleans, he didn't request we go to The Fireman's Band or any other night spot in the French Quarter. Perhaps he was afraid someone might ask him about it.

30. BUBBA: A TRIBUTE TO MY MENTOR

A Brother Who Is More than a Brother

Bubba, Marilyn, and me

My older brother Berry Lee was my hero from my earliest recollection. By the time I was six years old he had graduated from high school and was a student athlete at the University of Arkansas. As an All-American high school football player, he received a full scholarship to play as a Razorback. As if that alone were not enough, Berry Lee was the valedictorian of his high school graduating class.

He was injured playing football during his second year in college but continued on a full scholarship although his playing days for the Razorbacks were over. His academic achievements continued, however, and he graduated summa cum laude from college and was then valedictorian of his graduating medical school class. Many people including myself thought he was too brilliant to limit himself to a private medical practice, but would surely remain in the academic field and be involved in research of some kind. However, following his internship year at Parkland Hospital in Dallas and two years of active duty in the US Air Force, he decided to join our dad in his family medical practice in El Dorado.

Our mother had died from breast cancer before I was two years old. Our sister Marilyn was five, and Berry Lee was thirteen at the time of her death. I don't know for sure, but I suspect in her last days, our mother told Berry Lee he needed to make certain he watched over us and protected us after she was gone.

Berry Lee was always "Bubba" to Marilyn and me. I can't remember a time when I called him by his given name. In today's culture, the name Bubba has certain connotations, but he fits none of them. He never owned or drove a pick-up truck with a gun rack, never wore a baseball cap, nor ever had a chew of tobacco in his mouth. He never drank a beer or even a sip of beverage alcohol, and as far as I remember, he never said a cuss word his entire life. Nevertheless, he was our Bubba.

Bubba taught me how to play every sport, from throwing a football, to shooting a basketball, to hitting a tennis ball, to rolling a bowling ball, and even to playing ping pong. He was very good in all sports, but I can remember very well when my skills in basketball, tennis, and ping pong exceeded his, and I was able to beat him in all three. For me it was the equivalent of winning three Olympic gold medals!

On at least four occasions while Bubba was in college and medical school, he wrote me four-to-five-page hand-written letters in which he gave advice and encouragement which usually a father would give to a son. The advice covered a number of life issues which young men face, but the gist of each letter was I should keep myself clean and free from the wicked influences of the world. Living a life pleasing to God would honor the memory of our mother. Marilyn said she received similar letters from him. I have kept each one of these treasured letters.

The greatest impact Bubba had on my life was yet to come. Following my training as a general surgeon and completion of my active-duty requirement in the Air Force, my wife Cathy and I decided to move back to my hometown in 1971 to establish a private practice in surgery. By this time Bubba had experienced a spiritual conversion four years earlier and was very open and zealous in his faith. He could tell Cathy and I were religious but did not have a personal relationship with Christ. We tried our best to avoid any discussions concerning religion with him. At his urging we attended a Christian conference in Dallas in 1977, and, while there, both Cathy and I received Christ as our personal Savior. Everything changed for us. As we grew in our faith our love for each other increased, our marriage improved greatly, and I started assuming my God-given role as spiritual leader in our home.

Bubba began urging me to apply the principles of faith in my surgical practice. I knew he prayed with all of his patients and had led many to a personal faith in Christ, but I never considered doing those things as a part of my practice. For all the years of training and the two years in the Air

Force, I had never seen any doctor except Bubba pray with a patient. Prior to my conversion I had considered such a thing as an unwelcomed intrusion of a physician into the personal life of his patient. Bubba challenged me to pray with each of my patients before operating on them by saying, "You are taking your patients into a life-threatening situation in the operating room, and this might be their last chance to hear the gospel." At first, I was very reluctant to pray with each one and my early attempts were awkward to say the least. Many of my patients had been referred by Bubba, and I later discovered he had been checking up on my faithfulness by asking them, "Did my little brother pray with you before the operation?" I didn't know this until, at a follow-up visit, one particular patient told me what Bubba had asked.

From the time of my spiritual conversion until he departed this life in 2009, my relationship with Bubba was one of a spiritual father to his son. He encouraged me to memorize large portions of scripture while spending daily time in the Word. We were involved in several men's Bible studies together, and for one period there were two other physicians who joined us. They too had spiritual conversions and were active in their witness to patients. For a short time, Bubba and I taught a couples Sunday school class together. These were times of rapid spiritual growth for me, and it seemed he was making a conscious effort to pour as much truth into me as possible.

Years later when Cathy and I moved to Fayetteville, Arkansas, in order to be close to our daughter Ginny and her family, my personal time with Bubba was reduced to the few times each year when we returned to visit our son John Aaron and his family. We spoke often on the phone, and he continued challenging, encouraging, and occasionally rebuking me regarding my spiritual life. At the end of every phone conversation, we prayed for each other.

Bubba departed this life at age eighty-one after spending the last ten years of his life as care giver for his beloved wife LaNell. She had developed progressive dementia, and Bubba retired early from his medical practice in order to provide for her. He finished his journey well by setting this example of unconditional love while modeling marital faithfulness for better or for worse, in sickness and in health.

Bubba was not perfect by any means and by his own admission had "lots of faults." He never disappointed me in his role as older brother. Even though I thought he was too rigid and meticulous in the way he approached most problems, he remained my hero because of his wonderful character. The spiritual impact he had on Cathy, our children, and me was huge and will continue on for generations.

It would be an understatement to say I miss him, but I know very soon I'll see him again at the feet of our Savior. Following several million years of worship and praise of the Lord Jesus, I will be very glad to report to our mother that Bubba did a mighty fine job of watching over Marilyn and me, and impacting our families for Jesus's sake.

31. "MURLYN, I'M SCARED. CAN YOU TURN ON THE LIGHT?"

An Older Sister Kept Me Safe

Bubba, Marilyn, and me

My sister Marilyn has been a strength and an inspiration to me for my entire life. Our mother died of advanced breast cancer when I was one and a half years old and because Marilyn was three years older, I depended on her for much of the love and nurture one would normally get from their mother. She helped teach me to read and write and often read stories to me at night when it was time for bed. We shared a bedroom in our early years, and because I knew she was older and braver, I would always call out to her if I awakened scared. As a small child I didn't pronounce her name correctly, and it would come out as "Murlyn." Later when Pop married our step-mother Athie whom we called Mom, she would occasionally hear me call out in the middle of the night, "Murlyn, I'm scared. Can you turn on the light?" She never failed to turn the light on for me and to calm whatever fears I had and didn't fuss at me for being scared.

Marilyn was also much wiser than I and had a calm reassuring demeanor toward me. I don't remember her ever being stumped by any question I posed, or being emotionally rattled by a frightful situation. Our Bubba loved trying to scare us at night by turning off all the lights in our home by the main power switch in the stairwell to the basement. He would come up the stairs of our darkened two-story home, clomping his feet and talking in a low scary voice saying, "The wicked monster is going to get all the little children and swallow them up!" While we huddled together in our bedroom as quietly as possible, I knew if I could hold onto Marilyn, she would save me from this "wicked monster." I don't remember what caused the monster to give up, but I thought it must have been something Marilyn had said or done.

She never scolded me nor spoke a harsh word to me, although I know there were many times I needed correction. She must have had to bite her tongue often! In thinking about that one quality that she demonstrated toward me, I believe I would have been terrified had she ever been harsh or unkind.

During our teenage years, I was not as close to Marilyn for several reasons. She was not as interested in sports as I was, and she was spending lots of time with her many friends, and also she was dating. I always checked out the guys she dated to make sure they were suitable for my big sister. When she decided to attend the University of Texas, I couldn't believe she would go to a school which was such a bitter rival of my beloved Arkansas Razorbacks. It turned out to be the absolute best decision for her, because it was there that she met a handsome guy from Lubbock named George Berry. They dated for more than a year and were married in El Dorado on July 27, 1957. Although I liked George very much and was certain he was the right person for Marilyn, when the wedding was over and I was alone, I remember crying pretty hard. For some reason I thought Marilyn was gone from my life, and I wouldn't see her very much anymore.

George was blessed with a highly intelligent mind, and he earned a doctorate in banking and finance from the University of Texas. It was always fun for me to tell friends that my sister was married to "Dr. Berry" since that was the name which many people in El Dorado called Pop.

George began his career as a professor in the Department of Banking and Finance at Texas Tech University in Lubbock. After spending seven years there he made a transition into the business world as a financial consultant.

Throughout his years in the consulting business, George has been highly sought throughout the state of Texas because of his wisdom and skills in financial matters. As a result of his success, they moved to Austin in 1978.

Marilyn and George have four sons who are now wonderful men with very successful careers. James, the eldest son is a professor in the Department of Anesthesia at UT Southwestern Medical Center in Dallas and has achieved national prominence in his field. His wife Elizabeth has her doctorate in medical ethics from Rice University and is also a professor at UT Southwestern. She has authored textbooks in her field and now travels world-wide conducting seminars and filling teaching assignments. James and Liz have two daughters.

Their second son John lives in Houston with wife Pat, and they have two sons. John graduated from the University of Texas with a degree in business administration and has become very successful as a financial leasing broker. John and Pat's strong Christian commitment has brought them through the recent trial of an extremely serious accidental injury to their oldest son, Brad. He is recovering, and the entire family is gaining greater strength as a result of their trials.

Robert, their third son, is an attorney in Austin and specializes in bankruptcy cases. He has a compassionate heart for people who find themselves in serious financial crises because of poor decisions, and he is making a difference for those who will follow his wise counsel. Robert has not yet married.

Their youngest son David is a physician practicing in Austin, specializing in maternal-fetal medicine and was just presented the inaugural award for the most outstanding physician in Austin. David has four daughters and he and his wife Lisa are strong Christians and role models for their family.

Marilyn and George are active members of Hyde Park Baptist Church, which has been their church since moving to Austin. Marilyn teaches a Sunday School class for senior adult ladies and has done so for over ten years. Prior to this, she taught in the children's ministry.

Cathy and I had the privilege of serving with Marilyn and George in the International Congress on Revival for ten years, 1995 to 2005. We travelled extensively in Europe and in Ireland as part of a ministry of encouragement to pastors and their wives. In our first year together in the ICR ministry, we went with the team to Israel and experienced God's power released in each of our lives in new and fresh commitments to Him and to others. Since that shared experience in Israel, the close relationship between Marilyn, George, Cathy, and me has grown even closer and stronger.

In His Sermon on the Mount recorded in Matthew 5, Jesus said, "Ye are the light of the world. A city that is set on a hill cannot be hid . . . Let your light shine before men, that they may see your good works and glorify your Father who is in heaven." Marilyn has been letting her light shine since she was a four-year-old while turning on the light for her little brother, who was scared in the dark and afraid the light might never come back on for him. She has been letting her light shine for her husband, her children, and grandchildren so they may become all God wants of them. She is shining the light of her life for the sake of a group of elderly ladies, so that in their latter years they may experience Jesus in a new and fresh way. She is indeed an inspiration to everyone her life touches and will freely admit, it is because The Light of the World lives within her.

32. GROWING UP IN EL DORADO

Remembrances of Happy and Carefree Days

Growing up in a small southern town in the 1940s and 1950s was wonderful for me. Life was simple, the environment was safe and except for the odor emitted from the local oil refineries there was no pollution. I had lots of good buddies with whom I loved playing baseball, basketball, golf and tennis; enjoyed hunting and fishing, swimming, and water-skiing in a stump-filled river; and enjoyed just plain having fun in a relatively stress-free life. If there were any dangers to us regarding serious crime, I was not aware of them, and I don't remember our making an effort to lock the doors of our home upon retiring at night.

Television was unknown to me until the early 1950s when I was a teenager, and the idea of each person's having a hand-held device to talk to another person miles away was only seen in Dick Tracy comic books. Going to the movies was a weekend ritual, and my buddies and I couldn't wait to see the latest installment of the serial cowboy movies shown at the Majestic Theater. Those were the equivalent of our present weekly television series, except that it cost us ten cents to attend a movie, at least until you were fourteen years old when the price jumped to a staggering twenty-five cents! The more sophisticated theater in town was the Rialto, but the movies shown there tended to be more of what I called "love story movies," like *Gone with the Wind, It's a Wonderful Life, The Philadelphia Story,* and *Giant,* and I wasn't particularly interested in them. The high price I had to pay out of my fifty-cent weekly allowance was also a deterrent to seeing very many of those "love stories." I was looking for the real excitement of cowboy movies starring such heroes as John Wayne, Roy Rogers, Gene Autry, Tex Ritter, Lash LaRue, Johnny Mack Brown, Red Rider, and the Lone Ranger.

Summers were always exciting because life generally centered at the Boy's Club playing baseball. As soon as the school year ended, the kids were organized into teams according to age and location of residence, and the entire summer was spent in competition with each other. I generally played on the Gulf Refining Company team because that was the team which included kids on my side of town. Our uniforms were not at all like the matched uniforms the kids have today. We got a white t-shirt with the Gulf Refining logo printed on the front and back along with a matching ball cap and that was it. The remainder of our attire included blue jeans and baseball cleats, which we had to provide. I only wore my Gulf Refining shirt and cap for scheduled games so they would last the entire season. Our team was always competitive, and for a couple of years we won the city championship in our league.

The real prize for the best players in the league was to make the all-star team. Twice I was chosen for the prestigious team as third baseman, and one of those years we won the state championship tournament held in Hot Springs. Going to the state tournament meant getting a complete uniform for the three-day event and having all our expenses paid while there. It made us feel like real major league stars! Some of the better players over a four-year span were Berlie (Beryl Anthony), John Lee (John Lee Anthony, Berlie's brother), Moody (Jim Moody), Mook (James Mook), Bussey (Richard Crawford), Buck (Jim Weedman), Norris (James Norris), Jody (Jody Mahoney), Pesnell (Larkus Pesnell), Tom (Tom McRae), Tommy (Tommy Murphree and Tommy Reeves) and Boo Boo (Jeff Murphree, Tommy's younger brother). These guys were highly motivated toward success on the ball field and later in life became prominent citizens, such a US Congressman, a federal judge, a candidate for governor of Arkansas (who came in second to Bill Clinton), an Arkansas state senator, a touring PGA professional, a college football coach, an owner and CEO of a major surgical instrument company, and three physicians. Not one of us however, was thinking about future careers when we in the midst of the competition at the Boy's Club.

During our high school years, many of my friends gave up sports during the summer and opted for summer jobs to earn serious spending money when the top wages for a student was on the order of one dollar and twenty-five cents per hour. Good jobs were at a premium but were available to those who were persistent. I remember Pop's telling me, "You need to have fun and just play while you are young. The time will come when you have to work and won't have the option to play!" He was right, but I just couldn't enjoy such a leisure lifestyle while most of my buddies were working.

Some of my most memorable summer jobs included working at Richardson Oil Company in maintenance, at the Lion Oil Refinery in the chemistry lab, at Southern Poultry as a "chicken plucker," and at Hanna Furniture Company for four weeks during their close-out auction. From those job experiences I learned how to relate to adults other than my parents and the parents of my friends. Some of the conversations and a few of the stories I heard from the adults with whom I worked were not things I heard at the Boys Club, but I was getting older and needed to learn how to filter the language and those stories through my maturing mind.

Fortunately, I was also receiving some spiritual training in the youth department at First Baptist Church. Several of my baseball buddies attended the same church so frequently our conversations tended to revolve around sports instead of the truths from that particular Sunday's Bible lesson. Our teachers tried their best to keep us focused, but such wonderful men as Mr. J. D. Beazley, Mr. Mac McCollum, and Mr. Homer Frisby taught us more by their examples of faithfulness than from their specific knowledge of the Bible. I knew they were just ordinary men, but if they had any major faults in their lives, I wasn't aware of them nor was I trying to discover anything.

If I could script the ideal setting and pick the right individuals to associate with our grandchildren in order to offer them the best opportunity to develop character and purpose, it would be similar to the ones I experienced. We did not have cell phones, iPads, iPods, video games, Facebook or Twitter, but we had good friends who enjoyed camping out, talking non-stop, playing sports, eating fast foods, and dreaming about owning and driving fast cars. I lived in a safer time at a slower pace, but it is not my desire to go back to the past. The challenges for young people today are greater and the temptations to stray are more numerous, but God's eternal promise for us is that his grace abound in us. When this happens, he is able to make us abound in everything we do. Cathy and I have raised our three children to love Jesus with all their hearts, and they are now teaching their children to do the same. We face tomorrow with a steadfast confidence in him.

33. "I'LL BE WAITING ON YOU"

A Brother's Remembrances of Our Mother

Lydia and Berry Lee, May 1934

I was born in 1939, the third of three children born to Berry Lee (Pop) and Lydia (Mimi) Moore. My brother Berry Lee Jr. (Bubba) was born in 1928, and our sister Marilyn was born in 1936. Shortly after my birth, Mimi was diagnosed with advanced breast cancer and began treatment in New Orleans under the care of Dr. James Nix, a personal friend of both Pop and Mimi. I do not know any more details of her treatment because it was too painful for Pop to relate those to me even years later when I became old enough to understand.

As a surgeon I know the rapid advance of her disease was directly related to her pregnancy with me, and the vast majority of doctors then and now would have advised a therapeutic abortion for Mimi to save her life. She died at age thirty-seven from the disease in April, 1941, when Bubba was thirteen, Marilyn was five, and I was one. I have no recollection of her at all, but have been told by many people a lot of wonderful things about her life and character.

Bubba was especially close to Mimi and through the years was the one most consistent in reminding me of her Christian faith and her unfailing love for Pop and her three children. My Aunt Lillie Mae (Smith) once told me the following account which really caused me to choke up: "I'll never forget one day when your mother was near the end of her life and was barely strong enough to stand, but she was holding you in her arms. She looked into your face and with motherly tenderness said, 'Oh, I just wish you knew how very much I love you.'"

After Pop married our step mother Athelene West in 1943, we immediately received her as our new mother, and I called her Mommy. As I grew older and more "sophisticated," I called her Mom. Pop never openly spoke to us about Mimi while Mom was anywhere around. He still loved Mimi and missed her greatly, but out of respect to our mom, he stayed silent on the matter in her presence.

After Cathy and I married and moved back to El Dorado to raise our children, there were a few occasions when Bubba would either show one of the few photographs he had of Mimi or mention a remembrance he had of her. I believe he wanted to remind us and our children of the heritage we had through our birth mother. We all certainly loved Mom (Gram Moore) who lived until she was ninety-four years old, and we all have wonderful memories of her. Gram Moore stories are usually a topic of some of our conversations when we are together.

Bubba departed this life in 2009 at age eighty-one following a short but fatal illness. Several months prior to his death, while Cathy and I were in El Dorado visiting our son John, his wife Gina and our three grandchildren went to Bubba's house to visit him and wife LaNell. As we were preparing to leave, we were standing at their back door, and Bubba for some reason was speaking about heaven.

> I know I will soon be making my way to heaven and can hardly wait to see our Savior face to face. After some period of time, I know I will again see our Mimi. Sometime later John, it will be time for you to make the journey, and I believe the first person to greet you after the Lord Jesus will be our Mimi. She will be anxiously awaiting you to tell you how proud she is of you. I want you to know I will also be waiting on you and will be the next to welcome you home!

Despite Bubba's advanced age over mine, I always believed he would outlive me. He had been an avid exerciser his entire adult life, with regular, long-distance running, and had better cardiac health than our dad and granddad. When he said he would be waiting on me, I thought it would actually be just the opposite. I am still learning how unwise it is to try to predict one's own or another's departure from this life. The Word of God does teach we are to live each day in gratitude and thanksgiving to the Giver of Life and to encourage all others to follow him. I am grateful to have had these truths reinforced by the life of my mother (Mimi) whom I don't remember and my brother (Bubba) whom I remember well.

34. THE YOUNGS OF FORT LAUDERDALE

Cathy's Family Legacy

Cathy, George, and Nancy, circa 1945

In the fall of 1964 when I was an intern at Grady Memorial Hospital in Atlanta, a friend named Marsha Moore arranged for me to have a "blind date" with Cathy Young, a fellow elementary teacher at her school. Marsha was married to a close friend and fellow intern Dan Moore, whom I had known since college days at the University of Arkansas in Fayetteville. This double date that night in Atlanta fifty-five years ago started Cathy and me on a beautiful and wonderful life journey and was the beginning of a life of grace together which was established in heaven.

After Cathy and I had been seriously dating for several months, I had the privilege of meeting the first member of her family from Fort Lauderdale, Florida, her mother, Virginia Young. At the time, Virginia was President of the Florida School Board Association, and she was in Atlanta for a national meeting of state school board presidents. I think the real reason she came to Atlanta was to meet the young man who had been steadily dating her younger daughter, and she had gotten word we were considering engagement for marriage. The evening I met Virginia (Mom), I was just coming off ER duty at the hospital and still had on my all-white uniform. There were a few spots of blood on my coat and pants leg from the day's work, and for years afterward, Mom would tell people, "When I first met John Henry in Atlanta, he had been on ER duty and was covered in blood!"

The Youngs were a pioneer family of Fort Lauderdale. Cathy's grandfather, George W. Young, came to Fort Lauderdale from northern England in the early 1900s and began a construction business, which was the first of its type in the city, and it became one of the premier construction businesses in all of South Florida. Cathy's dad, George F., joined his father in the 1930s and became known for his mastery of custom design in homes while developing skill as an expert on steel and concrete. Many of the businesses on historic Las Olas Boulevard along with the Riverside Hotel and the Governor's Club Hotel were built by Young Construction Company. During those busy years the company employed as many as one hundred and eighty laborers.

Cathy's mom was an outstanding person and unsurpassed politician in Broward County. For the decades between the 1970s and 1990s she was the best-known woman in South Florida. In addition to raising three outstanding children alongside her husband George (Dad), Virginia (Mom) was deeply involved in the educational and political life of the people of Fort Lauderdale. From her position as State School Board Chairman, she ran for and won a seat on the City Commission. For two separate terms, she served as mayor of Fort Lauderdale, and to this date is the only woman to hold the position. She also served two terms as vice-mayor and later mayor *pro tem* during her years of service for the city. When her time on the City Commission ended, she served on the Downtown Development Authority (DDA) for seven years helping preserve historic landmarks and direct new business development for this booming city.

The Young's three children, George, Nancy, and Cathy, were able to grow up in a beautiful ocean-side city where it was safe enough for young people to play on the beach unaccompanied by adults. Neighborhoods for the most part were not dangerous, and children could play without fear of kidnapping. Walking the streets and playing in yards in the evening and into the night could be done without parental observation.

Following high school graduation, Cathy and her older siblings continued their education by attending Florida State University in Tallahassee. George led the way in 1955 and pursued a degree in education leading to his PhD in 1966 with a focus on student affairs. His first and only position outside of Florida was as dean of students at Valdosta State University in Valdosta, Georgia, and he and his wife, Dawn, moved there in 1966. By this time, they had two small children, Jenifer and George IV. He served this growing college between the years 1966 and 1969 and was offered a similar position as dean of students at Broward Community College in Fort Lauderdale. This was the same year I was commissioned as a medical officer in the US Air Force at Moody Air Force Base in Valdosta. Cathy and I were initially excited to live in the same town as George and his family but discovered they had decided to move. One of George's last good deeds in Valdosta was to locate and secure for Cathy, our young son John Aaron, and me a beautiful home which we rented for the two years we were stationed at Moody AFB. George continued in his role as vice president of student affairs until his retirement in the early years of 2000. He was such a recognized national leader in his profession that he served 1979–1980 as president of NASPA, the National Association of Student Personnel Administrators. With his election he became the first administrator from a community college to have been elected as president of this prestigious organization.

Nancy followed George in obtaining her degree in education at Florida State, a program which she completed in 1961with a BA with honors. She obtained her masters degree from FSU in 1965, also with honors. Nancy's first teaching position was in Sopchoppy, Florida, where she taught in the elementary school. She moved to Titusville, Florida, on the east coast with her young son Clay and continued teaching until she became an elementary school principal in the late 1960s. At the urging of friends and colleagues, Nancy decided on a career in law and moved with Clay in the early 1970s to Gainesville, Florida. She got her JD degree from the University of Florida in 1977. By this time, she had met and married Norman Smith from Kissimmee, Florida, and she joined Norman in his law firm of Brinson, Smith and Heller in 1977. She practiced law for over thirty-five years in her new firm—Brinson, Smith and Smith.

Besides her love of law, especially family law, Nancy was an avid bass fisherman who knew and fished all the lakes of central Florida, especially Lake Toho (Tohopekaliga). She was such a recognized expert on bass fishing that she had a regular column in the *Kissimmee News-Gazette*, providing tips on where and how to catch the largest of the largemouth bass of Florida.

George and Virginia Young (Dad and Mom) each had tremendous impacts on the lives of people in Fort Lauderdale while raising three outstanding children who carried on the Young legacy. In my opinion the youngest of the Young children is the most outstanding member of a very wonderful family, and she happens to be Catherine Reta (Cathy), my wife for the past fifty-three years. I will admit to extreme prejudice, while at the same time am very grateful to the Lord for the blind date in Atlanta in 1964!

35. AN EXPENSIVE GALL BLADDER

Pop's Most Expensive Surgical Procedure

My Dad (Pop) was one of the last of the generation of GPs (General Practitioners), who treated almost every medical problem presented to them. In addition to treating ongoing medical conditions, he also performed surgery on the patients who were in need of a particular procedure. Except in an emergency situation, he didn't do neurosurgery or cardiac surgery since both of these specialties were in their infancy. Someone once asked him if he was a specialist to which he remarked, "Why yes, I specialize in the skin and its contents!" Because he had additional training in surgery at Charity Hospital in New Orleans, he enjoyed and became very proficient doing some very complicated operations. One of his colleagues in training was Dr. Michael DeBakey, who became world-famous as a pioneer in cardiac and cardiovascular surgery.

Most of Pop's patients were ordinary, hard-working people with average incomes. The local area had experienced an economic boom thirty years earlier when a large oil field was discovered, and overnight a few of the fortunate landowners became millionaires. My Dad had only three or four patients who were so financially blessed by the boom. One couple who had become wealthy with oil royalties were faithful patients and also good friends with Pop. The husband had done so well financially he had founded an oil production company, which was managed by his family. Mr. HPS had farmed all of his adult life until this windfall, and he continued wearing bib overalls except when he went to church. To those in the area who didn't know him, he was generally not recognized as a wealthy man. There were a few things on which the couple splurged however; and according to one of Pop's nurses, Mr. HPS once bought his wife a red Cadillac and had a chauffeur drive her wherever she needed to go.

During one prolonged period, Mrs. HPS experienced debilitating abdominal discomfort which fortunately was intermittent but continued for months. In those days, sophisticated diagnostic tools were not available, so many illnesses were treated symptomatically. This method of treatment was generally effective, but in her case it didn't work. She continued having pain and symptoms despite trying most of the available medications for abdominal disorders. Pop and Mr. HPS agreed upon a consultation at the world-famous Mayo Clinic in Rochester, Minnesota. She was seen and treated with medications by a large team of well-qualified physicians, and she seemed to be improving initially but had a relapse several weeks later. She had not been advised to have an operation.

Pop told both of them he was confident her problem was not in her stomach, but was a diseased gall bladder. In his opinion an operation was the only solution to her puzzling situation. They assured Pop they trusted his wisdom and skill and saw no need to return to the Mayo Clinic for an operation. They had failed to correctly diagnose her problem, and Pop was capable of doing the needed work. The operation was successful in removing the diseased organ and accompanying gall stones, and her wound healed quickly with no complications. It took her about six weeks to gain back her strength, but then she gladly reported she was free from the terrible pain and "felt better than she had in a long time." On her final post-operative visit, Mr. HPS sat in Pop's office and as he took out his check book he said, "Dr. Berry, let's get settled up on your bill."

In this generation because so few people had medical insurance, many struggled greatly to pay their medical bills. The surgical charges were very low then by today's standards. In some instances, wealthy people were charged a little more than the usual and customary fees, in order to balance the large number who were not able to pay anything. The usual and customary physician fee for gall bladder surgery in those days was two hundred and fifty dollars. Pop said to Mr. HPS, "I have thought and prayed for a long time what would be the proper fee for your wife's operation. You and I both know they couldn't diagnose her problem at the Mayo Clinic." Mr. HPS said, "You saved us a whole lot of money by not sending us back up there, and we want to pay whatever you say." Pop was still hesitating and perhaps feeling a little guilty when he slowly said, "Mr. HPS I've decided to charge you five hundred dollars!" As he began writing out the check for that doubled fee Mr. HP said, "Dr. Berry, you could have said five thousand dollars and we would have thought we got a good deal." Years later Pop confided in me at the moment when he heard what Mr. HP said, he wished that he had said five thousand instead of five hundred! He quickly said, "Oh well, it's just money."

36. THE LOST ART OF HOUSE CALLS

Pops Makes an Interesting House Call in Florida

Early on I was fascinated with most of the "doctor talk" I heard at home. My Dad (Pop) made medical house calls, so our phone rang constantly. The calls were seldom for me, but I frequently answered, hoping one of my buddies was calling to invite me to join in some type of game. When I happened to answer a patient's call, they occasionally would voice their complaints to me, and I tried to be a sympathetic listener. It didn't take long to recognize the voice of some of the frequent callers, and I knew the nature of their complaints even before they voiced them.

Pop was a dedicated servant to the people of our hometown. When anyone called for him to come to their home for a medical problem, he would go, usually without complaint. Emergency Room visits then were less frequent than now, probably because many fewer people had medical insurance then. I recall numerous phone calls after midnight when I would sleepily awaken and hear him tell the person on the line, "I'll be right over." An interesting characteristic of his was that he would frequently slip his trousers over his pajama bottoms so when he returned home, the time necessary to get back in bed was shortened!

As a young boy I occasionally accompanied Pop on his house calls. Because he was so busy during the post-World War II years, I seldom got to spend much time with him, so going with him on calls gave us great times together. Mom wouldn't allow me to go if the hour was later than eight p.m., so I could get to bed at a respectable hour. I loved spending time with Pop, because I got to hear his exciting "doctor stories." Additionally, he allowed me to carry his large, black medical bag, which was heavy and contained numerous "mystery items." An added benefit was that some of the patients called me "Little Doc." I loved having the title until I no longer thought I was little. I especially enjoyed going with him into the rural areas since many of the farm families would have a meal prepared for "the doctor and his helper." Those country meals were always plentiful and delicious.

One of Pop's favorite house call stories occurred in Miami, Florida, where he was attending a medical convention early in the 1940s. He had met a Miami surgeon who asked if he ever made house calls in south Arkansas. Pop responded that house calls were an important part of his practice to which his new surgeon friend responded, "Why don't you go with me on this call I'm about to make? I think you'll enjoy it." They arrived at a very exclusive home in Coral Gables and knocked on the door. The man who opened the door was introduced by the Miami surgeon, "Dr. Moore, I'd like you to meet the brother of my patient. This is Al Capone!" While the doctor attended Al's sister, this well-known gangster from Chicago offered my dad some refreshment and invited him to join him on a tour of the garden. Pop said this man, who was responsible for so much crime and so many deaths, couldn't have treated him any nicer during that house call. Al had recently been in federal prison, and was out briefly on parole to visit his sister who had been quite ill.

None of Pop's patients at home were celebrities or nationally-known gangsters, but were ordinary folks who had a loving and caring doctor whom they trusted. They knew they could depend on him to come to their aid regardless of the time of night. If they were unable to pay for his services, Pop would always tell them, "I'll just put it on the books." I'm confident that the amount of money which was "on the books" was much greater than the amount he ever collected.

With the advent of fully-staffed emergency rooms and greater availability of health insurance, the necessity for medical house calls vanished from the scene. Pop continued this part of his practice until he departed this life, because he knew he was providing a needed service for his patients who couldn't afford an expensive ER visit. He was a beloved physician not only to his grateful patients but to an adoring "little Doc."

37. THE QUALITY GROCERY STORE

An Unusual, Family-Operated Business

I received my first up-close experience with the grocery business when my mom and her sister Aunt Tooky (Thelma) bought the Quality Grocery Store in El Dorado in 1948. Aunt Tooky was a very special aunt from St. Louis, Missouri, and at the time was the wealthiest person I had ever met. Her husband, Uncle Max Manne, owned the Artistic Furniture Company and had made his fortune building moderately priced furniture. He once told me that he had invented the sofa hide-a-bed concept, but the Simmons Company had stolen the idea from him and had made millions with the product. Aunt Tooky was the one who personally introduced me to two of my heroes at that time—Stan Musial and Roy Rogers.

Neither Mom nor Aunt Tooky had any interest in the grocery business. Their brothers Ed and Paul West had just returned from serving in the US Army in World War II and needed work, so this seemed like a good option for them. After the purchase was finalized and the store was operational, Aunt Tooky decided to live with us for several months to help mom with the management of the store. Uncle Paul and Uncle Ed handled the meat market and the produce portion of the business.

They had one other employee, a delivery man named Clarence, who was in his early twenties in age. As a young man, he became the brunt of many pranks by my uncles who were masters at that sort of thing. They were always telling Clarence he needed to "find a good woman to marry," and they were going to help him find just the right one. Clarence would usually tell "Mr. Paul" and "Mr. Ed" he wasn't ready to "take that step just right now." Because the store was not making much profit, they were not able to purchase Clarence either a truck or a motor scooter to make deliveries. He had a bicycle with a basket on front which was large enough to hold most orders. The majority of his deliveries were within a two-mile radius, so bicycle deliveries were manageable. Clarence spent most of his working day making deliveries which prevented him from spending much time in the store. He would probably would have endured more pranks had he been in the store more often.

Bobbie Fike was working as a maid in our home during this period, and her service was invaluable to us since Mom spent most of her days in the store. Sister Bobbie not only kept the house spotless, but her noon lunches were so delicious my sister Marilyn and I still reminisce about them when we're together. Mom had known Sister Bobbie for several years before she and Pops married because Sister Bobbie had done domestic work for her back in the early 1940s. Both Uncle Ed and Uncle Paul had known her since those days, and she also became the object of a few of their practical jokes.

Mom's personal grocery shopping became much easier while managing the store because she could call Sister Bobbie for the things needed at home and have Clarence deliver them to her on his bicycle. Our home was about a mile away and usually there was another order close by, which would make his deliveries more efficient. By the time Clarence had made four or five deliveries to our home, he commented to Uncle Paul that Sister Bobbie was not very friendly to him. Uncle Paul teasingly said to him, "You had better be careful how you treat Bobbie Fike. She is one of the meanest women I have ever known." Clarence responded, "She don't look all that mean to me, and I ain't gonna try to make her mad anyhow." Uncle Paul said, "If you don't believe me, ask Mr. Ed just how mean she is. He has known her a long time and remembers one of her former husbands." When Clarence got Uncle Ed alone, he asked him about Sister Bobbie and told him what Uncle Paul had said. He picked up on the joke and began laying the ground work for another prank. He told Clarence, "Bobbie Fike has a terrible temper and once when she got into a fight with one of her husbands, she stabbed him with a butcher knife. He was lucky to live, and he got a divorce from her the next week." He expanded on the story, "Another time, a delivery man knocked on the back door and when she didn't hear, he knocked so hard on the door, it made the door rattle. She came to the door with a pan of boiling water and threw it in his face through the screen door, telling him he shouldn't make so much racket. It caused all the skin to peel off his face and he was in the hospital for two weeks before he could even eat." Clarence said, "You and Mr. Paul are telling a big story on that woman, and I don't think she could be that mean." But the seeds of doubt had been planted.

About a week later, Sister Bobbie called Mom and told her she needed a large number of groceries and in particular some items she needed that morning to prepare lunch. Mom gathered the two sacks of groceries and asked Clarence to deliver them to the house. Uncle Paul overheard and decided to spring the trap on Clarence. Mom didn't know anything about the tale her two brothers had told him. Uncle Paul then called Sister Bobbie and said they wanted to pull a joke on Clarence. He told her, "When Clarence knocks on the back door, wait an extra minute or two to make him knock louder and longer than usual. Get a small pan of *cool water,* and when you go to the door throw it through the screen door and tell him he is making too much racket." In about thirty minutes when Clarence arrived, he found Sister Bobbie was not in the kitchen as usual so he began knocking louder and at the same time calling out her name. When she finally arrived, he noticed the small pan in her hand, and he began backing up remembering what Mr. Ed had told him. When Sister Bobbie shouted he shouldn't make so much noise and threw the cold water through the screen, he was so far back from the door that very little water got to him. Both sacks of groceries were thrown in the air, and he made a scramble to get to his bike and away to safety. Sister Bobbie called Mom and told her Clarence had dropped both sacks on the back steps and had made a big mess! The only real loss was the quart of milk in a glass bottle. When Clarence got back to the store, he told Mr. Paul and Mr. Ed she really was the meanest woman he ever met. As the two jokers laughed about the incident, they told Clarence they had put her up to it and she was not really a mean woman. In fact they said Sister Bobbie was such a good cook she might make him a good wife. Clarence dismissed the idea completely by saying, "she is way too old for me."

During the next year or so while the Quality Grocery was owned by our family, Clarence continued delivering groceries in the neighborhood and also to our home. He knew he had been the object of a prank and understood Sister Bobbie didn't intend to hurt him. Whenever he delivered to our house he would set the groceries on the back steps, knock on the door and quickly get on his bike. By the time Sister Bobbie arrived at the door he was half way up the driveway.

38. LETTERS FROM BUBBA

Letters Which Became Cherished Treasures

I have written in other posts that my hero from earliest remembrance is my brother Berry Lee, whom I always called Bubba. Because he was eleven years older, he seemed grown to me and certainly acted that way toward our sister Marilyn and me. He never told me, but when our mother died at age thirty-seven from far advanced breast cancer, and Marilyn and I were very young, he felt a very real and urgent sense of responsibility in caring for us. I suspect that in her last days, our mother Mimi told Bubba she was leaving us in his care, and he needed to be more than just an older brother.

As a young boy I tried to emulate some of the things I saw in Bubba or saw him do. I tried to walk like him with a slight pigeon-toed gait; I practiced my cursive writing to look like his; and at times I even tried to dress the way he did. As he grew older, his children told him he looked and dressed like Mr. Rogers of television fame. I was glad I hadn't gone that far to look like him despite my personal admiration for the character of Mr. Rogers.

I remember the sadness I felt watching Bubba drive away to college. He owned a red Model A Ford that he kept in perfect condition, and I stood at the end of our long driveway waving to him until he turned left onto North Madison and disappeared from sight. I wondered if he would ever return because I didn't understand what it meant to go to college. I did know he was going to the University of Arkansas, and he was going to play football for the Razorbacks. I was told I wouldn't see him again for a long time, but he would be coming back.

When he did come home for semester breaks and for Christmas, it was a very big deal for me. We played catch with the football, shot baskets on the basketball goal, and played pitch and catch with the baseball. He taught me the basics of all those sports, and I thought he knew everything about every sport . . . and just about everything else.

There were so many intangible things he taught me, but the tangible things he gave me are real treasures now. When I was a struggling teen with all the insecurities which accompany that stage of life, I received several hand written letters six pages or more in length. He was in medical school and then later an intern at Parkland Hospital in Dallas and had precious little time to spend writing letters, yet he made the time for my sake. Those letters were written before his life was filled with Christ, but he wrote words of encouragement saying I should strive to be the "best man and most loving man I could be." He added that if I did my best to live up to Christian ideals, I would have a greater influence in the lives of others than I would ever imagine. I have four letters from this period of time, and the theme is much the same in each one. He was obviously thinking a lot about me and the heritage given me which I should pass on to others. Bubba was the only man who ever sent me letters like that, and I not only read them multiple times but have saved them for these sixty-five plus years. Marilyn told me she also received long letters from Bubba and how much they meant to her also.

Several years following Bubba's spiritual transformation in 1967, Cathy and I moved to El Dorado to begin our life there. In 1977 Cathy and I were born again and everything changed for us. Bubba no longer wrote letters to me, but for every birthday he would send a card on which he wrote some special message to encourage me. Some of the words were humorous but most were intended to strengthen my faith. On the card he sent on my fiftieth birthday he wrote, "John, you are so special! I thank the Lord for giving me a brother like you. When Mimi was pregnant, I'm almost sure I prayed for a lil' brother—and He answered that prayer in a special way—not just a brother to have fun with—(Marilyn was sweet and a wonderful sister, but she wasn't interested in boy's things)—but the Lord gave me a brother who shares the same hopes and desires in Christ—and whom I love—as my best friend. From your Bub, Berry Lee."

If there is someone in your life who has been special to you, I would encourage you to take the time to write them a letter (or even an email) to tell them what they mean to you and how they have blessed your life. Who knows, they might still be reading those words sixty-five years from now!

39. RAZORBACKS FROM EL DORADO IN WAR MEMORIAL STADIUM

Bubba Plays in the Stadium Inaugural

Ark. (40) vs. Abilene Christian (6), War Memorial Stadium, Sept. 18, 1949. Berry Lee Moore (#70), Ray Parks (ball carrier)

When War Memorial Stadium in Little Rock was officially opened on September 18, 1948, it was the finest football stadium in the state. Constructed at an approximate cost of one million two hundred thousand dollars, it would seat about thirty-one thousand fans, and it became the flagship stadium for Razorback fans statewide. The stadium on the campus of the University of Arkansas in Fayetteville has always been home for the Razorbacks, but its location in the northwest part of the state has made it less accessible for a large majority of the fan base. For many years following the opening of the Little Rock stadium, there were at least three Razorback football games played there every year. For the past several years, the number of games has diminished to one game per year.

The opening game for the Razorback 1948 football season was with Abilene Christian University, and it was played in the just completed War Memorial Stadium. There were two Razorbacks from El Dorado who played in that game, Ray Parks, a halfback, and Berry Lee Moore, a tackle. Both had played for the El Dorado Wildcats under Coach Guy B. (Skipper) Hayes, and both had done so well they were selected to the All-State and All-Southern Teams. In those days, an All-Southern selection was the equivalent of a current All-American pick.

Berry Lee (Bubba) was an amazing football player for his size. He was 6′ 2″, weighing 185 pounds and played on the offensive and defensive lines as a tackle. It was very common for players to play both offense and defense, and the two-platoon system didn't become usual until the 1960s. The average weight for linemen in the 1940s was two hundred pounds or less, so Bubba was usually playing against men his size. As a comparison, the Razorback offensive line for the 2015 season averaged 328 pounds.

A significant handicap for Bubba was his vision. He was far-sighted and needed his glasses for near vision. Contact lenses were available but were much larger than now and very painful to wear. He tried them for a while but soon returned to his special plastic sports glasses. Occasionally he tried to play without glasses, and I noticed in the photograph above he doesn't appear to be wearing glasses. He once told me that without glasses he occasionally blocked or tackled the wrong man!

All who knew Berry Lee would attest to his quiet and gentle spirit, but put a football uniform on him and his competitive "Mr. Hyde" nature appeared. (I've written about his tough side in "Coach Fischel's Worst Moment on the Gridiron.") I once had a conversation with Dewey Blackwood, one of Bubba's assistant high school coaches, and he told me the following story: "When Berry Lee finished his high school career and went to Fayetteville to become a Razorback, I ran into one of his line coaches and asked him how my boy Berry Lee was doing. He said he was doing great and was becoming a very good football player. In fact, he said if Berry Lee weighed as much as 225 pounds, we would force him to practice on the opposite end of the field from the rest of the team. He would injure too many of the players with his tough and aggressive play." Coach Blackwood was pleased to tell this story, and I wasn't surprised when he told it.

Bubba said his favorite game as a Razorback and also his last was the one at War Memorial Stadium against Abilene Christian. He sustained a right knee injury early in the game, and the cartilage tear prevented him from further contact sports. The injury according to Bubba happened in the following manner: "I was supposed to stun the tackle in front of me, slide off, and block down field for the halfback. I guess I stunned the tackle so hard he fell across my right knee and caused the injury. I continued playing because I wanted to get in as much playing time as possible. After the game my right knee swelled so badly that I couldn't bend it." Our Dad's advice to him at the time was to avoid an operation and rehab the knee back to proper function. Arthroscopic surgery had not been devised then. Today many athletes are able to return to full capacity within months of such a cartilage tear.

Since that initial game in War Memorial Stadium, there have been some outstanding El Dorado Wildcats who have played as Razorbacks and starred on that gridiron, including Bill Fuller, Jim Mooty, Wayne Harris, Jim Gaston, Buddy Reuter, Richard Branch, Tommy Brasher, and Glen Ray Hines from the 1950s and 1960s. All these players were coached in El

Dorado by the legendary Garland Gregory. There perhaps were other El Dorado football players during this time span who played for the Razorbacks, but I don't recall their names.

The stadium has undergone expansion and renovation for the past several decades, and the seating capacity is now approximately fifty-four thousand. Over the years since 1948, there have been approximately two hundred Razorback games played there. I had the privilege of attending all the games played there during the years 1960–1964 while I was a medical student at the University of Arkansas Medical Center in Little Rock. The following year, 1965, the Razorbacks won the national championship in football. The contract between the University of Arkansas and War Memorial Stadium will expire following the 2018 season, and some people fear there will then be no more Razorback games played in Little Rock. That decision will obviously impact many thousands of fans statewide.

As for my family and me we had a great start in 1948, and we are partial to the Razorbacks continuing to play in War Memorial Stadium in Little Rock if only for one game yearly. [NOTE: The Razorbacks do, indeed, continue to play at War Memorial Stadium. The 2023 season opener against Western Carolina will be held there on September 2.]

40. THE VISITING DOCTOR HAS A BAD DAY

Not All Doctors Are Suited for the Operating Room

As a fourth-year surgical resident at Charity Hospital of New Orleans in 1969, I considered myself to have "seen it all and operated on at least one of everything." I was a young, enthusiastic surgeon and wanted my family to share in as many of my medical experiences as possible. On many occasions, I tried to get my wife Cathy to come into the operating room dressed in a surgical scrub suit to watch her "famous husband do miraculous deeds!" She always graciously declined by saying something like, "I'd rather not draw attention to myself by getting sick."

Cathy's brother George and his wife Dawn, who lived in Valdosta, Georgia, at the time, were visiting us one particular weekend I happened to be on call for emergency surgeries. I had reached the enviable status I could take calls from home unless there was a case which was too difficult for the junior resident to handle. Our enjoyable time together was being interrupted by numerous calls from the junior resident who just needed reassurance he was making the right decisions, and I didn't need to be there. I had told George that in case I did have to go to the hospital for an operation, he could accompany me if he desired, and he could see first-hand what a "great surgeon" his brother-in-law had become!

George was the Dean of Students at Valdosta State College and had an earned PhD in Higher Education. With his title, "Dr. Young," it would be much easier getting him into the operating suite without arousing any undue concerns. He said he was hoping he might have the opportunity to observe what takes place in that environment so he could share the experience with the students at his college who had an interest in the medical field.

Just after lunch on Saturday the resident called to say he had two patients who were trauma victims needing emergency surgery and a third patient who was in immediate need of a vena cava ligation. This patient was throwing multiple blood clots into his lungs and the operation would be life-saving, so I knew I had to get to the hospital as quickly as possible. The junior resident was capable of handling both of the trauma patients. While driving to the hospital I told George I would introduce him as a "visiting doctor," and he could simply observe rather than scrub up and be part of the operating team. His lack of knowledge of those procedures would be an immediate giveaway that he was not an MD, and I didn't want any unnecessary attention drawn to George.

We got to the twelfth-floor operating suite and quickly donned our scrub suits. Because this was his first experience in such an environment, I wasn't too concerned about the initial anxiety I could see in George's face and detect in his voice. Charity Hospital was a huge facility, and there were twelve operating rooms on each of two sides of the large operating suite. The two trauma patients awaiting their procedure were on the gurneys outside their respective rooms, and both patients though stable were receiving blood transfusions. My attention was focused on the patient on whom I was to operate, so I wasn't paying close attention to George. I had simply introduced him to the many doctors and nurses in the hallway as "Dr. Young a visiting doctor from Georgia." As we were waiting to take our patient into the room, a student came rushing up to George and asked, "Dr. Young, the patient by Room 10 has received two units of blood already. Do I need to start a third unit?" George quickly said, "I'm not sure. You need to ask Dr. Moore." Fast thinking for the visiting doctor.

Our operation began with George's standing at the head of the table next to the anesthesiologist where he could get an unobstructed view. After I made a very long incision and quickly exposed the vena cava, I pointed out to George various organs and what we were planning to do in this procedure. George was leaning over the table intently observing, and he seemed to be absorbed in his new learning experience. I did notice he was not asking any questions. When I had to focus all of my attention to the delicate portion of the procedure, I didn't notice that George had left the room. When it came to a point where I could turn over the responsibilities of the operation to the younger resident, I took off the sterile gown and began looking for George.

When I asked one of the nurses if she had seen Dr. Young, she said he was in the utility room adjacent to the OR. I found George sitting near a window which had been opened, and his head as close to the window as possible. A student nurse was fanning him and giving him as much comfort as possible. George said to the nurse, "That's the last operation I will ever watch. I darned near passed out!" The nurse said, "Oh Dr. Young, please don't quit surgery because of this." George said, "Ma'am, I'm a PhD, not an MD, and this is the last one for sure." The nurse responded, "In that case, you better lie down!"

We didn't talk much on the way back to our apartment where I knew our wives were anxiously awaiting a report of our experience. Finally, George said in a refreshingly honest way, "I don't mind if you tell them I fainted because I've seen all the surgery I ever want to see." To this day, I've not been able to convince George that every doctor has at least one bad day in the OR.

41. THE MOST DELICIOUS APPLE (ONION?) I EVER ATE

Hypnosis Causes Me to Eat an Onion

As a young person, I developed a passing interest in the field of hypnosis. I don't recall much about the circumstances nor even the name of the performer, but a magician and hypnotist performed in El Dorado at the high school auditorium when I was a pre-teen, and I had a front row seat. I was fascinated by the many card tricks and the appearance and disappearance of birds and bunnies, but I was especially captivated by the hypnotic feats he performed with a volunteer from the audience. I never discovered whether the volunteer was randomly chosen, or if he was a performer who worked for the magician. Like most in the audience, I assumed the former. While he was in a hypnotic state, he was given commands to do certain unusual things he might not have otherwise done, especially in front of a crowd. A few things I remember were his walking on all fours, barking like a dog, and then begging for a bone. Before he was hypnotized, the man did not appear to be an extrovert, and it didn't seem like he was acting while barking and begging. The hypnotist said a person could not be given a hypnotic suggestion to perform a lethal act or do something which would be personally harmful. Who knows what calamities that might lead to? In the following months I read a few articles about the hypnotic state, but because I wasn't challenged by any friends to continue, I lost interest.

About a year later, my brother Berry Lee (Bubba) and wife LaNell were in El Dorado for a brief visit during Bubba's Christmas break from medical school. He began talking about a course he was taking on medical hypnosis offered as an elective by the Psychiatry Department. My sister Marilyn and I had lots of questions, particularly on the medical indications and the long-term effects hypnosis might have on a person. Not surprisingly, Bubba was well read on the subject, and it seemed he had enough knowledge to be considered an expert. One of us asked the question, "What type of person is the best candidate to be put into a hypnotic state?" His answer was something like this: "The person must have lots of trust in the hypnotist and believe in his ability to hypnotize them. Now which one of you wants to try it?" Because he was looking at me, I quickly said, "I'll go first." In reality I was so competitive I didn't want Marilyn to beat me out on something good.

I don't have a clear recollection of what occurred, but this I do remember: The doors to our large living room were closed, the curtains drawn, the room lights dimmed, and the room very quiet. Only the four of us were present—Bubba, LaNell, Marilyn, and me. Bubba's voice was the only sound I heard, and he spoke in a very hushed tone. I remember his telling me I must allow every muscle and joint to relax so I had no sensation of any impulse coming to me except the sound of his voice. I can recall the complete relaxation I was experiencing in that distraction-free environment, and that is all I remember. What occurred from this point on I was told later by Bubba and LaNell, and it was confirmed by Marilyn.

While Bubba was inducing the hypnotic state in me, either LaNell or Marilyn had gone to the kitchen and retrieved a large white onion. When he believed that I was ready to proceed, Bubba told me he had the most delicious red apple he had ever seen and wanted me to eat as much of it as I wanted. When he handed me the onion, he said I quickly took a huge bite out of it and seemed to savor each crunch as I chewed and swallowed the juicy apple (onion). I believe he allowed me to take another large bite, and I was in the process of chewing and swallowing the bite when he took the onion away from me. I suppose he couldn't bear watching me eat the entire onion, though I was apparently enjoying it. When he awakened me from the hypnotic state, he showed me the onion and told me what I had done. I remember thinking I don't remember taking two bites from the onion, but the taste in my mouth confirmed it.

I don't think Bubba had any other experiences with inducing a hypnotic state in an individual and certainly not in me. Perhaps he saw the ability one could have in affecting another's behavior even to the extent of doing something they would not choose to do. Medical hypnosis has been used for years for many varied things such as smoking cessation, weight loss, dealing with the pains of labor and delivery, and treatment of all forms of phobia.

When I worked for a short time in an industrial surgical clinic in New Orleans, one of the surgeons in the clinic was certified in medical hypnosis, and he treated patients with severe warts with hypnosis. He said his cure rate was at 80 to 90 percent. I never saw him treat a patient in that manner during the two months I worked there. I personally prefer Huckleberry Finn's treatment for warts. (You'll have to look it up).

Over the last forty-plus years, I have not enjoyed raw onions on any food, thus I always ask the server to leave them off. Cathy knows I don't care for onions and doesn't prepare a dish with raw onions for me. I can't say with certainty, but it may have something to do with that delicious red apple I was devouring many years ago when Bubba made me stop!

42. GRAM YOUNG, AKA MADAM MAYOR

Cathy's Mom Wore Two Hats

Mayor Virginia Young, 1974

Cathy and I were introduced to each other in October of 1964 by Marsha Moore, whose husband Dan Moore was a physician friend of mine. She and Cathy were teachers together at an elementary school in Atlanta, Georgia. Cathy had just graduated from Florida State University, and this was her first teaching assignment. I was an intern at Grady Memorial Hospital, and Dan and I had both graduated from the University of Arkansas Medical

School in Little Rock, so we had been friends for a long time. Cathy was born and raised in Fort Lauderdale, Florida, and I had never known anyone from that city prior to our meeting. My understanding of the city was based on viewing the movie, "Where the Boys Are," which was a far cry from the reality of a very beautiful and culturally significant south Florida metropolis.

After the first few dates, I was stricken not only by Cathy's beauty but by also her sweet and sensitive spirit. I just couldn't believe she wanted to continue dating this Arkansas hillbilly, but I didn't complain, and the seriousness of our intentions toward each other escalated. After dating for about six weeks, I wasn't surprised her parents wanted to meet the young man who was seriously dating their daughter. Cathy's mom, Virginia Young, was president of the Florida School Board at the time, and she had a meeting scheduled in Atlanta. This was her opportunity for us to meet.

On the evening of our meeting at her hotel I was on call in the Emergency Room at Grady Hospital and had just finished my shift for the day. I was still wearing my white uniform since I didn't have time to drive to my apartment to freshen up and change clothes. She told people for years afterwards the first time she met me I had on my white uniform which was covered with blood. I really think there were only a few scattered blood spots, but they had surely caught her eye. Overall, I was pretty certain I had made a good first impression despite the blood.

Cathy and I continued to date throughout the year and both of us decided that God had meant for us to spend our lives together in marriage. In March, 1965, with her father's permission, I asked her to marry me, and so we were in Fort Lauderdale on August 7, 1965. I had already moved to New Orleans the prior month to begin my four-year training in general surgery on the LSU Service at Charity Hospital. We had a small but nice apartment in Kenner, which was near the elementary school where she had a teaching job. A surprise wedding present we endured along with all the residents of New Orleans was Hurricane Betsy which came on September 8, 1965.

Cathy's mom and dad were very supportive of us throughout their lives, but we were especially blessed by them in the early years of our marriage. Gram Young kept in close touch with us by phone, and it was not uncommon for her to call three or four times per week. Those calls were very important for Cathy because many nights she was alone in our apartment while I worked at Charity Hospital. Her mom's calls kept her current on her family and the things happening in Fort Lauderdale.

Mom Young loved to travel, and she visited us more often than any other family member throughout her life. Financially we struggled because the salary I was paid at Charity Hospital kept us under the federal poverty guidelines. It was only Cathy's modest salary as an elementary teacher which enabled us to cover our apartment rent and the few other bills we had each month. We loved receiving a "care package" from Mom Young, because often it contained two or more nice dresses for Cathy and occasionally a dress shirt or a good book for me. As an added blessing, she frequently sent large sacks of limes from their Key lime tree. Cathy was an expert in making the most delicious Key lime pies I had ever eaten. In fact, before we married, I had never had eaten a piece of Key lime pie, and it is now my favorite.

Mom became more involved in Fort Lauderdale politics when she ran for the City Commission in 1971 and was elected, thus becoming the vice mayor. The city's by-laws stated the commissioner with the most votes became mayor, while the second largest vote-getter was named vice mayor. In 1973 following the next election, Mom became the first woman to have ever been elected as mayor of Fort Lauderdale. She served until 1975, when she was again elected vice mayor. She served in that position until 1981 and then assumed the unexpired term of Clay Shaw as mayor, continuing until 1982. The city of Fort Lauderdale underwent major changes during the eleven years she served on the Commission, and it was always exciting and fun for us to be on the "inside" of all of those changes.

Following completion of my surgical residency in 1969, I entered active duty in the US Air Force as a major in the medical corps. Our country was near the height of the Vietnam War, and trained surgeons were needed. We thought I would surely have to go overseas, but instead I was sent to Moody Air Force Base in Valdosta, Georgia. One of the benefits of living in South Georgia was that it meant an eight-hour drive down the interstate to Cathy's hometown of Fort Lauderdale. We were able to visit her parents and her brother and sister much more frequently. As we began having children Mom's name was changed to Gram Young

During those years we were able to witness up-close Gram Young's skill, both as a grandmother and an outstanding city administrator. I was amazed at her ability to deliver as many as six speeches to various organizations in one day without the use of notes. I always wondered if she ever was confused about the organization to whom she was speaking and called them by the wrong name. I don't think it ever happened. When she was home, she took off her political hat and was very content to be a wife and grandmother. The only evidence in their home of her importance to the city was the number of phone calls she received daily. This was prior to the universal use of cell phones, and she was able to get some relief from all the calls by going with us to the shopping mall or the beach.

Near the end of her life, she was honored by the city of Fort Lauderdale by two significant presentations: A city park and a new and magnificent elementary school were named for her and both had great personal significance. Throughout her adult life she worked diligently to make Fort Lauderdale more family friendly, and she also made public education an equally important priority. Whenever Cathy and I go back with our family to visit Fort Lauderdale we never fail to visit these two sites and reminisce over just how important Mayor Virginia S. Young was to the city. More significantly she was a great wife to her husband George, a wonderful mother to her children George, Nancy, and Cathy and a magnificent Gram to all her grandchildren.

43. "GEORGE, YOU DON'T TALK MUCH, DO YOU?"

Cathy's Dad Was Known as a Quiet Man

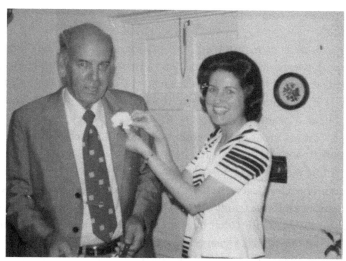

Cathy and her dad

I have already written about the wonderful legacy Cathy's dad, George Young, left for his family and friends and some of the wonderful character traits which marked his personal life. He was a master builder who owned the oldest building-contractor business in Fort Lauderdale. He purposefully kept the business small so he could assure every customer the work done on their particular project would have his personal attention and would be of the highest quality. His reputation as a quality builder was widely known in Broward County and south Florida.

Dad Young was a quiet and thoughtful man who did not easily share his personal thoughts with any but his closest family members and not all of them. According to his son, Dr. George W. Young, Dad had a stuttering problem as a child and was able to overcome that problem with time and personal discipline. I don't believe his parents retained any professional help for Dad, and I'm confident this struggle affected him greatly. Cathy has told me on many occasions about the empathy her dad had for anyone with a speech impediment.

Another characteristic of Dad Young was that he didn't like to travel outside of Broward County. On one occasion when Cathy and I were visiting her brother, the younger George obtained tickets to a Miami Dolphins football game, and Dad agreed to go with us. I was excited to not only see a Dolphins game but to also have a chance to spend time with both men, whom I admired greatly. Early in my marriage to Cathy, I bonded with Cathy's brother George, and he helped me understand many of the family dynamics. He drove me all around Fort Lauderdale pointing out landmarks and especially homes and businesses that Young Construction Company had built.

The football game in Miami was exciting, although I don't remember the opposing team or the outcome. As we were driving home after the game, I asked Dad how long it had been since he had made the forty-mile trip to Miami. He responded, "About forty years." I said, "I know the roads are much better now and it is easier to get there. When do you think you'll go back?" In his usual quiet manner and with a little chuckle he said, "In another forty years."

He told me the following story concerning his travels (or lack thereof), and this is one of my favorites. It probably occurred ten to fifteen years prior to my entrance into the family in 1965. He had a trip scheduled with another man to go to Atlanta for either business purposes or for a training seminar. Dad was not one to make leisure trips, and I don't recall his ever travelling with anyone except Mom. Back then, the interstate system in Florida was not as well-developed, and an automobile trip to Atlanta might take as long as twelve hours depending on traffic and the number of stops one made. According to Dad, when they were about fifty miles outside Atlanta, the driver looked over at him and said, "You don't talk much, do you George?" This was when they realized not one word had been exchanged between the two of them since they left Fort Lauderdale eight or nine hours earlier. They each had a good laugh knowing how quiet they were.

Dad was very content within himself to be quiet, since, for most of his life, he was with people who had a need to talk. It was such an obvious quality known by everyone who knew him, and when Dad did speak, everyone stopped to listen, because it would always be relevant.

He never raised his voice toward me in correction or rebuke, but if it had happened, I would have been shocked. The only time he verbally showed some displeasure toward me was in his misunderstanding of something I had said. Cathy and I had just arrived on a visit from Valdosta where I was stationed in the Air Force. Mom had just been elected the mayor of Fort Lauderdale, and we were very excited to hear all about the election and her new role. As Dad was helping me unpack our car and we were alone in the garage, I innocently asked, "How does it feel to be married to the mayor of Fort Lauderdale?" He stopped what he was doing, looked me in the eye and said, "What do you mean by that?" He must have thought that in some way I was demeaning him, and he felt judged. I quickly said, "Oh, I didn't mean anything except as a compliment to her and to you. Cathy and I are very proud of her accomplishments!" He picked the bag back up and made no other remark. I assumed my explanation cleared the air and nothing else needed to be said. Thank goodness it didn't take eight or nine hours for us to re-engage in conversation.

44. "GEORGE, DID YOU DO THE WORK?"

A Man's Word Is His Bond

Cathy' s dad, George F. Young was one of the most remarkable men I have ever known. When Cathy and I first met and began dating in 1964 while I was an intern at Grady Memorial Hospital in Atlanta, I had never met anyone from Fort Lauderdale. I met her mom Virginia in Atlanta after we had been dating for several months because as president of the Florida School Board, she was in town for a meeting. Cathy's dad and granddad George W. Young were well-known building contractors in Fort Lauderdale in a business which her Granddad founded with his brother Will in the early 1900s. The two of them were master cabinet makers from England. When I met Cathy, her dad's construction business was the oldest one of its type in the city of Fort Lauderdale, and they had built such landmarks as the Riverside Hotel and the exclusive shopping area known as Las Olas.

When I finally met her dad during the Easter weekend in 1965, I had heard many stories about him from Cathy, and what a brilliant man he was with outstanding character. I had a bit of anxiety prior to our meeting, because I wanted to make a good first impression. I was planning to ask for his blessing for our marriage the following August. The first thing I discovered was that he was a man of few words. At our initial meeting, and seemingly for several years afterward, I don't recall his initiating a conversation with me. He was not impolite or rude, but I was never quite certain in those early years whether he liked me or approved of me as Cathy's husband. Her mom, on the other hand was open and verbal, and I was confident of her approval, so that was sufficient. I believed if Virginia (Mom) approved, then George (Dad) approved also.

I always loved sitting with my own dad (Pop) and listening to his stories relating to his life and the many people with whom he'd interacted. I wanted to have the same type of relationship with Dad Young, but it was not possible because of his basic quiet and private nature. Mom Young however was a story-teller like Pop, and she loved telling stories almost as much as I loved hearing them. One of the stories I have repeated often best characterizes Dad Young's character and the reputation he had in the city of Fort Lauderdale.

A wealthy man and his wife contracted with Dad to remodel their beautiful and expensive home. Normally Dad's fee was on a cost-plus basis, but in this instance, he had agreed to a contract price. Throughout the remodel, the wife made numerous changes to the agreed-upon project, and Dad made those changes knowing the final price would be higher than the contract price. He assumed the husband would honor the added expenses and pay for them accordingly. When the work was completed, inspected, and approved by the owner, Dad presented the final bill, which was considerably higher than the contract price. The customer told Dad he was only going to pay the contract price despite Dad's explanation of the added amount. Dad went home telling Mom they were just going to have to absorb the loss since the homeowner was adamant in his refusal. Mom said, "George, this is just not right and we are not going to stand for this. We are being forced to take legal action." In all of their previous dealing with customers, they had never filed a suit in small claims court.

An attorney was engaged and on the appointed court date, both Mom and Dad appeared with the necessary documentation for the work and presented the detailed accounting to the judge. The judge very carefully examined the documents, looked at Dad and asked, "George, did you do this work?" Dad said, "Yes Judge, and that is my bill for the work." The judge looked at the defendant while striking his gavel on the stand and said, "The court orders the defendant to pay George Young the full amount of this bill." The defense lawyer objected, "Judge, we have not presented our defense." The judge quickly said, "There is no need for you to speak. Everyone who has lived in this community for any period of time knows the integrity and honesty of George Young. If he says he did the work and this is his bill, then you must pay it because it is fair and reasonable. Case dismissed."

Our children were fortunate to have known their Granddaddy Young before he departed this life. They were also blessed to have seen a more talkative and open man than he was at an earlier age. He told us he enjoyed coming on visits with Grammy to Arkansas even though he didn't like the colder weather they occasionally encountered. All of their visits were filled with surprise gifts from Florida, lots of conversation with jokes and laughter, and plenty of good stories, which have made many wonderful memories in our hearts. In remembering him it has been the prayer of Cathy and me that our children and grandchildren (and especially the men) will have the character and reputation which marked their Granddaddy Young.

45. MY RIDE IN A HEARSE

I Thought I Was Going to Die

Cathy and I were married shortly after I began my surgical residency at Charity Hospital in New Orleans in 1965. In addition to the stress of the many hours of training required to become a surgeon of excellence, Cathy and I were faced with the challenge of dealing with the usual changes which occur in the lives of newlyweds. Our premarital training with a mature married couple never happened, and there was very little resource material available then to assist young couples in facing common marital issues. There was certainly no training which could have prepared us for dealing with a serious medical illness.

We doctors in training through the LSU surgical program were "farmed out" from the main Charity Hospital in New Orleans to the smaller Charity Hospitals in Lake Charles and Lafayette, Louisiana. I selected the hospital in Lake Charles because the residents who preceded me had said I would do more surgical cases there. That was all of the encouragement I needed.

Following one year of experience at the main hospital, Cathy and I moved to Lake Charles for a three month stint beginning in June 1966. There were small apartments available on the hospital grounds which made it very nice and convenient for me to get back and forth to work and to take the required emergency room calls. Although our apartment had very few amenities, Cathy and I had not developed expensive tastes and were more than happy with it. The fact that it was provided at no cost made it all the more attractive to us. We still had to pay for our New Orleans apartment, to which we would return when our term in Lake Charles was completed.

After I had been working about three weeks in this new location, I began experiencing flu-like symptoms. I had a low-grade temperature and generalized aches in my muscles, particularly in the upper body. I took a day off from work, but, because our operative schedule was full of procedures which needed to be done, I returned to work still feeling poorly. For the next week, I had the increasing symptom of extreme tiredness. At the end of each day, I would be exhausted and return to the apartment in the early evening and go to bed. After sleeping for eight to ten hours, which was very unusual for me, I would awaken rested. Within ten to fifteen minutes in the OR, I would feel so tired I had to call for a chair to sit down. Within another day or so, I knew I needed to be seen by a physician. Cathy and I went to a local internist in Lake Charles, and he immediately asked me, " How long have you been jaundiced?" When I looked into the mirror at his office at my eyes, I saw I was, indeed, deeply jaundiced. As a physician trained to look for such things, I had not even noticed the color change in myself.

He told me I had to be hospitalized, and, because we only had hospital insurance with the Charity Hospital system, I had to be admitted there instead of in a local private hospital. The internist at Charity Hospital was not a favorite of mine, because he had issues with alcohol abuse several years earlier while in a private practice setting. He had a rather eccentric personality, but I had no other option but him.

As a surgeon in training, I was particularly susceptible to needle sticks from other personnel in the OR who were also in training. Procedures done deep within body cavities with multiple hands in narrow spaces can be hazardous to the operating surgeon as well as the other personnel.

I was diagnosed with serum hepatitis, probably from a needle stick, and my laboratory tests related to liver function were getting worse each day. I became so sick and nauseated that even the smell of food was repulsive. As a physician I knew that if my condition continued deteriorating, complete liver failure was a certainty, resulting in my death. Cathy was very frightened, and I suppose I was too sick to be scared. Cathy pleaded with my mom in El Dorado to come to Lake Charles to help her make some important decisions. My dad (Pop) had died earlier the same year from heart failure, so Mom was dealing with her own issues of life adjustment.

I distinctly remember that on the evening Mom arrived at the hospital, the dietary department had just sent me a huge plate of red beans and rice to encourage me to eat more nutritious food. Cajuns believe a meal like this will cure anyone of any illness. Normally I liked this dish, but this time I gagged at the sight of it. Mom said, "That's it, Cathy. We're taking him to El Dorado." The doctor happened to come into the room at the time and told her, "You can't move him from this hospital," to which she responded, "You just watch me!" If I hadn't been so ill, I would have laughed out loud.

When Mom called the ambulance company in El Dorado the same night, she was told they would send their best and most comfortable vehicle the next morning. When the driver arrived, he was not in an ambulance but in a brand-new Cadillac hearse! It didn't matter to me, because I was headed home, and if I didn't make it, at least Cathy and I would be with family and friends in familiar surroundings. The only vehicle we had driven to Lake Charles was my 1964, red, Corvair Monza convertible with a stick shift, and Cathy didn't know how to drive a car with standard transmission. But she had gotten a rush course in driving it from one of the doctors the previous night in the hospital parking lot.

Cathy's trip by herself in our convertible was not only frightening for her but also frustrating. It seems the windshield wipers quit working for some unknown reason, and she had to drive through a rain storm. Praise God, he protected her, and she made the five-hour drive with no accident. My driver was polite and gracious but inexperienced as a limo driver. Within minutes of beginning the trip, the air conditioner failed, and this was late July in south Louisiana. On top of this, after I'd endured two hours of the sweltering heat in the rear of the hearse, the driver allowed the vehicle to run out of gas. This sounds like a horror movie in the making. We had to wait for about forty-five minutes before help arrived with gasoline. Fortunately, the remainder of the journey was trouble-free, and I arrived at Union Medical Center hot and exhausted but alive. There is a lot more to the story, but I did begin improving in the El Dorado hospital. I remained there for four days and worried more about my hospital bill than I did about my health and recovery.

Cathy and I celebrated our first wedding anniversary the day after I was discharged. I forgot to get her flowers or even a card; I blamed it on my weakened condition, which was a weak and pitiful excuse. She loved me in spite of my forgetfulness and provided things I was not even aware during such a scary time. For certain we grew more mature while learning to handle adversity, and I haven't forgotten any more anniversaries. We were not believers at the time, and I don't recall one prayer I offered for Cathy or for myself. But God was faithful and merciful, knowing in a few years we would both turn our lives over to him in repentance. As a result, my next and final ride in a hearse will be a victorious one!

46. A WEEK AT THE GREENHOUSE

A Special Relaxing Week Became an Embarrassment

During the years Cathy and I lived in El Dorado, most of our out-of-town shopping trips were either to Monroe, Louisiana to the Pecanland Mall or to Little Rock to one of several malls there. We seldom travelled to Dallas because it was a long six-hour drive, and we dreaded the traffic in Dallas. After living in a small town where it takes five minutes to drive downtown and park right next to the store, the idea of visiting a city of one and a half million is not only unattractive but intimidating.

On rare occasion when attending a conference or a sporting event in Dallas, we did shop in a few of the nicer Dallas stores. I remember that on two occasions we visited the world-famous Neiman-Marcus Department Store just to rub shoulders with the rich and famous of Dallas. Cathy found and bought some item she needed, so our name was automatically placed on their mailing list. For several years we received the beautiful Neiman-Marcus catalog with its gorgeous clothes and outlandish prices. We looked forward to seeing what they had to offer especially the "His and Hers" gifts. One I recall was a five-star African safari for three weeks, which included a formal dinner party with the US Ambassador in Kenya. The price tag was a mere seventy-five thousand dollars.

One particular offering which caught Cathy's eye was an invitation to spend a week at the Greenhouse Spa. This exclusive spa was built in 1965 in Grand Prairie, Texas by owner Stanley Marcus and featured the very latest and finest amenities certain to pamper those who could afford it. It attracted a clientele from Dallas and across the nation. Like so many of our friends Cathy was at a stage in life in which she was constantly on the go with our three children, who required transportation to school, to friends' homes after school, to sporting practices and games, and to piano lessons and recitals. In addition, she had to shop for groceries, household items, and clothes among many other things. All the while, she was maintaining our home and keeping our marriage relationship vibrant and fresh. I knew that the thought of having a week of rest, relaxation, and total pampering might be appealing, and one which she had certainly earned. One evening, I told her that I would consider underwriting a week at the Greenhouse for her and her mom. Cathy's mom, Virginia Young,was the mayor of Fort Lauderdale at the time and was in the midst of a re-election campaign. I thought she might also welcome a relaxing week following her victory.

A few days later, Cathy had a phone conversation with her mom, and told her I would send them both to the Greenhouse for a week if they wanted. She briefly explained the function of the Greenhouse and said it might be a relaxing time for both of them. Her mom's only comment was, "That might be fun." Nothing more was said about it during the exchange.

It was not unusual for Mom (Mayor Young) as part of her official duties to give two or three talks per day at various official functions. During a re-election campaign, however, she might have seven or eight stops with a speech at each place. I was always amazed at her knowledge base, her memory, and her ability to speak without the use of manuscript or notes. She never used a teleprompter nor did she need one. She probably knew more about Fort Lauderdale and its history than anyone of her era.

One afternoon at one of her scheduled campaign stops, this at a large condominium near the beach, she spoke to a group of a hundred or more interested citizens about what the city council had been doing for their benefit. She said that, as their mayor, she was best qualified to continue those policies. During the talk she spoke about her family's heritage as early settlers of the city and proceeded to tell them about her own children and their families. When she came to Cathy, she said she was married to a surgeon, and they had planted their roots in South Arkansas. And then she said something to this effect: "My son-in-law is so generous he offered to send Cathy and me for a week of relaxation at The Green Door." She had forgotten it was the *Greenhouse*! According to her, this was all she said concerning the offer.

When the meeting was over, one of the ladies pulled her aside and, after congratulating her on an excellent talk, said, "Virginia, I would advise you to not ever mention that your son-in-law in Arkansas was sending you and your daughter to the *Green Door*." Virginia asked, "Why? I thought it was a sweet and generous offer." The lady said, "Are you aware that The Green Door is an X-rated business out on Sunrise Boulevard?"

When Mom told us the story, we had a good laugh. At the same time, we were prayerful that no one who heard her thought or believed there was anything unwholesome about my offer. We were later very thankful when the election was over Mom was once again re-elected to the city council. She and Cathy never did make it for a week or even a day at the Greenhouse. I still believe that they both not only earned it, but that they would have had a great time there.

47. THE US AIR FORCE MEDICAL CORPS BOOT CAMP

Training Doctors in Military Protocol

Major John H. Moore, 1969

During the years of my medical training in the 1960s, the United States was involved in very serious foreign engagements which could have escalated into global nuclear conflicts. The Cuban Missile Crisis occurred in 1962 when I was a sophomore in medical school, and for thirteen days the nation was on the brink of all-out war with Russia. We had advisory troops already in Vietnam, and the situation there escalated into a full military engagement before the end of that decade. The impact those engagements had on the medical profession was substantial, for all able-bodied doctors just out of their medical training were subject to being drafted into active military duty. It was much better for us to enlist in the military right after med school and complete our service requirement early on, rather than begin a medical practice and wait to be drafted.

I enlisted in the US Air Force in 1960 when I was a freshman student in medical school with the understanding I would go on active duty when my medical training was completed. I was commissioned as a second lieutenant, and as I progressed in training and service, the Air Force promoted me in rank. At the completion of surgical training, I was promoted to captain, and when I finally received my orders to serve in 1969, I was promoted to major.

The promotions were made quickly in the Medical Corps so the salaries offered by the military would be somewhat comparable to those of a physician entering private practice with that level of training. The photo above was taken during my week of orientation upon reporting for active duty. The serious and almost sinister look on my face should have been enough to scare all enemies of the state to surrender unconditionally! Perhaps, through a military error, the Vietnamese never saw this particular photograph.

My initial military experience began at Sheppard Air Force Base in Wichita Falls, Texas, where I began a temporary assignment of three weeks training at the Medical Services School. Cathy was unable to accompany me, because she was four months pregnant with our second child, Mary Kay. Instead, she spent the three weeks with her family in Fort Lauderdale, Florida. There were three hundred other doctors in my class, and the majority of them had no military experience. I had two years of ROTC in college, so at least I knew how to put the insignias on the uniform and knew the proper protocol for saluting a superior officer and returning the salute of a soldier with inferior rank.

Our training consisted mostly of classroom lectures on military history, military protocol, and our particular medical responsibilities, both in the US and in the war zone. Every morning before class, we were taken to a practice ground and taught how to align and take marching orders. We practiced marching for at least an hour each day. My ROTC experience was most valuable for this part of our training. These three weeks came during the month of August, and the Texas sun made for a very hot hour of marching even though we began at 8:00 a.m. The culmination of all of this training on the practice grounds was to occur on our last day there. There was to be a grand march around the formal base parade grounds past an official reviewing stand bearing high-ranking officers of the base.

The parade was to begin at 9:00 a.m., and we were ordered to gather at 8:45 in order to get properly aligned and prepared. We were to line up behind the base marching band, with about a hundred members. It was going to be an impressive show for the dignitaries—a marching band of a hundred followed by three hundred marching doctors! The commander for our group was selected not for his marching skills, but because he was the tallest doctor among the majors. There were approximately seventy-five majors and the remainder were captains. One major was taller than I, and I was greatly relieved he was one inch taller. He had no experience in commanding marching men except for one practice run the previous day.

Our commander was told that when the band struck up their marching tune, he was to give the order "Forward march," and we were to follow the band around the parade ground and past the reviewing stand. Sounded pretty simple and straight-forward. The officers present on the reviewing stand included the wing commander who was a brigadier general, the base commander who was a colonel and a group of at least four other officers who were either colonels or lieutenant colonels. They all seemed proud that this was the largest class of physicians to graduate from the Medical Services School at Sheppard AFB.

The program began promptly at 9:00 a.m. with the raising of the flag in the center of the field and the playing of the National Anthem, while we all saluted. That was enough to make it a memorable service. But the best was yet to come! A master sergeant who had been assisting us with our marching training alerted our commander to "remember to follow the band." With his eyes on his troops and listening to the band's prompt, he waited for the music to begin. What he missed, because he wasn't watching the band, was the band had a musical introduction to their marching tune, and it was only at the end of that phrase that they were to begin marching. When our commander heard the introductory bars, he loudly gave the order, "Forward March!" With this order, about a half of the marching doctors marched right up into the midst of the band, who had not yet moved. I was in the half within the band, so I saw what took place next. The trombone player's slide caught the hat of the man ahead of me, knocked it off, and sent it spinning among the legs of the band members. The astonished trombonist stopped playing while the hatless doctor scrambled between legs to retrieve his hat. The band stopped playing, and our commander screamed, "Stop," thus losing all sense of military protocol. The commander then gave the order, "About face," at the urging of the master sergeant. I was well aware of the principle that when an order is given, it is to be obeyed whether it is the correct order or not. I am convinced the right thing was for the band to begin marching forward to untangle this mess. Approximately one half the doctors thought the same, and they didn't move when the about-face order was given, but the other half obeyed the order. Now there was a situation wherein about a hundred doctors were facing each other. The commander tried again, repeating the order, "About Face," which everyone then obeyed, so there were still doctors facing doctors. In total exasperation, the commander screamed out, "Get the h–l back where you are supposed to be!" We quickly walked back to our original position and held still. I took a quick glance at the reviewing stand and saw all of the general officers either laughing or bowing their faces into their cupped hands. I feel certain they had never seen anything like this fiasco. The remainder of the marching review went without incident and was really very impressive and awe-inspiring.

At an evening reception for the graduates hosted by the general staff, all the generals and colonels were having a good time laughing and recounting the morning's review. I overheard one of them remark, "Well, what more could you expect from three hundred intelligent doctors without a lick of military sense!" I was just grateful our training was over, and I got to be part of a "Gomer Pyle" event.

48. AN UNUSUAL APPENDECTOMY

Improvising at the Operating Table

The two years I spent on active duty in service to our country was in the US Air Force from 1969 to 1971. Those were good years for me professionally, because I had just completed my training as a general surgeon, and it was a good transition into private practice. I was the only surgeon assigned to Moody Air Force Base in Valdosta, Georgia, and it was perfect for Cathy and me. The war in Viet Nam was raging; surgeons were needed and were continually being sent there. I was fairly certain the Air Force was not going to suddenly move me from Moody to Vietnam.

I had the total flexibility of arranging my work schedule to suit my needs, but because I was eager to gain needed experience, I was aggressive in doing as many operative cases as possible. I developed a close working relationship with Dr. Bill Retterbush, a local Valdosta surgeon who had a large and growing private surgical practice. When I wasn't busy at the base, I assisted Dr. Retterbush with his operative cases, with the permission of the base hospital commander, and the extra pay to assist him supplemented my Air Force salary. Our hospital commander saw the benefits of my gaining additional operative experience and enhanced judgment at the side of a more experienced surgeon. It was a beneficial arrangement for Dr. Retterbush, the Air Force, and me.

I was able to treat or assist in the treatment of a number of unusual patients during those two years. One patient I remember well was referred to me on a Friday afternoon by the base pediatrician. He suspected appendicitis, and after examining the patient, I agreed with his diagnosis. The patient was a ten-year-old dependent of an active-duty airman, and his parents had not delayed in seeking medical attention. I was confident he had an early case of appendicitis and was not in immediate danger of perforation, which severely complicates the treatment. I scheduled an operation for him later in the afternoon and asked Dr. Parkhurst, the referring pediatrician, if he would like to assist me in the procedure. Earlier he told me if I needed an assistant, he would really enjoy the opportunity. He had never seen an appendectomy, but in the past year had referred several patients with the infection.

The time was late July, and the South Georgia weather was especially hot and humid. The air-conditioned hospital provided much-needed comfort for the patients and hospital personnel, but I was soon to discover just how essential a cool environment was to the treatment and recovery of surgical patients. I had been told the air conditioning unit in the OR had been malfunctioning, but the use of fans had made the situation more tolerable. I was confident in my ability to do the appendectomy quickly and be completed in forty-five minutes or less. I would have been much less likely to schedule a longer case because of the heat and humidity. This was mistake number one!

By 4:00 p.m. on Friday, most of the hospital personnel had gone home for the weekend. The only people left in the hospital were the emergency room staff, the inpatient staff, and a few laboratory and x-ray technicians. Our anesthetist was Captain Coleman, a career military officer and very skilled in her profession. She was very verbal, and in addition to keeping me aware of the patient's condition during procedures, she would engage in light-hearted chatter which helped lessen the usual tension in the OR.

At the beginning of the procedure, I noticed that she had decided to simply mask the patient rather than insert an endotracheal tube, which is routine for every major operation. She knew I was able to do an appendectomy quickly and, rather than traumatize the child unnecessarily, she could keep him asleep safely by mask for the forty to forty-five minutes needed. That was a mistake number two!

With Dr. Parkhurst ably assisting me, I located the diseased appendix quickly and placed the needed sutures securely before removing it. All the while, I was showing Dr. Parkhurst the anatomical landmarks which he had only been able to palpate externally. He seemed to be really enjoying the experience, and so was I. Within fifteen minutes of beginning, I was ready to close the wound and realized we had not heard a word from Captain Coleman the entire time. With my eyes fixed on the operative field, I asked her if everything was okay, to which I heard only a garbled response. I looked up to see her seated on her stool just at the moment her eyes rolled back in her head, and she began to topple backwards. I moved quickly behind her and caught her between my knees while grabbing the mask she had just released and keeping it on the boy's face. I didn't miss a beat in the administration of the anesthetic gas that was keeping him asleep. I told the circulating nurse to quickly move a gurney into the OR and get someone to help her get Captain Coleman on it. I was pretty certain she had simply fainted from the heat but was not sure whether or not she had a cardiac event also.

When I finally looked at Dr. Parkhurst, he had the most startled look at what he had just witnessed. I had never experienced anything like it, but I knew we had to get this operation completed and awaken this child as soon as possible. I asked, "Bob, have you ever closed a surgical wound?" He said he had not. I told him I could talk him through it easily enough and was sure I could keep the child asleep while he did it. I wanted to show strong leadership and confidence, because I thought if I got rattled, Dr. Parkhurst might faint. After what I had just seen, I figured anything could happen.

Just as Dr. Parkhurst began to follow my instructions, Captain Coleman recovered and even though still a little groggy insisted she could take over long enough for us to finish. Much to my assistant's relief, I rescrubbed my hands, donned another sterile gown, and finished the procedure. Despite this unbelievable turn of events, we still were able to finish in under forty-five minutes.

Thankful to say, the young man recovered quickly and was able to go home with his grateful parents the next day. They never knew what had happened in the OR other than we had removed his appendix. We all learned valuable lessons in the hot OR that afternoon, and we carefully stored them in our experience bank. In my forty-plus years of operating on thousands of patients, I never had another anesthetist faint during a procedure. It was quite a challenge for me and for Dr. Parkhurst. The experience was enough for him, because he never again asked to assist me in the OR.

49. GRANDPA AND GRANDMA LUTHER

The Two Greatest Soul Winners I've Ever Known

Grandpa and Grandma Luther

When our younger daughter Ginny married John Luther from Fayetteville, Arkansas, in 1995, Cathy and I became related by marriage to both the Luther and Bigger families. Both families have lived in Northwest Arkansas for several generations and are some of the most wonderful people and strongest Christians we have ever known. Both sets of John's grandparents were living at the time of the marriage, and the relationships we developed with them over the next ten years were life changing for us.

When we met them, Grandma and Grandpa Luther had lived on the same farm in Savoy, Arkansas, for the sixty-five-plus years of their marriage. Savoy is a picturesque community located near Lake Wedington about twelve miles west of Fayetteville. Both Grandma (Frances) and Grandpa (Fay) were born and raised in the community and never moved away for any significant period of time. He was an expert farmer and cattleman having learned the skills from his father and his brothers while working with them. After their father died, two of the nine brothers, Fay and Roland, stayed on the farm and continued farming and raising cattle.

Upon meeting the Luthers, we discovered what strong Christians they were and the heart each one had to witness for the Lord Jesus. Grandpa looked me in the eye and his first words to me were, "How old were you when you were saved?" I had a ready answer for him and said, "I was thirty-seven years old and am ashamed I waited so long!" He chuckled and said he was like me and had wasted a lot of living before he finally found Jesus. To every person I introduced to Grandpa following our initial meeting (including my pastor in El Dorado at the time), he asked them the same question.

Their modest home on their beautiful farm reflected their character and lifestyle— nothing fancy but warm and welcoming. When Cathy and I were living in South Arkansas and would come for a visit with our kids, going to Grandma and Grandpa's home was always on our agenda. Often Grandma would have a three-or-four-course meal prepared, and it included some of my absolute favorite dishes, like chicken and dumplings, fresh corn, home-grown tomatoes, home-made rolls, and her famous strawberry jam. I would brag on her jam so much she always insisted we take a couple of jars home with us.

Something I learned early about the Luther's was that they never locked the doors of their home. If the doors did have locks, they were long since rusted from disuse. On more than one occasion, they awakened in the morning to discover a visiting missionary couple in the guest bedroom, guests who had arrived after the Luthers had retired to bed. The visitors knew the house was unlocked and, rather than awaken the Luthers, they went to straight to the guest room. Grandma always told family and friends, "If Fay and I are asleep when you get here, come on in and make yourself at home!"

One Christmas Cathy and I received a letter from Grandma saying, "It was great to have visitors this year from California, Colorado, Tennessee, Oklahoma, Maryland, Virginia, and the West Indies to share our home that our Great God has given us to use. This isn't really our home. We are just sojourners here." I have every letter Grandma wrote to us, and they are treasures.

Of all the things I admired and loved about them, the one that stands out above the others was their continuous witness for the Lord Jesus. Every conversation led to a discussion of God's amazing grace and how fortunate they were to tell folks the good news that Jesus saves. I have had the privilege of knowing and serving with some of the greatest preachers in the world, but I have never known soul winners who compared to the Luthers. Who could imagine that this simple farm couple from a tiny community in Northwest Arkansas would lead over *twelve hundred people per year to Christ for over a forty-year period*? Only God could do that through them.

Their method for soul winning was as uncomplicated as their lives. Each year during the farming season, they would save enough money to take a two-month break in the late summer and early fall during the county fair and rodeo seasons. They would drive their van with a small trailer attached, both packed full of clothes and supplies. They tried to attend every county fair and rodeo in a three-state area. They would sleep in their van to save the expense of a motel room. On the fairgrounds they would set up their booth, which included a long table with eight chairs. Grandma would sit at the table and tell the people seated with her about the wonderful love of her Savior. She made certain they knew he loved them and that he died for them so they might be saved. In the ten-to-fifteen-minute session, it was not unusual for three or four of her guests to make a profession of faith to receive Christ as Savior. Grandma's testimony was sincere, compelling, and very convicting.

While Grandma was making her presentation, Grandpa's responsibility was to walk around the midway talking to everyone he encountered. He was extremely friendly and a master at making conversations with total strangers. He invited them into their booth to "hear some good news from Frances." He was so convincing with his invitations people were usually standing in line waiting to sit at Grandma's table. All the while they were waiting, Grandpa was telling them how wonderful it is to be saved, and God wanted to do this for them. In the course of the six to eight weeks of the fair and rodeo season, they would lead as many as *one thousand four hundred people* to a saving knowledge of Jesus Christ. They were an incomparable team!

By the time we met the Luthers, they had been doing their county fair and rodeo ministry for over forty years and were in their mid-eighties. The fairs and rodeos always came during the hottest time of the year, and they would stay at their booth from nine o'clock in the morning until the fair closing in the evening. The few times we visited during a fair, the temperature was so hot I had difficulty staying in the heat for more than a few hours. Grandma once told me, "Oh, Dr. John, I just wish Fay and I could do more. I don't know who will take our place when we leave here!"

It was so special to see them in public, such as at a Razorback basketball game, which they loved to attend. They would be sitting, holding hands, and Grandma would usually be napping with nineteen thousand crazy fans jumping and screaming all around them. When she awakened, she would always say what a fun time she had at the game.

Fay and Frances departed this life when they were both in their mid-nineties, having been married for seventy-five years. Frances died about a year before Fay. Throughout the following year, while waiting for the Lord's timing, whenever I saw him, he would say, "I miss Frances more than I ever thought. I just wish I had told her more often I loved her." I'm confident he is now making up for lost time.

When they finally entered their rest and were greeted by their Savior, I can imagine he said to them, "Well done my good and faithful servants. You have sacrificed much by loving so many in my name and have brought these precious souls into my kingdom." I can see him turn and point to the fifty thousand or more cheering and grateful saints they loved and led to him.

50. GRANDPA BIGGER'S WALMART STORY

An Offer to Become a Very Rich Man

Bob and Bonnie Bigger and Claire Luther (great-granddaughter), 2005

When Cathy and I moved to Fayetteville in 2000 after our eight month sojourn to Largo, Florida, we were thrilled to be back in Arkansas for several reasons. First, I was not a good fit for the medical clinic at the First Baptist Church of Indian Rocks, which I helped open and direct, and second, we were coming back to our home state where our children lived.

In Florida, we found ourselves isolated from our children and grandchildren, and the separation anxiety proved to be greater than anticipated. I was blessed to quickly find a medical position as one of the directors of the Wound Care Clinic at Washington Regional Medical Center, and Cathy and I were able to purchase a beautiful new home within a few miles of our daughter Ginny and her husband John Luther.

After becoming established as residents in northwest Arkansas we discovered an unusual thing about this part of our beloved state: A large number of people had a Walmart story. In the past, I had not paid much attention to the meteoric rise of the corporate giant, but as new residents, we saw that much of the region's economy was Walmart driven. There were rags-to-riches tales in which individuals had purchased original Walmart stock before the company went public, and their investment made them wealthy. Other stories involved missed opportunities. The best story I ever heard came from a extended-family member, an account I had not heard prior to our move to Fayetteville.

John Luther is blessed by the fact he and his brother James grew up under the direct godly influence of both sets of grandparents, who lived in the Fayetteville area. I have written about the spiritual impact that Fay and Frances Luther, his paternal grandparents, had on everyone including Cathy and me. Bob and Bonnie Bigger, his maternal grandparents were also spiritual giants in our opinion. We had such an affection for them that we called them Grandpa and Grandma Bigger as a measure of our love and respect.

Before retiring, Bob worked forty-two faithful years for Southwestern Electric Power Company in Fayetteville (SWEPCO), first as a lineman and then in supervisory positions. I have heard him tell stories of being called out at all hours of the night to help restore lost power from storms, accidents, and extreme icy conditions. There were times he would be separated from home and family for extended days and even weeks until full power was restored to all SWEPCO customers. He said his work was never routine or dull, and the conditions under which he worked could be very risky and often uncomfortable weather-wise.

Shortly after our move to the area Grandpa told his Walmart story at the urging of John Luther. Back in the early 1950s while Grandpa was working as a lineman, his routine included having coffee with a group of friends every Tuesday when he wasn't out of town because of work responsibilities. The men had some common interests such as raising cattle, but in general had just been friends for years. One of the men, whom they called "Mr. Sam," also had some Ben Franklin stores.

One day following coffee, Mr. Sam approached Grandpa and said he was making plans to incorporate his retail business, and he needed a total of $250,000 to finance the transaction. He was seeking ten investors to put up $25,000 each and had found nine men already. There was one option left, and he was offering it to Bob, who responded, "Mr. Sam, you know I have an ordinary job with SWEPCO, and with a wife and two young children, we don't have that kind of money in savings." Mr. Sam told him he understood, but if he would borrow the money from his bank, he (Mr. Sam) would co-sign the note. Grandpa told him he needed to discuss the proposition with his wife. They would pray about it, and he would give him an answer the following week. Mr. Sam told him there was no pressure, because if he didn't want the option, there was another man who was a manager of one of his stores who wanted it.

The following week, Grandpa told Mr. Sam he and Bonnie had prayed about it and were at peace with their decision that this investment was not the thing for them to do. He and Mr. Sam shook hands, and Mr. Sam told him he understood completely. Mr. Sam was Sam Walton and the ten initial investors did extremely well financially with their $25,000 investment into what became Walmart Corporation!

The manager who took Grandpa's option was Charlie Baum. Fast forward forty years and Mr. Baum had done so well with his investments that he was able to donate over two million dollars to the University of Arkansas to help fund the building of Bud Walton Arena for basketball and the new baseball stadium for the Razorbacks, which was named Baum Razorback Stadium. At his death in the 1990s, Mr. Baum's estate was reported to be valued in excess of a hundred million dollars.

When Grandpa told his story, I said, "If you had only borrowed the money, we would not have to struggle to get Razorback baseball tickets, but would be sitting in an air-conditioned box in Bigger Stadium and would be riding to the stadium in a chauffeured limousine instead of your pickup truck! Don't you wish you had the chance again to purchase the stock?" He chuckled when he replied in his usual humble manner, "No, I'm not sorry at all Momma and I didn't borrow the money. God has taken good care of us. We were able to pay our bills and didn't have want for anything. If we had had that kind of money, we might have had more problems than we could have handled."

Every time I tell this story and consider his honest reply to my questions, I ask the Lord to give me a grateful, humble heart like Grandpa Bigger's. He was thankful to God for things given him which were good, but also thankful for things which were withheld because they might have harmed. His Walmart story reminds me of God's promise: "Our God shall supply all of our needs according to His riches in glory by Christ Jesus" (Phil 4:19).

51. A MISSION TRIP TO "DONAMEEKA"

A Huge Mistake Leads to an Eternal Benefit

You may not have ever heard of Donameeka, or know where it is located, or know it is a fertile field for mission work. I learned all about the little country when we first met Grandma and Grandpa Luther.

The Luthers were the paternal grandparents of our son-in-law John Luther, whom our daughter Ginny married in 1995. They lived on the family farm in Savoy, Arkansas, a beautiful community about twelve mile west of Fayetteville. They were a simple, unpretentious couple, but I soon learned after meeting them that they were the two greatest soul winners I have ever met. They worked for Child Evangelism Fellowship for over forty-five years and personally led thousands of people to a faith in Christ every year. I have recounted their lives in the story, "Grandpa and Grandma Luther."

One evening I was talking with Grandpa about Cathy's and my experience with overseas missions. We had been discussing the responsibilities of all Christians to go around the world and carry the gospel message, and we were recounting our recent trip to Budapest, Hungary. Grandpa told us he and Grandma had recently gone to "Donameeka" to take the good news to the island. Since I had never heard of the island, I had him repeat the name, and he clearly said "Donameeka." After a few more questions concerning the island's location and its approximate size, I finally determined that the site of their mission trip was Dominica, which is a tiny Caribbean island in the Lesser Antilles region. When I thought I knew the actual name of the country, I said to Grandpa, "You mean the Republic of Dominica?" He replied with a chuckle and one of his typical responses, "I guess that's it—whatever you want to call it!" He continued calling the island "Donameeka." We have heard him say it so often it is now what we call it. It is hard for me to pronounce it "Domineeka." When Grandpa described their trip to the island, their experience had an unusual "Luther twist," just like the name of the country.

About six months prior to their journey, both Grandma and Grandpa were attending a Child Evangelism Fellowship conference in Florida. There they heard a missionary from Dominica speak of the opportunities for witness for the Lord Jesus and the open doors which were present on the tiny island. They heard that the country had a total population of less than eighty thousand (similar to ancient Nineveh), and it was the prayerful goal of the Dominican missionaries that the entire population would soon be saved. The Luthers began praying for the people of the island and that the missionaries would have the supernatural power to witness to every person. After praying for the missionaries for several months, Grandma told Grandpa the Lord had told her they needed to go to Dominica to aid in the mission effort. Grandpa told her to "buy the tickets and we'll go there, if this is what the Lord told you." She contacted the Dominican missionary to coordinate the best dates for them, and when a date was settled for their arrival, the missionary would meet them at the airport. He told them the flight from Miami would arrive around midnight.

They drove their van to Miami in order to save the money of an expensive flight from Northwest Arkansas. It took almost two days, and they slept in their van at a rest area in Alabama to save the additional cost of a motel room. They boarded the plane in Miami for the two-and-a-half-hour flight, and when they arrived, the airport was very small with only a few people there. As they entered the terminal, the missionary was nowhere to be found.

After about an hour's wait, they asked the only person at the airline counter if he knew the missionary they were seeking, and he said he had never heard of him. He also told them he knew most of the missionaries on the island bearing the Dominican Republic! Grandpa said in his usual loud voice, "I thought this was supposed to be Donameeka!" In the midst of this new surprise and confusion, they discovered when Grandma called the airline to book their tickets, the agent misunderstood her and booked two seats on a flight to the Dominican Republic. Neither Grandma nor Grandpa had checked their tickets to discover the error.

They asked the agent at the terminal what could be done, and according to Grandma, the only thing he knew was contact a local law enforcement officer whom Grandma called the "Chief of Police." When he finally arrived, he told Grandma she needed to accompany him to his headquarters, where he could make the necessary phone calls to get them back on their journey. In the meantime, Grandpa had gone to the restroom without telling Grandma where he was going, and when she couldn't find him, she went alone with "the Chief" to his station. When Grandpa began searching for Grandma, he was told that "she went off with the police chief." Grandpa just sat down and waited.

When she finally returned about an hour and a half later, she had obtained tickets for a flight back to Miami where they could book another flight to their intended destination of Dominica. Apparently, there were no flights from the Dominican Republic to Dominica. She also told Grandpa she had a chance to witness the love of Jesus to the "police chief," *and he had prayed to receive Christ as his Savior.* Grandma never missed an opportunity to witness for her Savior, and she had this law officer all to herself for over two hours!

They finally made it safely to Dominica and connected with the missionary. They said the time spent in "Donameeka" was a wonderful learning experience for them, and they were able to tell countless people on the island that Jesus loved them and that he came to earth as a man to save them. In recounting this story to Cathy and me, Grandma and Grandpa were not sure just how many people on "Donameeka" were saved during their trip, but they did know for sure the "police chief on that other island" was saved.

He could have been the very reason God sent them on this particular mission trip (with a slight detour).

52. "YOU'RE NOT MUCH OF A WITNESS"

An Effort to Witness Christ at Walmart

Grandpa Luther was never at a loss for words, and often his words would cut through all the pretense of pride and focus on the main thing. For him the main thing was his witness for the Lord Jesus Christ. Whenever Cathy and I were with either Grandpa or Grandma Luther, the conversation invariably led back to Christ and his redeeming work on the cross.

Grandpa never met a stranger, and he would often initiate a conversation with someone he didn't know by saying something like, "I'll bet you didn't know I have two birthdays. How many birthdays do you have?" Regardless of the answer, Grandpa used his opening line to give his natural date of birth and then tell when he was born again into the Kingdom. His follow-up question was always, "Have you had your second birthday?" One of his favorite opening lines when he met a woman was, "I know someone who loves you." Usually she would ask, "Who is it?" Grandpa followed with, "Jesus loves you so much he died on a cross to save you. Have you been saved?" For Grandpa and Grandma Luther every encounter and every conversation led to Jesus.

Grandpa told me about an encounter he had with a man while on a shopping trip with Grandma to "Walmarks." He always called the giant chain "Walmarks," and to this day it is difficult for me to remember it is Walmart. Grandpa was waiting for her to finish shopping and was sitting on a bench in the foyer. He said that "an old man" came in with his wife, and, while she shopped, he sat down beside him. I asked Grandpa just how old the "old man" was since Grandpa was in his late eighties when he told the story. He said in his usual loud voice, "Oh, I don't know. Probably fifty or sixty." Grandpa was hard of hearing despite wearing hearing aids, which never worked very well for him.

The two of them sat without speaking for five or six minutes when Grandpa asked loudly, "Where do you go to church?" The man said quietly, "I'm a Jehovah's Witness." Grandpa had no idea about Jehovah's Witnesses, including their doctrine denying the divinity of Jesus Christ. To Grandpa, one was either lost or saved and was either a Christian or a non-Christian. When the man told Grandpa that he was a "witness for Jehovah," Grandpa responded with, "You're not much of a witness! We've been sitting here for over five minutes, and you haven't said a word about Jesus!" At this point, "the old man got up and left."

In Grandpa's world, everything was either black or white. If you love Jesus and claim to be his witness, you need to tell everyone around you how wonderful he is and that he will save you if you are lost. Grandpa didn't intend to be unkind to the "old man," but rather was challenging him to be more faithful. Grandpa and Grandma Luther lived and witnessed on a different level from any other Christians I have ever known. Consequently, they led many thousand people to a saving knowledge of Jesus Christ. When I think of their witness, I am convicted that what Grandpa said to the "old man at Walmarks" can also be said about me.

53. FINDING TAFFY

Mary Kay's Lost Dog Is Found

Mary Kay and Taffy

Our family loves pets, and through the years we have had some memorable dogs, cats, ducks, turtles, and a few fish. We never experienced the "joys" of owning rabbits, gerbils, parrots, possums, or racoons. When we get together for holidays and special events, the conversation occasionally comes around to discussing and laughing about a particular pet who impacted us in a positive, but occasionally in a negative way. We have even been taught spiritual lessons unexpectedly through some of our pet experiences. One such lesson occurred through the life and adventures of Taffy.

Taffy was a beautiful, female Sheltie (Shetland Sheepdog) whom we bought for our daughter Mary Kay from the daughter of our veterinarian in El Dorado. Because the registered name of the mother of our puppy was Candy, Mary Kay chose to name her "Taffy." Her coat was a lovely golden color similar to that of the Silver Dollar City taffy which a few of us in the family loved. Taffy was a cute and playful puppy, and we all fell in love with her at first sight!

Mary Kay was ten years old at the time she had wanted a Sheltie, and we were pleased to declare Taffy as "Mary Kay's dog." For Cathy and me, this also meant that Mary Kay was responsible to feed and clean up after this small puppy. Our back yard was large and fenced, which made a perfect playground for an active puppy who loved to run and herd. None of our pets were "inside pets," but we had a large basement for shelter during stormy or severely cold weather.

Taffy grew to adult size within a year, and we had her spayed to avoid the problems associated with breeding and puppy care. Because she was so active and playful, she didn't have the problems of weight gain and lethargy some spayed, female animals experience. Two characteristics of Taffy were her high-pitched bark, which I called a "yap," and a characteristic twirling motion she executed when she was excited or saw Mary Kay. Little did we know these peculiar characteristics would play a critical role in Taffy's future.

When Taffy was approximately three years old, we discovered her missing one day. It was not unusual for her to be outside the fence, because our yard was large, and occasionally when one of the gates was accidentally left open, she would run into the neighborhood. In all previous instances, Taffy would return home within an hour or so following her neighborhood exploration.

This time she didn't return. We thoroughly searched the neighborhood until dark, and hoped that when daylight came, someone would find her and bring her home. Her collar had all the necessary information needed to contact us. That night we all prayed for her safe return, and within our little prayer circle, there were a few tears shed thinking she might be hurt or worse.

Days led to weeks of no word concerning Taffy, and I must admit I gave up ever seeing her again. I had lost special dogs in the past, and it was easier for me emotionally to assume they were dead rather than continue hoping for a return. Cathy, Mary Kay, John, and Ginny didn't give up and continued to pray for her at every meal and during evening prayers. I certainly didn't discourage them or make them think I didn't also miss Taffy and long for her return.

About a year from the date of Taffy's disappearance, I received a phone call at my office on a Saturday morning from a lady who had been a surgical patient in the past. At the beginning of the conversation, she said, "I know where your dog is!" I said, "You know where our Sheltie is?" without thinking that was the only dog we had missing. She said a woman friend of hers had found the dog a year ago and decided to keep her despite knowing the dog belonged to us. I knew the lady who supposedly had taken our dog, because she had also been a surgical patient. I asked why she was just now letting me know since she had known about it for so long. Her answer was, "I felt bad knowing where your dog was, and I got into an argument with the lady and decided to get her into trouble!" I thanked the caller for her information.

I looked up the address of the alleged dog kidnapper in our office files and called home to report this startling news. I picked up the girls, and we very anxiously drove several miles to the lady's address. Upon arrival, we found a small, poorly kept single-dwelling home with a fenced backyard. There was evidence of a recent fire at the residence with significant damage. There was no one at home, so we went to the corner of the fence, and Mary Kay began calling Taffy's name. Within seconds a bedraggled-looking Sheltie ran around the house in response to the call. We couldn't be sure this was Taffy because this dog was thin, her coat was duller in color, and she seemed more lethargic than our Taffy. When she spotted Mary Kay, she began "yapping" and twirling in an unmistakable fashion. We immediately knew this was our Taffy! We were so excited to have found our dog, and Taffy kept up her yapping and twirling in celebration with us of her reunion with her family.

Within a few minutes, a car drove into the driveway, and I recognized the lady at the wheel. On exiting the car, she was crying and kept saying, "I'm so sorry, I'm so sorry, I'm so sorry." When she calmed down, she confessed she knew Taffy was ours, but when she found her roaming in her neighborhood, she had just lost her own dog and believed we could "easily get another pet." Because we were so glad to have found Taffy, we never considered pressing any charges against her. We told her we forgave her, and then prayed with her concerning the fire damage to her home and belongings. Our attitude toward her later opened a door to share Christ and his forgiveness of her, and she prayed for forgiveness of her sins to be saved.

The following week we took Taffy to the veterinarian, and she was found to have heart worms because of her poor care. She almost didn't survive the treatment, but began improving to become a healthy and happy

Taffy once again. The above photograph was taken about a year after the ordeal. We all learned some very important life lessons concerning our yapping, twirling Taffy. Forgive quickly those who have harmed you. Never give up hoping for someone (or some dog) who is lost that they will be found, and by all means pray without ceasing! (1 Thess 5:17). Someone's eternal future may be hanging in the balance.

54. GIVING UP "BOOTS," AKA "HARRY"

Ginny's Lost Cat Was Found and Given Away as A Gift of Love

"Boots" in his chair

Our daughter Ginny loved cats, and I have told her she must have inherited the love from her mother, because I don't care much for cats. My sister Marilyn always seemed to have a cat when we were growing up, and because her cats aggravated my dogs, they aggravated me also. I did my best to return the favor whenever possible.

Cathy had numerous cats during her childhood, and she had lots of "cat stories" from her past. In a moment of extreme weakness, I even gave Cathy a Siamese cat for her birthday in March of our courtship year. I was so in love with Cathy and wanting to please her so much, I failed to think I would be living with Ming the following August when we were married.

Because our other daughter Mary Kay also inherited cat love from her mother, I was destined to always have one or more cats living around our home. Our son John inherited his disdain for cats from me, and we tried our best to agitate them with our pet dogs as often as possible. We never intended any physical harm for them.

At one point when Ginny was approximately eight years old, we came into possession of a cat who was part Siamese and part some other breed.

As I recall the kitten had been abandoned, which was all our merciful girls needed to know. Ginny was first in line for a new kitten, so this one became hers. The kitten had distinctive white paws and was a male, so Ginny named him "Boots." I was thankful the kitten was male, so we didn't have to take him to the veterinarian for a spaying. Boots was seemingly more playful and friendly with me than our previous felines, so I think I kind of liked Boots.

Our across-the-street neighbors were the Clydes, and their younger daughter Elizabeth (Bitsy) was close friends with our kids, especially Mary Kay and Ginny. Bitsy loved animals, and, in fact, she became a veterinarian and now lives with her family and practices veterinary medicine in Mattoon, Illinois. Whenever we went on vacation, we engaged Bitsy to watch over and feed our animals, which she not only loved doing for us but also appreciated the extra money we paid for her kindness.

One year in March when Boots was approximately two years old, we took a family vacation to Fort Lauderdale to spend time with Cathy's parents and family. To cover our ten-day absence, we again enlisted Bitsy to feed Boots and make certain he was safe. As I recall we didn't have a dog at the time, which was rare for us. Upon our return, Bitsy sadly reported she hadn't seen Boots for about five days and had no clue of his whereabouts. He was pretty much a home cat and to our recollection had never been gone for such an extended period of time. That night all of us, and especially Ginny, asked God to return Boots safely home.

Within the next month when there was no sign of Boots, we all gave up hope of his return—all except Ginny. She prayed multiple times during the day, at all our meal times when it was her turn to pray, and especially at night as we listened to and agreed with her pleas to our heavenly Father. She never stopped praying for Boots when some of us had long since given up.

Approximately eight months later on Halloween evening, our kids were preparing to go into the neighborhood for their annual "trick or treating" when our front door bell rang. It was Bitsy, who was short of breath from running. She told us excitedly, "I've found Boots!" "Where in the world did you find him, and why didn't you bring him home?" we asked. "He is at Mrs. Reeves house and when I knocked on her door to trick or treat, there was Boots standing beside her."

Gladys Reeves, the widow of Harry Bryant Reeves, lived two doors down from us on the same side of the street. She had been owner of the iconic B. W. Reeves Department Store in downtown El Dorado. Harry's father had founded the famous store during the oil boom days of the 1920s, and everyone in the surrounding area was familiar with the store. Harry had died about five years earlier from heart disease, and Gladys lived alone in their beautiful two-storied home.

When Bitsy saw Boots at Mrs. Reeves feet, she asked her why she had Boots. She responded, "Do you recognize this cat? He came to my door about six months ago, and I thought he was a stray cat. He had no collar and was very hungry, so I began feeding him. He was happy to stay with me." Bitsy told her Boots was his name, and he belonged to the Moores. She had been feeding him while we were out of town, and one day he disappeared. Mrs. Reeves was shocked at this revelation and told Bitsy, "This cat has decided to stay with me, and he's now an inside cat. I have had him de-clawed, neutered, and named him "Harry" for my dear, departed husband. Harry never leaves my side and even sleeps in the bed with me! I just can't give him up."

Ginny was so excited Boots had been found and wanted him home with her. But now Mrs. Reeves was saying she couldn't live without "Harry." I immediately phoned her, and, while she was recounting the story Bitsy had told us, she began crying uncontrollably at the thought of returning Boots to us. I told her we would explain this to Ginny, allow her to decide, and then would let her know.

As we sat down with Ginny to explain the dilemma of Boots, she also began crying so we prayed with her as she made her decision. She went into our yard, picked some flowers and walked the short distance to Mrs. Reeves house to knock on her door. I think Mrs. Reeves was a little surprised to see Ginny with her flower gift and was almost shocked when Ginny told her, "I want you to have Boots as a gift from me." She hugged Ginny and, through tears, told Ginny what a sweet girl she was for this gift while promising to take good care of Harry.

We were all very proud of Ginny's loving generosity in giving up Boots, and I promised her I would find another cat for her very soon. Ginny's attitude helped reinforce to us we must hold our possessions in an open hand so when our Father decides to move them to someone else, we can give freely and cheerfully. He always gives back more than we had in the beginning (Luke 6:38). I can't be sure, but I think we found two more cats for her to replace Boots. I am sure Harry had a much more luxurious life with Mrs. Reeves than he ever had with us.

55. BORROWING MONEY FROM GRAM YOUNG

A Loan Paid Off Brings Dividends

1969 Fiat Spider

When Cathy and I lived in New Orleans during my surgery residency days at Charity Hospital, we were doing surprisingly well on poverty level income. For my first year of residency and our first year of marriage, the hospital paid me the paltry sum of $125 per month, which based on a one-hundred-and-twenty-hour work week, this amounting to approximately twenty-six cents per hour. Not bad for a hospital to hire a surgeon at that wage even though I was still in training. Cathy's salary as an elementary school teacher, although small by today's standard, kept a roof over our head and food on our table. At one point that first year we asked an official of the state of Louisiana if we qualified for food stamps and were told from a financial standpoint we did qualify, but the state would not issue food stamps to a medical doctor. Go figure! Because we had no indebtedness and were frugal in our spending, neither Cathy nor I considered ourselves poor.

During my second year of residency, a representative group of interns and residents at Charity Hospital appealed to the hospital board and the state of Louisiana for a significant raise in salary, and it was granted. I was then paid the unheard-of sum of $500 per month, and Cathy and I thought we suddenly had struck it rich! We had learned to live on so little we were able to put money into a savings account for the following year. In July, 1967, we were blessed with the birth of our son John Aaron, and our new expenses caused us to begin using our savings. We had two automobiles, which we each owned before marriage, and had no indebtedness on either.

In the fall of 1968, we decided we could get along well with only one car so we sold my Corvair Monza and traded Cathy's Cutlass for a Dodge station wagon. I was able to ride to and from Charity Hospital with my surgical colleague Jack Welch, who lived nearby. That arrangement worked very well for us during my last year of residency because I seldom had to go back to the hospital at night, even when on call. I simply allowed the third-year resident to resolve problem consultations, because they were required to stay in the hospital on their call nights.

Upon completion of my training, I had a two-year commitment for active duty in the US Air Force. I was certain I would be sent to Vietnam, because the war there was near its peak, and I was a fully trained surgeon from the "battlefields" of New Orleans. In the wisdom of the military, however, I was assigned to the Air Training Command Base at Valdosta, Georgia–Moody Air Force Base. Several months before I was to report for duty, Cathy and I realized we again needed a second vehicle, since we would be living in town, and the base was a ten-mile drive away. Our problem was our ability to pay for an automobile, even an inexpensive one.

While visiting Cathy's parents in Fort Lauderdale, we discussed our situation with them, and her mother (Gram Young) offered to loan us enough money for the car stating "we could pay her back when we could afford to." That sounded like a great plan to us, but we set a two-year limit on the payoff, and we agreed to send her a check each month.

We shopped for a suitable car in Fort Lauderdale, and I found the perfect one for me, a 1969 Fiat Spider. The car was purchased in my name with a check given us by Gram Young. We used the bank interest rate at the time to calculate the two-year payout, and Cathy and I signed a hand-written promissory note to Gram. She said we didn't have to do that, but we insisted, not wanting to take advantage of her generosity.

For the next two years we faithfully sent her a check each month, and I included a hand- written note telling her how we were doing and what our plans were for the following month. Every time we saw her and many of the times when we talked with her by phone, she would tell us how she enjoyed our notes.

Finally, near the end of our two years in Valdosta, I mailed her the last payment on the Fiat, and Cathy and I breathed a sigh of relief to again be debt-free. For years afterwards, whenever she thought about it, Gram would ask, "Can't I make you another loan? I loved getting those notes from you each month!" I now regret having stopped writing her, but we did talk with her often by phone and made frequent family visits to Fort Lauderdale. She and Granddaddy Young came to El Dorado at least twice each year and would stay with us for five to seven days. I have to admit Gram Young was the most generous and wonderful creditor we ever had!

PS: We sold our 1964 Corvair Monza convertible to Cathy's Uncle Bobby Shuman for $500. He got a great bargain. Today the same vehicle would sell for ten times that amount!

56. WATCHING "THE RUMBLE IN THE JUNGLE"

John and I Watch a Historic Boxing Match

With the recent death of Muhammed Ali, there have been a tremendous number of articles written in the media along with televised comments from a wide range of people regarding their remembrances of this boxing champion. His reign in the boxing world occurred during an era when professional boxing was at its peak in popularity and before the rise of televised mixed martial arts fighting.

Although I never participated in boxing, I have loved watching boxing matches dating back to the mid-1950s when Pop and I frequently watched televised matches. It was a time I especially loved, because it was something we regularly did together, seldom missing one of the *Pabst Blue Ribbon Bouts* on Wednesday night or the *Gillette Friday Night Fights*. This was before the introduction of color television, and we would choose either the "black trunks" or the "white trunks" as our favorite for any particular fight.

As well as I can remember, Cassius Clay (aka Muhammed Ali) never had one of his bouts televised on a free television channel. As his popularity rose quickly when he became the heavyweight champion, one had to pay a high fee to watch one of his fights on a closed circuit which was transmitted only to theaters and large auditoriums.

One particularly expensive and disappointing match for me was his first fight with Sonny Liston on February, 1964, in which he won the heavyweight championship. I was a senior in medical school and had very little extra money available for expenses and certainly none set aside for boxing matches. Jim Weedman, a fellow senior medical student, and I paid $25 each to watch the match on a closed circuit screen at Robinson Auditorium in Little Rock. We were hoping to watch Sonny Liston demolish the brash talking Clay, but just the opposite happened. Clay scored a TKO in the seventh round over the seemingly invincible Liston when Liston couldn't answer the bell for the round. In today's economy, the $25 we spent is equivalent to $190!! (Cassius Clay changed his name to Muhammed Ali when he joined the Nation of Islam shortly after becoming the heavyweight champion.)

Fast forward to 1974 when Muhammed had lost his heavyweight crown because of his refusal to serve in the military. George Foreman was at the top of the heavyweight boxing world. He was huge, menacing, and mean with knockout power in both hands. Muhammed Ali appeared to be past his prime, but was proclaiming wherever anyone would listen that he "was the greatest boxer who ever lived." I always hoped some fighter would knock out "The Louisville Lip" as he was often called.

Our family was on vacation in Fort Lauderdale in October visiting Cathy's family and enjoying the warm weather of South Florida. On the return trip in our car, we decided to stay overnight in Montgomery, Alabama, which was approximately half way to El Dorado. We arrived in Montgomery around 5:00 p.m. and were getting settled into our motel room when I read in the local newspaper about the heavyweight championship fight between Foreman and Ali that night. It was being held in Kinshasa, Zaire (now the Republic of the Congo). I noted in the advertisement that the fight was entitled "The Rumble in the Jungle" and was being shown on closed circuit television in a downtown auditorium. I asked Cathy if she would mind if I took John Aaron, who was seven years old and go to the auditorium to watch the fight. She said, "You can take John and go, but don't count on us girls to go with you. We're staying here to rest and watch a movie on TV."

The fight was scheduled for 7:00 p.m. Montgomery time, so John and I got directions from the motel to the auditorium and set out. We arrived forty-five minutes before fight time, and a large crowd had already gathered outside. The crowd was mostly grown men aged forty or more, and I estimated the racial mix included approximately 65 percent Black American. I was very uneasy being there, because this was six to eight years past all the racial unrest in Alabama, and Montgomery was the city where lots of demonstrations and riots had occurred.

I stepped up to the counter to purchase a ticket and told the agent, "One adult and one child, please." He said abruptly, "There ain't no child tickets." "You mean I have to pay $25 for a seven-year-old?" I asked. "If you want to take him inside you do." I grudgingly paid the $50 for our tickets, which were general admission since there were no reserved seats. I found two seats as near the aisle as I could about half way down front. I looked around at the guys close to us for a man who might have some compassion for a dad and young son in case of any riot-like event. I spotted at least two large men nearby who fit the profile, but I didn't introduce us.

The fight began on time, and I don't believe it was any louder at ringside in Zaire than it was in the Montgomery auditorium. Our crowd, which numbered about three hundred and fifty, seemed to be split about half for Ali and half for Foreman. As all boxing enthusiasts know, Ali knocked out George Foreman in the eighth round because he used a defensive technique he called the "rope-a-dope." It was designed to cause Foreman to wear himself out through delivering multiple punches to Ali's forearms and hands.

In typical bragging fashion, Ali said after the fight he learned the technique from Stepin Fetchit, a black American movie actor of the previous two decades. Ali always seemed to have a funny poem or quote to punctuate each fight, and this was one of his best. I still wanted to see him knocked out because of his anti-war sentiments.

John and I made it safely back to the motel about the time the girls finished their movie, but I believe we had a better time than they did. I just had to keep putting it out of my mind how much we had to pay for our "good time." I definitely would do it over again, because John and I were watching an exciting boxing match together like Pop and I did many years before.

PS: What really saddens me about Muhammed Ali is his final destination. The Bible clearly teaches those who are not for the Lord Jesus are against him, because the god of this world has blinded their eyes. All who have not received him as Savior and Lord in this life will be condemned into eternal punishment forever. All the accolades of men will not change the result of one's earthly choice regarding him.

57. THE FINAL FOUR IN 1978

Great Connections to Obtain Tickets

When I was an undergraduate at the University of Arkansas in the late 1950s, the basketball team was pretty uninspiring, and I was not alone in my assessment. Our fraternity required all freshman pledges to attend the home games because the attendance at Barnhill Arena was so poor. On a good night there would be fewer than three thousand in attendance, and this number included the student body, who would be loudly cheering for their beloved Razorbacks. Coach Glen Rose was a good coach, but his talent pool was not able to regularly compete in the Southwest Conference. He was followed by two coaches, Duddy Waller and Lanny Van Eman, who collectively coached from 1967 through 1974. Arkansas basketball needed re-vitalization, and it came with the hiring of Eddie Sutton in 1975.

Coach Sutton was a disciplinarian and drilled sound basketball fundamentals into all of his players. There was no shot clock in those days, and the game was slowed to such an extent that many games were won by a team who scored only forty points. There was a premium on ball control and pinpoint shooting, especially free throws.

In his second year of coaching at Arkansas, he recruited three players from Arkansas who helped transform the Razorbacks into a national power—Marvin Delph from Conway, Ronnie Brewer from Fort Smith, and Sidney Moncrief from Little Rock. They later became known as "The Triplets" and individually set Razorback records for scoring, rebounding, and assists.

Their first year together, they led the Razorbacks to the NCAA Regionals, only to lose in the first round to Wake Forest. The following season was their best, and they made it to the Final Four, which was played in late March, 1978, at the Checker Dome Arena in St. Louis.

As soon as I knew the Razorbacks were in the Final Four, I called Uncle Harry Gosling who lived in St. Louis. Earlier he told me he was best friends with the facilities manager of the Checker Dome. I asked if he could get four tickets for the games through his friend, and he thought surely it would be possible. I anxiously awaited his call the following Monday, but Uncle Harry sadly reported the words of his friend, "Harry, if my own mother wanted tickets for the tournament, I couldn't get them. They've been sold out for almost a year!"

After asking several friends in El Dorado if they had any connections to get tickets, I remembered Russell Marks would be a good source. His dealership, Marks Ford Company, supplied the use of a new vehicle each year to the Razorback coaching staff, and he was a personal friend of Frank Broyles, the athletic director. Mr. Marks told me he didn't have tickets, but I must have lots of confidence in his ability to secure tickets. He said, "I'll take this as a big challenge and see what I can do!"

Several day later, he called to say he had quite an experience in his ticket search and was only partially successful in the quest. He couldn't get tickets through the Razorback athletic department but had gotten not four but two tickets from the president of St. Louis University, who was also a personal friend. Mr. Marks apologized for his inability to get the four tickets I had requested, but said, "I think you'll like these two because they are really good seats." Indeed, we discovered later how successful was his search. The two seats were on the second row behind the home bench because they were the personal seats of the university president, whose team, the Billikins, played their home games in the Checker Dome.

The Final Four games were played over the Easter weekend, and because Cathy's mom and dad were visiting from Fort Lauderdale, I thought it would have been rude for John and me to leave and be absent on Easter Sunday. We gave our two tickets for the Saturday games to the El Dorado Wildcat head basketball coach, Jim Atwell, so he and a guest could attend the semi-final games. John and I scheduled a Monday flight to St. Louis so we could make the final game which was on Monday night.

We were hoping the Razorbacks would defeat the Kentucky Wildcats on Saturday and then play for the championship on Monday night, but it was not to be. The Wildcats had some very large and talented players, and they muscled their way to a 64–59 victory with aggressive rebounding and accurate shooting. The play was so rough one of our forwards, Jim Counce, had to be hospitalized following the game with an injury to his kidney.

In those days, there was a consolation game, so we were scheduled to play Notre Dame on Monday night prior to the championship game between Kentucky and Duke. Although John and I were disappointed in not getting to see our team play for the title, we would see a great game with Notre Dame and then watch the National Championship game live! We arrived at the airport and Uncle Harry met us and took us to our motel room. We were to call him following the game and he planned to drive us back to our motel, which was several miles away.

We were very excited by the crowd and the noise outside the arena, and fans from Kentucky and Duke were anticipating that their team would win the grand prize. I approached a man holding two fingers in the air and asked him if he had two tickets to sell, to which he replied, "No, I want to buy two!" I asked what he was willing to pay, and he said, "One thousand dollars apiece." I felt those expensive tickets in my coat pocket and for a brief moment considered making a quick two thousand dollars and going back to the motel to watch the game on television. I knew, however, Mr. Marks would discover my deceit before we got back to El Dorado.

The game was everything predicted and even more. Near the end of regulation time the game was tied, and we had the ball on our end of the court with only ten seconds left. There was a timeout called while the coaches planned their strategy. My heart was beating so hard I asked the man next to me if I had a heart attack, would he please see that John got back home! He laughed and said, "Don't worry Doc. You'll both make it fine."

Ron Brewer got the in-bounds pass and walked the ball down court with the fans of both teams loudly screaming. When he got to the top of the circle and there were two seconds left on the clock, he quickly shot a jumper that hit the bottom of the net, and we won the game. It was the most exciting basketball game John and I ever saw together. And yes, we both did make it! I survived the heart scare and John got back home.

PS: Kentucky beat Duke, so at least the team which beat us was the national champion!

PS 2: Fast forward thirty-eight years and Dr. Jim Counce, noted heart surgeon in Fayetteville who was injured in the Arkansas-Kentucky game performed an open-heart, triple-coronary-bypass operation on me in 2016. I not only survived but did well and have not lost my enthusiasm for Razorback basketball.

58. A DIVINE LEGAL APPOINTMENT

A Routine Appointment
with a Lawyer Reaps Life-Long Benefits

When a physician gets a phone call from a lawyer's office, it can strike fear in his heart. There is often an overriding anxiety of a medical malpractice suit lurking somewhere in his mind whether he will admit it or not. Even the wording of the allegations in a malpractice document, such as "did willingly and knowingly commit the error of, " are painful and distressing for a conscientious doctor. Just the mention of certain lawyers' names evokes the same fearful response. Such was not the case when I received a phone call at my office one Monday afternoon from the El Dorado attorney Dennis Shackleford. I made an appointment to be in his office on the following Thursday afternoon.

Dennis was a personal friend, well-known in Arkansas for his outstanding legal defense work in medical malpractice cases. He occasionally asked me to review a case for him regarding allegations made against a physician from another part of the state but never against a local doctor. In addition to the generous monetary benefit I received from such a review, I really enjoyed the legal discussions with Dennis because I always learned something new from him. At one point during my training years, I considered law school in addition to my medical training and had an abiding interest in the law. Pop used to tell me in a half-kidding way, "If you have a degree in law in addition to a medical degree you can write your own ticket working for a big insurance company!" I liked the part of "writing your own ticket," but was not enthused about the "big insurance company" part!

Before my discussions began with Dennis, he would frequently ask about our son John who was in law school during the late 1980s and early 1990s. When John graduated from the University of Arkansas School of Law in Fayetteville in 1992, he began searching for just the right professional fit to begin his practice. He and his wife Gina enjoyed their three years living in Northwest Arkansas, and had many friends and a great church in the First Baptist Church of Springdale (now Cross Church). Initially their preference was to remain in the area, but available positions for a new and inexperienced lawyer were scarce. Gina had a good job working as an accountant for J. B. Hunt Trucking, which supported them financially, and to supplement her income, John got a job in the produce section of Harp's Grocery. He also worked for a short time at George's Chicken in general maintenance. Cathy and I were greatly concerned for our lawyer son doing such non-legal work and were very diligent in those days to pray for John's employment.

This particular afternoon when Dennis asked about John's status, I told him John had graduated but was having difficulty finding the right fit for employment. By this time John had taken and passed the Arkansas Bar examination, so he was ready to start his legal career. Dennis said, "I've got a good suggestion for him. Judge Harry Barnes from Camden has just been appointed by President Bill Clinton as Federal Judge for the Western District of Arkansas, and he is waiting for confirmation from the United States Senate. Federal Judges always hire legal clerks to assist them, and those clerkships are highly sought by young, aspiring lawyers. "Why don't you give Harry a call and see if he would consider hiring John as his clerk? I doubt he has hired anyone yet."

I was acquainted with Judge Barnes because about a year earlier, another attorney friend, Worth Camp, invited Cathy and me to join him and his wife Janice along with Harry and Mary Barnes for an evening meal. Cathy and I really enjoyed our time spent with the Camps and Barneses.

I went back to my office and called the number Dennis gave me, and Judge Barnes immediately answered, which I considered miraculous. I identified myself and the judge remembered our dinner meeting. I told him about my conversation with Dennis and wanted to know if he had already hired a clerk, which he hadn't. I told him about John, and he said he would love to interview him because he had "a stack of applications" from all over the country but liked giving preference to local people. "When can John be here for an interview," he asked. I said, "I think he can come down from Fayetteville tomorrow afternoon." "I look forward to meeting him," the judge said as we concluded the call.

John was excited to meet and interview with Judge Barnes the following afternoon, and they immediately clicked. At the end of the interview Judge Barnes told John that if he was confirmed by the Senate, then he would be his law clerk. How excited we all were with this sudden and unexpected blessing! Both Cathy and I firmly believe Judge Barnes saw the outstanding character qualities in John and made the best choice for his first law clerk.

The two years John spent clerking in Judge Barnes's office were the perfect beginning for him. He not only learned the many intricacies of jurisprudence from an outstanding judge, but was also able to meet and know a large number of attorneys in the Western District of Arkansas. The law department at Murphy Oil Company, whose national headquarters are in El Dorado, saw the great potential in John and hired him as an associate attorney in 1995. He has since risen in the corporate ranks of Murphy Oil, and, when the corporation split to form Murphy USA in 2013, John became senior vice president and general counsel for Murphy USA.

We never know the impact of a phone call or a meeting until looking back we see where God has directed. His promise is made real when we trust him with all of our heart and don't lean on our own understanding (Prov 3: 5–6). Cathy and I will always believe the appointment that afternoon with Dennis Shackleford was ordained by God.

59. WHO BURNED DOWN HUGH GOODWIN?

Anxiety Over a Sex-Education Talk

Hugh Goodwin Elementary School

Physicians in small towns are frequently asked to do any number of civic-minded activities apart from practicing medicine. I usually welcomed opportunities to give back to the people of El Dorado if I felt qualified for the task for which I was invited. For more than twenty-five years, I served as the team physician for the El Dorado Wildcats and thoroughly enjoyed my role in the position. I was invited to serve on various boards, most of which

I had to decline because the meeting times conflicted with my schedule as a general surgeon. Early in my career, I was invited to participate in a teaching function at the elementary schools, and I was told by the person who invited me that this role was usually reserved for the "younger doctors." At the time, I certainly qualified from an age perspective. In retrospect I wish I had disqualified myself on grounds I was really not qualified. The teaching opportunity I was given was the annual "sex talk" given by physicians and nurses to the fifth graders in each school.

The format for the talk had the students separated into boys and girls classes, and a twenty-minute slide presentation was shown. It was very general in nature, showing the reproductive anatomy on plastic models and the physiology of fertilization using drawings. There was nothing graphic or objectionable about the slide show. Following the slide presentation, the lights were turned on, and the expert (me) was available to answer questions from the boys. The nurses were scheduled as experts for the girls to avoid possible embarrassment.

The first year I was scheduled to be the expert at Yocum Elementary School, which traditionally had been equivalent in academics to Hugh Goodwin, my boyhood school. As a Hugh Goodwin alum, I always considered "my school" to be superior, but I admit my prejudice. I had rescheduled my surgical cases for the appointed morning and arrived on time, but with some trepidation in my spirit.

I was shown my room and told that the usual teacher had called in sick that morning and wouldn't be there that day. I should have insisted on a substitute monitor, but bravely said, "I think I can handle it with no problem." The school nurse was there to show the slides, which went well. When she finished, she turned on the lights and excused herself. I then stood up and asked, "Are there any questions?" An older-appearing boy immediately raised his hand and asked an X-rated question, which I will not repeat here. The class instantly broke into uproarious laughter with most of the boys slapping their sides and slapping one another as if they had gotten away with talking dirty. When I tried to quiet the class with a few loudly spoken words, the perpetrator of the question turned to his buddy next to him and said something I couldn't hear, and the laughter escalated.

I happened to look in the chalk tray behind me and saw a long wooden pointer which I thought I might use to make a loud sound to get their attention. I slammed it down on the desk too hard and before I could say, "Get quiet," the pointer broke in half, and I was left holding a stub. The class was totally out of control with shouting and laughter. I simply laid the stub down and walked out of the room. As I walked down the hall, I could hear the boys still laughing when I happened to approach one of the nurses. I told her what happened and said she could do as she pleased with that rowdy bunch, but I had patients at the hospital whom I needed to see. That afternoon I got a phone call from the assistant principal, who profusely apologized, saying it should never have happened that a school monitor was not present. He promised that if I would consider returning the following year, he would personally be in the room. The next year I reluctantly agreed, and the assistant kept his word. I knew him to be a stern disciplinarian, and the boys were polite and respectful, asking a few good questions, which I was able to answer easily. Overall, I was pleased with the boys and with my performance this time.

The third year I was assigned to be the reproductive expert at Hugh Goodwin, and, based on my previous experience, I made certain with the scheduling nurse I would have a monitor in the room. She assured me there would definitely be a school official in the room. The presentation was to be on a Monday morning at 9:00 a.m., and I made certain I had no appointment conflicts that particular morning.

About 10:00 p.m. on Sunday evening, I received a phone call from a Hugh Goodwin representative telling me there had been a fire about an hour earlier, and a significant portion of the school had been damaged. The school would be closed for several days. Plans had to be made for temporary class room space and the reproductive class would be cancelled for this year. I hung up the phone and praised the Lord that no one was injured in the fire. And I was given a reprieve from the "sex talk" for another year.

The next morning, I went into the doctors' lounge at Warner Brown Hospital, and the usual five or six doctors were there having morning coffee. Before I could say anything, one of the doctors said, "John, word on the street is you are the one who set fire to Hugh Goodwin last night to keep from giving the annual sex talk!" My only response was, "I have to admit I thought about it, but I plead, 'Not guilty.'" Perhaps there was some suspicion that I, indeed, had set the fire, because I was never again asked to participate in this teaching project. Whatever the reason, I wasn't the least offended.

60. GRANDFATHER (OR FIANCÉ) OF THE BRIDE

Appearances Can Be Deceiving

Ginny, 1995

Cathy and I have been blessed to witness and experience the weddings of our three children to wonderful spouses. From the time we were saved and filled with God's Spirit, we began praying that God would lead our children at the proper time to strong and loving believers to whom they could join their lives in holy marriage. We purposed to not only teach our children about a Christ-centered home but to live the model in front of them. There were periods when we fell far short of the ideal and certainly would have changed some of our attitudes and actions, but God's grace overshadowed our failures.

Within a five-year period from 1990 through 1995, John, Mary Kay, and Ginny were married to their life partners to begin their own journeys. Great memories were made during the span, which involved the full range of emotions from heartaches to laughter, from doubts to confidence and from anxiety to peace. When we are all together now for special events and holidays, stories from that time are re-told so our grandchildren can better understand their heritage.

In 1990 when John announced his intentions to marry Gina Ratcliff from Texarkana, Texas, we came to love her and believe she was the perfect one for John. We wanted to do all we could to help make their wedding day as special as we could for them. Gina bought her wedding dress from Low's Bridal in Brinkley, Arkansas, of which we were unaware. Many brides from Arkansas and probably Tennessee and Mississippi travel to this small town in eastern Arkansas half way between Little Rock and Memphis to buy their elegant gowns at very reasonable prices. Cathy, Mary Kay, and Ginny made note of how beautiful Gina's gown was, knowing they might also be shopping at Low's one day.

The following year when Mary Kay and David Janke announced their plans to marry, both Cathy and Mary Kay made the trip to Low's Bridal, where Mary Kay found the one special dress for her big day. It was beautiful. And we were all so pleased with Low's that when Ginny and John Luther planned their wedding in 1995, another trip to Brinkley was in order.

Ginny and John planned an early June wedding, so Cathy and Ginny visited Low's several months in advance. On their return home they told me they had found the perfect gown, and because of alterations which needed to be made, the gown could be picked up in several weeks. As time for the return trip to Brinkley neared, Cathy suggested I drive Ginny so the two of us could have some special father-daughter time. Despite the fact I knew I would be far out of my comfort zone at Low's Bridal, the thought of spending six or seven hours alone with Ginny driving there and back was enough for me. We scheduled an 11:00 a.m. appointment for a Saturday.

The three-and-a-half-hour drive to Brinkley passed quickly as we had no complications or undue delay due to Little Rock traffic. I admit to having some anxiety concerning Low's, because I was fairly certain there would be no men there with whom I could have conversation. I prepared myself emotionally to accept the environment and make Ginny know I was so glad to share this moment with her, even if it meant a bridal store.

I was very surprised to find such an elegant store in a small farming town which was better known to guys as a duck-hunting mecca. My suspicions concerning the clientele in the store were entirely correct. There were at least twenty-five people there and not one man. It was fairly easy to identify the brides because of their young age, and they were all accompanied by middle-aged women and a few much older women, presumably their mothers and grandmothers. I had nothing in common with anyone in the store, so conversations with them was not an option.

As Ginny disappeared into the dressing room to try on her new dress for final inspection by the sales personnel, I faded into a far corner of the store to just watch the action. Now and then I'd briefly watched a television show called *Say Yes to the Dress* when Cathy had it on, and I thought I was getting an up-close and personal version of the show.

The place where I was standing was near the checkout counter, and a very nicely dressed lady much older than me was standing behind the counter. I presumed she was the owner of the store, but I didn't think it proper to ask her about it. We simply exchanged initial greetings. I had my eyes on the dressing room Ginny had entered, and after about ten minutes she emerged in her new dress. I believe the following is a traditional thing at this store and possibly all bridal stores. When Ginny exited the dressing room, everyone in the store stopped, turned, and focused on her in her new dress and almost with one gasping voice said, "Oh what a gorgeous bride and beautiful dress!" I agreed completely in my mind, but just didn't join the chorus. She was beautiful!

The older lady behind the counter was one of the chorus of voices when she turned to me and said, "Isn't she just beautiful?" to which I responded, "She certainly is!" Then she asked, "Is she your granddaughter?" I have to admit Ginny looked several years younger than her twenty-two years, and it could have been possible age-wise for her to be my granddaughter. But before thinking, I said quickly back to the store owner, "No ma'am. She is my fiancé. I am a very rich man." She put her hand to her mouth and said, "Oh, I'm so very sorry. I just didn't know." I let her stay like that for a few more moments, and broke into laughter telling her Ginny was really my daughter not my fiancé, and I wasn't a rich man after all. (I inwardly feared the price of the dress might have gone up!)

I didn't tell Ginny about my checkout story until we were on our way back home. I sure didn't want her to feel embarrassed around those ladies and in particular the store owner. It did liven up my one and only experience in a bridal store. The cost for the owner was a little embarrassment, but for me the time alone with Ginny was priceless. It is possible I could have another opportunity for a bridal store experience with a real granddaughter, but have an idea that Cathy won't be sending me there without her!

61. A MISTAKEN IDENTITY

Incorrect Identification Can Cause Anxiety

Dad Young, 1970s

When Cathy and I first met and began dating, we were living in Atlanta where she had her first job as a fifth-grade teacher at John Clancy Elementary School. I was an intern at Grady Memorial Hospital, and we were introduced by the wife of a friend and fellow intern, Dan Moore. Marsha Moore and Cathy were both teachers at the school. For several months I resisted a blind date despite the fact that Marsha had told me how beautiful her new friend Cathy Young was and what marvelous character she possessed. I had known Dan and Marsha for several years before to moving to Atlanta, and it seemed she was always trying to "fix me up" with a potential wife. She told me Cathy was "different from the others" she had in mind for me. I finally agreed and we all went on a double-date so the initial meeting wouldn't be so awkward. When I met her at the door of her apartment, I was stunned by her beauty, and my first thought after seeing her was to wonder why had I resisted for so long? For me it was love at first sight. Cathy was from Fort Lauderdale, Florida, and I had never met anyone from that city. Our courtship began in September, 1964, and within several months we both began to believe God meant for us to join our lives in marriage.

I met her mom in Atlanta within the first few months because she was attending a national school board meeting there, and I believe her initial impression of me was a good one. It was the following year during Spring Break I scheduled a trip to Fort Lauderdale to meet her dad and the remainder of her family. It was then I was planning to ask him for permission to marry her.

Cathy had told me many things about her dad, George Young. He was a building contractor and owned the oldest contracting business of that type in Fort Lauderdale. His father had started the company in 1912, and together they had built some of the most impressive and beautiful businesses and homes in Broward County. From all she had told me I felt I had a good grasp on his character and his personality long before our initial meeting. She said there were some physical similarities between her dad and me, but our personalities were different. In his type of business, he was accustomed to hard physical labor in the Florida sun. In my profession, my work is always indoors and required no manual labor at all. Despite the fact he had crews of men working for him, he was quiet and introverted, and I am definitely not introverted. He was tall, slender, and balding, so we had these similarities, but otherwise I didn't think we looked alike.

Dad Young was so quiet when I was with him early in our marriage that I was sure he didn't think very much of me. I thought I could have a sustained conversation with anyone I spent more than a minute or two with, but not so with him. He was polite to answer any specific questions I had, but we didn't have many common interests at this point. I knew absolutely nothing about the construction business, nor did I even know the names of many of the tools he commonly used. I was certain he didn't know anything about the surgical tools I used each day. I discovered I was more interested in learning about his tools than he was in learning about mine. Dad's quietness with me bothered me for a long time until I understood this was just his way whether he was with friends or family. (In "George, You Don't Talk Much Do You?" I've recounted the story of his riding with a friend to Atlanta years before, a trip where they realized they'd not exchanged a word for over eight hours.)

After Cathy and I moved our family to El Dorado her mom and dad would visit us two or three times each year and would usually stay for five to seven days. We made the trip to Fort Lauderdale at least once each year and would have gone more often, but it was more difficult for us because of my surgical practice and the many activities of our kids.

Throughout the years of spending time with them and especially Dad, I learned at least three significant things about him and from him. First, part of the reason for his quiet demeanor related to his childhood stuttering problem, and early on it was embarrassing for him to speak at all. I never learned how he overcame the affliction, but by the time I knew him, he spoke very clearly and had a masterful understanding of the English language. He often was seen searching his giant *Webster's Unabridged Dictionary*, located next to his easy chair. I never heard anyone stump him on the definition of any word. One of his favorites was "eleemosynary."

Second, I never heard him say a critical word about anyone or participate in any gossip taking place in his presence. I have often thought about this strong quality Dad possessed, and realize how essential it is for me and for all Christians to mirror this quality the Lord Jesus taught us to have.

Third, he had a wonderful sense of humor. When Jerry Clower became a popular humorist, I started playing his tapes for Dad whenever we were together, and it was really fun to watch him belly laughing while listening to Jerry's colorful stories. On one occasion we were able to go to a live performance by Jerry Clower when he appeared in El Dorado. It was just as much fun watching Dad as it was to hear Jerry's stories.

After Dad retired from his business because of health issues, he had lots of time to read and sit on the patio by their pool with his faithful dog Maude at his side. The location was visible from the sidewalk in front of their beautiful two-story home in the Rio Vista subdivision. Friends and neighbors walking by usually saw Dad sitting there and would wave and occasionally stop for a brief conversation. It was such a relaxing spot whenever we visited that this was also my favorite place to sit when he wasn't there.

When Cathy and I were in Fort Lauderdale in 1983 for the sad occasion of Dad's funeral, I was sitting in his chair by the pool in the early morning hours on the day of his burial. An older gentleman I didn't know was slowly walking by, and as he looked toward me, I waved to him not thinking anything more than just being friendly. He did a distinct double-take in his look toward me and without waving he doubled his pace in moving away from the house. I believe he thought I was George and, knowing of his recent death, he must have thought he saw a vision of some type. I can only imagine what he told his wife when he got home from his walk!

In pondering the mistaken identity that the neighbor had of me, I have thought I would surely like to have others see in me some of the wonderful qualities Dad Young possessed. The Bible says in Ephesians 4:29, "Let no corrupt communication proceed out of your mouth, but that which is good to the use of edifying, that it may minister grace unto the hearers." I am grateful for Dad Young's model to me of controlling his small but powerful muscle, the tongue. However, of all the outstanding accomplishments of Dad Young, by far the greatest for me was to father the most wonderful daughter in the world, my wife Catherine Reta.

62. SILVER DOLLAR CITY

Uncle Harry Introduces Us to Branson

Silver Dollar City, 1977: The Moores

Cathy and I had never heard of Branson, Missouri, where we now live, until 1975 when we had a conversation with Uncle Harry Gosling from St. Louis. Uncle Harry and Aunt Ruth were favorites of ours, and in the early 1970s, we were lamenting the fact we seldom got to see them. Uncle Harry said, "Why don't we meet in Branson, Missouri, which is about half-way between El Dorado and St. Louis? My band plays at a real nice motel on the lake and we could all stay there." We said, "That sounds like great fun, but where in the world is Branson?" We found it on the map and began making plans to go there in the summer of the same year. The motel was the Rock Lane Lodge on Indian Point on Table Rock Lake, a large man-made lake created by damming the White River.

For those who are unfamiliar with Branson, Indian Point is about seven miles west of Branson off Highway 76 at the end of Indian Point Road. As you turn off Highway 76 toward Indian Point, you drive past Silver Dollar City, one of mid-America's best theme parks. Founded in 1960, it captures the 1880s in a family-friendly way and attracts hundreds of thousands of visitors to the area each year.

When we discovered the Branson area and subsequently the Rock Lane Lodge, we were introduced to the traffic jams of the area, which seemed unusual for a place with such a small year-round population. Highway 76, affectionately known as "The Strip," is also known as the world's largest parking lot because of the continuous flow of traffic at a very slow pace. Much to our delight, we discovered that the road from Silver Dollar City to the Rock Lane Lodge has very little traffic, so whenever we wanted to visit the theme park, we didn't have to face the traffic jams. We seemingly had the best of both worlds.

The Rock Lane Lodge is located right on Table Rock Lake, which is unusual because the Corps of Engineers, who built the lake, does not allow many commercial properties to be located directly on its shores. We found that the lodge was very nice but rustic, and thus was ideal for families. In addition to the boat docks with rentals for fishing and skiing, there were swimming pools, tennis courts, volley ball and shuffle-board courts, and a video game area for the teens. The restaurant was full service and offered wonderful meals at reasonable prices. Our family still talks about some of the dishes regularly served such as their breakfast grits which were "the best we ever had."

We met Uncle Harry and Aunt Ruth on our first visit to Branson and the Rock Lane Lodge, and spent the next five days with them seeing as many attractions as possible. We spent two of those days visiting Silver Dollar City, which was our favorite activity by far. I especially enjoyed all the food venues, and the funnel cakes which I had never eaten before. I know I had eaten salt water taffy previously, but it was especially fun watching all the different flavors being crafted; and they just seemed to taste better there.

In those early days of the city, two of the better attractions were "Fire in the Hole" and "Rube Dugan's Diving Bell." The waiting lines were relatively short, and we rode each one two or three times each day. Like all the other tourists at the City, we purchased a lot of things we normally wouldn't buy (and in most cases didn't need) including lye soap, hand crafted baseball bats, walking sticks, toy pop guns, Ozark Mountain toys, and train whistles. I was always intrigued by the vast number of craftsmen throughout the park who were demonstrating their skills and selling their products. As a surgeon I spent more time watching the wood-carvers and would always leave the park thinking about purchasing a set of carving tools and learning this particular hobby. I am sorry now I never acted on either impulse.

On our first visit to the City, we discovered the Tintype Studio, where 1880-vintage photos were made, and we had our first of many annual photos taken. In the photo above, I was dressed as a stern-faced preacher-father, ruling over his flock with the Bible and a long-barreled pistol. Cathy was the beautiful, well-dressed matriarch surrounded by her dutiful daughters and slightly rebellious son toting his jug of moonshine. The collection of photos made through the years are treasures to all of us, and occasionally when we're together, we'll bring out the photos and have a good laugh. The grandchildren seem to be amused at the sight of their parents in funny costumes.

In visiting Silver Dollar City today, one finds a number of new attractions including at least four world-class rides which make me queasy just watching. If those had been available when our children were younger, I feel certain they would have wanted to ride them multiple times. I suppose we would have had to take some additional older family member to accompany them, because under no circumstance would Cathy or I have voluntarily gotten on even one of them. Despite the expansion, the City has not lost the charm of its early days and is a credit to the foresight of the Herschend Family Entertainment Corporation, who own and manage the attraction. It is still a fun family park!

One morning, I had an interesting conversation about health care with one of the managers of the Rock Lane Lodge. I asked him, "If one of our family members had a health issue, would you recommend using the local (Skaggs) hospital?" He replied, "If you have a cold or need a few stitches, I would let them take care of it at Skaggs. If it is a more serious illness or injury, I would recommend bypassing them and going to Springfield." I had no idea that thirty-five years later, I would be a staff member of Skaggs Regional Medical Center, which offered full service treatment and what I consider excellent medical care. The hospital was bought by the Cox Health System and is now call Cox South Branson.

There are many reasons for our gratitude that God moved us to Branson in 2005. We have been close to our Branson kids, Mary Kay and Dave Janke and our two granddaughters, Becca and Sara Beth. We have a wonderful church family at First Baptist Church. We have been part of a wonderful ministry at The Free Medical Clinic of the Ozarks, and, to top it all off, we still love going to Silver Dollar City for the crafts and the funnel cakes. Forget about all those scary rides!!

63. SURGICAL LESSONS LEARNED FROM POP AND BUBBA

A Great Start to My Surgical Career

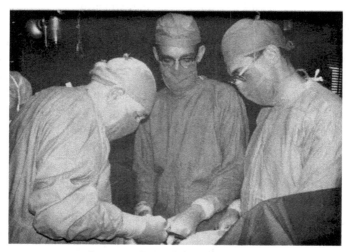

Pop operating with his sons assisting

Pop practiced medicine and surgery in El Dorado from 1934 until his death in 1966. The first eight years were especially wonderful for him, because he had the privilege of practicing with his dad, Dr. J. A., whom he greatly admired and loved. Their personalities were totally different because Granddad Moore was very serious in demeanor, seldom joked in his conversations, and only occasionally smiled. Pop was jovial, extroverted, ready with a joke, and masterful at story-telling. Their personalities were professionally compatible, however, and together they developed a large medical and surgical practice during that eight-year span.

Pop became a physician later in life than his peers, because he spent his early adult years in vain pursuit of multiple careers. His Dad was long-suffering concerning him, and when Pop was twenty-eight years old and had been married to Mimi for six years, he finally decided a career in medicine was suited to his talents and gifts. Granddad and Grandmother (Deeji) Moore assisted them with their finances, and it must have been very difficult for all of them because this was during the Great Depression.

After receiving his MD degree at the University of Arkansas in Little Rock in 1932, Pop, Mimi, and Bubba, who was four years old, went to New Orleans for a two-year, medical-surgical internship at Charity Hospital. One of Pop's fellow interns was Dr. Michael DeBakey, who later became the most well-known heart surgeon in the world. Pop had some interesting stories about Dr. DeBakey and his other colleagues there. I even have photos of their intern baseball team which was coached by Dr. Arthur Vidrine, the superintendent of Charity Hospital. Dr. Vidrine later became well-known as Huey Long's personal physician and the one who unsuccessfully operated on him when he was shot by an assassin in Baton Rouge.

When his training in New Orleans was complete Pop, was not only qualified to treat patients with medical problems; he had a large repertoire of surgical procedures he'd learned at Charity. He and Mimi had decided years before that they wanted to live and raise their family in El Dorado, where Pop could practice with his dad. They were general practitioners who treated medical illnesses, delivered babies, provided pediatric care, and treated surgical problems. When one of their patients required an operation, Granddad would administer the anesthesia and Pop would do the procedure. In those days the preferred method of general anesthesia was open-drop ether or chloroform, which is no longer used because of safety issues.

The economy of the country was beginning to recover from the Great Depression of 1929, but the winds of war were blowing in Europe and Germany with the rise to power of Adolph Hitler. When our country's involvement in war was inevitable, several physicians from El Dorado enlisted in the Army Medical Corps, which made the work load much greater on the doctors remaining at home. Because Pop was thirty-seven years old, he was exempted from active duty.

In 1954, Bubba graduated from the University of Arkansas Medical School and he and his wife LaNell moved to Dallas where he completed a one-year rotating internship at Parkland Hospital. Those were the years of the Korean War, and young physicians just out of training were required to serve in the military. Their active-duty assignment was Brookley Air Force Base in Mobile, where they spent the next two years. Then they decided to move back to El Dorado where Bubba joined Pop in a medical-surgical practice similar to the one Pop and Granddad had had fifteen years earlier. I graduated from high school that same year, which was also the year our sister Marilyn married George Berry. There were lots of changes in the Moore family in 1957.

During my high school years, Pop would occasionally allow me to spend time in his office observing how he interacted with patients and learning some of the medical vocabulary. By this time, I was absolutely convinced I would pursue a career in medicine and probably become a surgeon. When Bubba joined the practice, I began spending more time in the office. He initially had more free time than Pop because his practice was new and relatively small, and he loved teaching. Between the two of them, they taught me the principles of wound care and suturing, and I learned the art of handling instruments as well as the essentials of sterile technique. Upon entering medical school, I could suture a wound as well as any intern.

During college and medical school years Pop allowed me to assist with his surgical cases when I was home for Christmas, spring, and summer breaks. On their operative cases, Bubba was always the first assistant, and I was the one who got to hold the retractors—the most physically taxing of the OR jobs and the most boring! But I was so excited to be in the OR environment that I was seldom bored. Prior to beginning my formal surgical training as an intern and resident, I had assisted Pop and Bubba with as many as fifteen operations and had sutured at least twenty patients who came to the ER with various minor wounds. In today's atmosphere of malpractice litigation, the things I was allowed to do then would not be tolerated even under the close supervision of Pop and Bubba.

The techniques I used in the forty years of my own surgical practice I learned from many gifted surgeons, including the men I served with at the Surgical Clinic of South Arkansas in El Dorado. Those surgical techniques were essential for the *science* of medicine, but an equally important aspect of any practice is the *art* of medicine. I was fortunate to have a grandfather, father, and brother who were gifted at both the art and the science of medicine. I am very grateful to the Lord for the heritage of medical service Pop and Bubba received from Granddad Moore and then passed on to me.

64. FOUR GENERATIONS OF MEDICAL MINISTRY

An Unusual Family Legacy

Dr. J. A. Moore, 1936   Dr. Berry Lee Moore Sr., 1932

Dr. Berry Lee Moore Jr., 1954   Dr. John Henry Moore, 1964

Dr. James Michael Berry, 1984   Dr. David Lee Berry, 1991

I was born into a family of medical doctors. My dad (Pop) was a second-generation physician and had been in practice with his father, Dr. John Aaron Moore, for five years prior to my birth in 1939. Granddad Moore began his practice in Union County, Arkansas, in 1898 in the community of Lisbon and later moved his family to El Dorado in 1912, where he continued to practice until his death in 1943.

The small, quiet town of El Dorado, Arkansas was transformed into a boom town with the discovery of oil in 1921, and the population quickly grew from just several thousand residents to near forty thousand within a few months. The medical needs of the town grew exponentially, and Dr. J. A.'s practice responsibilities were huge. The economy during the 1920s was booming, and people were better able to pay for the medical care they needed. There was no such thing in those days as medical insurance, so everyone paid either cash for their care or bartered with their physician using such things as fresh vegetables, chickens, hogs, or rabbits. No one was ever turned away from receiving medical care by Granddad Moore because of lack of money. That principle of reimbursement for medical treatment begun by Granddad was continued throughout the next two generations of Moore's who served the people of South Arkansas.

Upon completion of his medical training in 1934, my dad (Pop) joined his father in a general medical practice in which they treated every medical condition including delivering babies and doing all forms of surgical procedures. Following medical school graduation in 1932, Pop had taken two years of additional surgical training at Charity Hospital in New Orleans and was qualified to do most general surgical procedures in addition to orthopedic procedures. They continued their practice together through the economically-depressed era of the 1930s and the beginning of World War II. Granddad Moore had severe coronary artery disease and died as a result of a heart attack in September, 1943. Pop continued in a solo practice through the 1940s and 1950s during the maturing years of my older brother Berry Lee Jr., our sister Marilyn, and me.

My brother Berry Lee (Bubba) joined Pop in a general medical practice in 1957 after he completed his internship at Parkland Hospital in Dallas and had served two years in the US Air Force at Brookley Air Force Base in Mobile, Alabama. Bubba learned the skills of a few surgical procedures such as Caesarean section, hernia repair, and skin lesion removal, but generally left surgery to Pop, assisting him in the OR when necessary.

Their practice location was on the second floor in the Masonic Building in downtown El Dorado on the west side of the square. Granddad was the Worshipful Master of the Masonic lodge responsible for constructing the building in the 1930s. As a young boy visiting my Pop's and brother's clinic, I recall the odors of a medical office filling my nostrils upon climbing the first steps of the Masonic building.

Near the end of Pop's life in the early 1960s, plans were being made to build a new clinic on Grove Street situated between the two hospitals, Warner Brown Hospital and Union County Medical Center (now Medical Center of South Arkansas). The clinic was completed and dedicated several months after Pop's death from heart disease in January, 1966.

I completed my surgical training at Charity Hospital in New Orleans in 1969, and was required to spend two years in the US Air Force in Valdosta, Georgia. In 1971, Cathy and I moved to El Dorado where I joined Bubba in The Moore Clinic on Grove Street. My practice was primarily general surgery, but because I was associated with Bubba, I also did some general medicine and shared night and weekend calls with him.

I continued in this practice model until 1974 when I joined The Surgical Clinic of South Arkansas with three other general surgeons. In this new setting, I limited my practice to general surgery exclusively. Both Bubba and I agreed this would be a better situation so other family practitioners would be more likely to refer their surgical patients to me. Bubba continued referring all of his surgical patients to me, and he was freed from the responsibility of assisting me in the operating room on the more complicated procedures.

In 1977, when Cathy and I had a spiritual conversion to make Jesus Christ our Savior and Lord, our lives were transformed in every respect. Bubba, who was a dynamic and witnessing Christian, was instrumental in our faith conversion, and he offered to mentor me as a Christian who served and ministered in the practice of medicine. This was an entirely new life and lifestyle for me, because in all my prior professional years, I had never seen a physician who ministered Christ and Christ-like attributes to his patients. For the next twenty-two years while living and practicing in El Dorado along-side Bubba, he poured his wisdom and encouragement into me.

When we moved to Fayetteville, Arkansas, in 2000 and then to Branson, Missouri, in 2005, my medical practice was in wound care exclusively and no longer in general surgery. Bubba and I continued to talk regularly with each other by phone and occasional visits, and he continued mentoring me until his departure from earth on August 7, 2009. He had retired from medical practice in 2000 in order to care for his wife LaNell, who had developed an illness requiring his close attention.

The three generations of Moores practicing medicine in El Dorado continued uninterrupted from 1898 to 2000, while the fourth generation of physicians in the family had begun serving and ministering in Texas beginning in the 1980s.

Our sister Marilyn graduated from high school in 1954 and went on for her first year at Lindenwood College in St. Charles, Missouri. For her second year, she transferred to the University of Texas because of the friendship and influence of Mary Ann Nowlin, a classmate at Lindenwood from Houston. It was at the University of Texas she met George Berry from Lubbock, whom she dated, fell in love with, and married in 1957. She tried to persuade me to attend the University of Texas, but I told her I had too much Razorback blood in my veins to move to Texas.

George earned his doctorate in banking and finance and began a teaching career at Texas Tech University in Lubbock. He continued in his academic career for nine years and then decided to make the transition into the business world as a financial consultant in banking. They moved initially to Midland for nine years and ultimately moved back to Austin in 1978. He and Marilyn had four sons—James, John, Robert, and David. Their oldest, James Michael, and their youngest, David Lee, decided to pursue careers in medicine, and they became the fourth generation of medical doctors from the lineage of Dr. J. A. Moore.

It was exciting for all of us concerning their decisions, and both James and David were able to spend some time in El Dorado in the summer months during their training years with both Berry Lee and me. They were able to shadow us to learn some of the practical applications of their medical training with actual patient care. They assisted me in the operating room with many surgical cases, and I encouraged both of them to consider careers in the surgical field. Both young men were not only gifted intellectually, but had excellent eye-hand coordination skills, well suited for a surgical specialty.

James received his MD degree from the University of Texas Medical Center in Houston in 1984 and decided on anesthesiology as his specialty. From the outset he has had an outstanding career in the academic and patient practice world. In addition to providing anesthesia care for many tens of thousands, he has helped train several generations of new anesthesiologists. While in Houston, one of his responsibilities was in the field of hyperbaric oxygen (HBO) therapy, and he was in charge of the huge, multi-place chamber at UT Houston. During those years he encouraged me to become certified in HBO therapy which I did, and this led to my transition into primary wound care for the last twelve years of my medical practice life.

James moved with his family in 2001 to Jackson, Mississippi, where he became a professor and head of the department of anesthesia at the University of Mississippi Medical Center. It was there he began his design and subsequent construction of a revolutionary device for reclaiming exhaled anesthetic gasses. When he moved again in 2003 to Nashville, Tennessee, to become a professor and head of anesthesia at Vanderbilt University, he was able to put into practice his Dynamic Gas Scavenging System (DGSS). The previous cost to Vanderbilt University for anesthetic gas was approximately a million dollars per year, but with James's system in place, the cost dropped to about one hundred thousand dollars, a 90 percent savings! This device is patented and now commercially available, being used in a number of hospitals nationwide.

James moved with his family back to Texas in 2018, where he is now a professor of anesthesiology and on the staff of the University of Texas Southwestern Medical Center in Dallas. In addition to his many other responsibilities, James has served for years on the American Board of Anesthesiology as an examiner for the oral portion of the certification process for all anesthesiologists completing their training.

David attended medical school at the University of Texas in Galveston, where he graduated with an MD degree in 1991. He decided on a career in obstetrics and gynecology and took additional training in maternal fetal medicine. He has practiced his specialty in Austin, Texas, since 1997, when he founded The Austin Perinatal Associates. His specialty, also known as High Risk Obstetrics, treats expectant mothers who have had complications with their pregnancies in the past. Some have illnesses such as diabetes which can lead to high morbidity and mortality rates for their newborns. His patients also include those with suspected or known abnormal conditions of the fetus. David's skills, which are unique, include prenatal diagnoses, invasive diagnostic and invasive procedures for the baby who's still in the uterus, and critical care obstetrical procedures. Because there are fewer than six maternal fetal specialists in Austin, the demand for his expertise is huge. The population of Austin and all of central Texas may approach close to two million. In his practice for over twenty-two years, David has successfully treated thousands of grateful mothers and safely delivered their babies under very stressful conditions.

In March, 2017, David was privileged to safely deliver the Hodges family quintuplets at Seton Hospital—the first set of quints delivered in Austin since 2009. The events surrounding the labor and delivery of their babies were the subject of a documentary on The Learning Channel (TLC), which aired in the fall of 2017 with the title, *Hodges Half Dozen*. (They already had one child prior to the quintuplets). The show became a reality television series, and David was prominently featured in the first episode.

David, his wife Lisa, and their family members are strong Christians in their beliefs and witness. In July, 2018, he was ordained as a minister of their church, The Throne of Grace in Austin. They are involved in multiple ministries and outreaches in the Austin community through their church because of their personal devotion to the cause of Christ.

God gifts us all differently, and we are to use those gifts for the benefit of others to the glory of God. I don't consider the profession of medicine any greater or more important than any other profession. I am honored to have had the opportunity for all my professional years to have served others with my medical and surgical skills and to have been in a family of so many physicians. Perhaps there will be yet a fifth generation of physicians in our family, but regardless, we are fully committed to loving and serving others in the name of the Lord Jesus Christ as long as we are here.

65. "DO YOU HAVE A BROTHER NAMED BERRY LEE MOORE?"

An Unexpected Family Friend Brings Comfort

This question has been asked of me on many occasions and under lots of different circumstances throughout my life. On one occasion I was asked about Berry Lee (Bubba) in an unusual setting, and the conversation which followed brought me a lot of peace and comfort.

For the past seven years, I have been adjusting to one of the health problems of advanced aging for the male members of the Moore family. My paternal grandfather, (Granddad Moore), my dad (Pop), and my brother (Bubba) all had coronary artery disease of varying severity, and it ultimately caused the death of all three. Pop had other health issues which, combined with his heart disease, led to his seemingly premature death at age sixty-three. Because both Bubba and I were keenly aware of our genetic weaknesses, we became regular aerobic exercisers from our mid-thirties until late in our seventies. Neither of us were smokers, nor did we drink beverage alcohol in any form, in part because those two bad habits are huge risk factors for heart disease.

Recently I have experienced a marked decrease in exercise tolerance which has concerned both Cathy and me. I plead guilty for acting like many physicians in that I had not seen a doctor for my health for at least five years, so I had no idea what was happening. I suspected advancing, coronary atherosclerosis (hardening of the arteries) because of our family history. At Cathy's insistence and the pleading of our children, I agreed to consult a cardiologist, Dr. David Churchill, in Fayetteville. I had known him and about his excellent reputation when we lived there over ten years previously.

At our first consultation, I discovered I had developed atrial fibrillation (abnormal and uncontrolled heart rate) which was part of my overall problem and totally unsuspected by me. So much for my cardiac self-diagnosis! Dr. Churchill set into motion a series of invasive examinations over the next several weeks, and I was plunged deeply into the modern medical world in which I was now the patient and not the provider.

I decided early on I would be completely compliant with my doctor's orders and not become a grumpy and demanding old doctor with my heels dug in! Having the loving encouragement and complete devotion of Cathy at my side plus the concerns and sweet prayers of our children, grandchildren, other family members and friends, has made the journey a lot less uncomfortable.

I was quickly scheduled for a TEE/DCC (Transesophageal echocardiogram/Direct current conversion), which, in simple terms, is shocking the heart back into normal rhythm. This was done at the Walker Heart Center, a highly sophisticated heart center in Fayetteville. Cathy and I had been there the previous week when I underwent a left heart catheter (diagnostic) procedure which went well, and this next procedure was to be therapeutic (treatment) and not diagnostic in nature.

The Walker Heart Center is quite large with as many as twenty to thirty patients having invasive and non-invasive procedures done daily. We arrived two hours early for the usual preparation procedures such as recording health history, acquiring vital signs, placing the intravenous line, and drawing blood for the appropriate tests needed. At approximately the correct hour, a nurse came in to tell Cathy she should remain in the holding room because the planned procedure would only take twenty to thirty minutes, and I would be back in the room within the hour. At this she wheeled my gurney down the hall and up one floor on the elevator.

My gurney was placed in the hallway of the multiple procedure rooms, where I was to await my designated room. The nurse told me, "We have come up a little early, and there will be another fifteen-to-twenty-minute wait here in the hallway." As I lay there feeling exposed and vulnerable, many professional people passed back and forth without ever acknowledging my presence. It was near the lunch hour, and I assumed some were headed to the cafeteria. At one point my cardiologist passed by, and I don't think he recognized me because he simply said, "Hi", and that was the full extent of his greeting. I had the overwhelming sense I was simply a specimen and not a person, more specifically a diseased heart needing a shock. I don't believe it was a case of self-pity, because I don't think I was treated any worse (or better) than any of the other patients in the heart center. At this point I quoted to myself the wonderful words from 1 Corinthians 6:19–20, reminding me that my body was "the temple of the Holy Spirit," that I was "not my own," and that I was "to glorify God in my body!" My spirit began to immediately lift despite what was taking place around me.

I was then moved into Procedure Room #10, which was filled with gigantic and highly technical equipment of which I had no professional knowledge. The technicians in the room, although efficient and knowledgeable, were not particularly personable. An older technician, perhaps in his mid-forties, passed by the gurney holding my health record and disappeared into the control room without speaking.

In a minute or two, the older tech came walking over to me and asked, "Do you have a brother named Berry Lee Moore?" My initial thought was that he was too young to be a contemporary of Bubba, but he might have once been one of Bubba's patients back in El Dorado. I said, "Yes sir, Berry Lee was my brother and we practiced medicine together for many years." This man then said something totally unsuspected: "My grandmother was Dr. Berry Lee's office nurse as long as he lived, and I am Marty Leach, her daughter's son. You Moores are just like family to my family!"

I was pleasantly stunned by his introduction. Mary Alice Cross was Bubba's nurse for the entire fifty-five years he practiced general medicine, and now her grandson Marty was bringing me great comfort in this flood of memories from the past. I shook his hand and thanked him on behalf of his family heritage, while on the inside I thanked God that he just "happened to have Marty Leach in the room" where I was feeling a bit lonely. I could hardly wait to get through this examination and cardiac conversion and then back to the room to tell Cathy whom God had waiting for me in Procedure Room #10! "Blessed be the God of all comfort who comforts us in all our trials" (from 2 Cor 1:3–5).

III. Friends Along the Journey

Friends are used of God to make important and often life-changing investments in us. Understanding their value may make us more sensitive to their needs and more alert to keep our relationships fresh and free of anger, resentment, or jealousy.

66. KISSES FROM LILLIAN

A Loving Caregiver for Life

Lillian Singleton

My mother developed breast cancer while pregnant with me in 1939. I do not know any details of the discovery and diagnosis of the cancer, but as a physician, I know the high concentration of hormones present during pregnancy greatly accelerates the growth and spread of breast cancer. In most patients diagnosed with breast cancer during early pregnancy, the recommendation of many physicians is termination of the pregnancy in order to save the mother's life. My mother literally sacrificed her life to give birth to me. Despite aggressive treatment following my birth, she lived only a short time and died at age thirty-seven when I was one and a half years old. My brother was thirteen and my sister was five years old at her death.

Our grief-stricken Dad was left with the daunting task of trying to raise three small children while maintaining his very busy medical practice. There was an additional burden on the medical personnel in our town, because this was near the beginning of our country's involvement in World

War II. All the doctors left at home were working at high-stress levels. Fortunately, my dad had lots of physical and emotional support from family and friends, but he still had to hire several ladies to do the cooking and cleaning in our home. Unfortunately for me, I don't remember any of the people or events until I was five or six years old.

One of the ladies I do recall is Lillian Singleton. The reason I remember her so well is she worked intermittently for our family for the next eight to ten years. She would later tell me stories of my childhood, of things I had said and done and how she had "fallen in love with my brother, my sister, and me from the very beginning." Lillian was only fifty-five at the time of her employment but seemed to be a very old but sweet lady to me. She and her husband Will lived in a modest home in the "colored quarters" across town. These were the years of racial segregation all across the South. Will and Lillian had no children, and I'm certain some of her attraction to and affection for us was related to her mothering instincts.

Lillian wore a starched white uniform with a black apron which was typical for domestic help at the time. I remember her uniform was always spotless despite the many things she did including cooking meals and cleaning the house. Her graying hair was pulled back and neatly pinned. Most often, she had a wide smile revealing teeth which appeared a bit too large for her mouth. Her upper teeth were so white and perfectly formed they had to be dentures. I never asked her.

When Lillian spoke, her lips didn't seem to move much, but I had no trouble understanding her because she talked slowly while emphasizing many of her words. I don't remember her ever scolding me even though I was spoiled and, like all children, needed to be rebuked and occasionally spanked. Lillian knew all the foods I enjoyed, and I could depend on her to prepare whatever I asked. There were very few things Lillian withheld from me. She would occasionally tell me, "Now don't let on all the things I let you have, because the Doctor doesn't want me to spoil you." She told me later after I was grown, she "always felt sorry for us children because we didn't have a mother." I remember she hugged me a lot, and frequently kissed me on the cheek with what seemed like "big, juicy kisses." During my pre-teen and teen-aged years those expressions of affection were always embarrassing when any of my buddies were present.

Dad remarried when I was six years old, and our step-mother, "Mom," raised my brother, sister, and me and loved us as her own. She and Pop never had children together, so I always thought that Mom made an exceptional sacrifice to provide a loving and caring home for children to whom she had not given birth. After Mom assumed her role, Lillian continued working, but much less often. I never knew the reason and never asked, but I suspected there was tension between the two of them. I didn't see Lillian very often after I left home to begin college. Many years passed, and I would only see Lillian once a year for a brief visit.

Upon completing my training, my wife Cathy and I returned to El Dorado to establish our life and raise our children. It wasn't long before Lillian re-entered our life. Her husband Will had died earlier of heart failure, and she was living alone. She had retired from domestic work and, once every few weeks, would drive to our home for a visit to establish a relationship with Cathy and our three children. She especially loved telling them what I was like as a little boy, and particularly how she had spoiled me in spite of "what the Doctor had said." Our children loved hearing her stories, and each one hoped Lillian might somehow spoil them in the same way. Each visit, before she left our home, she would hug each one and kiss them on the cheek as she had done for me. Our daughters remembered how "wet and juicy" were the kisses that Lillian planted on their cheeks.

When Lillian became physically unable to drive her auto, we would go to her home for visits, usually on a Saturday or Sunday afternoon. Her eyesight had become so poor her usually spotless house became more and more cluttered and dirty. Cockroaches took advantage of her disabilities, but we never told her about them, thinking it would hurt her feelings. On a number of occasions, Cathy and the girls would dust and clean her house as much as possible and especially the kitchen. We had the carpet replaced throughout her house, and, in exchange, Lillian insisted on giving us her antique RCA radio console, which we had always admired. All of us remember how hot she kept her house during the winter months, so to visit with her for more than an hour was extremely uncomfortable. With each visit we carried food and something sweet like cake or pie, and she was always grateful. At the end of each visit there was always the "big hug and the juicy kiss on the cheek."

In remembering the past, I am confident God sent special angels to watch over three little children who had lost their mother. One of the brightest and most loving of those angels was Lillian Singleton, who instead of having wings had long and strong arms capable of tireless work. They were also agents of love expressed by huge hugs, which were not common from domestic help in a segregated South. As one of the children so blessed, I thank God for Lillian Singleton. Her life and love remind me I should live out Jesus's words when he said (in Matt 25:40), "As ye have done it unto the least of these, my brethren, ye have done it unto me [juicy kisses and all]."

67. THE LIMO TRIP TO SMACKOVER

Ike Shows Off His Driving Skills,
and It Affected His Church Attendance

Ike Wilson was one of Pop's best friends, and the two of them could spin some of the funniest tales I ever heard. When Ike came to our home, which was usually in the evening, the two of them would begin telling stories of growing up in South Arkansas, and I would sit and quietly listen for hours at a time. I never knew whether any of their tales were true, but since I heard them so often, I assumed they were. Regardless of the number of times I heard them, they were always funny to me because of the gestures they made while mimicking the voices of their subjects. I'm confident they loved telling them because I was a good listener and laughed along with them. One of Ike's tales which I especially loved occurred years before and involved his owning and driving a limousine.

In the mid-1930s, Ike was a young man in his late twenties and was quite an entrepreneur. Despite the fact the Great Depression had devastated the nation's economy, El Dorado was still enjoying some of the prosperity brought about by the oil boom of the 1920s. The phenomenal rise of the automotive industry increased the demand for oil and gasoline products, and the refineries in El Dorado were producing them as rapidly as possible. Huge fortunes were being made in South Arkansas by fortunate landowners and wildcat speculators, and good jobs were available. At one time, Ike owned and drove a limousine, which was appealing to some of the executives and speculators who were constantly travelling in and out of the area. He would lease the limo by the ride or for a specified period of time, and he worked as the chauffeur.

On this particular day by mid-morning, Ike had not been hired and was in his usual parking spot next to B. W. Reeves Department Store on the northwest corner of the square two blocks from First Baptist Church, and in a good location for attracting passersby who might require transportation. The pastor of First Baptist, Dr. John Buchanan, was walking towards the square and saw the limo with Ike sitting alone. Since Ike was a member of the church and well-known to him, he stopped to ask how he was doing and how his business was faring. During the conversation, Ike asked Dr. Buchanan if he had ever ridden in a limo, to which he responded that he had never been given the opportunity. Ike said, "Then hop in and I'll drive you up to Smackover and back."

Smackover is a small town twelve miles to the northwest of El Dorado and was founded as a result of the oil boom. The area surrounding Smackover was known among oilmen as the North Field and was rich in the oil and gas produced from the Smackover Formation. The road to Smackover, although well-traveled, was narrow and marked by many curves. It was quite different from the four-lane highways we have today. Ike told me he made the trip to Smackover and back to the square in approximately twenty-five minutes. Under normal conditions the trip usually took thirty to thirty-five minutes. Upon their return, Ike asked, "How did you like the limo ride, Dr. Buchanan?" He replied, "Ike, I have never been more scared nor prayed more in my life than I have in these last twenty-five minutes. Just so you will know how I felt and how scared I was, I am going to call on you to pray the next time you come to church!"

Ike said he knew Dr. Buchanan was serious because of how pale and frightened he looked when he made the statement. Dr. Buchanan frequently called on men of the church to pray publicly, but these men were deacons who were accustomed to it. Ike had never prayed in front of such a large group. Because of his anxiety, Ike didn't attend church for several months. He continued attending the Men's Bible Class to which he belonged, but went home promptly after Sunday school. He didn't want to face the embarrassment which might follow if he stuttered and stammered while praying.

His mother, Cousin Annie, couldn't understand why Ike was missing so many church services for such a long time. He said he was not about to tell her because she was likely to say something to Dr. Buchanan, which would make him even more aware of the promise he had made. Finally, after another month or two, Ike decided to risk attending church, thinking that surely Dr. Buchanan had forgotten about the ride and his promise. He waited to be seated until after the offering was taken, because it was always prior to the offering Dr. Buchanan would call on a deacon to pray. Ike said that all during the sermon, he never heard a word the pastor said, because he was worrying Dr. Buchanan would spot him and remember his promise. At one point he was certain their eyes met. Ike said, "I was really beginning to sweat, because I knew what was about to happen." About five minutes before the sermon ended, Ike stood up and slipped out the back door of the church. No one but Ike and Dr. Buchanan ever knew why Ike left church early that morning. Ike didn't say whether he and Dr. Buchanan ever had another conversation about the incident, but I am certain the pastor never requested another limousine ride with Ike!

68. COUSIN ANNIE AND SOUTHWESTERN BELL

Cousin Annie Gets Pranked

Cousin Annie's phone

Isaac (Ike) Wilson was my Pop's best friend, and I loved it when he would come to our home for a visit. Both men were master story-tellers and their repertoire seemed endless. They could remember the names of people with whom they had connections, and some of their stories dated as far back as thirty years. Usually, I wouldn't say a word but would sit, listen, and laugh. I think having an audience of just one spurred them on. Most of their stories I had heard often, but they could add some different twists and still make them funny.

We were related to the Wilson family through Ike's mom, Annie. Her maiden name was Sheppard, and they could trace their ancestry back to the Three Creeks community in South Arkansas, where the Moore and Sheppard families were original settlers in the 1840s. Annie's mother and my great grandfather were siblings, so Annie was called Cousin Annie by our family. When Pop was in a playful mood, he would call Ike, "Cud'n Ike."

Ike did not inherit his joking and outgoing personality from his mother. Cousin Annie was quiet, thoughtful, and very serious. When she was told something, she accepted it as fact, and was lovingly known by many as being gullible. She became the object of numerous pranks, mostly from family members. Ike had learned early not to tease his mother too often, because it bruised her spirit, and he would get into trouble with her. Others in the family, however, were not as thoughtful. Dr. Jack Sheppard, a distant cousin, had the reputation as the number one practical joker in the family. He and his brother Dr. Julius were general-practice physicians and both were well-liked and respected.

One morning when his patient schedule was slow, Jack placed a telephone call to Cousin Annie and disguised his voice to give her some much-needed information concerning her telephone service. At the conclusion of the conversation, Cousin Annie thanked the caller and promised she would follow his timely advice. She had no idea she was talking to Dr. Jack.

Ike was at work that morning and was planning to have lunch with his mother. She had lived alone for years following the death of her husband, but, in addition to her only child Ike, she had very good neighbors who checked on her frequently. She never felt alone and was fortunate to have such excellent neighborly and family support.

When Ike arrived home, he noticed something very strange on the table which held her only telephone. The receiver was off the hook; it was wrapped in a damp towel and lying next to the base of the phone. Ike said, "Mother, what in the world have you done to the phone? If anyone tried to call you, they would only get a busy signal, and you would never know they called." (This was years before call-waiting and voice mail.) Cousin Annie said, "Oh, Ike don't worry. I'm just following the advice of the president of Southwestern Bell who called this morning." "Well Mother, just what was his name and what did he tell you?" "He said his name was Mr. Smith and he wanted to warn me about something about to occur today. He said the company was having a system cleanout, and they would be blowing out all the lines so that the phones would work better. There was a good chance that all the carbon and soot in the lines would blow into my home as a result. He recommended I take the phone off the hook and wrap it in a large damp towel. He was trying to save me a lot of unnecessary house work, so I thanked him for his concern and did exactly what he recommended."

Ike didn't tell his mother she had been pranked again. Instead, he told her, "I think the clean-out is already over, so I'll just remove the towel and put the phone back on the hook." Ike immediately knew the perpetrator of the call. Only Dr. Jack could think of such an outlandish prank knowing Cousin Annie would fall for it. She was grateful for the advice she received that morning from "President Smith" and never noticed even a speck of dust or soot from the system clean-out.

69. BROTHER MOSE AND SISTER BOBBIE

Housekeepers Who Loved Me Like Family

Brother Mose

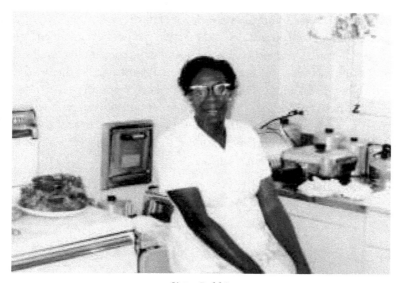

Sister Bobbie

Growing up in South Arkansas in the 1940s and 1950s exposed me to a cultural setting which has long since passed away. In many respects life was simple and reduced to such burning questions as how late I'd be able to stay up tonight, what sports I'd engage in the next day, and who were the other players? There was an entire other culture of young people living in El Dorado whom my friends and I never considered joining in any kind of activities.

We were isolated from black kids, not necessarily by our choices, but by society over which we did not have control. We lived in separate neighborhoods, attended separate schools, and were separate in every aspect of life, including hotels, restaurants, movie theaters, grocery stores, department stores, and even doctors' offices. I participated in varsity sports in high school and college and never competed against a black athlete during those seven years. The only significant contact I had with any black person were with those who worked in our home over a fifteen-year period.

Mose Graham began working for our family as a yard maintenance man in 1947 when I was eight years old. Over the next fifteen years during which he worked at our home, he became one of my best friends and confidants. It is sad to remember, but a black man was never identified as "Mister." A term of respect which was frequently used was "Brother;" thus Mose Graham was known to my family and me as Brother Mose.

Brother Mose was in his late forties when he began working for us, but he always seemed to me to be an old man. He was five feet, eight inches tall, weighed one hundred and fifty pounds, and had thinning grey hair. Unfortunately, he had poor dental hygiene and had only a single incisor in his upper gums along with multiple other upper teeth which were in poor condition. He called his front tooth a "snaggle-tooth," and often bragged he could strip a barbecued rib as fast as anyone with a full set of front teeth. His lower teeth were also in poor condition. Dental care was out of the question for Brother Mose since there were no black dentists in the area, and, to my knowledge, white dentists did not accept blacks as patients.

Brother Mose was always cheerful, and I never saw him angry or upset. When he was working or concentrating on anything, he was always humming or singing one of several familiar tunes. His favorite song was "Precious Lord," and by the time I was ten years old, I had sung it with him so often I knew every verse. There were other songs he sang, and I remember them as well. Even now, more than seventy years later when my sister Marilyn and I are together and reminisce about Brother Mose, we will occasionally sing some of the songs we heard and learned from him. His only vice I remember was playing cards in a tavern called Lonnie Mitchell's, located in the black section of town known as Saint Louis. His favorite card games were Pit-T-Pat and Coon Can. He never taught Marilyn or me to play either game, probably because he didn't want to corrupt us in some way.

In addition to Brother Mose, our family was privileged to have a maid working in our home. During the time of Mose's employment, we had several different women doing domestic housework for us, but my favorite by far was Sister Bobbie Fike. When I remember her, I think about her fried chicken and hot-water cornbread (hush puppies). They were absolutely delicious and close in quality to our mom's, and I think it was Sister Bobbie who taught my Mom to cook them so well.

Most of the time, she and Brother Mose got along with each other pretty well, but occasionally she would get aggravated with him. It bothered her how slow Brother Mose moved from one place to the next, and how long it took him to complete a task. It didn't seem to bother him at all, and when she fussed and fumed, he would respond with a "yessum, you sho' is right." A characteristic response of Brother Mose, when he was some distance away and called by Mom or Sister Bobbie, was to answer with a high-pitched, owl-like "Hooo." No one else could make a comparable sound, and I could recognize it from three to four hundred feet away.

I dearly loved Brother Mose and Sister Bobbie, and when I was with them and could get them to stop their work, I would ask about "the old days" and different people in their lives. Often, I could get them to sing their favorite songs, and I would sing with them. Sister Bobbie's favorite song was, "There Will Be Peace in the Valley." If I kept them singing too long or was asking too many questions, either one or the other would say, "Masta, we gots to get to work. Miz Mo' will be comin' any minute now." I didn't know the salary Brother Mose and Sister Bobbie received for their work, but I know it was not much. Every week when I was given my allowance of one dollar from Pop, I always gave ten cents to each of them. I don't think Pop knew of my gifting, but I feel certain he would not have objected. I never asked them to call me "Masta," but this was the name they gave me. By the time I was in junior high school and certain I was going to be a doctor, they started calling me "Docta" or "Docta John."

Brother Mose and Sister Bobbie were in my life prior to the civil rights movement and desegregation, but those laws would have not changed my relationship with them. I never thought of them or treated them as anything other than family. It sorrows me to think how shamefully blacks were treated, and, had it been in my power, all racial barriers would have been torn down years before. The truth is when we allow our precious Lord to take our hand and lead us on, all prejudicial and racial barriers will be broken down. At their fall, there will be a fresh measure of peace in the valley, about which Sister Bobbie, Brother Mose, Marilyn, and I frequently sang.

70. LIVE RIGHT IN THE SIGHT OF THE LORD

The Philosophy of My Friend, Mose

Brother Mose Graham was hired by my Pop to maintain the large yard and grounds at our home, and he faithfully worked for us for about fifteen years. He was a fun-loving, kind, and gentle man whose philosophy of life still impacts me today. His tenure with us was prior to the civil rights movement in the 1960s, but we treated him as family as much as the culture of the day would allow.

I knew Brother Mose better than anyone in our family and probably better than most of his friends. The simple reason is because I spent so much time with him listening to his stories and songs, watching him dance little jigs, and learning his philosophy of life. After my sister Marilyn married George Berry in 1957, George got to know Brother Mose like all of the family, and for years we loved recounting our remembrances of him.

One of the stories I often heard from Brother Mose concerned his boxing match with the star of a travelling troupe. During the depression years of the 1930s up to World War II, there were many travelling shows who passed through small-town America. They provided various forms of entertainment to the locals who couldn't afford the expense of travel to the larger cities. One such troupe which came to El Dorado was a boxing team featuring a star boxer named "Battlin' Red." Any local who was brave enough to pay one dollar and stay in the ring with Red for at least one round without getting knocked down would earn five dollars. Mose was a young man then in his twenties and was nimble on his feet. He said he was able to get in a few good licks on Red but mostly dodged his blows long enough to earn his five dollars. He said there were other men were not so fortunate and lost their dollar to ole "Battlin' Red."

Brother Mose loved to sing and could even play a few songs on the guitar. When I purchased my first guitar in 1956 for ten dollars from "Cousin" Willie Dykes, Brother Mose showed me how to play his favorite (and only) vocal guitar piece, "I Walked All the Way from East St. Louis." His a cappella repertoire was more extensive, and his favorite song, which he constantly sang or hummed, was "Precious Lord." Other songs which we remember and can still sing today include "The Foxes Love the Low Ground, the Gooses Love the Hills"; "Let the Wind Blow Low"; "Who Been Here Since I Been Gone?"; "Poppa Didn't Raise No Cotton and Corn"; and "There Will Be Peace in the Valley." Marilyn and I heard those songs so often we can sing them today.

A belief which Brother Mose had which neither Marilyn nor I challenged concerned a name he thought was ascribed to God. I don't remember how the conversation began, but he told us he knew "another name" for God. When asked to explain, he said the other name was "Hallow." "How do you know that Brother Mose?" one of us asked. He said, "In the Lord's Prayer it says, 'Our Father which art in heaven; *Hallow* would 'a bein' thy name." One of us replied with smiles, "We didn't know that!"

The only bad habit we saw in Brother Mose was that he loved to smoke "ceegareets," as he pronounced them. When I acquired the taste for cigarettes at the tender age of ten along with a neighborhood friend, John Lee Anthony, we would frequently "bum" a smoke from Brother Mose. He made us promise to not let "Dr. Mo'" know about our little secret, because it would get him in a heap o' trouble.

Brother Mose worked for our family during the years of racial segregation. Nation-wide and locally there was complete separation of the races to the shame of our nation. Neither Brother Mose nor Sister Bobbie, who also worked for us, were allowed to eat their meals in our dining room. I didn't know about the restriction until I was about six or seven years, but when Marilyn and I were at home alone with them, we tried to get them to join us for a meal at our table. They simply would not do it because segregation was so ingrained in them. If either of them had any anger toward us concerning this injustice, we never knew it.

I didn't know much about Brother Mose's home life except that he was married to Eloise. They never had children together, but helped raise two small children to adulthood and considered them their own. I don't think they remained very close to them after the children were grown. Mose and Eloise worshipped at Morning Star Baptist Church, but I don't know how regular they were in attendance.

Many times both Marilyn and I heard Brother Mose summarize his philosophy of life: "Live right in the sight of the Lord." And I believe he did. He was kind, loving, generous, forgiving, and without any guile. As I think back on his life and the circumstances he endured, I consider him to be one of the most outstanding men I have known.

When he was in his late sixties, he developed lung cancer from the many "ceegareets" he smoked over a lifetime. He received very good end-of-life medical care at the VA Hospital in Little Rock. I was in medical school at the time and was able to visit him on several occasions. I only wish I had prayed with him at his bedside during those visits and told him how much I loved him. I know he knew it, but I regret it just the same.

At his death, his funeral was held at Morning Star Baptist Church, and I took time off from medical school to drive the hundred miles from Little

Rock to El Dorado to attend. Mom and I were the only Caucasians in the church, and they gave us a place of honor near the front. We were asked if we wanted to give a testimony concerning Brother Mose, and to this day I regret that we politely refused. During the service, the choir sang "Precious Lord," and both Mom and I broke down and cried harder than any family member present.

I believe eternal life is received as a free gift of grace from the Lord Jesus, and no amount of good works will secure it. I also believe between the moment of our conversion until we meet Him face to face, we must live obedient to His command to love Him supremely and love others as He loves us. I am confident Brother Mose loved the Lord with all his heart, and I experienced the way he loved two small children who were quite different in color and culture. He was the first person I saw who overcame his trials and tribulations by "living right in the sight of the Lord!"

71. BROTHER MOSE SERVES THE GARDEN CLUB

He Brings Out Water in Our Finest Glasses

Stories concerning my wonderful childhood friend Brother Mose Graham abound in my memory. In the racially-segregated South in the 1950s, a black person was always addressed by his first name, and I don't recall anyone's ever using the title "Mr." in this context. Our family loved and respected Mose Graham so much we called him "Brother Mose." I never heard anyone address him as Mr. Mose, and I'm certain he never heard it either.

His responsibilities at our home included maintenance of our large yard and grounds and heavy-duty housework such as moving furniture or any objects too heavy for Sister Bobbie. He occasionally would stay after hours to babysit my sister Marilyn and me when needed, but this was rare. He never sat in any chair in the house except on a stool in the kitchen while having lunch. He never even considered using one of the three bathrooms inside the house, but he and Sister Bobbie had the use of a small room attached to our home which we called "the Servant's Quarters." The quarters contained a bed, a chair, a small lavatory, and a toilet. They would also use the Servant's Quarters for short rest periods during their workdays, which lasted seven to eight hours.

As a young boy I didn't understand why Brother Mose wouldn't use a bathroom in our home or sit beside me at the table when I was eating alone in our breakfast room. On many occasions when he was eating in the kitchen, I invited him to join me at the breakfast room table, but he politely refused by saying, "That's alright Masta. I'm jes' fine right here." He and Sister Bobbie called me "Master," not because they were ordered to or I demanded it, but because they loved me and had given me the moniker much like a nickname. In the beginning I was embarrassed, but I came to accept it as a loving name from them.

When Mom had a social event at our home with ladies from her garden club or from the church, she depended on Brother Mose to arrange the furniture and make certain everything was clean and orderly. As the ladies arrived, he remained in the background—usually in the kitchen in case Mom needed any extra help. He never mingled with the ladies or interacted socially although most of them knew him by name. He never wore a special white jacket for any social event, but only his usual work clothes. He liked suspenders, so he never wore a belt.

On this particular occasion, Mom had invited her garden club to our home for their monthly meeting. I assume the meeting was rotated to the other homes also, since I don't remember having the garden club in our home very often. As the ladies arrived, Mom had some cookies and small cakes on the living room table but there were no drinks on the table. When she asked if anyone would like something to drink, one lady responded, "I would love a glass of water." Several other ladies responded they too would love water. Mom went into the kitchen and asked Brother Mose if he would bring a tray of glasses of water for the eight ladies in the living room. "Yes'um, I'll be glad to."

Mom noticed it took Brother Mose an unusually long time to bring the water, but she didn't go into the kitchen to check on his reason for delay. When he finally arrived in the dining room, Mom knew the reason. He had gone into her cabinet and found one of her large Sterling silver trays, but when he saw the tray needed cleaning, he took time to clean it with silver polish. And right in the midst of the beautifully-polished tray were eight of what Brother Mose considered our finest serving glasses—Welch's jelly glasses! In those days Welch's grape jelly came in a colorfully-decorated glass. When the jar was empty, it could be washed and used as an orange juice glass for children. My sister Marilyn and I loved having our juice each morning in a Welch's glass.

When Mom saw the glasses, she quietly and politely asked Brother Mose if he would exchange those colorful glasses for plain glasses which the ladies would prefer. I believe they would have enjoyed their water while looking at the classic Disney character painted on the outside. Brother Mose was so loved by all of us that Mom never faulted him for his choice of glasses, and he probably continued thinking he was serving the ladies with our very finest. Such was the unpretentious nature of Brother Mose!

72. OLLIE AND THE MEAT CLEAVER

A Childish Prank Which Worked

Whenever our family gets together and swaps old stories, Cathy usually asks me to tell this one. In writing the story, it loses some of its flavor, lacking the sounds and hand gestures necessary to convey the full impact. The setting was in my childhood home almost seventy years ago.

One of my best buddies and inseparable companions during our preteen and teenage years was Eric Richardson. We hunted, fished, camped out, water-skied, rode in his Model A Ford, worked on my motor bike, and spent the best part of every summer day together. Eric's grandfather and father owned and operated Richardson Oil Company, and they gave Eric and me our first jobs during the summer of 1955. Our job titles would probably be "general handymen." We didn't accomplish much meaningful work but sure had a great time while getting paid the whopping sum of fifty cents per hour. I still have the first check I ever received as an employee. Of course, it's a cancelled check.

I have written about Brother Mose who worked for our family and just how much I loved him. I believe Eric loved Brother Mose almost as much. We enjoyed all his funny stories and songs, and we loved teasing him about his snaggle-tooth, a practice which didn't seem to offend him. When we had a little extra money, we would buy a cigarette or two from Brother Mose for a nickel or a dime. That was an exorbitant price to pay because a pack of cigarettes sold for twenty-five cents, but we dared not go to the store to buy a pack. We feared the store owner might tell our parents, but we knew our secret stayed with Brother Mose, because it was profitable for him and he didn't want us to get into trouble.

During one brief period, Pop had hired a cook and housekeeper named Ollie. I don't know who recommended her, but she undoubtedly was very efficient and was also a pretty good cook. Ollie was slender in build, quick in her movements, and short-tempered in nature, especially with Brother Mose. She couldn't seem to tolerate his slow but steady pace and seemed to think he must either be lazy or not very bright. The songs he was always singing or humming must have added to her impression that Brother Mose would try to get by with as little work as possible. If for no other reason than she didn't like my friend Brother Mose, I didn't care much for Ollie. She usually didn't have time to talk with me, and she would answer any questions I had with either a short yes or no. She was more interested in getting her work done than in having a relationship with me or with any of my friends. I suppose this was a good thing for Pop and Mom, but Ollie just wasn't much fun to us.

One day when Eric was at our house and we were near the kitchen, we heard Ollie open the back door and with a loud voice call out to Brother Mose, who was far away in the back yard, "Mose, get yo' lazy self up here in this kitchen and sweep and mop it right now like Miz Mo' has told you." Mose responded in usual slow and polite manner, "Yes'um, I'll be right there in jes' a minute." Eric and I couldn't stand hearing her mean voice and seeing her attitude toward our pal. For some reason Eric said, "Ollie, did you know that Old Mose has epilepsy, and when someone yells at him and threatens him, he will have a seizure?" I picked up on his spontaneous (but untrue) story by saying, "When Mose has a seizure, he doesn't know what he is doing and turns violent by striking out at the one closest to him." While speaking, Eric spotted the meat cleaver which always hung on a rack by the kitchen sink and continued to enlarge on our concocted story. He said with a straight face, "Once when a housekeeper in this very kitchen yelled at Mose, he had a seizure and grabbed this cleaver and buried it in her forehead right between her eyes! She died right where you are standing." Ollie said she didn't believe this story and asked, "If he killed the lady, why didn't he go to prison?" We said that Pop loved Brother Mose, and when he arrived to check the lady, he testified that she'd died of a heart attack. He signed that on the death certificate, so there was never an investigation. Ollie said, "You two boys are telling a big story that ain't true, and I ain't got time to listen to no more of yo' lies." We said she had better listen and keep a close eye on Brother Mose. The trap had been set in her mind, but we needed to let Brother Mose in on the scheme.

Eric and I made our way to the back part of our large yard where Mose was raking leaves and asked if he would like to make an easy fifty cents? "I shore would. What are you two boys up to?" We told him all he had to do was when he went into the kitchen and Ollie started fussing and complaining, he needed to grab the meat cleaver and act like he was going to use it on her. He said he could do that, so Eric and I each gave him a quarter.

Within five minutes, Brother Mose made his way to the kitchen where Ollie was working at the sink with her back to the door. As soon as Mose entered the room, Ollie began her usual tirade, "I don't know why you took so long getting here, and you ain't done what Miz Mo' told you. Where you been all this time? You know what you supposed to do." As she turned around to face Mose, he had the cleaver in his hand and according to him, all he did then was show it to her and say, "Here's what I'm gonna' do!" Mose said her reaction was instant as she squatted down with both hands in the air as if she was about to receive the deadly blow to her forehead. She screamed, "Ohhh, Lawd Jesus, hep me." She then burst out the back door in a dead run and ran half-way up our long driveway before she stopped. When Eric and I heard the commotion and came into the kitchen Brother Mose was doubled over in laughter. He said Ollie had "run off." Eric and I went quickly up the driveway to tell Ollie it was a big joke, and Mose would never hurt her. It was safe for her to return to the kitchen and continue working. We were afraid she was going to report us to Pop or even worse to the police.

Ollie never fussed or complained again to Brother Mose following this incident, but I don't think she ever fully trusted him. She kept her eyes on him not knowing whether he might really have epilepsy or some other strange malady. Within a month she turned in her resignation to Pop saying she had found another job. None of us were particularly sad she was gone, and I never told Pop this story. If I had told him, I think he would have had a big laugh over it especially the part about the death certificate.

73. "MIZ MO', SHE SAID SHE SAW YOU KISSING SANTA CLAUS!"

Brother Mose Relays a Telephone Message

Brother Mose was the central character of many of the funny stories of my childhood and youth. I spent so much time with him and knew him so well that even now as I remember those experiences, I find myself laughing and enjoying them all over again. My sister Marilyn and I are the only remaining ones in the family who knew Brother Mose, and we love reminding each other of the impact he had on us. I know Cathy and our children have grown weary of hearing me tell stories about Brother Mose and Sister Bobbie, but that generation has passed from the scene forever. Our children will never experience some of the good things we did and hopefully none of the bad things we allowed. Cathy and our children did know Lillian Singleton, and I have written an account of our collective remembrances.

Although Brother Mose was hired to do yard maintenance and heavy cleaning in the house, he would occasionally answer the telephone, and some of his phone conversations were hilarious. Not infrequently he would answer the phone with the following, "Dr. Mo's residence. Dr. Mo's porter speaking." I don't know where he came up with that title, but Pop didn't require it. On one occasion, Pop jokingly introduced Brother Mose to his close friends as "my footman."

This particular telephone conversation occurred in the early 1950s when a recording of Jimmy Boyd's hit song "I Saw Mommy Kissing Santa Claus" came out. It was so popular that record stores could not keep up with the demand, and our local store, Samples Electric City, was no exception. Mom had begun trying to purchase the record in August to have it available for the Christmas season, placing her name on a long waiting list. It was taking so long, she said she had forgotten about it.

Mom had a meeting in early December in our home with some ladies from the First Baptist Church and had asked Brother Mose to remain in the kitchen to help with the serving and clean-up. The telephone rang, and Brother Mose answered with his usual greeting. The lady on the other end said, "I'm calling from Sample's, and I have her record of 'I Saw Mommy Kissing Santa Claus.' Would you tell her for me?" Brother Mose did not understand her message at all and said, "M'am, excuse me, what was it you said?" The lady politely repeated her words, but it still didn't compute for him. "Could you say that just one more time, please 'em (please M'am)?" Brother Mose was then sure what he heard but wasn't sure how he would tell Mom with all those ladies present. Mom said he sheepishly came into the room and stood there for a few moments with a quizzical look on his face. She asked, "What is it, Mose?" and he answered, "Mrs. Mo' could I have a private word with you?" She was a little aggravated but stepped into the hall way and again asked, "What do you want to tell me?" Mose said, "A lady from Sample's called and said to tell you she saw you kissing Santa Claus." Mom looked at Mose and said, "Mose, what in the world are you talking about?" He repeated what he thought he'd heard, and suddenly Mom remembered her reservation for the record. She said, "Thank you Mose for the message." He seemed relieved that he got that embarrassing message delivered in as discreet a manner as possible, and none of the church ladies would be any the wiser. When we got the record, I played it for Brother Mose a couple of times and told him I thought the fellow was singing about Mom and how she got caught kissing Santa Claus. I don't believe Mose thought it was funny. He certainly didn't want me talking about it to anyone else.

74. "SISTER ALBERTINE, CAN YOU BRING ME A COKE?"

My Favorite Childhood Nurse Had a Huge Servant's Heart

Sisters of Mercy, 1950

The only hospital in El Dorado, Arkansas from 1921 until 1965 was Warner Brown. From my earliest remembrance, Warner Brown Hospital played a large part in my life because of my family's investment in it from its beginning. My granddad, Dr. J. A. Moore, was one of the founding physicians. Granddad, Pop, Bubba, and I were members of the medical staff, and each of us served at some point as chief of staff. In 1965, a second hospital, Union Memorial, was opened, and both served the community of South Arkansas as full-service hospitals.

Warner Brown was operated by the Sisters of Mercy from 1927 until the mid-1970s, when they turned the management of the hospital back to the community. I have nothing but wonderful memories of all the Sisters of Mercy. As a child I frequently accompanied Pop to the hospital when he would make evening rounds or attend to a patient in the emergency room. One of the prime reasons I enjoyed going with Pop was that I would get to visit with one or two of the sisters on duty that evening. I think they had a special place in their hearts for me, not only because of their love for Granddad and Pop, but because my mother had died of breast cancer when I was an infant.

There were several sisters who were special favorites. I remember with fondness Mother Ursula, the hospital director. She was an elderly but robust woman, and the first one I remember wearing the strange-looking dress (nun's habit). When she saw me, she would say, "There's my favorite little doctor," and always give me a big hug and squeeze. It seemed as if I was being buried into her fresh smelling and always starched black dress, which crackled as I was being engulfed. In those days, no one hugged me quite as well and as lovingly as Mother Ursula. A few years later, Pop told me Mother Ursula was very sick as a patient in the hospital and was not expected to live much longer. He said she would love to have me visit her, so I was excited to go. It shocked me to see her in bed, and, although she was well covered with the bed covers, I had never seen her without her habit and never seen her hair which was closely cropped. Despite her weakened state, she was still able to lean over and give me another big hug.

My favorite nun was Sister Albertine, who was the supervisor of the operating room and recovery room. Whenever she heard I was in the hospital with Pop, she would make a special effort to find us and visit with me for a few minutes. She would say things like, "Be sure and call me if I can do anything for you." I was certain she meant what she said because, even at age four or five, I was able to call the hospital. This was a few years before dial telephone service was available, when one simply picked up a receiver and a telephone operator would say, "Number please." I would just say "Warner Brown" and the operator would connect me by plugging into the three-digit switchboard number. The hospital operator was Mrs. May Wall, and I would tell her I wanted to talk with Sister Albertine. She easily recognized my voice and always connected me. Sister Albertine later told me I would usually say, "Sister Albertine, I'm out here all by myself. Would you send me a Coke?" She knew I was not alone but my favorite drink was Coca-Cola. Often, she would get the hospital orderly, Richard Holt, to drive to our home with an ice-cold Coke. I don't think I ever abused the privilege and probably only made the request a couple of times. More often when I called her, she would ask what I was doing and when was I coming to the hospital to see her. I loved hearing her voice, and she always made me feel important. She never made me feel I was imposing on her time. Sister Albertine served at Warner Brown Hospital until the 1960s, when she was transferred to St. Edwards Hospital in Fort Smith. I lost contact with her for many years.

In the Fall of 1989, our daughter Mary Kay, who was a freshman at the University of Arkansas, was horseback riding with a friend in a mountainous area south of Fayetteville. She was an excellent rider but had an uncooperative horse she was unable to control. She was thrown from the horse and sustained serious pelvic injuries which required hospitalization. Because of her proximity to Fort Smith, she was admitted to St. Edwards Hospital in the middle of the night, and Cathy and I were called. We immediately dressed and began the six-hour drive from El Dorado to Fort Smith arriving there about 8:00 a.m. We were thankful we found Mary Kay well cared for and stabilized, but she still required significant amounts of pain medication for the serious and painful injuries.

When we were certain Mary Kay was out of immediate danger, I asked the nursing supervisor if Sister Albertine was still working there. She responded, "Yes, and she is on duty today." I had her paged, and, when she answered, I said, "Sister Albertine, this is John Henry and I am here in St. Edwards in Room 410 all by myself. Can you bring me a Coke?" She said, "I'll be right there." When she arrived, she had an icy Coke in her hand, and we embraced and praised the Lord we could meet again. Sister Albertine was seventy-nine years old but still energetic and with the same sweet personality which had made me feel so special years before. We got caught up on the years which had separated us while Cathy and Mary Kay also got to know this special sister they had heard me talk about so often.

Sister Albertine lived to be ninety and was buried near her birth place in central Arkansas. I'm certain God gave her long life in order to minister to the needs of others, and especially to the least of these, like little three-year-old boys who are lonely and could use a kind word and an ice-cold Coke.

75. DEPUTY SHERIFF BARNEY SOUTHALL

A Tough Lawman with a Tender Heart

One of the more colorful characters from my childhood was "Mr. Barney," who was a deputy sheriff of Union County. He served the people during the 1940s and 1950s. It was a sign of great disrespect for a young person of my generation to call an adult by just their first name, so Deputy Barney Southall was known by me and almost everyone in the county as "Mr. Barney." He appeared to me as a giant, not simply because he was over six feet tall and weighed in excess of two hundred and fifty pounds, but because of the respect everyone had for him. When I first learned of his exploits, he had been in law enforcement for over twenty years and had earned the respect from young and old alike.

My dad (Pop), was a general practitioner in medicine, and it seemed that he knew everyone in El Dorado and Union County. Because he made house calls almost every night and some of the calls were into unsafe neighborhoods, Pop would occasionally have a deputy sheriff follow in his patrol car to keep watch during the time of the visit. Usually, Mr. Barney was the deputy on call, so he became one of Pop's best friends and guardians.

I don't remember Mr. Barney's wearing his deputy's hat, but he was so polite he may have removed it when I was in his presence, which was typically indoors. As I recall, his service revolver was a pearl-handled thirty-eight caliber, and according to his nephew Barry, who inherited the pistol at Barney's death, it "was rusted from disuse." The one weapon he carried which was well-used was a black slapjack. He kept that instrument in his right rear pocket and was known to use it liberally on any Saturday night when there was a dispute or disagreement in one of the more dangerous areas of town. It was said Mr. Barney could remove that slapjack from his pocket and deliver a paralyzing blow so fast the shiftiest character did not have reflexes fast enough to avoid the blow.

It was told that on one Saturday night in the volatile, all-black St. Louis section of town, Mr. Barney was called to investigate an altercation. Two young men who had been drinking alcohol to excess were fighting, and the fight couldn't be stopped. When Mr. Barney held one of the combatant's arms and told him he needed him to leave the premises and go home, he jerked his arm away. He said, "You ain't my Daddy to tell me what to do!" With that, the slapjack flashed from Mr. Barney's pocket and a quick blow to the man's temple left him on the floor in a semi-conscious state. His companions gathered around him and said, "You know who yo' Daddy is now. Mr. Barney is yo' Daddy!"

Mr. Barney was a master in settling disputes, and quite often he could get it done in a non-violent fashion. Pop told me this story, which involved a married couple who lived in another racially-segregated area of town called Fairview. It seems they had a physical altercation with each other almost every weekend when they were drinking alcoholic beverages. Invariably Mr. Barney was called to their home to separate them and to get one or the other to the emergency room for suture repair of the injuries. On this occasion, Mr. Barney said, "Now listen I'm sick and tired of breaking up your fights. You two can't seem to get along, so do you want to get a divorce?" "Yes suh, Mr. Barney, we wants to get di-vorced." Barney told them to place their right hands on his badge and answer this question, "Do you James and you Sally desire to divorce each other?" "We do," was their reply. "By the authority given me by the state of Arkansas and the county of Union, I now declare you divorced." According to Mr. Barney, James and Sally continued living together but never had another altercation requiring Mr. Barney's attention. I was not told whether they gave up drinking alcohol, but I suspect they did not.

Deputy Barney Southall had a long and faithful record of service to the people of Union County, and I believe he was never paid a salary reflective of the value for his service. His greater value and true legacy have been recorded in the memory of his family and friends who knew and loved him. There were countless people like James and Sally with whom he made a lasting difference by his firm but sometimes unusual methods of law enforcement. I just wish there were a few more Mr. Barneys around.

76. BON APPÉTIT

The Mayor and His Wife on a Cruise Ship

A well-known citizen in El Dorado for the decades of the forties through the seventies was Irving Leon Pesses. He was better known by his nickname, Izzy Pesses, and was a prominent businessman who owned and operated Pesses and Marks Pipes and Supply Company. Izzy was from New Orleans and had graduated from Tulane University as a civil engineer. He and his family were members of the small Jewish community in El Dorado and worshipped at the Temple Beth Israel.

Izzy was a tireless businessman and civic leader, and I was told he seldom travelled outside of Union County for either business or pleasure. He served the town as Mayor from 1967 through 1976, working very hard to improve the streets and infrastructure of a town, which had declined in wealth and population since the oil boom days of the 1920s. One of his famous campaign slogans was "Izzy's Been Busy," and he truly lived out that slogan.

I was told he had made a promise to his wife upon his retirement that he would take her on a long vacation to Europe. As he neared the time he decided to retire, she reminded him of his promise made years before. He told her to schedule the trip, but reminded her he was not flying because of his distrust of airplanes. She scheduled an ocean voyage to Europe which left out of New York City. They travelled to New York by rail and boarded the giant ocean liner for the five-day trip across the Atlantic.

They obviously had no experience with ocean travel, but quickly discovered they were assigned regular seating for every meal in the dining room with the same travelers. They did not meet their table companions until the first meal of the first day, which was in the evening. One of the four other guests at their table was a gentleman from France who was returning home after visiting relatives in the US. He could not speak English and neither Izzy nor his wife could speak French. As they were seated the first evening, there was some initial discomfort with the strangers at their table. The gentleman from France seated directly across from Izzy spoke first and said, "Bon Appétit," to which Izzy held out his hand to shake and said, "Pleased to meet you. I'm Izzy Pesses." Izzy's conversation for the remainder of the meal was with his wife and the others at the table since he couldn't understand a word the Frenchman said.

The following morning, they gathered at the table for breakfast and immediately upon sitting, the Frenchman said, "Bon Appétit." Izzy was a bit taken back, but held out his hand again to shake and said, "I'm Izzy Pesses." No other words or gestures were made between the two. The lunch meal seemed to come too quickly following breakfast, but again, shortly after sitting, the Frenchman said, "Bon Appétit." Izzy responded again with a handshake and his name, Izzy Pesses, but summoned the table steward and whispered, "Is that man sitting across from me crazy? He has introduced himself to me three times, and each time I told him my name. This could go on for the whole trip." The steward asked," What was it he said?" "He said his name was Bone Appetit." The steward said, "That's not his name. He was just saying, have a good meal in French." Izzy said, "Well, that makes a lot more sense. Thanks."

In the evening as the guests were again being seated, it was Izzy who looked across the table and politely said to the Frenchman, "Bon Appétit," to which the Frenchman reached across the table to shake hands and proudly said, "I'm Izzy Pesses!" They both laughed without either one knowing what the other had said. The correct meanings of the spoken words escaped both men, but the cordial spirit of each one bridged all the language and cultural barriers. They had a pleasant crossing, enjoying the voyage, and probably continuing to greet and introduce themselves at each meal!

77. MEETING ROY ROGERS
How I Met My Cowboy Hero

The Day I Met Roy Rogers

Every young man whom I knew as a pre-teen had a western hero. Prior to television, the prime source of entertainment in El Dorado on weekends was attending movies at either the Rialto or the Majestic theater. Both these theaters in the 1950s were segregated, and the only integrated movie theater was the Ritz. We didn't call them "theaters" in those days, but rather "picture shows." The Rialto was more sophisticated and didn't feature the Western (cowboy) movies we loved. They were shown at either the Majestic or the Ritz, so those venues were our favorites. There were a large number of Wild-West stars such as Roy Rogers, Gene Autry, Tom Mix, Johnny Mack Brown, Joel McCrea, the Durango Kid, Lash La Rue, the Lone Ranger, Sunset Carson, and the favorite of many, John Wayne. I loved all of them, but my favorite by far was Roy Rogers. This became especially true after I got to meet him.

I was fortunate to have an aunt in St. Louis who took great interest in things which were important to me. Aunt Tooky (Thelma) was an older sister of Mom, and she and her husband Uncle Max had no children. Their marriage relationship was always strange to me, because Aunt Tooky lived alone in a very exclusive and beautiful apartment and only saw Uncle Max on occasion. Mom told me they had been separated for many years but were not divorced. At the time, Aunt Tooky was the wealthiest person I had ever met, and all I knew was that she had "millions."

My parents received a phone call from Aunt Tooky in the summer of 1949, and she said she had just read that Roy Rogers was bringing his rodeo to town. She suggested they take a few days' vacation and bring me to the rodeo so I could see him in person. Pop said he needed a few days off and would enjoy going to St. Louis. He bargained with Mom so she and Aunt Tooky would be responsible for taking me to the rodeo without him.

The decision was made to take the all-night train ride to St. Louis, which left El Dorado about 8:00 p.m. The excitement of spending the night on the train was huge and only added to the enormous thrill of getting to see Roy Rogers. I packed my finest cowboy outfit for the event, and we boarded the train.

The trip was uneventful except for the fact I could hardly sleep thinking what lay ahead. The noise and the swaying of the train were a little disturbing at first. When I saw that neither Pop nor Mom were concerned, I decided this was a small price to pay for what I would be able to tell my buddies on returning home.

Aunt Tooky met us at the train station, and she immediately saw my excitement. I had donned my cowboy suit and wanted Roy to know I was "one of the boys" in case I accidentally ran into him. The rodeo was scheduled for the afternoon of our arrival, so the wait was not so long, although it seemed that lunch would never end. Mom, Aunt Tooky, and I headed for the downtown arena about an hour and a half before the scheduled rodeo time so we could park and find our seats. Aunt Tooky had reserved our seats, and I have no idea how much they cost. They seemed to be some of the finest seats in the arena. At the appointed hour, the lights dimmed, and the giant spotlight focused on one end of the arena while the announcer shouted, "Now heeer's Roy Rogers!" As the crowd roared I could barely catch my breath when I saw Roy riding Trigger into the center of the arena waving his hat to the adoring crowd. Aunt Tooky said I never took my eyes off him for the entire first part of the show, and she had never seen me so focused. Intermission came far too soon for me, but Aunt Tooky asked, "Would you like to go with me and see if we can meet Roy?" "Yes Ma'am!!" I quickly said. The question was like asking a starving man if he would like to have a gourmet feast!

Mom decided to remain in our seats, so Aunt Tooky and I made our way down a number of long corridors which seemed to lead toward the basement area. The number of people we encountered became smaller and smaller until it seemed we were the only ones present in the corridor. Suddenly a guard appeared and said we were not allowed in this part of the arena. Aunt Tooky told him her nephew had come all the way from Arkansas to see Roy Rogers, and wondered if he could arrange the meeting. As she spoke, I saw her reach into her purse to get a hundred-dollar bill and slip it into the guard's hand. In our present economy, this would amount to approximately seven hundred dollars. As he placed the bill into his pocket, he said, "Stay right here, and I'll see what I can do." In less than two minutes, I could hardly believe my eyes. There was Roy Rogers riding Trigger down the corridor and approaching us! He said, "Son, I hear you have come all the way from Arkansas to see Trigger and me." From this point on I don't remember one thing I said. I think I just listened. With my mouth wide open from sheer disbelief he asked, "Would you like to climb up on Trigger?" as he extended his hand and pulled me into the saddle behind him. I wanted to just touch those beautiful pistols in his holster but dared not. He said a few more things to both Aunt Tooky and me, and then said he needed to get back so the second half of the show could begin. He helped me dismount Trigger. As we walked back to our seats for the remainder of the show, I was trying to think just how I was going to tell this unbelievable story to all my friends. I wanted them to know I now had a new pal in Roy Rogers. They would just have to dream about what I had gotten to experience first-hand in St. Louis. There would be some who wouldn't believe my account. If only I had a photograph of me sitting behind Roy Rogers on Trigger.

Roy Rogers died in 1998 at the age of eighty-seven having lived a life providing clean, wholesome entertainment for millions of young people over many decades. I always regretted as an adult that I never wrote Roy a thank you letter for the act of kindness and love he showed an adoring nine-year-old fan. He certainly had nothing to gain from our encounter except the sheer joy of seeing on my face how much I loved him. I feel certain the guard never told him about the money he received from Aunt Tooky.

78. THE DAY I MET STAN THE MAN

My All-Time Baseball Idol

Most young men who love playing and watching baseball games have at least one hero whom they admire and seek to emulate. I had several heroes during my Boys Club baseball playing days in the early 1950s, but my absolute favorite was Stan Musial of the St. Louis Cardinals. He was affectionately known by all as "Stan the Man," and he lived up to his nickname in almost every category one could name. One of the reasons I so admired Stan the Man was because my beloved Aunt Tooky was also from St. Louis, and she spoke often in glowing terms about what a good man and great baseball player he was. She did not know him personally but had several friends who did.

Aunt Tooky (Thelma Manne) was my mom's older sister and lived in St. Louis. She also was a hero to me because several years earlier she had arranged a private meeting for me with Roy Rogers. Because of her wealth and status in St. Louis, she knew a number of dignitaries and could get things done which others couldn't. She lived alone in the Chase Apartments, which were exclusive and very expensive dwellings adjacent to the well-known Chase Hotel. She and Uncle Max had lived separate lives for at least ten years but had remained friends. The only explanation I was ever given concerning their marital status was, "They had trouble getting along," and this satisfied my curiosity. (I have written two other stories of the impact Aunt Tooky had on me as a child—"The Quality Grocery Store" and "Meeting Roy Rogers.") During the months in the late 1940s when she lived with us in El Dorado while managing the Quality Grocery Store, I told her how much I admired Stan the Man and hoped one day I could meet him. This planted a seed in Aunt Tooky's mind, and I knew she loved surprising me.

As my baseball playing career with the El Dorado Boys Club began flourishing in the early 1950s, my admiration for Stan the Man increased.

I knew most of his playing statistics and easily quoted them with family and friends whenever conversations turned to Major League Baseball. This was at least ten years before the availability of televised games, and my information was acquired through newspaper stories, occasional movie news clips, and very infrequent radio broadcasts of St. Louis Cardinal games. On one family visit to St. Louis in the summer of 1948, my Uncle Harry (Aunt Tooky's brother-in-law) had taken me to a baseball game at Sportsman's Park. I'm sure I sat there in wonder the entire nine innings with my mouth open while watching men I had only read and dreamed about play. I never thought about getting an autograph, because it would have been impossible with so many thousands in the stadium. I had never been in a stadium with forty-five thousand spectators, which was double the number of people who lived in El Dorado.

During the summer of 1950, I was developing into a pretty good third baseman for Gulf Refining (El Dorado Boys Club), but we were not at our best and missed the playoffs that year. Mom wanted to make a week-long visit to St. Louis to spend time with Aunt Tooky and Aunt Ruth, her other sister who lived in St. Louis. It was her husband who had taken me to the Cardinals game two years earlier. I was excited to stay at Aunt Tooky's apartment, especially because she had a television set on which I could watch shows like *Captain Kangaroo*, *Howdy Doody*, and *Art Linkletter*. It was the summer Aunt Tooky asked, "Would you like to meet Stan Musial?" She didn't have to hear my answer; she just went ahead and said she had a friend who would set up a meeting the very next morning. I didn't know Stan the Man owned a restaurant until she said we would drive to his restaurant and meet him in the morning. It had to be a morning meeting because he had a game to play that night. I don't remember sleeping much that night because I was so excited.

Aunt Tooky drove a Chrysler, two-door convertible, and riding in her car with the top down was such fun. It compounded the whole experience. Fortunately, Aunt Tooky had an attorney friend named Arnold Kovin who was good friends with Stan, and he arranged the meeting. (Mom didn't go with us so I could get the full impact of such a momentous occasion.)

Stan co-owned a well-known restaurant named "Stan Musial and Biggie's, which had opened about a year earlier. "Biggie" Garagnani was an experienced restaurateur who knew that adding Stan Musial as a business partner would only mean greater success. Aunt Tooky knew exactly the location and drove straight there to keep the 10:00 a.m. appointment in front of the building. As she pulled into an empty parking spot at exactly the appointed time, he was standing out front. He was dressed in a suit, which surprised me, because I had only seen him in his Cardinal uniform.

As I stepped out of the car, he said, "You must be the young ball player from Arkansas," while extending his hand to shake my hand. I don't remember one thing else he said because I was in such awe of this celebrity who acted as if he wanted to meet me. I do remember his kind and gentle manner as he looked into my eyes and handed me a new baseball in its own case. He said something like he was glad to meet me and thanked me for being a Cardinal fan. His parting words indicated he hoped to see me again soon. It all happened so fast the next thing I remember was riding back to Aunt Tooky's apartment looking at this treasure I held. As I opened the box there was a new baseball inscribed, "To John Henry, Best Wishes Stan Musial." Had I been given the Hope Diamond I don't think I could have felt wealthier.

Aunt Tooky had come through again. First Roy Rogers and now Stan Musial. In my childish amazement, I considered her ability to make dreams come true to be unlimited. I couldn't wait to get back to El Dorado to show my baseball buddies what a celebrity I had now become.

79. "I DIDN'T KNOW YOU WOULD BE MY NEIGHBOR"

We Plan Our Homes but Not Our Neighbors

In my medical practice life of forty-five-plus years, I have had the privilege of serving with many outstanding doctors. The two most outstanding to me were my dad, Dr. Berry L. Moore Sr. (Pop) and my brother, Dr. Berry L. Moore Jr. (Bubba). When Cathy and I moved to El Dorado, Arkansas, in 1971 to begin my general surgical practice, I met some very colorful men who were practicing medicine there at the time. All were older men with lots of experience, and I was excited to have the chance to learn as much as possible from them. Pop had died from heart failure six years earlier, but Bubba was near the top of his practice experience and wisdom.

Mom was still living in our family home on North Madison, but the home and gardens were far too large for her to continue living there. A decision about her future residence would soon have to be made. Living next door on the north side of Mom's home were Dr. Frank and Lillian Thibault. They had been good neighbors to Mom and Pop for years and never caused any significant neighborly problems. Their yard and grounds were not neat and well-manicured like Mom and Pop's, but they didn't have a boat and trailer or a junk car in their yard, and they had their yard mowed at least once or twice each summer. They had not been very sociable with Mom and Pop and pretty much kept to themselves. I don't remember seeing either one of them in our home or hearing any account of their having Mom and Pop over for a cup of coffee.

The stories concerning Dr. Thibault were myriad, and most were focused either on his personal appearance or his automobile-driving exploits. For reasons known only to him, he seldom had a clean-shaven face. When seen at his medical office or the hospital, he had a three- to-four-day growth of facial hair which was never groomed. In addition, he wore bedroom slippers the majority of the time. I don't remember seeing him in a pair of shoes. Perhaps he had a medical issue with his feet which made the wearing of regular shoes painful, but I never heard this explanation. Our county coroner, Dr. John Henry Pinson, told of once overhearing on his frequency a radio transmission from an Arkansas state police officer. The trooper called in to report an individual with no personal ID who had been stopped for speeding on the highway near Sheridan, Arkansas. The individual identified himself as Frank Thibault, an El Dorado physician, and the trooper wanted to know if anyone could confirm the identity of such a person. Dr. Pinson keyed in on the frequency and identified himself to the trooper, telling him he was a friend of Dr. Thibault. He told the trooper that if the individual was "clean-shaven and wearing shoes," he was an imposter.

Another story told me by Dr. Thibault himself involved a later traffic stop by a different state trooper. The doctor had just purchased a new Pontiac and was "breaking it in" by driving to Little Rock to attend an Arkansas Razorback football game. About half-way to his destination, he was pulled over for excessive speed and given a ticket. When he asked what the fine would be, the trooper said, "It will cost you fifty dollars which you can pay now." Dr. Thibault handed the lawman a hundred-dollar bill and told him, "I'll be coming home tonight around 10:00 following the game, and this will cover that fine."

Dr. Thibault had a long career practicing family medicine in El Dorado, and I think he had a large number of loyal patients who depended on him. He never referred any patients to me for a surgical procedure, but we collaborated on a few acute trauma cases assigned to us as on-call doctors. From my observation of his patients, he had sound judgment and current medical knowledge. I heard several people who had been patients of his for years say that they believed, despite his unusual personal traits, that he was a "brilliant doctor." I had no reason to doubt their assessment, but he was definitely different.

I was in the emergency room at Warner Brown Hospital on a cold December afternoon when Dr. Thibault was brought in having sustained a shotgun injury to his right hand. He had been duck hunting that morning and was getting out of the boat while pulling his shotgun out of the boat barrel-first. The gun was still loaded with the safety off, and, when he pulled on the weapon, the trigger struck an object and the shotgun discharged through the middle of his right palm. I assisted the orthopedic surgeon Dr. J. C. Calloway in an operation to save his hand. The operation was successful, but for the remainder of his life, Dr. Thibault had a severely deformed right hand which hampered his doing any more surgical procedures. His gun safety judgment was certainly faulty.

I heard Pop once say, "Old Frank is strange, but I think he is a pretty good doctor. He and I get along just fine." As a teenager I was present in our sideyard one afternoon when Pop made this comment tongue in cheek to Dr. Thibault: "Frank, the Lord says in the Good Book I should love my neighbor like myself. But he didn't tell me Frank Thibault would be my neighbor!" Frank laughed out loud without making any comment. When Cathy and I moved into the family home years later, I occasionally reminded Dr. Thibault of Pop's comment about being his neighbor and told him I concurred with Pop. He always laughed and once he retorted, "Unfortunately we don't get to pick our neighbors."

80. LESSONS LEARNED FROM MISS ELLIS

My Grade School Principal Taught Me as a Child and also as an Adult

Hugh Goodwin, 4th grade class (the author, next-to-last row, second from the left)

I remember that when I entered the first grade at Hugh Goodwin Elementary School, I was excited, thinking I was being sent to a playground where everyone played all the time. All I knew about school was what I saw as I rode by in my parents' car and watched all the kids playing on the huge playground. When I didn't see them outside playing, I assumed they were inside taking a nap and getting ready for the next play period. Hugh Goodwin was one of the four elementary schools in El Dorado at the time and was the school which my brother Berry Lee and sister Marilyn also attended. They'd told me it was "the best school in town" so I thought they must surely have the best games to play.

I remember the names of all of my elementary school teachers and at least one of the qualities which set each apart from the others. In those days, there were no men who taught school at that level. The one individual who was a constant in my grade school experience for the entire six years at Hugh Goodwin was the principal, Miss Nola Ellis. My childhood remembrance was she was short in stature and had bright red hair. I didn't think she was much taller than most first graders. She moved quickly from one place to another with short rapid steps which seemed louder than others because of the black, quarter length heels she wore. My friends all said they were scared of Miss Ellis, and the last thing they ever wanted was to be called into her office. A summons to her office was never for a congratulatory message or award, but for an offence which could not be handled by your teacher. I knew where her office was located but tried not to pay much attention to either its location or the furniture behind the closed-door marked "Principal's Office." My attitude was that if I avoided her and her office, perhaps I could get through the six years at Hugh Goodwin, and she wouldn't know my name or anything about me. That was about to change when I got to the fourth grade.

Perhaps I was becoming bolder in my more "mature" state, or I wanted to become more popular with the so-called tough guys. Whatever the reason, I got involved with a gang of spit-wad shooters. Spit-wad shooting was expressly forbidden at school, and carrying rubber bands was punishable by a trip to Miss Ellis's office. Repeat offenders were occasionally expelled from school for several days. I won't go into further details except to say I was caught one morning with a small pack of rubber bands in my sock and was immediately sent to Miss Ellis's office. I was terrified to the core as I walked down the long hallway, and I probably promised God a large number of things if he would bail me out. As I sat there with two other perpetrators, she looked at me and said, "John Henry, this is not like you, and because this is your first time to my office, you just have to stay after school for an hour each day in detention hall the rest of this week. Don't ever do anything like this again." I said, "Thank you Miss Ellis. I promise I will never to do anything like this for the rest of my life." That was my one and only trip to her office throughout my grade school career. Whenever the thought of a misdeed crossed my mind, I recalled the terror of the walk to Miss Ellis's office and my thinking that my useful life was over.

Years later following a Christian seminar which Cathy and I attended, we were challenged to think of some person from our past who had meant a great deal to the development of our character. I remembered the incident involving Miss Ellis which had occurred over thirty years earlier, and I wrote her a detailed, two-page letter thanking her for her influence in my life. I told her she epitomized discipline with mercy and was an ideal grade school principal. I was grateful for her many years of dedication to excellent childhood education in El Dorado. I received a thank you note from her within a week, and I still have her note written on May 21, 1979.

Within a few months of the letter, Miss Ellis came to me as a surgical patient. She had been in excellent health for her previous eighty-two years, but had developed a malignant condition which required a major operation. She recovered well and was cured from the malignancy. The blessing for me was that I had the privilege of spending many hours with Miss Ellis while she recovered and got to witness Christ to her and pray for her. She told me many stories about her wonderful career in education and her influence on so many children.

Miss Ellis lived another ten years and departed this life in 1989 at age ninety-two. She had a quiet but vibrant faith in the Lord Jesus, and she is with him now. Thank you, Miss Ellis. You will always be one of my heroes.

81. THE DAY WE SET THE WOODS ON FIRE

Playing with Fire Has Consequences

The first four years of my life, I was raised by baby sitters, maids, and house keepers, because my birth mother died of advanced breast cancer when I was eighteen months old. My brother Berry Lee (Bubba) was thirteen years old and my sister Marilyn was almost five years old. Our dad (Pop) was emotionally devastated but had to continue his busy medical practice to support us and to provide as much parental support as possible. Our maternal grandmother lived with us for several years, but her home was in Little Rock, and it didn't work out for her to stay on a permanent basis. I believe there was significant tension between Pop and her regarding our care. By the time I was four, Pop had met, courted, and married Athie West, who became our step mother. Since I was too young to remember my birth mother, my new mom filled this void in my life, and it was not until years later I was able to understand the significance of her sacrifices.

Mom had no prior experience at parenting, and she wanted only the best for us. She knew about dresses and frilly things for girls and seemed to have no problems with Marilyn, but for me it was different. I am told that as a child, Mom kept me spotless in appearance and usually wearing the latest in children's clothing. Whenever I got dirty playing outside, I was quickly cleaned and dressed in another outfit. I must have assumed this was the way it was supposed to be for boys. I don't remember complaining about it or thinking I was different from other little boys. This all changed when I was seven years old and the Anthony boys moved into the neighborhood.

Beryl Franklin Jr. (Berlie) and John Lee were the only sons of Beryl and Oma Lee Anthony. There were two older daughters, Patsy Sue and Carolyn. The Anthonys were part owners of a family timber business in South Arkansas and North Louisiana, and they moved to El Dorado from the small town Calion in the mid-1940s. In addition to other holdings, the Anthonys owned a large sawmill in Calion, which supported an adjoining community of sawmill employees. A company store there sold all the necessary household supplies and groceries for the community. That store later became a source for John Lee and me to obtain cigarettes for our smoking pleasure at the ages of nine and seven respectively. Needless to say, our parents did not suspect this for a long time.

Berlie and John Lee played a huge role in my growing and maturing experience as a young boy. We rode bikes together and played baseball, football, and basketball depending on the mood and the season. We wrestled in the grass, mud, or whatever happened to be on the ground at the time with no thought from either of our parents of trying to clean us up. We would hunt and fish together at Calion near the sawmill and were probably under the watchful eye of some adult without knowing it. Berlie was a year older than I, and I looked up to him for his great wisdom and worldly experience. John Lee was two years younger, and occasionally, because of his inexperience and immaturity, Berlie and I would exclude him from our deliberations. If Berlie wasn't available, then John Lee became my best friend.

I'm not certain of our exact ages, but somewhere around seven or eight, I was introduced to cigarettes by the Anthony boys, primarily by John Lee. The cigarettes never made me sick, but I do remember feeling I was a big man when I would light one up. I am pretty sure I could look and talk tougher whenever I had a Lucky Strike in my mouth. Even though this was an era when smoking was commonplace and Pop even smoked cigarettes, I did not dare let him know I was smoking. Bubba was in college at the time, and he was an excellent athlete. I knew he had never smoked cigarettes, but this didn't matter to me. I asked him once if he had ever smoked, and he said he tried it and it made him sick. Since it didn't make me sick, I was sure this was my indication I was supposed to smoke.

One morning near lunchtime, John Lee and I were in the wooded area adjacent to their home and decided to make a small campfire in order to make our smoking more enjoyable. Perhaps we had in mind making some coffee, which is what we had seen John Wayne and some of his sidekicks doing in the movies. As I recall there was a slight breeze, which made lighting the fire a little more difficult, but when it was well-lit, caused it to burn better and faster. By the time we added a few small tree limbs and pine straw, we had a roaring fire and thought perhaps we needed to reduce it a bit. The more we tried, the larger the flames grew, and as I was trying to stamp out the fire, I saw John Lee start crying as he ran towards home. He decided to leave the fire control to someone older and wiser. Not sensing that I was up to the task, I gave up and also started running home, which was two blocks away. Before I reached our front porch, I heard the sirens of a fire engine and assumed it was headed our way. I don't know why, but I ran to my bedroom, pulled off my britches, and climbed into bed. Mom saw me and asked, "What are you doing, and what is that siren I hear?" My response was, "I don't feel very good, and I don't know anything about the siren."

The wooded area was not completely burned, but several large beautiful pines were destroyed. I wasn't punished for my misdeeds, but John Lee's parents were not as forgiving. He got a significant spanking. His mom and dad always thought I was so sweet that I couldn't have possibly thought about starting a fire like that, so it must have been John Lee's idea. I never let them think otherwise and still have a little bit of guilt concerning my silence.

I have wonderful memories of those days with the Anthonys, and I'm grateful they were a big part of my early maturing process. By God's grace and mercy, we did learn cigarettes and smoking were dangerous to wooded areas and to health, and we quit smoking within a few years. The Anthony boys turned out well. Beryl Franklin became a US Congressman from the Fourth District in 1979 and served faithfully for seven terms. John Lee became president and CEO of Anthony Forest Products and made a significant contribution to the growth of the timber industry in South Arkansas. In that role, part of his responsibilities involved the planting, growth management, and harvest of pine trees on tens of thousands of acres. He more than made up for the few trees we destroyed in our fire. I just wish I had confessed my guilt concerning the fire to Mr. and Mrs. Anthony. I doubt they would have spanked me.

82. WILDCAT BASKETBALL

Lifelong Friends Made on a Basketball Team

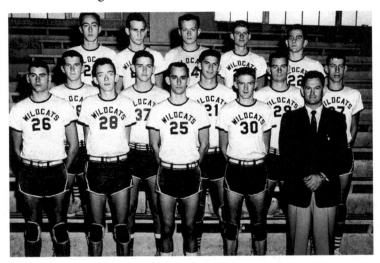

El Dorado Wildcat basketball team, 1956–57

From my earliest remembrance, I have loved all types of sports. My older brother Berry Lee (Bubba) was good at most of them, and he was my idol. He excelled at football and was a high school All-American at El Dorado High School. He was selected for a scholarship to play tackle for the Razorbacks at the University of Arkansas from 1946 through 1948. He would have played all four years had he not suffered a career-ending knee injury his sophomore year.

Because he was eleven years older, he was a father-figure in many ways. He taught me to play football, basketball, tennis, ping-pong, and bowling. My sports goals were to beat him in everything but football, and, by the time I was a teenager I was able to able to do it. My first love in sports was football, and I would have tried out for the team in junior high school had I not been so skinny. I chose basketball for junior high and high school competition. I didn't make the team as a ninth grader, so I played Boys Club basketball that year. I was leading scorer on our team in every game, averaging fifteen points per game. By the tenth grade I made the Wildcat B team and again was the leading scorer.

I spent hours shooting basketballs from the perimeter outside the circle, and my favorite spot was from the left, which is now in a three-point area. When the gym was open in the off-season I preferred practicing there, but usually I practiced on the playground at Hugh Goodwin Elementary

School. During every practice period of a couple of hours, I would shoot at least a hundred free throws. My strong point was shooting and not rebounding since I was not heavy enough nor strong enough to "mix it up" on the inside.

By the twelfth grade, I finally made the starting lineup for the Wildcats. Our coach was Pel Austin (first row, far right) who was quite a colorful figure. Coach Austin had once played left field for the El Dorado Oilers, a Class C League professional baseball team, in the late forties and early fifties. He was the best hitter for the Oilers and well-known for his home-run power. He was known as "Pelting Pel from Peach Orchard" because his home town was Peach Orchard, Missouri. I thought he was an excellent basketball coach and a good motivator of young men. He was stern in discipline but not profane in his language, which I especially appreciated. He was physically larger and stronger than all the players on the team, so no one would dare think of challenging him in any way.

Most of our team players were skinny like me, and I was one of the taller players at six feet, two inches (#28). The stronger players and good rebounders were Richard McCuistion (#21) and James Norris (#29), who were also excellent football players for the Wildcat football team. By far our best player was Bill (Spider) Jones (#30) who had a twenty-point scoring average for the season. As a small forward, he had the ability to score from the inside despite his relatively small size (six feet two, and weighing a hundred and sixty pounds). The players in our conference who were bigger and stronger couldn't stop Spider, who easily made the All- State first team and earned himself a full scholarship to play for Arkansas State University in Jonesboro.

The high school campus was located where the El Dorado branch of South Arkansas University now sits, and our practice gym was the on-campus gymnasium. It's still standing and has been designated a state historical building. As an aside, I was present in this gym at a game in the early 1950s when the Harlem Globetrotters played a game against a locally organized team. The star Globetrotter was Reese "Goose" Tatum, whose home was El Dorado and was a very well-known national sports star. He was nicknamed the "Clown Prince of Basketball." Some of his family members still live in El Dorado, and his sister became a surgical patient of mine forty years later.

All of our home games were played in the Barton Junior High School gymnasium, which would hold more fans than our practice gym. Most of our games were well attended, but, in those days, even parents of the players were less likely to attend than now. I cannot remember my Pop and Mom attending even one home game, and I did not think it strange then. The 1950s preceded the civil rights movement, and I never played against a team with a black player. The black students in El Dorado attended Booker T. Washington High School, and the building is still in use, now named Washington Middle School. We never played against the Washington High Hornets but probably would have lost.

Our most memorable accomplishment my senior year was beating Little Rock Central High School on our home court. The Little Rock Tigers were almost invincible each year because it was the only high school in our state's capital city. Their enrollment made it one of the largest high schools in the nation. As a comparison, it would be like our playing an all-star team from twelve high schools in a big city. We beat them by eight points that night, and I was able to score twelve points in the game. We caught them on an especially bad night and were emotionally pretty high since we had not beaten them in four years.

Some of our better players included Billy Ray McGaugh (#25) who was our second leading scorer; Tommy Murphree (#22) who went on to a successful coaching career at Ouachita Baptist University; Max "Buddy" Barron (#26) who attended West Point after graduation and had a career in the Army, including a teaching post at West Point; and Tommy Stegall in the photo standing to the right of Tommy Murphree.

After graduating from high school, I attended the University of Arkansas in Fayetteville and thought I would try out for the Razorback basketball team as a walk-on. Glen Rose was the coach, and after one day of practice, I realized that those players were above my skill set. I decided it best to walk-off! That one year I had a growth spurt and gained fifteen pounds in weight and two inches in height. When I went home for our spring break, I ran into Coach Austin. When he saw my current size, he said jokingly, "Johnny, if you had been this big last year, we would have won the state championship!" Of course, he was kidding, but I loved the compliment. Incidentally I was known as "Johnny" by my teammates.

83. REVERSAL OF A TECHNICAL FOUL

A Foul Years Earlier is Remembered Prior to an Operation

Football was always my favorite sport, but there were several reasons I never tried out for either the junior high or high school teams. I was tall and skinny, and it seemed I could not gain enough weight despite eating as much as I possibly could. There was little emphasis then on strength training, so I was not particularly strong. I had to wear glasses, and without them, it would have been impossible to play football. Contact lenses were new and not adapted for sports, so whatever sports activity I participated, I had to wear my glasses.

Basketball and tennis were the two sports on which I focused during those years. I had discovered my skill level in tennis while attending a summer camp at Camp Stewart in southeast Texas when I was fourteen. I won both the singles and doubles titles for the camp, and from then on, I was hooked on tennis as a secondary sport, with basketball as my primary interest. It also worked well for me because basketball was a fall and winter sport and tennis was a spring sport.

I spent many hours practicing basketball during the junior high and senior high years, and I ultimately became a starter on the Wildcat squad in my senior year. I have many wonderful remembrances of that year and have written about some of them in "Wildcat Basketball." Although I was six feet two, I wasn't heavy enough or strong enough to be a very good rebounder. I played mostly on the perimeter as a shooting guard and seldom "mixed it up" underneath the basket. As a perimeter shooter, I didn't get many personal fouls and never fouled out of a game during the two years I was on the varsity squad. On one occasion I did get a technical foul, which is more serious than a regular foul. Two technical fouls and you are tossed out of the game.

There are various reasons for being assessed a technical foul, but the one I received was for making a smart aleck remark to the referee. He had called a regular foul on me which I didn't think I deserved, and I said something like, "That was a terrible call. I didn't even touch the guy, and you missed it!" The referee held his hands to signal a technical foul on me, which gave the opposing player two extra free throws. My coach Pel Austin was not at all pleased with me but left me in the game after a good scolding on the sidelines.

I remembered the incident well and also the official, who was a regular high school referee named Dub Martin. He was a native of El Dorado and well-known in the area for being a man of great character—an excellent, no-nonsense referee. He and his family were very active members of Marrable Hill Chapel under the pastorate of Brother Sam Shepperson. His son Charlie became a prominent Southern Baptist pastor. Years later I was privileged to serve on the staff for Brother Charlie Martin at the First Baptist Church of Indian Rocks in Largo, Florida.

As a general surgeon for almost twenty-nine years in El Dorado between 1971 and 1999, I had the privilege of serving many people with whom I had experiences during my formative years there. One of those patients was Dub Martin. He had an uncomplicated surgical problem which needed repair, and he came to me as a patient for that procedure. I had not seen him in years, but certainly knew about him and his reputation as a kind and godly man. I was pleased and honored he selected me for his operation and made it known to him how grateful I was for the trust.

The night before the procedure, I was visiting with him and explaining what he might expect during the operation and also the anticipated recovery time for such a procedure. I could tell by his demeanor I would be able to add some levity to the situation so I said, "Brother Dub, before I pray with you about the operation and your healing, may I ask you a personal question?" He said, "Sure Brother John, what is it?"

"You may not remember what happened thirty-five years ago, but in a basketball game the Wildcats were playing against Camden, you called a technical foul on me because you thought I was disrespecting your call of a foul on me. I got in serious trouble with Coach Austin over it, and I have never forgotten about it. Before I take you into the operating room and put you to sleep to do this operation, do you want to re-consider that technical foul?" I was grinning when I told him the account, and he knew I was having fun with him. I didn't expect his retort.

"I have often thought about that call Brother John," he said. "I was a referee for many years and made thousands of calls. In all those years I now believe this was the only call I made which was wrong, and right now I am reversing that technical foul!" he said laughingly. "It's never too late to ask forgiveness," we both said joyfully before we shook hands and prayed together for his healing.

Brother Dub healed nicely, recovered well, and I was set free from the stigma of a technical foul!! I just wish Coach Austin could have been there to hear it.

84. TRUCK AND TRAILER

Two Brothers Well Known by Townsfolk

There were a number of colorful characters who lived in El Dorado during my formative years, and they added their own flavor to the spice of life in this small South Arkansas town. Some of the ones who come to mind are James Mook, a close friend and high school classmate; Flying Saucer, whose real name I never knew; Donald Dollarhide, an acquaintance who worked at P. I. Lipsey's, a well-known hamburger joint; Tony the hot tamale man who pushed his tamale cart around town for over ten years; and Buzzy Sutherland, another friend and class mate, who was known for his fiery temperament, but who had a spiritual change and became a well-known pastor. And then there were Truck and Trailer, two of the most colorful men about town. I never knew them but heard stories of some of their exploits.

I don't know the first names of the Goodwin brothers, but only their nicknames of Truck and Trailer. They walked everywhere they went, because they didn't own an automobile and probably didn't know how to drive. I don't believe that they were ever employed for any length of time, so doubtless they couldn't afford the luxury of a car. They received their nicknames because wherever they were seen walking, Truck was always walking ahead of Trailer. Because their living conditions were probably sub-optimal, their personal hygiene suffered. I was told by a local merchant nicknamed "Perk" that you could usually smell Truck and Trailer before you saw them. This particular merchant owned a drug store on the square, an establishment which had had a small soda fountain serving lunchtime sandwiches and drinks. For a period of time, Truck and Trailer came daily to the store for coffee, usually between 11:00 and 11:30. As they sat at the counter, Perk noted that a few of his regular lunch customers would separate themselves as far as they could from the brothers. He said a few of his customers finally told him they would no longer come in for lunch if the brothers did not do something about their body odor. In as gentle and gracious manner as possible, he told the brother that they needed to bathe and use some type of deodorant before coming in for coffee, because their body odor was so offensive it was keeping some from enjoying their food. The brothers said they understood and consented to improve their personal hygiene.

They didn't come in for another week or so, but when they finally returned, Perk said he could smell them from ten feet away. He intercepted them before they were seated and told them in a firm but polite voice that he was unable to seat them because their odor was still too offensive. They left without argument, but were heard saying as they left, "What we thought about this place is true. They only allow big shots in here!"

Another story I heard about the brothers involved a court case in which they were seeking a judgment against an individual who had accidentally struck and injured Trailer with his automobile. Trailer sustained a broken leg requiring several months to heal. The accident occurred in the west side of town on a hill known locally as Goodwin Hill. The hill was not named for the brothers, but for Dr. Don Goodwin, who owned the land and had his veterinarian clinic there. The driver of the vehicle was also named Goodwin, but was not related to the two Goodwin brothers. The plaintiff, Trailer Goodwin, alleged that the driver of the car swerved off the road and side-swiped him causing the injury. The defendant, Mr. Goodwin, told the jurors that Trailer Goodwin was not paying attention and stepped out onto the road, and he could not avoid striking him. The lawyers for both parties were getting the Goodwin names all confused and especially because the accident occurred on Goodwin Hill. Finally, the judge asked the defendant the following question: "Mr. Goodwin, it is alleged you have poor eyesight and could not tell when your auto veered into Mr. Goodwin causing him to sustain a broken leg. Tell me, Mr. Goodwin, just how far can you see?" Mr. Goodwin thought a moment, scratched his head and said slowly, "Well Judge, I can see the moon." The judge said, "I've heard enough of this case. Judgment in favor of Mr. Goodwin!" When I heard the story from a relative of the judge, I never got it straight which one won.

85. AN IMPORTANT LESSON LEARNED FROM MRS. TURNER

One of Pop's Patients Taught Me about Patience

My dad (Pop) was a family doctor in a generation of physicians far removed from the present doctors. He learned many of his doctoring skills from his dad, Dr. J. A. Moore, who was a family doctor in South Arkansas from 1898 until his death in 1943. Medical technology in the first half of the twentieth century did not advance as rapidly as it did in the second half. The success of a medical practitioner was dependent on his interpersonal, relational skills and his ability to make an accurate diagnosis with only a few diagnostic tools for help. CAT and PET scans were unheard of, and even x-rays were not as widely used as now. Listening carefully to a patient's complaints was paramount and required unusual patience. When I entered medical school, I remember Pop's telling me, "Listen to what your patient is saying without interrupting much, and more often than not, they will tell you their diagnosis." He emphasized the critical importance of observation and the necessity of careful palpation while not overlooking the sense of smell. He said, "I can smell a person and diagnosis kidney failure without running one lab test!" I later discovered what he meant when I began treating people with renal failure.

Pop never had an unlisted telephone number. There are few if any current physicians who do not have unlisted numbers. He said he wanted his patients to be able to find him when they needed help, and that made an impression on me. I never had an unlisted number in the forty-six years I practiced medicine. It made an impression on Bubba also, because he practiced family medicine for fifty-four years, and his home phone was always listed. He would get twice as many medical calls at home as me, and I asked him once if he ever thought about an unlisted number. He answered the same thing as Pop: "I don't want a patient who needs me to be unable to call for help."

Pop had certain patients who called on the telephone at least once per day. Some called more than once. This was long before the invention of cellular phones, so he was contacted either on his office phone or on our home phone. The frequent callers to our home recognized my voice when I answered and would call me by name. Likewise, I could recognize many of them before they identified themselves and asked to speak to Dr. Moore. One of those regular callers was Mrs. Turner (not her real name), and her calls were regular and predictable.

Mrs. Turner knew our family always had our evening meal together at approximately 6:00 p.m. Pop was so busy and would leave for work so early each morning that the evening meal was the only time we were all together. It was not uncommon for him to go back to the hospital or make a house call following supper. When the phone rang in the evenings, usually my sister Marilyn or I would answer, hoping it was one of our friends calling. Most of our friends knew not to call around 6:00 because that was meal time. When Mrs. Turner made her evening call, Pop would usually be the one to answer.

On this particular evening at precisely 6:00, the phone rang and Pop answered. Mom, Marilyn, and I were seated at the table along with Pop, and our meal had already begun. By the tone of his voice and the words spoken, I could tell it was Mrs. Turner. He spoke to her in a kind and patient voice, and whatever he said seemed to resolve her particular problem that evening. When he hung up the receiver, I just couldn't resist saying what I had thought for a long time but had never spoken out loud for our family to hear. "I can't believe Mrs. Turner continues to call us at 6:00 every night knowing we are eating, and she is disturbing our meal." I continued with my indignant commentary by saying, "I doubt she has ever had anything really wrong other than being a needy, grouchy person!"

With my last words Pop held up his hand without speaking, and I knew this was his signal for me to be quiet and listen. He said, "I want you to know Mrs. Turner has put clothes on your back, food on our table, and kept you in school. Whatever problems she may have, I don't want you talking about her anymore." All I dared say was, "Yes sir." There was dead silence at the table when Pop said, "Now let's continue our meal."

As a result of Mrs. Turner's call that particular evening, I learned several important lessons, some of which I applied when I began my own medical practice. First, it was not my concern nor my right to comment on a person's medical condition unless I had first-hand knowledge of their problem. Those comments could then be discussed privately with the person or one of their immediate family members or another health care professional involved in their care. My personal opinions concerning the validity of a person's complaints must be kept to myself. Probably the most important lesson Pop (and Mrs. Turner) taught me that night was that I needed to listen more and speak less (Jas 1:19). I later met Mrs. Turner when I accompanied Pop on a house call, and she was very polite to me and glad I had come with Pop to see her. I was never able to tell her how she helped me become a more compassionate doctor in the years ahead.

86. WATER SKIING ON CALION LAKE

A Fun Outing with Friends Almost Turns Tragic

Calion Lake is well-known to South Arkansans but is little-known to folks outside of the area. Perhaps the reason is because the lake is relatively small and there is not much room for anything but fishing. Over the past forty to fifty years, bass fishing, which attracts many fishermen, has not been very good in the lake so it is not on the radar of the serious bass fisherman. The lake is only ten miles north of El Dorado, and, because it is so convenient to the locals, it is the recreational spot for many. At different seasons bream fishing is very good, and I have heard from some that white perch fishing is also good.

During the years I was a teen and always looking for something new and exciting, Calion Lake presented an option. Water skiing didn't sound too exciting because there were lots of stumps in the water, and the lake was not wide nor long enough to ski for very long stretches without having to turn around. Also, none of my good buddies had one of those sleek and speedy ski boats, so it seemed that skiing on Calion, or any lake for that matter, was not an option.

My closest friend was Eric Richardson, and the two of us spent many hours during the summer months camping, hunting in the woods, and fishing on the Ouachita River with its sloughs and tributaries. Many times, I had no idea where we were, but I depended on Eric and his knowledge and expertise to keep us from getting lost or in serious trouble. GPS technology had not been developed, so knowledge of the rivers, lakes, and large tracts of land were very important.

Although Eric did not have a ski boat like a few of our wealthier acquaintances, he did have a very nice flat-bottom, aluminum boat with a eighteen-horse-power Evinrude with which we safely and quickly navigated the waterways. We had considered giving a try at water-skiing behind his boat but had never acted on it until one beautiful Saturday morning when the weather was perfect. The closest body of water for excellent skiing was D'Arbonne Lake in Farmerville, Louisiana, but it was at least an hour's drive away, and Calion seemed like a very good option for our initial skiing adventure. We had heard that most of the stumps in the middle of the lake had been removed, which made if safer and easier to maneuver in tight turns. We also heard that a ski jump had been added in the middle of the lake for the really adventuresome skier, but this option was completely off the table for us.

A story which was circulating said that Frank Thibault Jr. had attempted going over the jump while skiing barefoot. Frank, who was a year younger than us, was well-known for some of his antics, and the story didn't surprise us. I never checked with Frank to verify the story, but we believed it was true.

Eric's next-door neighbor, Jimmy Moody, was with us that morning, and, although he was a bit reluctant at first, he was in complete agreement with our plan. Jimmy had friends with nicer ski rigs so he was a more accomplished skier than either Eric or I. In those teen years, we were each skinny and didn't believe our individual weights were too great to prevent the relatively small motor from pulling us behind the boat. When we arrived at Calion, we launched the boat with ease. Neither Eric nor I had any experience skiing with a single ski, and although Jimmy knew how to slalom ski, we believed the motor was not powerful enough to pull even a skinny slalom skier.

I remember only one or two other boats with skiers that morning, but we still were going to be cautious and conservative because of the small size of the lake. There would certainly be no attempts at going over the ski jump! None of the three of us were as brave as Frank Thibault and skiing bare-foot was totally out of the question.

Jimmy went first since he was the "expert," and with Eric driving the boat and me as spotter, Jimmy was successfully pulled up on the skis. What great fun it was that morning with the wind in our faces and the sun on our backs, flying along at ten to fifteen miles per hour! Despite our small size, the speed generated at full throttle was barely enough to keep us up on skis. No matter–we were successfully skiing despite the fact we looked the part of three rednecks skiing behind a fishing boat!

I was next and was able to get upright on my first attempt. I made a couple of rounds on the lake, even though I was pretty sure Eric was making more turns than necessary trying to get me to fall. Eric was mischievous enough to do that. When it came Eric's turn to ski, I was the designated driver. I had previous experience with the boat and motor from many of our fishing and camping outings.

I got Eric up on skis on the first attempt, and things were going smoothly as I made a couple of good turns while Eric stayed up. What happened next is a little blurred, but here is my recollection. The motor began to sputter while losing power and speed. As we slowed, Eric sank into the water twelve to fifteen feet behind the boat. With Jimmy in the front, I began pulling on the rope crank to restart the engine while Eric remained in his position behind the boat. I assume that a spark from the ignition and a little spilled fuel in the bottom of the boat were the culprits, but a rather large fire ignited in the floor of the boat very near the large gas can! Jimmy would have no part of a possible rescue attempt, so he dove into the water swimming as fast as possible to get some separation before the expected explosion. I figured since I was now captain of the ship, I had to at least try to save the boat. There was a lot of screaming and shouting while Eric used the ski rope to pull the boat closer. Without climbing into the boat, he was able to reach the gas connect from the motor to the gas can and we moved the gas can as far away from the flame as possible. We were able to extinguish the fire with water from the lake while stability and a measure of calmness was restored. Jimmy stayed afloat about ten feet from the boat and swam back when the fire was extinguished. A nearby boat with skiers was watching this scene and came over pull us back to shore. We were glad we still had a boat left to pull.

We never blamed Jimmy for abandoning the boat when he saw the flames, and, in fact, I was about ready to dive into the water with him when Eric came to the rescue. I believe his fear of losing his boat and motor gave him the extra motivation to attempt the rescue. We were all glad he did. The boat and motor survived to run once again, but they were never used again for skiing to my knowledge. Besides, within a year or so, we had all gained too much weight for this rig.

87. AN ELVIS SIGHTING IN EL DORADO

An Icon Performs Early in His Career

I was never a fan of Elvis Presley nor of the style of music he and so many others like him made popular in the fifties and sixties. He was at the forefront of a music revolution which swept the nation and the world, and his music is still being listened to and enjoyed sixty-plus years later. Living in Branson, Missouri, we are annually treated to shows featuring Elvis tribute artists and even Elvis look-alike contests, none of which Cathy nor I have seen.

Elvis died tragically on August 16, 1977, of a reported pain-medication overdose, but there are still some who believe his death report was a hoax. There have been reported "Elvis sightings" every year since his death, but these sightings are considered on the same order as UFO sightings and reports of appearances of Big Foot. But, I am able to report an actual Elvis sighting in El Dorado, Arkansas, in 1955.

I was a sophomore in high school and was at the school early one spring evening practicing for a Latin play. I was such a nerd then I took Latin as an elective subject taught by Mrs. W. E. Durrett. The play practice ended at approximately 8:30 p.m., and several of us were leaving the campus and walking together to our vehicles. Our path took us past the auditorium, and, as we neared it, we noticed a large number of parked cars and heard music coming from the stage. I asked one of my fellow Latin nerds what was happening, and he said it must be the concert scheduled for that night. I couldn't imagine what kind of concert this might be in our auditorium, because the music I was hearing was what we used to call honky-tonk. If one drove past The Howdy Club on East Hillsboro in the late hours on a Saturday night, the type of music one would hear would be the same we were hearing from the Wildcat auditorium stage.

With our curiosity piqued, several of us peered through a window at the stage and saw a most unusual sight. There was a band consisting of several guitar players, a bass player, a drummer, and the main attraction at center stage. The performer was of medium height, with long black hair combed into a duck-tail, and wearing a green shirt and purple pants. His appearance was certainly unusual, but his music style and bodily gyrations were something I had never before seen on stage. We listened for a few minutes, and my only comment to my friends when we left was, "I don't think he'll get very far with that kind of performance. Does anyone know his name?" Someone responded with, "I think it's Elvis something or other." I had never known anyone with the name Elvis.

Later the same evening about 11:00, while driving north on North West Avenue, we spotted an individual standing on the street corner holding a guitar case. As we got closer, I noticed the green shirt and purple pants and recognized the performer we had seen just an hour or so before. His location on North West Avenue was near 5th Street where the Canary Court used to be. It appeared he was waiting for his ride or hitch hiking, but we didn't have any reason to pick him up since we were not going his way.

About a year later, that purple-pants performer recorded "Blue Suede Shoes" and the career of Elvis Presley began to sky-rocket to unprecedented heights. Few performers in the history of popular music have even come close to his world-wide popularity. Instead of calling his musical style "honky-tonk," it became known as "rock and roll," and his gyrations on stage were widely mimicked.

Elvis performed on one other occasion in El Dorado before he became so popular. He appeared at Memorial Stadium as part of a larger performing group, and I have no knowledge of this one. I do regret I didn't at least pull over that night at the Canary Court to introduce myself and inquire if he needed a place to stay for the night. I can't even imagine what my parents would have said had he accepted. Who knows, he might have offered me a spot in his band since I was a fledgling guitar player? But then in those days when I had hair, I never could get it to combed into a duck-tail!

PS 1: So much for my prediction concerning the future of the purple-pants performer I saw on stage that spring evening!

PS 2: That course in Latin helped me more in my subsequent medical training than any other subject I took in high school.

88. A 1950S CULINARY TOUR OF EL DORADO

Favorite Eating Places in a Small Southern Town

Dairyette, El Dorado, Arkansas

Life in middle America in the 1950s was care-free and casual. It was a wonderful time to be a teen because people were positive, our nation had survived and won the greatest war we had ever fought (World War II), the economy was rebuilding, and the future looked bright. Yet I don't remember feeling all that positive about my future since I was an ordinary teenager with what I considered major concerns for the present.

My anxieties centered on my hair (Did I have the right amount of Butch Wax applied to keep my flat-top upright?); my skin (Did I have any new and undetected pimples which would permanently scar my face?); and my size (Was there anything I could do to add pounds to my skinny frame?). Like many of my teen friends, I also wasn't very happy about my hometown, El Dorado, Arkansas, because it seemed so boring with "nothing to do." I dreamed of living in a big city like Little Rock or Dallas where life would be full of excitement and adventure on a daily basis. Despite these huge potentials for life failure, there were some very positive elements to life in El Dorado, and I was aware of them and grateful. One positive feature was the seemingly large number of great places to eat.

North West Avenue (known then as "The Strip") was the address of many of the finest dining choices El Dorado offered in the fifties. The favorite hangout for teens and young adults was the Dairyette, located on a large lot on the east side of the street where Mellor Park Mall now sits. The aging drive-in was owned by Jack Smith, to whom I was never introduced, but am certain I recognized back then. There was a pinball machine inside and a jukebox connected to outside speakers, which were constantly blaring. The burgers and fries were outstanding, but the attraction was the crowds and not the food. Seemingly the coolest teens and young adults stopped by each day if just for a short visit. Someone told me the Dairyette was the one place in town to get "dope." I believed they were talking about marijuana, but I never saw or smelled anyone smoking it. This was at least ten years prior to marijuana use becoming widespread. The two biggest vices for teens in the fifties were cigarettes and beer, and one couldn't buy beer at the Dairyette.

Further out North West Ave. toward Smackover was my favorite restaurant, the Old Hickory. It was located on the land where Oriental Gardens now sits. The restaurant was owned by the Parker family, and their daughter Patty was in my high school class of 1957. I don't remember ever seeing her there, because I was looking for those delicious barbecue-beef sandwiches with their famous baked beans in signature brown bowls. The Old Hickory was one of the few restaurants in town with curb service, so my family seldom dined inside. One could buy bottles of their barbecue sauce and replicate the Old Hickory taste at home. However, no matter how well Mom prepared barbecue sandwiches, they just never tasted as good as the Parker's. (I never said those words to Mom.)

Driving south from there on North West Avenue was the best place for ice cream, the Dairy Queen, which stood on the property where Andy's Restaurant now sits. The Frazier family owned the restaurant, and their only daughter Dixie was also a member of my graduating high school class. Mr. and Mrs. Frazier were always friendly to me, and when I happened to be alone in the restaurant for a burger or a milk shake, the conversation usually centered on what Dixie was thinking and how well (or even how poorly) she was doing in school. This is the first restaurant in which I experienced soft-serve ice cream, and to this day I'm convinced it was the best. One of their chocolate milk shakes was a supreme treat, and with as many of them as I drank, I'm surprised I was so skinny then.

When our family was hungry for a steak or a hamburger steak, our number-one choice was Lloyd's Stadium Drive Inn. Located on North West Avenue (Where else?) directly across the street from the Boys Club baseball field, the restaurant was owned by Lloyd McCarty who was a long-time pal of Pop. Lloyd had learned to cook steaks and burgers on the locally-famous "Hamburger Row" during the El Dorado oil boom days of the 1920s. He was relatively short in height (shorter than the Moore men, who were all over 6 feet) and had a particularly characteristic shuffle to his gait. I never saw him without his signature, white, butcher's apron with the large greasy spot in front. Pop said the shuffle was characteristic of all the cooks on Hamburger Row, but I never understood the reason for it.

Lloyd's steaks were absolutely the best tasting in town. The hamburger steak was also a favorite. He featured a steak sandwich which he called the "Jack Perry Special," and one of those three items were my only choices. Obviously, the sandwich was the only item which Mr. Perry ordered, and he was a frequent enough customer to have his name attached to it. Pop always said the key to the special taste of the meats at Lloyd's was the seasoning of the grill itself, which never looked clean to me.

Pop knew what he was talking about because he had once cooked for and even owned a "joint" on Hamburger Row when he was a young adult in his twenties. One other thing I remember about Lloyd's Drive Inn is that he had a "room in the back" for only a few of his adult men friends. The doors to the room were always shut, so I never entered. Pop said the room was where a select few men could eat and drink liquor. It was against the law to serve liquor in a restaurant, but apparently Lloyd bent the rules for some of his buddies, who reportedly were some of the elected high officials of Union County.

When our family dined out on Sunday, our usual choice was the Garrett Hotel dining room. Located on the block now occupied by The First National Bank, it was one of only two downtown hotels. They both opened in the 1920s during the days of the oil boom. One thing I remember about the hotel besides the dining room food is the lobby, which had a large screen television (fourteen inch), which could pick up channel KNOE from Monroe, Louisiana, and occasionally on a clear day, the Little Rock channel KATV. There was a gigantic antenna on the roof of the hotel, which allowed for such good reception. The dining room featured a number of delicious entrées, but our favorite selection was their chicken and dressing. The giblet gravy had a certain unique flavor. Their yeast rolls were outstanding, and no other restaurant in which I dined could come close to their taste. I could easily eat four of them, and if my sister Marilyn wasn't too hungry, I could get one or two of hers. Even though Mom wanted me to gain weight, she said too many yeast rolls were "not good for my stomach." I never questioned her wisdom on this, but would try to eat a couple of extra ones while she was not watching.

I don't recall eating out as a primary source of delight as a teen, but in thinking and writing about some of my culinary experiences, I realize I gained early expertise in the art of "fine dining" on North West Avenue. Neither Cathy nor I enjoy fancy restaurants now and are always looking for ordinary cafes or delis with extraordinary dishes. I'm still looking for another joint like Lloyd's. I would recognize any cook with a shuffle like his.

89. THE SPUDNUT SHOP

The Most Famous Donut in El Dorado

If you ask someone who has never been to El Dorado what they think about a Spudnut, you will likely get a quizzical look and a remark something like this: "I've never heard of a Spudnut. What in the world is it?" But ask anyone who has been to the Spudnut Shop in this South Arkansas town the same question, and their response will likely be, "There is no better doughnut in the world, and if they weren't so fattening, I'd eat them all the time!" For those of us who have lived in El Dorado and moved away, when we return to visit family or friends, one of the places we want to visit again will be this small, locally-owned franchise on West Faulkner Street.

Spudnuts were introduced to the citizens of El Dorado in the late 1940s by the Stringfellow family. Daisy Stringfellow and her husband Howard were travelling out west and happened to have one of these unusually named doughnuts in a newly-opened franchise and decided this might be a good investment for them.

The initial franchise was begun in 1940 in Salt Lake City, Utah, by the Pelton brothers. They had discovered that by using potato flour as a base ingredient, a very tasty doughnut with an almost addictive quality could be made. A franchise could be purchased early on from the Pelton brothers for $1500, which included equipment and floor plans. After the Stringfellows purchased the franchise, Daisy managed the shop because

Howard was employed at Monsanto Chemical Company and did not have the time necessary to get a new business started. They hired one employee, Bud McCann, who became the on-site operating manager after he learned the formula from the Peltons and was able to make the Spudnuts quickly and efficiently. The original store was on Oak Street adjacent to Rumph Mortuary, within two blocks of the new Barton Junior High School, and approximately six blocks from El Dorado High School on Northwest Avenue. In those days there was an open campus policy for lunch and large numbers of students chose the Spudnut Shop for a quick lunch of a hamburger, fries, and a Coke, with a Spudnut or two for dessert. Business was booming from the beginning, since this was the only doughnut shop in town.

Beginning at 3:00 a.m., Bud began preparing the hundreds of dozens of doughnuts needed for that day. By the time the shop opened at 5:00, he would have enough Spudnuts for the early morning customers but had to continue cutting, frying, glazing, and drying many more dozens for customers throughout the day. The store was open every day except Sunday. I once asked Mr. Stringfellow approximately how many Spudnuts he sold each day, to which he replied, "When the refineries in El Dorado were at full capacity back in the 1950s, we made and sold twelve hundred dozen Spudnuts one Saturday!" When one considers that one man was responsible for making them all, this is a staggering number.

In the early 1970s, Howard retired from Monsanto and could give more time to the business operation. His function seemed to be one of interacting with the regular customers and the newer ones who might stop in for a breakfast treat or perhaps a quick, light lunch. I always enjoyed talking with Mr. Stringfellow (I never called him Howard) because he was never at a loss for words and usually had a good story from the past. My favorite Uncle Dick (Smith) and he were good friends, and I could usually get him to tell me something about Uncle Dick I could use to tease him when I visited with him at H & V Sporting Goods.

The Stringfellows sold the business to their daughter and son-in-law, Nancy and William Varnell, in the mid-1970s, and the two of them managed the business until only recently. Bud McCann continued working another ten years or so until his health caused him to finally retire. Although I'm sure the Spudnuts tasted exactly the same, it just didn't seem right not seeing Bud over in the corner working his magic.

When Cathy and I had friends visit from out of town, we would frequently get a dozen Spudnuts for at least one of the breakfasts we enjoyed with our company. During the decades of the eighties and nineties when we were making annual mission trips to Eastern Europe, we invited a number of pastors and wives to El Dorado, and some of them came to have surgical procedures done. Each one of them got to enjoy a few Spudnuts during their visit and recovery. One couple, Costel and Mia Oglice, who are Romanians and missionaries for Kay Arthur's Ministry in Eastern Europe, always asked upon seeing us in Budapest or Salzburg, "Did you bring with you any "Spad-a-nuts?!"

There is another Spudnut store in Magnolia, only thirty miles away, and these two may be the only remaining ones in the South if not in the country. I have never visited the Magnolia store, nor have I desired to go there for a Spudnut. The one in El Dorado has always been special, and in spite of the fact now I might eat only one or two Spudnuts in an entire year, I still love them, and they are a part of my happy memories of growing up in El Dorado.

Note: Some of the historical information for this remembrance was obtained from articles written by Joan Hershberger, staff writer for *The El Dorado News Times.*

90. "I'VE KILLED THE MAYOR"

A Medical Student Error Has Consequences

Between my sophomore and junior years in medical school, I had the privilege of working in the medical office of Drs. Eldon and Julian Fairley in Osceola, Arkansas. I was there as part of the school's Preceptor program, which gave students hands-on experience working with family practitioners in small towns throughout the state. Our responsibilities as students included mostly observation, but, depending on the doctor and the trust they had in a particular student, they would allow more active participation in patient care. Both Osceola doctors were aware that my dad and brother were doctors and had taught me to do certain things most students at my stage in training had not done. I demonstrated to their satisfaction that I was very capable of suturing most lacerations.

One morning a patient came to the office needing repair of a minor laceration to his left index finger. He had been sharpening his pocket knife and carelessly cut his finger when he became distracted. The patient was in his mid-forties, of average height, but weighing about two hundred seventy-five pounds. He was a cotton farmer, so he was quite strong, with broad shoulders. He also happened to be the mayor of Osceola, so was well-known and beloved in the community. When Dr. Eldon examined the wound, he announced to the patient, "Mr. Mayor, we have the honor of having Dr. Moore with us, and he happens to be an expert in laceration repair. He has graciously agreed to repair your finger!" With such an introduction, I knew I had to do my best suturing job on this dignitary from Osceola.

The nurse set up the suture tray with everything I needed, and I had the mayor sit on the examining table without lying down. This was a critical error in judgment, one I never made again in my forty-seven years of medical practice. I took the syringe with the local anesthetic and began injecting the small laceration after I had very carefully cleaned the wound. I was holding his finger with the fingers of my left hand while numbing the wound, all the while telling him that this part would only take a few seconds. I was not looking at the mayor's face but was intent on getting the finger injected. I noticed he was gradually pulling the finger from my grasp, and I told him, "Just relax, it's almost numb." As the force of the pull increased, I looked into his face, saw his eyes rolling back, and heard him moan and gasp. I was so startled that I released my hold on his finger and quickly grasped his shirt as he was falling backwards off the table. My hold on his index finger was the only thing keeping him upright. He was so large, his weight pulled me with him off the other side of the table, and our combined size knocked over the IV stand and the light stand with a loud, reverberating crash. I could only think as I was falling over the table, "I've just killed the mayor of Osceola, and my career as a doctor is over!"

When I landed atop the mayor, he fortunately began to awaken from his faint and groggily asked what had happened. Dr. Fairley quickly entered the room to see this pitiful scene and teasingly said, "Dr. Moore, this is not quite what I had in mind for your suture job on the mayor!" I was very thankful the mayor was still alive, and I had the opportunity to continue my career in medicine. We examined him to make certain he had not sustained any injuries from the fall, and he was fine except for a bruised ego. My ego had also suffered from the fall. I did have enough presence of mind to repair the laceration after we got the mayor back onto the table, but I don't think it was my best suturing job. I'm confident the mayor didn't care, and he seemed glad to leave the office.

There was not another time in my long career as a surgeon whenever I sutured a finger laceration that I didn't remember this incident, and I never allowed another patient to sit up while I injected their finger. I did have a few other patients faint under different circumstances, but at least I didn't fall on top of them!

91. "IS YOU READY?"

The Fastest Labor and Delivery of my Career

Medical school is full of many surprises for every student from the lowly freshman to the "sophisticated and highly trained" senior. Some of the surprises are not very pleasant or comfortable while others are delightful, especially when remembering them years later. Some of the most interesting and wonderful training experiences happened for me when I was serving in the Preceptor program during the summer between my sophomore and junior years.

The University of Arkansas School for Medical Sciences instituted the Preceptor program in an effort to give medical students practical experience with family practitioners in small communities throughout the state. The students spent six weeks shadowing their appointed preceptors, while learning first-hand what it was like to treat patients. Up to this point in our training, we had spent most of our time in the class rooms and very little time with patients. Even though my dad and brother were doctors, and I had spent a lot of time in their offices, I was excited to get this different practice perspective. I was assigned to Drs. Eldon and Julian Fairley two brothers in Osceola, Arkansas, who had been in practice together for over fifteen years. Osceola lies in the heart of cotton-growing country in Northeast Arkansas and the cultural and agricultural environments are totally different from those of my home in the timberlands of South Arkansas where oil production and refining are a way of life.

Their practice was unique for many reasons. Dr. Eldon was a bachelor who was totally dedicated to his medical practice. His office hours were from 8:00 to 5:00 every day, including Saturdays and Sundays. The only time he took a break from the practice was to attend Sunday school and church. Dr. Julian was married, so his hours in the office did not include Saturday afternoons or Sundays. Both men made house calls and admitted patients to the hospital so they had to balance their office hours accordingly. Their patient population included a large number of black people because of the demographics of the area. These were the years of racial segregation in the South, and they had "Whites Only" and "Colored Only" waiting rooms. Since many people who lived in Mississippi County had incomes below the national poverty level, the office fees at the Fairley Clinic were extremely low compared to those in other towns in the state. They charged three dollars for an office visit, and, if an injection were given, the total charge was five dollars.

Another interesting element of their practice was that they delivered babies in their clinic. They had a special room designated for clinic deliveries, and they would deliver as many as ten babies per month in the office. The charge for a mid-wife delivery was twenty-five dollars, and the Fairley's thought their services justified a higher charge since they were doctors, so their fee for a clinic delivery was thirty-five dollars. The day I arrived, I was told I would be in charge of clinic deliveries, an assignment which both excited and terrified me. I didn't have extensive experience delivering babies. In fact, I had delivered only one baby at the medical center, and it was an uncomplicated delivery. The Fairleys assured me they would be within a few feet of the delivery room to give encouragement and help if needed.

It was about 4:00 p.m. on this particular Sunday, and the clinic staff including Dr. Eldon had left for the day since there were no more patients to be seen. I was alone in the library reading when I looked out of the window and saw a woman walking by herself toward the clinic backdoor. As I walked toward the door, I heard her knock. When I opened it, there stood a black lady in her mid-thirties, obviously pregnant and appearing to be in a hurry. She said, "Is you the doctor?" "Yes ma'am," I responded. "You better hurry!" I didn't have time to call Dr. Fairley for assistance.

I quickly took her into the delivery room which was next to the back door and helped her onto the table. As I was getting her prepped for the delivery, I asked her how many babies she had had, to which she responded, "This will make number eight." When I had the sterile drape in place and took my seat on the exam stool, she asked the important question, "Is you ready?" When I answered, "Yes ma'am," I noticed that she held her breath and pushed down as hard as she could. Her eighth delivery proceeded very quickly and could not have been any easier, both for her and for her young "doctor." As I was tending to the healthy baby, the mother asked if she could go to the rest room. I helped her there holding onto her with my right hand while holding the baby in the other arm.

I went back to the delivery room and got the baby cleaned and powdered while he calmed down from his initial crying. He was beginning to get used to his new environment and needed some rest from the ordeal he had just endured. I filled out his birth certificate and walked to the rest room door, and I asked the mother for his name to add to the certificate. "I'm calling him James," she said, "and would you mind calling me a cab?" I assisted her back to the delivery room where she held James for the first time, and they immediately bonded. I had her sign the birth certificate, and she paid me thirty-five dollars thus completing the business side of the whole transaction. The cab arrived and I helped her get into it with James, and they left for their home where presumably they would be greeted by seven excited siblings. I assumed since the father did not accompany her, he was no longer in the home. I happened to look at my watch, and the entire process from the initial back door meeting to the awaiting cab took a grand total of forty-five minutes!

For some strange reason I felt I had done a full day's work in that forty-five-minute span. I know I had just experienced something very few other medical students had. I was extremely glad I was training to become a doctor and delighted they had assigned me to the Fairley clinic for this once-in-a-life-time experience. Since this unusual experience in Osceola, I have always tried my best to "be ready!"

92. ONE NIGHT AT THE RACKENSACK

Playing and Singing at a Folk Society

The Rackensack Society is a folklore organization which began in Stone County, Arkansas (Mountain View), in the early 1960s. One of the founders who lived there and was a driving force in the organization was Jimmy Driftwood. He was a popular folk musician and song writer who gave us several nationally-recognized songs including "The Battle of New Orleans" and "Tennessee Stud." The purpose of The Rackensack was to preserve the folk music of the people of Arkansas, particularly people of the mountainous north central area. A year or so after the founding of the chapter in Mountain View, a second Rackensack group was formed in Little Rock under the leadership of George Fischer, a well-known political cartoonist.

When I entered medical school in 1960, I was very proud of the Gibson J-45 guitar Pop had recently purchased for me. He was not a musician and definitely not interested in the folk music I loved to play and sing. I enjoyed bluegrass and also the type of folk music heard from the Kingston Trio, who had just become nationally popular. I learned to play the guitar in high school, and by 1960, I had at least four years of experience in playing and singing. Pop told me when he paid the exorbitant price of one hundred and twenty-five dollars for the Gibson, "I'm getting you this fancy guitar for use in a backup career in case you don't make it as a doctor."

It wasn't long after school began when, on a Saturday evening sitting and jamming with a few students in the lounge of the Jeff Banks Dormitory, I met a classmate from West Memphis named Burt Renager. Burt was a pretty good ukulele player, and we knew the lyrics to many of the same songs. He could sing melody, and I thought I could sing pretty good bluegrass tenor, so we quickly became a duo. Our dorm rooms were so small they were not suitable for jamming, so when we decided to play, we would go to the large lounge with a piano and lots of comfortable chairs and couches. After one or two songs, we could draw a crowd rather quickly. Neither Burt nor I were as good as we thought we were, but we had lots of fun, and our friends seemed to enjoy it. Burt loved bluegrass music as much as I, and we learned a bunch of Flatt and Scruggs songs from albums we owned.

Burt and I had heard about the folk music society Rackensack, which met in the evening once a week at the Arkansas Art Center in MacArthur Park. We were told the program was open to anyone who loved to play and listen to folk music, and everyone was encouraged to bring their instruments and participate. That sounded like a venue in which we could showcase our much-heralded talents, so, in 1963, in the fall of my senior year, we ventured over to the park. Our greatest critics up to this point were mostly tone-deaf medical students. The evening of the meeting we were greeted by several officials of the Rackensack, and when they saw we were carrying instruments, they told us we could be first on the program since none of the other participants had arrived. We took our place on stage and tuned our instruments awaiting the official opening. Burt announced that our first number would be "Heaven," and that was his only introductory remark. It was a song we had heard on a Flatt and Scruggs album and was well suited for our playing and singing style. As I recall Burt did not play an instrument that night, so we sang only to the accompaniment of my guitar. We did a good job remembering all the lyrics and the blending of our voices that evening was better than usual. I was pleased when we finished the song, and we received a hearty applause. I stepped back from the microphone to give Burt room to announce the next number when the program director said, "Since this is your first appearance, we ask the performers to give some background of their songs, such as the writer of the song and what inspired them to compose the number." I was stunned thinking we would have to tell them we simply learned the song from a record album and had no idea about the origin. Burt was not the least bit fazed and immediately launched into the following explanation: "This song is almost a hundred years old having been written right after the Civil War." I couldn't believe what I was hearing and thought at any moment Burt would say he was just kidding, but he continued his account: "The author is unknown but he was imprisoned in Tennessee awaiting execution by hanging for some crime, which could have been desertion from the army or horse theft. As he was thinking about his life and remembering what his dear old mother had taught him about what heaven was like and how he would one day go there, he took a piece of coal off the floor of the prison and scribbled the words of this song. At some later time, an unknown individual joined the words on the prison wall to a melody, and thus was born the song we just performed." The members of the audience seemed to be nodding their heads in approval of Burt's explanation, and I nodded right along with them.

That night I learned several things. Burt is never caught off-guard with the lack of a story and is certainly not intimidated by a crowd of strangers in his story-telling. I also learned to never perform in a venue until I have checked out what they are expecting. From this point forward, Burt always introduced any songs we performed together, just in case an explanation of the song was required. We never performed again at the Rackensack, and I don't think we were greatly missed.

PS: I think we had other songs prepared for that evening, but I can't remember how Burt introduced them. I'm sure they were just as colorful and believable!

93. THE TUXEDOED PREACHER

Attending a Church with an Unusual Preacher

In the course of my spiritual journey, I have had the privilege of hearing some of the best preaching in the world delivered by some of the most wonderful men. I wish I could testify I have always sought to obey the challenges and heed the warnings of these great men of God. There were times I listened with a hungry heart, but also times when I was either a seeker living in disobedience or a believer with a cold and uncaring attitude. The first thirty-six years of my life, I was definitely in the seeker category.

When I was twelve years old, on Easter Sunday I walked down the aisle at First Baptist Church, El Dorado, and asked to be accepted into membership of this great church. While it is true that I wanted to please my parents, which I did, it was more important for me to do exactly what my good friend Richard (Bussey) Crawford had just done. I was soon baptized, which I thought at the time forever sealed my standing as a Christian and gave me the assurance of an eternity in heaven.

My church attendance was regular when I was living at home because I wanted to be with my buddies, most of whom were members of First Baptist. During the college years, my attendance was very sporadic, and I was not at all satisfied with First Baptist Church in Fayetteville. I thought the pastor was too harsh in his attitude towards the sinful behaviors so common among college students. I was more comfortable with the First Methodist Church, but was still only an occasional attendee there. It was important to me to report to my parents I was attending church somewhere. In medical school in Little Rock, I was even less inclined to receive any spiritual training at church, so I often excused myself with "I'm just too busy."

When I moved to Atlanta to begin my internship, I had drifted so far from any spiritual enrichment that I never considered church attendance. This was before I met a beautiful young woman named Cathy Young from Fort Lauderdale. On my first date with her, she told me how important faith was in her life, and I decided to take her to church the following Sunday. I definitely wanted her to believe faith was also important to me despite the fact my actions proved otherwise. I can't remember the church we attended, but it was probably a Baptist church. My attention and focus were on her and not on any preacher.

At some point in our dating relationship, it was suggested we might enjoy attending the Second Ponce De Leon Baptist Church on Peachtree Street because of the unusual preacher there. His name was Dr. Monroe F. Swilley, and we discovered he had been pastor of the church for over twenty years. There were two things unusual about him. First, he had the courage of his convictions because in 1957 when racial tensions were escalating all over the South, he joined with eighty other Atlanta ministers to sign the Manifesto on Racial Beliefs. This document clearly stated their collective opposition to racial segregation and violence and admonished all Atlanta residents to obey the civil rights laws implementing integration. This was a brave action for these men in those times. The second unusual thing about him was that he preached wearing a cutaway tuxedo. I had never seen a pastor wear such elegant attire. As I recall, he had grey spats on his black shoes.

My parents were eager to meet Cathy when she and I became serious in our intentions to marry, and they scheduled a weekend trip to Atlanta from El Dorado. One of the activities Cathy and I planned for all of us was to attend church to allow them see and hear this extraordinary preacher who "wears a tuxedo." As we took our seats at the beginning of the service and the pastor appeared, Pops said, "Why that's ole Monroe!" I said, "Pop, do you really know him?" "Of course, I know him, he's one of the Swilley boys from El Dorado!" I was stunned at this revelation but not as surprised as I might have been since I already thought Pop knew just about everybody. Following the service, we made our way to the front, and Dr. Swilley immediately recognized Pop, and they had a reunion of sorts. Of course, Dr. Swilley had no way of previously connecting me to my El Dorado heritage.

Knowing Dr. Swilley was from El Dorado perhaps caused us to attend church more regularly following our meeting and introduction, but a real and lasting spiritual change came to Cathy and me years later. We now know and understand faithful church attendance does not make one a Christian. Salvation is based entirely on a personal relationship with the

Lord Jesus Christ. One doesn't need to have a pastor who wears a tuxedo, although it is unique. One does need a faithful preacher of the Word of God, and also one who has the courage of his convictions to tell everyone including college kids how to act and live rightly.

94. REMEMBRANCE OF "SLOW DRAG"

A Jazz Icon Has His Operation at Charity Hospital

For over a hundred and seventy-five years, Charity Hospital of New Orleans was one of the premier hospitals in the country. Free medical care was provided there for any resident in the New Orleans area who couldn't afford care in a private hospital. In addition, Charity Hospital was the primary teaching hospital for LSU and Tulane Medical Schools. Pop took his postgraduate training there in the mid 1930s, and because he told me so many stories of his experiences, I set my sights on also training at Charity.

I began my surgical residency in 1965, the month before Cathy and I were married, and we spent the next four years living in New Orleans. I was thrilled to have been accepted into the LSU Surgical program, and although we are both loyal Razorback fans, the LSU program was much better suited to me than Tulane's. We had to tolerate a considerable amount of ribbing from loyal LSU fans, but I suppose we dispensed about as much competitive guff as we received!

In any residency training, the younger surgeons are given progressively more authority and opportunities as their judgment and surgical experience increases. By the time one enters the third year of training, he becomes the primary surgeon on a surgical ward consisting of about twenty-five patients. As a senior resident (third and fourth year), he does the more complicated procedures such as gall bladder and cancer surgery, and he delegates the less complicated procedures such as hernia repairs and amputations to the junior residents (first and second year). Because Charity Hospital served both the LSU and Tulane Medical Schools, patients who were designated as "emergency admissions" were admitted to the LSU service every other night. This system of emergency admissions worked well most of the time, but there were a few instances when the system broke down. If a patient had an undesirable problem, or if he was a particularly undesirable person, the emergency physician on the Tulane service might give that individual some medications to temporarily help and then say to him, "Be sure to return tomorrow so we can see if you are making progress."

I always considered the LSU admitting doctors to be more compassionate, not inclined to "slough patients" as this practice was called.

When I was in the middle of my third year, a particular patient with a tumor in his stomach was admitted to my ward. His name caught my attention because he had a distinct Cajun name, Alcide Pavageau. Because Mr. Pavageau had suffered a twenty-five-pound weight loss over the previous several months, the diagnosis was likely cancer of the stomach. Following appropriate pre-operative testing, it was clear he needed an operation as soon as it was safe.

He was a kindly looking black man with gray hair and a quiet and humble personality. His conversation was well-seasoned with "yas sir, naw sir; please and thank you" which attracted me greatly to his sweet spirit. He was scheduled for an operation within a week of admission, and, as the operating surgeon, I indeed found a large cancer in his stomach which I successfully removed before reconnecting his alimentary tract.

On the afternoon of his operation, I received a page from the hospital operator. She had a physician from Minneapolis on the phone who wanted to speak with me. I knew no doctors in Minneapolis and wondered why he specifically asked for me, so I took the call. After he identified himself, he asked if I was the surgeon who operated on "Slow Drag" and just how was he doing. I told him I was not aware of any patient named Slow Drag. He said this was the nickname everyone called Alcide Pavageau. I said I was indeed the correct surgeon, and I gave him the information he desired, thinking he was a friend of Slow Drag. He said he only knew him by reputation and had heard him play on just a few occasions. He told me Slow Drag was one of the most famous bass players of Dixieland music and was so great he was in the Dixieland Music Hall of Fame. Alcide had never told me about his musical expertise, nor did he say his nickname was Slow Drag.

Slow Drag had played with some of the most famous Dixieland bands in the country and, in his latter years, played in the Preservation Hall in the French Quarter. I loved going there, and on several occasions Cathy and I would sit and listen because it was free and the atmosphere was like a large jam session. On one occasion I was challenged to join the band on a number and briefly played the banjo for my one and only Dixieland gig. I don't believe Slow Drag was there that evening; at least I didn't remember him.

When Slow Drag began recovering from his operation, we had many opportunities to discuss his music and fascinating career. He had a family member bring some photos of his playing and several of the bands with which he had played through the years. I should have gotten his autograph but wasn't thinking about that sort of thing then. I lost contact with Alcide but read he had lived about one more year before dying with advanced metastatic cancer. I regret I never inquired about his spiritual condition and where he believed he would spend eternity. I was not a believer and such things were not important to me then. As kind and sweet as he was, I believe he must have known Jesus Christ as his Savior.

Fifteen years later after Cathy and I had moved to El Dorado, the Preservation Hall Band from New Orleans was on tour and played a one-night concert there, which we attended at the municipal auditorium. I didn't recognize any of the names on the program but several faces looked familiar. When the concert was over, I decided to go back stage and inquire if any of them remembered Slow Drag. The trombone player who was called "Frog" approached me and asked, "May I help you?" I said, "I want to thank you all for such a good concert. Do you remember Slow Drag because I was his doctor who operated on him fifteen years ago?" He hollered to all the band members, "Come meet this man. He was Slow Drag's doctor!" For at least ten minutes I reminisced with them over what a wonderful man and musician Ole Slow Drag had been. It was a sweet time, and I was thankful to the Lord that I had known him. Since those days in New Orleans, both Cathy and I have become Christians, and I believe I will see Slow Drag again in heaven. Perhaps I'll get to play in another Dixieland gig with him!

95. "TURN IT UP TO 300 AND HIT IT THREE TIMES!"

Payback Can Be Very Painful

I met and worked with some outstanding doctors and surgical residents during the four years I took my surgical training at Charity Hospital in New Orleans between 1965 and 1969. One of the surgical trainees with whom I did a large number of operations was Dr. John Piker from Clinton, Louisiana.

John and I rotated together from "Big Charity" in New Orleans to "Little Charity" in Lake Charles, Louisiana, during my third year of training and spent three months operating together at this facility. We were responsible for all the general surgical procedures done at the hospital under the supervision and assistance of a staff surgeon. John and I seldom asked the staff surgeon to scrub with us as we had become very confident in our operating abilities and self-sufficient in our management of surgical patients.

John was a few years older than most of us and had lots of other experiences outside of his medical training. He was an excellent story-teller and could spin some of the funniest tales I had ever heard from a Cajun. One of his funniest involved an episode when he was a medical student at the LSU School of Medicine. I will tell the account in the first person just as he told me:

I was in my senior year of medical school and had a two-weeks-long clinical rotation on anesthesia. My job was to assist an anesthesiologist in the operating room for that two-week period, and it included taking night call for emergencies when he was on call. The anesthesia resident, whom I will call Dr. Smith (not his real name), had the reputation of being especially hard on medical students. Perhaps he had been treated this way as a student and wanted to continue making life as miserable as possible for hapless and gullible students. He had a way of calling me "Piker" with a few added unmentionable adjectives which constantly irritated me, but I had to keep my mouth shut and my attitude hidden as much as possible. It was by far the worst two weeks rotation I had in medical school.

We had an on-call room with comfortable chairs and a TV to help pass the time when we were not being called out for an emergency. I tried to use the spare time to read and study, but Dr. Smith had the television on so loud it was difficult to concentrate. On this particular night, we were between emergency surgical cases when we got a Code Blue call from fifth floor, which was the medical floor. The patients there had various medical problems including MI (heart attacks), CVA (stroke), and diabetic emergencies. There were no surgical problems on the fifth floor.

Dr. Smith said, "Piker, get your lazy butt off the couch and bring the crash cart with you. We're going to fifth floor, and be quick about it!!" The crash cart had all the supplies necessary for a cardiac arrest, including a very large and antiquated defibrillator. The modern ones were compact, but this one was about ten-years old, stood tall on the stand, and required two people to operate it. One person had to set the dials on the console while the other one held the paddles to the patient. The one on the console was responsible for firing the electrical charge by means of a firing button located on the console.

When we finally got to the fifth floor and the patient's bedside, we found a typical scene for a person who had a cardiac arrest. It was a large open ward with approximately twelve beds, and this person was in a bed in the middle of the ward. The beds were all metal with wire springs. They were not like the modern ones with electric controls to raise and lower the bed and the head of the bed. A few had a manual crank for raising the head of the bed, but most did not even have this feature. The mattresses lay on springs which precluded any effective chest compressions should they be needed. This patient was a large woman in her late sixties, and probably had had an MI (heart attack) which caused her heart to start fibrillating. There had been several failed attempts to start an IV, and there were small puddles of saline on the floor beside the bed. In order to apply the paddles effectively to the patient, she had to be rolled slightly on her side to apply one to the front and the other to the back. Because of her size, Dr. Smith was stretched out almost to his limits and his knees were touching the side of the bed. He didn't notice he was standing in a small puddle of saline.

When he was in position, he said, "Piker, turn the power to fifty volts and hit it once." I did what he said and nothing happened. "Turn it to seventy-five and hit it again," which I did with the same result. "Come on Piker give me some power quick! Turn it to three hundred (maximum for this machine) and hit it three times." When I pushed the firing button after setting the machine to deliver three hundred volts, the electricity made an arc with Dr. Smith touching the side of the bed and standing in saline, and it was Dr. Smith instead of the patient who got the full charge. The electric shock lifted him up on his toes, caused his facial muscles to grimace and his arm muscles to straighten in spasm. You could hear air being sucked into his lungs with the spasm. I saw what had happened, but had my head turned slightly away from him toward the console and pretended I didn't see him being shocked. I hit the button the second time with the same results, and then for a third and final time!

When he finally came back down to neutral, the air rushed out of his lungs as he said with a grunt, "Don't hit that button again!" He thought I didn't see him being shocked and knew I was doing what he had told me, so he didn't blame me or punish me for shocking him. He did have a whole new respect for me though, and not once after that did he ever criticize or belittle me. I guess he was afraid I might think of something worse to do in retaliation. Maybe the shocks just made him sweeter.

96. THE GRACE OF MEETING THE BEAR

Bear Bryant Comes into My Front Yard

For football fans nationwide the bowl games are long-awaited treats at the end of the long gridiron season. Two of the bowl games are reserved for the top four teams, and the winners of those games will go on to play for the national championship. One of the more prestigious bowl games annually is the Sugar Bowl, which is always played in New Orleans on or after January 1. For many years prior to the opening of the massive Superdome Stadium in 1975, the Sugar Bowl was played in Tulane Stadium, the home field for Tulane University and the New Orleans Saints. The Saints began their initial season in 1967, and now both teams play their home games in the Superdome.

Cathy and I called New Orleans our home for the four years I was in surgical training at Charity Hospital. Initially we lived in the new Bissonet Plaza Apartments in Kenner, a fifteen- minute drive from the hospital. Cathy taught fifth grade for one year at John Clancy Elementary School in Kenner. Her second year of teaching was in Jefferson Parish on the West Bank, so we moved into a subdivision called Delmont Village on Pace Boulevard in Algiers, close to her school. It was only a ten-minute drive for me across the Mississippi River bridge to Charity Hospital when traffic was light.

We loved living in the Algiers duplex because we had some wonderful neighbors with whom we became close friends. In addition to other benefits, we had a small yard which we didn't have in Kenner. Our neighbors were able to offer Cathy some peace and protection during the long hours and frequent nights I had to spend at the hospital taking call and doing emergency surgical procedures. The couple in the adjacent duplex were Bob and Jerri Herold, who had recently moved from St. Louis. They were close in age to Cathy and me and had three young children. We bonded quickly with them, and Jerri became like an older sister to Cathy. An older couple, John and Jean Boyd, who were in their sixties and had retired from upstate New York, lived two doors from us and were like surrogate parents. They were particularly helpful following the birth of our son John, and it was nice to have a couple with so much life experience living nearby. I especially loved John because he was a good story-teller, and we swapped many tales, most of which were true.

The Christmas holidays of 1966 were uneventful for us. I had just recovered from the serum hepatitis I'd contracted in the early spring at Charity Hospital, probably from an inadvertent needle stick. Cathy was in the first trimester of her pregnancy with our first child, and we had spent our holidays there in New Orleans. The Sugar Bowl of 1967 was being played between Alabama and Nebraska in Tulane Stadium on January 2, but I had no plans to attend the game. I was not particularly interested in either team. Occasionally, a few doctors at Charity Hospital could get complimentary tickets for games played in Tulane Stadium, but I didn't even try this year. Although Alabama was undefeated at 10–0, they represented the Southeastern Conference, and in those days the Razorbacks were in the Southwestern

Conference. Had the Razorbacks been in the Sugar Bowl, I would have done everything in my power to obtain free tickets.

On the morning of January 2, I didn't have to report to the hospital, so I was enjoying a day of relaxation with plans to watch a few of the bowl games on television. It was about 9:00 a.m. and the weather was clear with a little chill, but not enough to warrant more than a light jacket. I happened to look out our front window and notice a man standing on the sidewalk of our front yard with his back toward me. Although I considered our neighborhood safe, it was very unusual to have a stranger standing in our front, viewing the apartments across the street. The distinctive thing about this large man was his hat, a black and white hounds-tooth. He looked familiar, but I couldn't tell for sure so I walked up to him.

As I approached him I said, "Coach?" to which he turned around. Sure enough, it was Coach Bear Bryant the famed head coach of the Alabama Crimson Tide! I asked him, "Coach, are you all right?" thinking perhaps he was waiting for a ride or may have been lost. He said, "Yes I'm all right. I'm just waiting on my wife. She is visiting a long-time friend who lives in this neighborhood, and I told them I was going outside for a little fresh air. She'll be finished soon because we need to get to Tulane Stadium."

I introduced myself and told him we were living in New Orleans while I was completing my surgical training. I also told him I was born and raised in South Arkansas in El Dorado knowing he was raised in Fordyce, a small town about fifty miles north of El Dorado. I knew this would encourage conversation about his earlier life, and we talked for about ten minutes about his life and experiences in South Arkansas. He asked a few questions about our life in New Orleans and whether we eventually planned to go back to live in Arkansas. I made sure he knew I was a loyal Razorback fan, and he commented something like, "They are a good team and well coached by Frank Broyles." Then he said he needed to go and convince his wife the team and coaches were expecting him at Tulane Stadium by 10:30 at the latest. We shook hands, and I told him it was a pleasure to have this brief visit with him.

As he left, the thought came to me how many loyal Crimson Tide fans would have paid large sums of money into the Alabama Athletic Foundation to have just a couple of minutes to chat alone with the famous Coach Bear Bryant. I had the pleasure at no cost and now the privilege of telling the story nearly sixty years later. That's one example of an undeserved gift which is called grace.

PS: Alabama soundly defeated Nebraska that day by a score of 34–7 and remained undefeated at 11–0, but still was not voted the National

Champion. Notre Dame received that honor with a record of 10-0-1. I suppose one could say Notre Dame received grace that year.

97. THE CHIEF OF NIGHT OPERATIONS

A Famous Person is Found at Charity Hospital

During my fourth and final year of surgical training at Charity Hospital in New Orleans, I was fortunate to receive the one and only political appointment of my medical career. Because of my personal friendship with Dr. Charles Mary, the hospital director of Charity, I was appointed as an assistant clinical director for the hospital for 1968–1969, wherein I served with two other physicians, Dr. John Buck and Dr. George Cook. It was quite an honor because Charity was the largest hospital in the United States at the time, with a staff of approximately two hundred and fifty resident physicians.

The two medical schools in New Orleans, LSU and Tulane Medical, used Charity as their teaching hospital, and the hospital was evenly divided between the schools. There was tremendous competition between the services, and each service thought they were the best. All three of the ACDs (Assistant Clinical Directors) were on the LSU Service for the year. The simple explanation is that Dr. Mary had been an internal medicine resident on the LSU Service prior to his appointment as director by Governor John McKeithen. I had gotten to know Dr. Mary as an internist since he had referred many surgical patients to me for three years, and we had a very good working relationship. The reason Charity had been so steeped in politics is that, at the time, the annual operating budget of the hospital was approximately thirty million dollars, fully funded by the state of Louisiana. That was more than the total budget of some states in those years, and in today's economy might be twice that much. Charity had been on the center stage of Louisiana politics for almost a hundred years, and every governor had some agenda regarding the hospital.

The responsibilities of the ACD were not complicated but required the ability to get along with all (most) of the doctors on staff and also the skill to settle disputes. LSU and Tulane doctors were constantly squabbling over which patients should be assigned to their service. There were some patients whom each wanted and some that neither wanted, and there was a daily turf war which had to be settled. The hospital director assigned those battles to his ACD's. He was busy with budget meetings, high level administrative duties, and meeting with all the political bigwigs of Louisiana.

Every night, the ACD was the acting director of the hospital, and every administrative decision was made by him alone. Most decisions were routine, but occasionally a decision would have far-reaching implications. Every third night, I was on call as ACD, and frequently the responsibility coincided with my duties as the fourth-year surgeon on call. This was before the days of cellular phones, but we used a beeper system, considered high-tech at the time. When I had a call from the hospital operator, my beeper would sound, and I would then call the operator to receive my call. It sounds very antiquated with our current technology, but it was a wonderful system allowing us to take call from home and also have the freedom to go to a restaurant or to a movie. The first time Cathy and I attended a movie with my new beeper and it went off, it caused great alarm to most people in the theater, who had never heard such a sound!

As ACD, I frequently got phone calls from politicians and state officials who wanted some political favor from the hospital. I once received a call from Governor McKeithen who wanted one of his friends with no medical insurance admitted to the Doctor's Infirmary. The Doctor's Infirmary was in a special section of the hospital, used primarily to provide medical care for the staff and occasionally for outsiders. Every room was a private room and the care provided was as good if not better than that of any hospital in New Orleans—and with an added benefit, it was free! Every patient had their own nurse and the only doctors allowed to treat patients in the Infirmary were the fourth-and-fifth-year residents along with the full-time staff physicians.

One of the most interesting calls I received all year was from a newspaper reporter in Paris, France. In his deep French accent, he asked if I could give him any information on a then-well-known opera singer who reportedly was a patient in Charity. I took the caller's name and number and said I would call when I could provide the needed information. I discovered after lengthy research that, indeed, the opera singer was a patient on the Psychiatry Service under the name "John Doe." He had been drinking large amounts of alcohol in numerous bars in the French Quarter and had been found lying unconscious on Bourbon Street. For whatever reason, he had no identification papers, so was brought to Charity and admitted to a general ward under the John Doe name. When he awakened several days later, he did not know who he was or any details of his life and was transferred to the psych. unit for rehabilitation. His memory very slowly returned, and, by the time I received the call from the Paris reporter, he was beginning to piece his life together. After I gave my report to the Paris newspaper, the story made international news because the singer was so well-known in the opera world. I began receiving other calls for similar information concerning him.

Cathy's Mom, Virginia Young who lived in Fort Lauderdale, called us a few days later and said I was quoted in the *Miami Herald* about the "world-famous opera singer." She sent me a copy of the article which headlined "Opera Singer Found in New Orleans." The article identified me as Dr. John Moore, the Chief of Night Operations at Charity Hospital. Mom Young teased me for a long time afterward and would ask if I only operated "at night." I would tell her I did work during the day, but did my best operating at night, so I was given the title "Director."

Since I lean more toward bluegrass music than opera, I don't remember the singer's name, but do remember he was finally released from Charity to return home and presumably continue his career. I never went to the psych. unit to meet him, but probably should have. I have to admit I enjoyed my year in Louisiana politics, but was glad to finally relinquish those duties and concentrate solely on patient care. Later, whenever she remembered the opera singer article, Mom would call me "the night operator chief."

98. MEIN LIEBER FREUND, ALFRED

A College Friendship with an Austrian Exchange Student
Lasts over Sixty Years

Alfred and me in Austria, 2002

For those who don't read German, the title says, "My dear friend, Alfred." I met Alfred Fischer in 1958 while in my second year of college at the University of Arkansas. I was a member of Sigma Alpha Epsilon fraternity, and one of the better traditions of our fraternity involved an annual ongoing relationship with an international student. Each year a selected international student would have lunch each day at our fraternity at no cost to the student. The purpose was to expose us to different cultures and broaden our world view. That year a student from Austria was selected to dine with us daily, and it was Alfred Fischer, who was a Fulbright Scholar and a pre-law student from Linz, Austria.

The first day I met Alfred I quickly noticed that he was quiet and reserved but had an open and receptive attitude toward new friendships. Since I was taking German as my pre-med language requirement, I was certain that a close friendship with him would greatly benefit me. His English was excellent, so I couldn't teach him very many language skills, but I knew I could tell him lots of good Southern stories and teach him some South Arkansas dialect to which he had never been exposed. As I recall, before the year was over, he was using the expression, "y'all."

Alfred did spend a lot of time tutoring me in German, and I did very well in the course. I know for certain I could communicate in German better than my classmates, because Alfred and I frequently spoke to each other in his native tongue. I was not able to carry on a prolonged dialogue, but it was fun for me since the only other language course I had taken was Latin as a sophomore in high school. I was hoping one day I might be able to travel to Austria and Germany and use my newly-learned skills.

Several times during the year, I invited Alfred to come to El Dorado to experience life in an American home, and he gladly consented. Mom and Pops thoroughly enjoyed having him visit, and, on one occasion, we even took him to a hunting camp for an overnight stay. Pops also took Mose Graham to the camp to help with the cooking and the clean-up, and Alfred was intrigued with Mose's ability to tell stories of life in the South from a black man's perspective.

At the end of that school year, Alfred had to return to Austria to complete his legal training, but we promised to stay in touch. In this connection, Pops promised that if I could get accepted to medical school after three years of college, he would finance a three-month trip to Europe for me in the summer between college and med. school. Needless to say, I studied much harder during my third year and was accepted for medical school for the fall of 1960. Alfred and I made plans to meet during the summer trip, and we spent two weeks together travelling in Austria and Italy.

I made the trip overseas with a friend from El Dorado who was several years older, and our interests in travelling and the sites we wanted to visit were different. We each had purchased a Eurail Pass which allowed us to travel first class on any train in Europe for any distance for a period of two months. About three weeks into our trip, we decided to split up, and he went to Rome to see the Summer Olympics of 1960. I didn't want to go there because it was extremely expensive despite the fact that I love track and field events. It was about this time that Alfred and I connected. We did spend four days with his mom and dad in Linz, and I'll write on that later. When we parted and I was returning to the states to begin my medical training, I wasn't sure we would ever be able to meet again.

Alfred completed his legal training with a doctorate, and with degree in hand, he began his practice of law, subsequently becoming a lower court judge. It always pleased me to address my letters to him as "Herr Doktor Alfred Fischer." When I completed my surgical training in New Orleans, Cathy and I were in the process of moving to Valdosta, Georgia for my active-duty service in the Air Force. I had to take a three-week training course in Wichita Falls, Texas, and because Cathy was pregnant with our daughter Mary Kay, she went to Fort Lauderdale to spend the time with her parents. While in Wichita Falls, I got a phone call from Alfred, and he said he was coming to the states for an international Rotary meeting and would be in Dallas for a few days. This worked out perfectly because I had only a two-hour drive to meet him, and I drove him back to Wichita Falls for a two-day visit. It had been almost ten years since we had seen each other.

Cathy and I were able to visit with Alfred and his wife Carmen and their two children on two other occasions when we were in Austria on mission trips. Alfred has been to the states on three separate occasions with his work for the Rotary Club of Linz, and on two of those trips, we were able to meet again. He happened to be in El Dorado in 1999, where he attended the retirement party given me by my office staff of the Surgical Clinic of South Arkansas. This happened to be forty years almost to the day from when we first met at the fraternity house in Fayetteville.

God has been so gracious to give me a life-long friend in Alfred. We have had many and varied great conversations through the years. I had the privilege of telling him how God changed both Cathy and me when we were saved in 1977, and just how it happened and what it meant. He remarked on several of our visits how much I had changed, and it opened the door to tell him how much God loves him and wants to have a personal relationship with him. I trust that when we leave this earth after our labor is completed, that "Mein Lieber Freund" Alfred and I will have another reunion that will be far greater than any one before.

PS: The photo above was taken in 2002 while Cathy and I were on a mission trip to Austria. The location is near Salzburg on Lake Attersee, where Alfred and Carmen have a vacation home. Their residence is still in Linz.

99. ARKANSAS RELAXING INCISIONS

Incised Marching Boots Give Much Needed Relief

I was excited to serve our country in the US Air Force during the Vietnam War. All physicians in those days under the age of thirty were mandated to serve for at least two years on active duty unless they were physically unfit. I was commissioned as a second lieutenant during medical school and was gradually promoted to the rank of captain upon graduation from medical school and completion of a one-year internship. Most young doctors went on active duty with the rank of captain, so the pay and benefits were higher than most other commissioned officers with no active duty experience. I was accepted into the Berry Plan, which deferred me for an additional four years to allow me to complete my surgical training. When I entered active duty in August 1969, I had been promoted to major.

At this stage in our life, Cathy and I had a son, John Aaron, and she was pregnant with our first daughter, Mary Kay. Our permanent duty station was Moody Air Force Base in Valdosta, Georgia, and we made plans to move there into a home off-base, which her brother George had found for us. I had to first report to Sheppard Air Force Base in Texas for a three-week, temporary duty assignment. Cathy was in the first trimester of her pregnancy, and the base in Wichita Falls would have been hot and very uncomfortable for her and John. We decided it best for them to spend the time with her parents in Fort Lauderdale, Florida. The three weeks assignment was a basic training course for doctors to prepare all of us for military service and some for their permanent assignment in Vietnam. I was shocked I was not sent to Vietnam, because I was a fully trained battlefield surgeon based on my four years of training at the famous New Orleans Charity Hospital.

Upon arranging for the Air Force to move our furniture and belongings from our duplex apartment in New Orleans to our new address in Valdosta, Georgia, I put Cathy and John Aaron on a flight to Fort Lauderdale, and I began my new adventure in the military. I drove my Fiat Spyder convertible from Valdosta to Wichita Falls, Texas. They had very nice accommodations for all the doctors in our class, and I was assigned one of the better rooms in the officer's quarters since I was a major amongst mostly captains!

One of our first jobs was to go to the Quartermaster Office to receive our uniforms with our brass, two pairs of shoes, and one very good pair of combat boots. Not many of the new medical officers knew how to properly place the brass on their uniforms and had to sheepishly ask one of the enlisted men to help. Fortunately for me, I had taken ROTC in college and knew where to place them, but I checked with the master sergeant just to be sure I had them correctly positioned. We were told when the boots were issued that we should wear them each morning during marching drill in order to break them in for the three-day field bivouac which was scheduled near the end of our training period. We were slated for an hour of close-order marching each morning at 8:00 before our classroom assignments began.

The majority of our basic training was spent in the classroom learning military protocol and all the new and somewhat strange military language. Classes began at 9:00 and lasted until 4:00 with a two-hour break for lunch at the officers' mess (dining hall). The early morning drill exercise was quite an experience with the three hundred physicians, most of them never trained to march in close order.

In the first few days of our classroom work, I met Bob Parkhurst from Michigan, who was assigned to Moody AFB as the base pediatrician. We were excited to get to know each other so soon, because we were to spend the next two years working very closely together providing medical care at our base hospital. Bob would be the only pediatrician, and I would be the only surgeon on the base.

I noticed an interesting thing at the drill each morning: Not all of the men wore their boots for the one-hour marching exercise. The weather was very hot in Texas in August, and the boots made the marching more uncomfortable. Many of those who didn't comply with the master sergeant's recommendation to break in the boots later had regrets.

In the latter part of the last week, we were ordered to be on the bus at 8:00 a.m. for transport to the field training area a one-hour bus ride away. Upon boarding the bus, Bob Parkhurst sat down next to me and said, "These boots are killing my feet!" He said he was one of those who didn't break in his boots, but they were too tight anyway. He also said, "If I have to wear these for three days, I think I'll be crippled for life." Since it was too late to go back and get a new pair, I told him I thought I could help if he would allow me. He pulled off both boots and gladly handed them to me. I said I had seen patients in New Orleans who were very poor, and the only shoes they owned were too small. They used their pocket knives to make some extra room. I had a very sharp knife, and I made very long cuts down the side of each boot. When he put the boots back on, there was a distinct look of relief on his face and he said, "That makes a huge difference, and I believe I can make it now!" I said I called those cuts "Arkansas Relaxing Incisions." His feet did look funny with his pinkie toes protruding out the side of his brand-new combat boots, but at least he could walk without pain.

A problem concerning the boots occurred very shortly when we had our first and only inspection of the men in our six-man tent. The inspecting officer Colonel Johnson came to each one of us who were standing at attention and made sure we were dressed properly for the bivouac. He saw Parkhurst's boots and asked, "What in the world is going on with your boots?" He told the colonel, "Sir, when I got on the bus this morning and discovered my boots were way too tight, Major Moore graciously put Arkansas relaxing incisions in them, and I can now walk without pain." The Colonel turned to me and asked, "Major Moore, have you ever done that before?" My reply was, "No sir, this was my first case, and I believe he will live." The colonel smiled, shook his head, and said, "Carry on!" Captain Parkhurst did survive, but on returning to the base, he threw those boots with my relaxing incisions into the trash. I should have kept them as a souvenir, because I have never since seen a funnier looking pair of combat boots. I am happy to report that Captain Parkhurst sustained no damage to his feet from his bivouac experience, and completed his Air Force duty assignment with no permanent disability.

100. SPAYING GRETA

The Veterinarian Turns Over His Operation

John Aaron and Greta, 1970

Cathy and I moved to Valdosta, Georgia in 1969 when I completed my surgical training at Charity Hospital in New Orleans. I had been commissioned as a major in the US Air Force Medical Corps for a two-year stint of active duty at Moody Air Force Base. We were very familiar with Valdosta, because her brother George (Dr. George Young) and his wife Dawn lived there while he served as dean of students at Valdosta State College (now Valdosta State University). The summer we received orders to report to Moody, we were so excited to live in the same town as George and Dawn. When Cathy called him to tell our good news, he reported the bad news (for us) that he had just accepted the position of dean of students at Broward Community College in Fort Lauderdale, where Cathy and George were raised.

Our son John Aaron was two years old and Cathy was pregnant with Mary Kay when we moved to Valdosta in September, 1969. Mary Kay arrived on the scene the following February. We rented a small but lovely, three-bedroom home on Azalea Drive in Valdosta, a place George helped us find before they left for Fort Lauderdale. The home had a fenced back yard, which was ideal because John Aaron was extremely adventuresome and prone to wander while exploring the neighborhood.

The base veterinarian was Dr. (Captain) Pete McKoy, whose wife Flonnie was also pregnant with their second child, and like Cathy was scheduled to deliver in February, 1970. We became friends very quickly. In conversation one day with Pete, I happened to mention we were looking for a suitable pet for John, one that might serve as a watchdog for our travelling young son. He said he had access to a German shepherd puppy which might be a good fit if we were looking for a larger dog. Our previous dog, Schnicklefritz, was a dachshund we owned in New Orleans. We had to part company with Fritz when John was born, because he was jealous of all the attention John received and snapped at him several times when John happened to grab some part of his fur.

The day our new puppy arrived, we instantly bonded and were happy with the name Greta, which her original owner had given her. Greta was a loving, friendly dog, and most importantly loved John and was fiercely loyal to him. Whenever John was outside playing, Greta was at his side. If John happened to get a little too rough or grab too much hair, Greta would simply put a little space between the two of them. Cathy learned that when she couldn't immediately spot John in the neighborhood, she could call Greta's name, and she would go to a position in the yard where Cathy could see her and immediately know John's location. The photo above shows John in one of his more benevolent moods, sharing some of his snack with Greta. On the back of the photo I had written, "Now get this straight – it's *one* for you and *two* for me!"

As Greta got older, we definitely did not want her to have puppies, especially in light of the fact our family had already enlarged with the arrival of Mary Kay. I asked Pete if he would consent to spaying Greta, to which he responded, "Sure. Bring her to the clinic tomorrow afternoon after duty hours, and I'll get that done for you." When my clinic finished the next day, I drove home, picked up Greta, and drove back to the base. Pete was finished seeing customers for the day, and the clinic was empty except for Pete, Greta, and me. I told him I would stay to keep him company and watch the procedure if he didn't mind. I helped him give Greta the intravenous medication and insert the endotracheal tube which would stay in place while she was anesthetized. He then shaved her abdomen and went over to the sink to scrub his hands in preparation for the procedure.

While he was scrubbing, I asked, "Pete, does the Air Force provide you with malpractice insurance while you are working here?" He turned around and said, "No they don't. Why do you ask?" I said, "You know Cathy, John, Mary Kay, and I have grown to really love Greta, and if anything happened to go wrong with this operation, I think I would have to sue you." Pete had not known me long enough to know I was joking, and a malpractice law suit is something I would never do. Pete quickly said, "Have you ever spayed a dog?" "No," I said, "But I'd like to." Pete responded, "Come on over here and scrub your hands!"

I had done a few hysterectomies in my training at Charity Hospital and assisted the base obstetrician with the procedure. Spaying an animal is the mini-version of a hysterectomy. Pete showed me several veterinarian techniques, and I was able to show him a few surgical techniques and surgical knots which would be useful for his practice. He and I had a grand time during that forty-five-minute procedure, as we talked and laughed together the whole time. Fortunately, Greta not only survived but did very well, and I was able to take her home later that evening.

Early in my surgical experience I learned and applied the following lesson: A wise and skilled surgeon should never operate on a member of his immediate family. Still, even though Greta was our family pet, I believed she fell outside this surgical maxim. I never told her I was the one who held the knife but, even if I had, I think she would have been all right with it. Within a day or two she began playing with John again and life was back to normal. I never had the opportunity to spay another dog, but had the occasion arisen, I was fully prepared.

101. THE INFLUENCE OF CHUNKY HARVEY

A Visiting Preacher Makes a Lasting Impact

REVEREND
RAYMOND FRANCIS HARVEY

Pastor Emeritus
Greenwood Missionary Baptist Church

June 20, 1918   September 22, 1992

There are some men whom God sent into my life at certain critical periods who have influenced me greatly. One of those men, Bill Gothard, was speaking at a conference about the saving knowledge of Jesus Christ at a time when my heart was open to him and both Cathy and I were saved. Another influential man was my brother Berry Lee (Bubba) who was the first man to offer encouragement to me as a mentor, and I sat at his feet to learn from 1977 until his departure to heaven in 2009. Not long after Cathy and I were saved, a guest preacher was invited to preach at the First Baptist Church in El Dorado, and he brought a series of sermons which moved me, girded my spirit, and strengthened my faith. I had been dealing with some personal issues of doubt and frustration in my Christian walk, and his messages spoke to my need. His name was Reverend Raymond Francis Harvey, affectionately known as "Chunky" to his friends. I had not met Reverend Harvey nor had I heard of him when our pastor Dr. Don Harbuck invited him to our church. He and Dr. Harbuck had been friends and colleagues for years, and they preached in each other's church on special occasions.

Reverend Harvey was the senior pastor of Greenwood Missionary Baptist Church in Tuskegee, Alabama, serving that congregation for over thirty-six years. Born and raised in Long Island, New York, he received his BD from Howard University in Washington, D.C. He continued postgraduate studies at Oberlin College in Ohio, Princeton Seminary, and Oxford University in England. He also received an honorary doctorate from Birmingham Baptist Bible College. His wife Lillian (Dr. Lillian Holland Harvey) had a distinguished career for almost thirty years as the dean of the School of Nursing at Tuskegee Institute (University) in Alabama.

Doctor Harvey spent most of his professional life serving in Tuskegee, where he was the active chaplain at Tuskegee Institute for several years prior to being called to Greenwood Missionary Baptist Church in 1955. The early years of his pastorate coincided with some of the most turbulent times in the nation's civil rights struggles, specifically in Alabama. He led his church and community with dignity and honor in peaceful dissent to the shameful and hurtful practices of segregation, and saw the fruit born nation-wide with the signing of the Civil Rights Acts in 1964, 1965, and 1968.

I was curious when Dr. Harbuck first announced the coming of Dr. Harvey to our church, adding that he was known as "Chunky." I was certain only his closest friends would use that name in addressing such a prominent pastor, and over the next several years after having met him and exchanged calls and letters, I could never bring myself to use that term when speaking to him. I never asked him the origin of the nickname, but suspect he had it since childhood or early adulthood.

The messages Dr. Harvey preached over the first three-day meeting in El Dorado were entitled "Not What [I Believe], But Whom," and he used the John Oxenham poem by that title to frame his sermons. His preaching was Christ-centered, topical, and delivered with an accent he must have acquired in Oxford. I could not detect any hint of an Alabama accent except on the rare occasion when, emphasizing a particular point, he would use the dialect of an Alabama black man. His overall style of preaching was fascinating to me, and I listened intently while taking notes. I wrote down the words of the poem and had them printed and framed, and it has been hanging in my office since. When Dr. Harvey returned home, I wrote him several letters expressing my gratitude for his timely messages to me and how they had ministered to a specific need I had at the time. I received a short but beautifully written note from him.

Dr. Harvey returned to First Baptist about a year later in December 1982, and I was able to spend a little time with him in Dr. Harbuck's office. I gave him a copy of the poem I had framed and again voiced my gratitude to him for ministering to me. The messages he preached on this visit were entitled "The Strength to Endure," framed by a quotation from Howard Cooke

Phillips, an American Baptist pastor. I have these messages on audio tape and occasionally listen to them recalling the power of his preaching.

The last time I heard from him was the following spring on the evening before Easter Sunday. I was sitting in my comfortable bedroom chair when the phone rang. Upon answering, I heard the deep resonating voice on the other end say, "Dr. Moore, this is Chunky Harvey!" He said he had been reading again the framed poem I had given him and wanted to know how I was doing. We had a wonderful visit for about ten minutes with his telling me among other things, about his wife's ministry as nursing director at Tuskegee and about his son, Dr. Paul Harvey, who was an internal medicine specialist in Michigan.

When Dr. Harvey died in 1992 at the age of 74, I was not aware of his departure until I received a note from his son. He said he had been reading some of his father's correspondence and noted several letters from me. He thought I might enjoy having a copy of the funeral service bulletin along with the poem entitled "The Long Road Home," read at the service. I loved the poem so much I had it framed, and it hangs in our bedroom. The two poems I have framed (the other being John Oxenham's "Not What, But Whom") remind me of my friend Chunky Harvey and how he blessed and impacted my life.

102. THE VALUE OF A QUARTER

A Good Lesson on Money Values

I am old enough to remember when a quarter was a lot of money. In the late 1940s when I was a young boy, I could buy a ticket for a dime to a Roy Rogers movie at the Majestic Theater in El Dorado. When I reached the ripe age of twelve, I had to shell out the exorbitant price of a quarter for that same movie. One piece of Fleers Double-Bubble gum was a penny, and one could get a PayDay candy bar and a Dr. Pepper for a nickel each. Some mighty pleasurable things could be purchased for a quarter. My friend and medical colleague, Dr. George Burton, taught me his evaluation of the worth of a quarter, but that lesson came in the 1970s when I was a relatively young physician El Dorado.

Dr. Burton was twenty-five years my senior and had been in practice in El Dorado as a radiologist for twenty-four years when I began my practice in 1971. He had the reputation for being eccentric and opinionated but far ahead of the time in terms of x-ray technology. For years El Dorado had only one hospital, Warner Brown, which was operated by the Sisters of

Mercy, but there was growing discontent in the community with the services they provided. Along with a small handful of physicians, he helped establish the Union County Medical Center in the mid-1960s. The hospital is now known as The Medical Center of South Arkansas. A bond issue had to be passed, and this small group of doctors were cutting across the grain of the vast majority of the medical community, so these men were not very popular with the other doctors. About 90 percent of the doctors had placed an article in the *El Dorado News-Times* opposing the building of a second hospital, but the vote by the public was overwhelmingly in favor of building. By the time I began my practice, both hospitals were operating to capacity, and Dr. Burton was the head of the radiology department at the new facility. He wouldn't even consider a staff position at Warner Brown.

Despite the fact George's professional life was strong and growing, his personal life was less than ideal. After more than twenty-five years of marriage, he and his wife divorced because of irreconcilable differences. George lived alone in the large house in which they raised their now-grown three children, and to say he didn't maintain it neatly is a gross understatement. He seldom had guests, and, when he did, he didn't spend much time tidying up. One of his hobbies was building airplanes, and he told me he assembled his latest plane in the living room. When he finally had to attach the wings, he was forced to move the assembly line to his back yard.

I once helped him assemble a grandfather clock at his home, and before beginning the project, he dumped all thousand pieces, small and large, out of the their boxes onto the floor of this same living room. He said he was more comfortable working there. We had a lot of fun working on that clock, and when it was finished, he gave it to me. Cathy and I had placed the clock in the entryway of our home on North Madison, and when we moved to Florida, we gave it to our son John Aaron.

George's economic lesson was taught to me early one morning in the cafeteria of the hospital. Dr. David Yocum and I were having breakfast prior to our scheduled operation later in the morning. Dr. Burton came through the line, placed the food items he desired on his tray, and was standing at the cashier's station to pay his bill. He seemed to be slower than usual trying to get the correct change from his front pocket, and I attributed it to the fact he was sleepy. From his overall appearance, it looked as if he had only been out of bed for ten minutes. As he fumbled in his pocket, a coin fell to the floor and rolled around a number of times, coming to rest within three or four feet of George. Everyone in the cafeteria including George heard the rattling sound. He paid his bill and without looking down for the coin came to our table and sat down.

I stood up and walked over to pick up the coin, a quarter, and gave it to George. He thanked me and started eating his breakfast. I said, "I'm just thankful to have breakfast with a man who is so wealthy when he drops a quarter on the floor, he doesn't even bother to pick it up!" Without looking up, George responded, "I learned about a year ago I don't pick up anything less than a dollar. It's too expensive." "Help me understand it George," I said, to which he responded, "Last year I dropped a nickel on the floor, and when I stooped to get it, I ripped the seat out of my britches. It cost me a dollar and a quarter to have them stitched up. I was out a dollar and twenty cents, so now I don't bend over for less than a dollar. It is too expensive!" Accordinging to Burton's current economics, a quarter wasn't worth so much as a stoop or even a squat. Now when I see a quarter on the floor, I wonder if it is worth the risk of retrieving it. I suppose it is my Scottish heritage which compels me to take the risk and pick up any coin (and especially a quarter).

103. "I AM A BLACK BELT KARATE"

Not All Men Are as Brave as They Claim

Some of the most humorous experiences I had as a surgeon came as a result of doing vasectomies for men desiring to have the procedure as an outpatient in my office. I had not been trained in the procedure during my residency training years. The skills I developed then were more focused on major operations such as gall bladder surgery, colon and stomach surgery, and numerous cancer treatment procedures. I did my first vasectomy while serving in the Air Force, and when word got out on our base I was doing them, the demand skyrocketed. I soon was scheduling as many as five vasectomy cases per week and was doing them every Friday. I continued at this pace for most of the two years I served in the military. When I began my surgical practice in El Dorado, Arkansas, I decided to continue offering the service with the blessings of the local urologist who was the only doctor offering the service then.

For a man to have the procedure, I required him to be in a stable marriage, and I would have both him and his wife come in for a consultation during which I would fully explain the operation. I would use a simple drawing to show exactly how it was done and allow either of them to ask any questions they might have. I offered a mild sedative to the husband to be taken a few hours before the procedure to help relieve any anxiety. With the sedative and use of a local anesthetic just prior to the procedure, there would be very little pain experienced. I also advised a simple shaving prep the night before which would shorten the procedure time and avoid some of the discomfort and embarrassment. I believed the time spent and the information given would lessen the fear factor every man had concerning this operation.

John E. and his wife came for a pre-op visit requesting a vasectomy, and I went through the entire process with them. I was acquainted with him from high school days, but didn't know him very well. He had always seemed friendly but had what is now referred to as a "red-neck" type personality. I recall on this visit his wife had a few questions which I answered, but when I asked if he had any questions, he responded with, "Nope. Let's get on with it!" I scheduled the procedure for the following week on a Friday afternoon.

On the appointed day, John came into the procedure room wearing his usual John Deere ball cap and with a cheerful countenance, which led me to believe he had taken the sedative. When I asked if he had taken the pill to help him relax, he had a quizzical look on his face and said, "I didn't know anything about a pill." I should have known he didn't hear a word I had said the week before. As I was getting him ready for the operation, I saw he also had not done the simple shaving prep I requested. I was a bit aggravated that I had to take the time to do what should have already been done.

With all the preliminary steps completed, John leaned back with his hands behind his head, and, with his cap still on he said, "I'm ready to go." I got the syringe with the very tiny twenty-five-gauge needle used for the local anesthetic, and he looked down and asked, "What is that for?" I again explained the use of a local anesthetic, and he said, "Doc, you may not know this about me, but I'm a black belt karate, and I have taken blows to my body which would kill a bull, and I didn't feel any pain at all. When I get myself psyched up, I just don't feel pain. I don't think I need an anesthetic shot." I said, "Well, since you are now psyched up, you won't feel this little needle stick which will only last for three to five seconds." The instant that needle entered his skin, his "psyched-up, black-belt karate" flew out the window and he screamed the loudest scream every heard in my office! He also used several crude, profane words, which I quickly let him know he could not use again in my office.

For the next ten minutes, he squirmed and sweated like no other man on which I had done a vasectomy, complaining all along that this was the worst thing he had ever endured and that I was killing him. I knew very well from long experience that the operative field was numb, and what he was "feeling" was due to a bad case of nerves. Just before I put in the final sutures, he suddenly sat up and vomited a huge amount of stomach contents directly on the operative field. The vomitus looked like partially digested chili. I let it sit there a short time while he settled down and I asked, "John, did you just eat?" "I had a bowl of chili just before I came in." "John, I told you last week not to eat lunch or anything for six hours before you came in so your stomach would be empty! If this gets infected it is all your fault." As he lay his head back and I began cleaning up the mess, John said, "I feel a whole lot better now." I didn't respond to his remark, fearing that I might say something which would be unkind and very unprofessional.

John and I both recovered from the trauma that afternoon. I'm happy to report that at his post-op check a week later, he couldn't recall many details of what had happened the week before, except that he had gotten sick. It took me several more days to see any humor in the whole affair. After talking with him, I think he still believed he could get himself psyched up to the point of feeling no pain. I never had another chance to prove him wrong, nor did I ever want to have the chance. That we both survived was good enough for me.

104. AILEEN'S APPLE PIE

A Generous and Gifted Patient Showers Us with Pies

Ask any member of my family what they remember about Aileen Ross, and without hesitation each one will say that she was one of the sweetest and most generous people they ever knew. They will also say that she made the most delicious apple pie they ever tasted, and I will agree wholeheartedly with both statements. In my estimation, we were the grateful recipients of at least fifty of her pies. She gave us so many pies over a two-to-three-year period that we lost count!

I had not known Aileen until she was referred to me by a physician friend because she was in need of a major surgical procedure. She was already in the hospital as a patient, and I went to her room to introduce myself and explain the details of the operation she was facing. During the visit, she was quiet and more subdued than usual, probably because she was not comfortable with a new physician, and also because of her apprehension of what lay ahead the following morning. After spending the necessary time explaining the details regarding the operation and allowing her time to ask the questions she wanted, I asked if I could have the privilege of praying for her. She said she would love that, and before I could bow my head she literally sprang from the bed and was on her knees at the bedside, leaving me standing with her chart in my hand. I didn't want to pray standing while someone was on their knees in front of me, so I laid the chart on her bed and joined her at the bedside on my knees. It was a sweet experience of prayer which remains etched in my memory.

Following a successful operation and a recovery which took approximately six weeks, I received a call from Aileen on a Saturday afternoon late in the day. During the conversation which took about twenty minutes, we talked very little about the operation, her recovery, or anything medical in nature. Instead, we discussed her family and their ministry in the community, their involvement in church, her pastor, and lastly what was happening in the lives of my wife and children. Toward the end of our conversation, she said, "Pete is on his way over there to bring you a little something!" Pete was Aileen's husband, and they had been happily married for nearly fifty years. Pete had a good job with a utilities company and he managed a tree service business with his sons, which provided needed supplemental income.

Within three or four minutes of Aileen's announcement, there was a knock on our back door, and Pete was standing there with a tray holding two freshly-baked pies, an apple and a cherry. I talked with Pete for perhaps a minute, because he seemed to be in a hurry. He always seemed to be in a hurry especially when delivering pies, and though I never asked him, I suspected he had more pies to deliver and didn't want any of them to get cold. Pete was not out of our driveway before I called Cathy and our children to come to the kitchen quickly. I was cutting into the apple pie, which was still warm and smelled heavenly. I can remember the first bite and my telling everyone present, "Without a doubt, this is the best apple pie I have ever eaten!" My opinion has not changed, and that was more than thirty-five years ago.

For the next two or three years, either Cathy or I would get a similar telephone call from Aileen. She called us at least twice a month, and for a short period of time it was weekly. Her call was usually on a Saturday afternoon lasting at least twenty minutes, and her lengthy conversations were interspersed with, "Honey, I'm telling you!" just to emphasize a particular point. When she finished talking, she would say the magical words, "Pete is on his way over there . . ." After the first two or three times she sent us pies, we offered to pay her for them, but our offer seemed to offend her. We quit asking to pay, and simply thanked her and thanked Pete over and over. We later learned there were at least ten other people for whom she was baking pies on a fairly regular schedule. For certain, her primary physician who referred her to me was on her pie list.

Aileen's gift of love to us and others was a model for our family of several Christian qualities. She had an ongoing attitude of gratitude, demonstrated by giving to everyone who had given to her. I believe she gave to many others she had never met but whose particular needs had been brought to her attention. Pies were definitely her special gifts, but she also gave her time and her presence—by visiting, phoning, praying, and just being there when someone was hurting. She had experienced the deep pain of the death of a son and was particularly sensitive to mothers in similar circumstances. We never saw Aileen discouraged or depressed, even when she seemed to have cause. I believe the reasons were the constant trust she had in the Lord Jesus Christ and her personal belief that God would meet all her needs "according to His riches in glory" (Phil 4:19).

We moved from our hometown to another state, and during our time there received word that Aileen had departed this life to meet her Savior. We were very sad that we couldn't be there for her family, but we called Pete to tell him and their children of our sorrow and our prayers for all of them. Her memory lives in my heart on several levels. I remember the sight and smell of her freshly baked apple pie and can almost taste the indescribable flavor. I remember the cheerful countenance with her wide, gleeful smile. I remember her neat appearance with a blouse and skirt which were always freshly pressed. But my most abiding memory is of her generous and loving spirit, best punctuated when I seem to hear her saying, "Honey, I'm telling you!"

105. A BEAUTIFUL PERSON

Cathy Befriends Someone Others Rejected

The world seems to have a fixation on beautiful people. Some of us who do not fit well into the category can be made to feel very unattractive. Physical beauty is assuredly relative, but there seems to be a standard which is promoted on television, in movies, and in all other visual media. The endless supply of beauty aids we are advised to purchase promise that, if we will use their particular cream or spray, we will be made beautiful. Our experiences with such products are typically that they do not work as advertised.

In the practice of medicine for many years, I have seen and treated hundreds of people who, through no fault of their own, have been physically handicapped and scarred. The emotional consequences of such handicaps can be far-reaching, ranging from thoughts or actions of self-destruction to withdrawal from social contact with anyone.

When we first met Judy Crumpler, we quickly discovered she was one of those who had withdrawn from most social contacts except those necessary for her existence. It was not in a medical setting we met her but rather in church where my wife Cathy spotted her sitting alone with no one within several feet of her. The most obvious reasons for the space were that Judy was extremely unattractive which made her difficult to look upon, and she had a foul body odor. No one except Cathy bothered to investigate the reasons for her difficulties, and neither of them were Judy's fault. She was born with a rare skin condition called elephantiasis, which caused enlarged and thickened skin folds over her body, most noticeable in the exposed areas of her face, neck, arms, and hands. These folds of skin prevented her from adequately bathing, and the excessive perspiration from the abnormal skin contributed to her body odor. Judy had other congenital abnormalities of which I was not fully aware, and even though she was in her late thirties, her mental capacity was that of an eight-to-ten-year-old. She was living alone in an independent living center, and a staff member was bringing her to church. She loved coming to church because her mother had taken her to church every Sunday when she was living at home.

Cathy took a seat next to Judy while the rest of us followed, and we all introduced ourselves to her. This was the beginning of a beautiful friendship, primarily between Cathy and Judy, but definitely involving the rest of our family. Our relationship with Judy forever changed our attitudes toward outward and inner beauty.

At first Judy was a little suspicious of us because in the past, others had reached out in friendship to her only to have the relationships fade because of Judy's multiple physical problems. Judy bonded first with Cathy, whom she called "Caffy," and as a family we determined we were going to include Judy in our friendship circle. She had our telephone number by her nightstand, and it was not unusual for her to call several times a day to ask Cathy an important question. When I answered, she identified me as "Shahn." Knowing every member of our family was available to her when she had a problem gave her more confidence in our love and concern for her.

Before long and while attending an evangelistic meeting at our church, Judy turned to Cathy and said, "Caffy, I want to have what the man is talking about." Cathy asked her to explain what she meant, and Judy responded, "I want to go to heaven when I die." Cathy took Judy into an adjoining room where along with another Godly woman, they explained God's plan of salvation to Judy in terms she could understand and receive. There was great rejoicing in the room and in heaven as Judy was born into the Kingdom.

For the next several years, Judy was included in many of our family gatherings, especially on holidays and for Judy's birthday. Cathy was able to help Judy with some of her personal issues, including better skin cleansing and the use of more effective anti-perspirants. She was also able to assist Judy in making arrangements for consultation at the University Medical

Center in Little Rock, which led to several corrective surgical procedures for her skin condition. With these improvements in her appearance and better control of her body odor, Judy gained increasingly in self-confidence.

One amusing aspect of her new health awareness involved her love for coffee. She was advised by one of her doctors to drink only decaffeinated coffee and was made to understand the concept by telling her to only drink "coffee from a green can and not coffee from a red can." One evening shortly thereafter, I received a call from Judy asking me, "Shahn, I can't remember. Am I supposed to drink red coffee or green coffee?" I reminded her to stay away from red coffee since it was not good for her!

Judy lived only for a few more years, and it was after we had moved from our hometown to another city that we received word Judy had departed this life. We were saddened to hear this news, but rejoiced in our confidence that Judy was in heaven with her Savior. One day very soon, Judy will receive a new body that will be perfect with no blemishes, and the same promise is for everyone who is a member of God's family. We all have imperfections, and the world will try to convince us we are displeasing to others and should live separated lives. Our Creator and Savior does not look on the skin or on the outer person, but on the inner person where his image is beautiful and growing stronger in us every day. Our sweet and beautiful friend Judy Crumpler reminded us of this, and for her life and friendship we are eternally grateful.

106. DR. JONES AND THE SPITTING COBRA

The Doctor Dispatches a Home Invader

As a missionary surgeon in the bush in Zambia for over twenty-five years, my friend Dr. Gordon Jones had a myriad of experiences and stories. He loved sharing those stories, and whenever he came home on furlough to El Dorado, I would listen with rapt attention.

Gordon received his training in surgery and tropical medicine in New Orleans at Charity Hospital where I trained and also in the Bogalusa Community Medical Center in Bogalusa, Louisiana. We had some mutual friends in the New Orleans medical community, and I could usually get him caught up on the latest news from South Louisiana. Just the fact he trained at the enormous Charity Hospital prepared him for almost any surgical problem he encountered in the Zambian bush. I particularly enjoyed having him assist me with my surgical cases during the months he was in El Dorado on furlough. He would show me different techniques he had perfected in his mission hospital, and I could show him newer technologies and techniques he had not yet seen.

Cobra bites were some of the more serious problems he regularly treated, an affliction that I was fortunate to never encounter in South Louisiana or South Arkansas. The cobra was a common reptile in Zambia and a frequent intruder into the homes and huts of the locals. The cobras were searching for mice and small animals and were not usually aggressive until cornered. Gordon said a major problem for all missionary doctors in Africa was in obtaining cobra anti-venom. They had discovered that an excellent substitute for the anti-venom was the use of a stun gun. This initially sounded to me like something out of a science fiction novel, but Gordon insisted it really worked. As he explained, within the first five minutes of an envenomation, if one applied the stun gun to the site of the bite and fired an electric current, the electricity neutralized the effect of the toxin and greatly reduced the risk of serious complications or death. I accepted his account and was thankful I didn't have to learn the use of a stun gun for such a purpose. When Gordon arrived in El Dorado, one of his first activities was to search every hardware store in town and purchase every stun gun in their inventory. He said that in the event he could purchase more of these instruments than he could use, he would mail them to some of his missionary colleagues in Africa who were in need of them.

I asked him if he ever had a close encounter with a cobra, and he related the following story: One morning while making his rounds at the hospital, a woman whom he knew came running in breathlessly asking if he could come quickly to her nearby home. She had just discovered a cobra in her bedroom that morning and was unable to coax him out of the house. She knew Dr. Jones kept a 410 shotgun for this express purpose. He went to his nearby home to get the gun and several shells and followed her to her home. As they slowly entered her bedroom and very carefully moved some furniture out of the way, the cobra came into view and, being threatened, reared his head. Gordon knew he was out of striking distance, so he began loading his shotgun. Gordon had a particular habit when he was doing something requiring concentration: He slightly opened his mouth with his tongue pursed against his lower lip. He said that as he slipped the shell into the chamber, the cobra did what they frequently do. He ejected (spit) venom toward the eyes of his victim. Fortunately, the venom didn't get into his eyes, but the entire amount went into Gordon's mouth!! Gordon said, "I began spitting as much of that stuff out of my mouth as I could, and told the woman to run as fast as she could back to the hospital to get the anti-venom. I didn't know if I needed a shot since I had never treated anyone who had a cobra spit into his mouth!" I asked him two questions: "What does cobra venom taste like, and what did you do to the cobra?" He said, "It has a nasty, salty taste, but I was spitting it out so fast I didn't think about the taste. As far as the cobra, I blew his durn head off." By the time the woman returned with the anti-venom, Gordon was experiencing no symptoms and decided that the risk of taking the anti-venom was greater than that of not taking it, so he didn't inject himself.

I asked Gordon if he had any advice concerning cobra encounters should I ever be in a place where I might spot one. I remember well his saying, "Don't get close enough to them where they can either strike or spit, but blow their heads off before they have a chance to do either." I resolved to do exactly what he said.

107. "I DIDN'T KNOW DOCTORS EVER GOT SICK"

One Empathetic Doctor

In all the years of my private medical practice, I don't believe I missed more than a total of five days because of personal illness. During the early training years such was not the case. I seemed to get an upper-respiratory-tract infection every other month, and would occasionally have to stay home to recover. I suppose most doctors develop a healthy immune system to protect them from the bacteria and viruses they are exposed to multiple times daily, and my immune system grew stronger as the years of my training progressed. On one of the few times when I did have to cancel an appointment because of illness, a patient told me on his return visit, "I didn't know doctors ever got sick." He was more right than wrong, but there were exceptions.

One of the family practitioners in El Dorado I had the privilege of knowing was Dr. Grady Hill. Grady had started in private practice about twelve years before I did, and for several of those years he shared office space with my brother, Berry Lee. When I moved back home to begin my practice Grady moved out of the office so I could move in since there was not enough space for three physicians.

Grady was tall, lanky in stature and moved slowly while never seeming to get in a hurry. He spoke in a slow Southern drawl, was mostly serious in demeanor, but would laugh heartily at a funny story or a joke. His hobbies involved hunting and fishing, and he seemed to me to be an expert on guns. Once when I was searching for a 9-mm German Luger, he not only knew all about the pistol, but he had one he eventually sold to me.

Bubba said his experiences with having Grady practice in his office were all good ones. Even though they shared office space, their practices were separate. They would use each other's wisdom in caring for their own patients and would speak together frequently during the course of a day. Bubba was impressed with Grady's compassion for his patients, saying he seemed to be kind and gentle with each one. He did say, however, when a patient would voice a particular symptom to Grady such as, "I have this pain in my stomach which hurts every morning," Grady would respond with something like, "I know what you mean, because I have a pain just like that!" It didn't seem to Bubba that a patient could voice any complaint for which Grady didn't have a comparable one, which made Grady appear very empathetic.

By his own admission, Grady had a "weak stomach." Several members of the medical staff including Grady would regularly have lunch in the doctors' lounge each day. All of the surgeons who had operations scheduled for the day would also eat in there between cases so there were usually six to eight doctors having lunch together. We all knew about Grady's weak stomach and usually avoided the frequent "doctor talk" about interesting things seen in the operating room, some of which were bloody and smelly. On a rare occasion, someone would tell a story about an unusual surgical finding which would make Grady gag while the rest of us had a good laugh at Grady's expense. Grady never thought any of such kind of talk was funny.

On one particular evening one of my surgical partners came through the emergency room of the hospital on his way to make evening rounds when he was stopped by the nurse on duty. She said, "I know you are not on call, but could you order something for nausea and vomiting for a patient we have in here?" My partner responded by asking if the patient had a family doctor. She said Dr. Hill was her doctor. My colleague looked through the treatment room door and saw the patient leaning off the examining table with her head near a waste can, and she was violently retching and vomiting. He asked the nurse if she had called Dr. Hill, and she said, "Yes I have, and he came out to see her, and now he is not in such good shape himself," while pointing to the corner of the room. There was Dr. Hill with his head down in the utility sink, retching and vomiting with great heaves. "Are you alright, Grady?" my colleague asked. He responded weakly, "I never could get used to a patient who was vomiting. It always makes me sick!" When I was told the story the next morning, I thought to myself that this was taking empathy a little too far. I was also told that both the patient and Dr. Hill were feeling much better that morning. Dr. Hill had not received an injection but rapidly improved as the patient stopped her vomiting.

108. THE NIGHT THE BAND WENT DOWN

A High School Prank Which Backfired

The year Cathy and I moved to El Dorado in the fall of 1971, I was approached by Dr. Paul Henley, a local surgeon and also president of the school board. He told me he had been the El Dorado Wildcat team doctor for over twenty years and was ready to step down. He said he was going to appoint me as the new team doctor with the intent of later appointing me as a member of the school board when he retired. I was definitely interested in the team doctor position, but was skeptical of serving on the school board. At the time, I didn't understand that despite Dr. Henley's good intentions, he did not have the authority to appoint me to the school board. He did, however, have the authority to appoint me as team doctor, so I accepted. I later discovered no other doctor in town wanted the responsibility of what I thought was a coveted position!

There were several good reasons I wanted to serve as team doctor. I am a sports enthusiast and wanted to use this opportunity to spend time with our son John, who was five years old when we moved. I knew we would be able to make some of the away games together, and for all the home games, he could be down on the sidelines with me. For one of the early out-of-town games, we rode in the team bus, but I soon realized we were taking two seats for players who otherwise might travel with the team. I drove my car on all subsequent trips, which gave John and me more time together without distractions.

Over the next twenty years, I really enjoyed my relationships with the coaches, the players and all the ancillary people involved in the high school sports scene at El Dorado. I got to know quite a few of the parents who regularly attended their sons' games and had to answer more than a few questions concerning injuries their sons might have had and the long-term consequences. Two men with whom I developed an excellent relationship as a result of my position were the superintendents, Dean Tommey and later Bob Watson. For the last few years of my service, Bob and I would ride together to many of the out-of-town games, and this was a special blessing for me.

The most unusual and potentially serious situation which very few team doctors have ever faced occurred one Friday night when we were playing an unnamed state school at home in Memorial Stadium. The weather was miserable as there was a constant drizzling rain throughout the entire game. Fortunately, there was no lightning so the game could be completed, but in hindsight, it would have been better in all respects had the game been cancelled. Our team was soundly defeated, and there were several players who sustained injuries which caused them to miss several games. The real problem occurred at the end of the game and didn't involve the football team at all. It involved about a half of the visiting team's band!

When the final buzzer sounded and I was preparing to go into our dressing room to evaluate any injured player, someone shouted that I was needed on the south end of the field at the twenty-five yard line. There was so much rain and with players and fans mingling on the field, I couldn't see what had happened. As I was hurrying there, someone said a visiting band member had fainted on the field. As I arrived at the student, she was lying on her back with her band cap still on and her eyes closed. With the rain beating on her face, she still had a blink reflex so I knew she was conscious. I felt her carotid pulse which was elevated, giving me more confidence that her condition was not life threatening. When I asked her what had happened, she said, "I think I've been poisoned." I asked, "How do you think that happened?" to which she responded, "Maybe it was the chips and queso I ate." It began to sound phony, because she was not complaining of stomach pains and had not vomited.

While I was talking with her, someone shouted, "There's another one down, and another, and a whole bunch!" I saw at least a dozen band members down on the ground, some rolling and moaning, while others were lying quietly holding their stomachs as if in pain. I hurriedly moved to three or four students, all band members, and made the same findings with nothing appearing serious. While kneeling and talking to one student in this mass of confusion, I saw gentleman standing upright, quietly looking down at this student. He seemed to be in control of his emotions, and I asked him who he was. He identified himself as the principal of the visiting school, and I asked him what he thought was happening. (His response is best not printed.) I responded, "The only thing I know is you need to be responsible for getting everyone who claims to have been poisoned to the emergency room of our hospital." We certainly didn't have ambulance space for this large number of students on the field, but they did have a band bus.

I went to the dressing room and alerted the ER that there might be as many as fifty students who were coming their way, claiming to have been poisoned. I told the ER nurse to call every available physician to come provide care for this mass-casualty situation. By the time I got there, Dr. Jacob Ellis, an internist, had arrived and had taken charge of the emergency situation. There were at least ten other physicians who had responded and were beginning to assess the students. After questioning the first student, I took Dr. Ellis aside and told him I believed I could solve this problem.

I asked if he would allow me to choose one student who was complaining the loudest, and I would insert a large gastric lavage tube into his stomach and pump all the contents from his stomach. It would empty his stomach within sixty seconds, but would be associated with much retching and gagging. When the other students saw this, they would quickly exit the emergency room unless they were truly sick. He declined, saying that medico-legally we were obligated to treat each one as a possible poisoning, which included blood work, toxicology screening, and observation for increasing symptoms. It took over three hours, but eventually all the students were deemed healthy and released. It had all been a giant prank!

The ER bill for all this work was sent to the visiting high school, but I never learned how it was settled. It was probably in the range of $10,000 to $15,000 for a prank these students devised. We later learned they had done the same thing in another town about a month earlier. I can only imagine the disciplinary action the school principal took on these band members.

I still wish I had been allowed to pump out that student's stomach. It probably would have saved the visiting school a lot of money. At least we learned that the chips and queso sold by our stadium concessions were safe to eat and did not contain some serious bacteria!

109. "DO YOU HAVE A COIL IN?"

A Misunderstood Phone Conversation

The following is one of many unusual and often hilarious stories told me by Dr. Bill Scurlock, my surgical associate for twenty-five years at the Surgical Clinic of South Arkansas in El Dorado. Dr. Scurlock has the wonderful skill of story-telling, and although some of his medical stories seemed far-fetched, I assumed all were truthful. I will relate this one in the first person just as I remember him telling me:

> I was on surgical call for this particular weekend and responsible for all surgical emergencies which might come to the emergency rooms of the two local hospitals. I was also responsible for any phone calls or surgical problems of my partners at the Surgical Clinic. The weekend was busy as usual, but by Sunday afternoon, I was taking advantage of some free time and taking a much-needed nap. After about thirty minutes of calm, my rest was interrupted by the ringing of the telephone. (This was prior to cellular phones.) I answered without identifying myself, and a black lady recognized my voice and identified herself as Lillian

J. from Warren (not her name or home town). I recognized her as one of my patients. I said, "Lillian, what in the world is wrong with you?" She said, "Dr. Scurlock, I've been bleeding." I knew she wasn't talking about gastrointestinal bleeding, but was concerned about gynecological bleeding, which was outside my area of practice. Thinking of ways I could refer her to someone else for her problem, I asked, "Good grief, Lillian, do you have a coil in?" I knew women with birth control coils in place frequently had problems with abnormal bleeding, and the coils had to be removed, usually by the doctor who inserted it.

"Y'as sir, I have a coil in," she quickly responded. I asked her who put it in, and she said her husband did. I exclaimed, "What? He can't do that Lillian. Your husband is not a doctor, and he's not authorized to do it. It's against the law for your husband to put in a coil." Seemingly astounded she replied, "I didn't know it was against the law for him to put a coil in. I thought we could *coil* you direct without going through a doctor!"

When I recognized we were talking about two completely different things, I started laughing while thinking what I might say next to straighten out this dilemma. "Lillian I wasn't talking about *coiling me* on the telephone. I was talking about a coil a doctor has to put in your womb to keep you from having babies. "Oh," she said. "I don't know nothin' about no coil in my womb. We was just *coiling* you to tell you I'm bleeding."

The hallmark for excellent medical care is the physician's understanding just exactly the nature of his patient's complaints and being alert and sensitive to what they are really saying when they express those complaints. In this particular instance it took Dr. Scurlock a little longer than usual to understand the problem with her *coil*!

110. IN NEED OF A RUSSIAN TRANSLATOR

Locating One to Help with an Operation

Cathy and I travelled overseas with the International Congress on Revival for over ten years and established wonderful relationships with some of the most godly people we have ever known. The purpose of the Congress (ICR), which was founded by Manley Beasley in the 1970s, was to encourage pastors and their wives to continue preaching the message of grace of the Lord Jesus Christ. The ministry started in Western Europe and spread to Eastern Europe, South Africa, Ireland, and Australia. Many of the Eastern European pastors at the time were laboring under conditions of discouragement and in some cases persecution for preaching the gospel. When Brother Manley died in 1990, God called Brother Bill Stafford to lead the ministry, and this led to Cathy's and my involvement in the ministry. We had been good friends with Brother Bill for the previous ten years.

The first year we attended the Western European conference, which was held in Salzburg, Austria, we met and became good friends with Mia and Costel Oglice. They were Romanians who lived in Chattanooga, Tennessee, while working and ministering with Precepts Ministry founded by Kay Arthur. Mia and Costel were ICR's translators for the Romanian and Russian pastors who attended the conferences. When Mia discovered I was a general surgeon who specialized in gall bladder surgery, she said, "I have seven pastors' wives who are suffering death on a daily basis because of gall bladder disease." I told her if she could get them to El Dorado, Arkansas, I would work out an arrangement with the hospital to have their operations done at no cost. Amazingly she was able to get four of the wives and their husbands to El Dorado where they received care through the generosity of the Medical Center of South Arkansas.

Late one Thursday evening, I received a phone call from Mia, who proudly announced she had arranged for Pastor Sasha and his wife Tamara from the Ukraine to come to Chattanooga in anticipation of travelling to El Dorado to have the hysterectomy she desperately needed. She said they would be in El Dorado by the weekend in order to have the operation the following week. I told Mia this was very short notice, but thought I could get it arranged. I said, "Of course you are coming with them, aren't you?" knowing her friends could not speak English. Mia said, "Unfortunately Costel and I are leaving tomorrow for a meeting in Moldova and already have our plane reservations." I told Mia I had to have a translator because there was no way I could take Tamara through a major operation without the proper communication. Mia's response was typical for her as she said in her heavy Romanian accent, "We will pray to the Lord he will provide the right one." I thought to myself, "I am already praying, but who in the world can I call?"

There was no one I knew in El Dorado who spoke Russian, and my only thought was to call Southern Arkansas University in Magnolia thirty miles away hoping to find someone on that campus who spoke Russian. I asked the switchboard operator if there was a Russian language department, and she said there was. "Please let me speak to the chairman," I said as I anxiously waited for her to connect me. When she came back on line, she said, "I'm sorry but he is out of town for the next two weeks." In a low tone I said, "I'm ruined now," to which the operator asked, "Is there any way I can help?" When I briefly explained the situation and how badly I needed a Russian translator, she said, "One of our switchboard operators is from Belarus. Perhaps she can help. Would you like me to connect you?" I held my breath as I waited for her to answer.

Innesa Divisova was, indeed, an exchange student at SAU from Belarus and worked part-time as a switchboard operator to help with her college expenses. She spoke excellent English, and agreed to come to El Dorado and stay with us for the week while Sasha and Tamara were there. She understood she would have to go into the operating room, at least for the first part of the procedure, and she assured me, "That will be exciting for me!" As we were making those plans, I could hear Mia's voice in my head, "We will pray to the Lord." I was embarrassed at my lack of faith.

The following week could not have gone better. Innesa was a delight to have in our home because of her cheerful, positive attitude. Pastor Sasha and Tamara were more subdued in their outward expressions, and Cathy and I thought it was because of fear and anxiety over what was taking place and their inability to openly communicate. The actual OR experience for Innesa went smoothly, and she had no problems with the sights, sounds, and smells of this new and strange environment for her. By the end of the week of healing and recovery, Sasha and Tamara were more relaxed and expressed gratitude for all that had been provided and done for them in the name of Jesus.

Cathy and I were grateful for the many doors of opportunity opened to us through the ministry of ICR. We experienced the joy of saying "yes" to using our skills and especially Cathy's hospitality in opening our home to brothers and sisters in Christ who were in need of medical care. At the hospital I was chided by a few physicians for having such an international referral practice but was confident God used the witness of those pastors and wives with all the hospital staff. The language of love of the Lord Jesus Christ is universal and transcends all cultural barriers.

111. SARA LEE COMES TO EL DORADO

The Original Cook of a World-Renowned Company Needs an Operation

The twenty-nine years I practiced medicine as a general surgeon in my hometown of El Dorado, Arkansas, were full of countless fascinating stories of the many thousands of people I had the privilege of treating. I believe the first few years of transition to a private practice were easier for me professionally because my brother Berry Lee (Bubba) was an established physician, and he referred most of his surgical patients to me. As I became better known in the community, my referral base of patients widened to several surrounding towns and counties.

One afternoon, I noted on my pre-op clinic schedule the name of a patient from Hampton, Arkansas, a small town thirty miles north of El Dorado. Hampton is the county seat of Calhoun County and has a population of approximately one thousand three hundred residents. There were two family physicians in Hampton at the time, and one of them referred her to me because of a serious circulation problem resulting in a major, lower-extremity wound.

She was an elderly black lady with short grey hair and a slightly stooped appearance. She was quiet with a humble and grateful demeanor. Before I determined the extent and severity of her wounds, I wanted to know more about her life and lifestyle, which would help me understand better how to advise her future care. I asked whether she had always lived in Hampton, to which she replied, "I was born and lived my early life in Hampton, but moved away when I finished high school. I moved to Chicago where I got a job and worked until I recently retired and moved back home. I lived in Chicago for over forty years."

"What was the company from which you retired?" I asked. She said, "I worked for Sara Lee for most of the forty years." "Wow, you must have known a lot of those recipes in working there for so long," I inquired. Then she revealed the extent of her Sara Lee involvement. "I was the original cook for Mr. Charles Lubin who started the company. We started out making and selling cakes and cheese cakes in the neighborhood in which he lived, and the business became so successful, we started selling all over Chicago. The company did so well in the city, he sold the cakes all over the country." I asked where he got the name for the company, and she said Sara Lee was his daughter's name. She said the name of the original creme cheese cake was Sara Lee Cheese Cake, and the cheese cake was so instantly popular that Mr. Lubin decided to call the company "The Kitchens of Sara Lee."

I said to her, "You must have been a real celebrity in the Sara Lee Company." She quietly answered, "I did have two presidents ask to have their pictures made with me." "Are you talking about two US Presidents?" "Yes sir, President Nixon and President Reagan toured the company and wanted to have their pictures made with the original cook, and I have those pictures hanging on my wall at home."

She had a very serious surgical problem requiring ultimately a limb amputation, and ensuing post-operative complications led to her death. Her underlying medical problems had so weakened her immune response and ability to recover from infection, she had no reserve when complications arose. She had only a few family members still living in Hampton, and her death was not mourned by a large number of relatives and friends.

The short time I had the privilege of knowing her and learning of her fascinating career in the corporate food business, I was blessed to have known such a pioneer in her field. I had spoken to her about her faith in Jesus Christ prior to her operation, and she assured me she had trusted in him as her Savior before moving from Hampton. One day, probably very soon, I will be able to get the rest of the story!

112. THE CALLING OF DR. COPPENGER TO FIRST BAPTIST

An Unplanned Conversation Opens a Very Important Door

Dr. Coppenger is new FBC pastor!

DR. MARK COPPENGER

The First Baptist Church at Main and North West Avenue in El Dorado voted Sunday to call Dr. Mark T. Coppenger as the new pastor of the church.

Dr. Coppenger, currently living in Jefferson City Mo., will move to El Dorado the first of December and will preach his first sermon as pastor of the congregation on Sunday, Dec. 4.

Coppenger is the son of Dr. and Mrs. Raymond Coppenger of Arkadelphia. Dr. Raymond Coppenger recently retired after many years of teaching at Ouachita Baptist University. The younger Coppenger received his B.A. Degree from Ouachita Baptist University in 1970 and received an M.A. Degree from Vanderbilt in 1972, and a Ph.D. from Vanderbilt in 1974. He also has earned the Master of Divinity Degree from Southwestern Baptist Theological Seminary in Fort Worth, Tex.

His wife, the former Sharon South, is the daughter of Dr. and Mrs. Rueben South. Dr. South is presently serving as executive director of the Missouri State Baptist Convention, and for 24 years was pastor of Park Hill Baptist Church in North Little Rock. Mrs. Coppenger also has a degree from Ouachita Baptist University. The Coppengers have two sons, Caleb and Jedidiah and a daughter, Chesed.

Dr. Coppenger is currently serving First Baptist Church of Stover, Mo. He has served on the faculty of Vanderbilt University and taught for six years at Wheaton College in Illinois. He holds the rank of Major, Infantry, U.S. Army Reserve. An author of many writings and other materials, Dr. Coppenger's most noteworthy book is "A Christian View of Justice."

El Dorado News-Times, December 1983

Over the past thirty-five years I have had the privilege of serving on four pastor search committees in three of the churches in which Cathy and I have been members. Two of the committee experiences were wonderful and resulted in the calling of pastors who were perfect fits for the churches. The other two experiences for me and for Cathy were disastrous. The very first committee on which I was asked to serve was perhaps the best.

Cathy and I moved to El Dorado in 1971 and soon thereafter joined the First Baptist Church without visiting any other church. FBC was my family's church home, and the church where I was baptized as a young boy. The pastor, Dr. Don Harbuck, had been serving the church since 1962. There had been some stormy years for him in the mid-1960s because of civil rights issues which affected the church. His social views, which many considered liberal at the time, involved inclusion of all people who wanted to worship at First Baptist regardless of race. His theological beliefs and teachings were considered moderate among fundamental Baptists. By the time we joined, Dr. Harbuck was well-liked among most who remained in the church, but there were a few who desired more fundamental teaching and a more theologically conservative church.

In January 1983, Dr. Harbuck's wife, Elizabeth, died suddenly. She had been dealing with chronic illness issues for many months, but her death was a total shock to everyone and especially her husband. In June of the same year, Dr. Harbuck resigned his pastoral position to become pastor of the First Baptist Church of Chattanooga, Tennessee. This was quite a surprise to most of his friends and church members in El Dorado, but many agreed a change might be good for him. A search committee was quickly formed and commissioned by the church, and I was one of seven members voted onto the committee. Our committee voted unanimously for Rodney Landes Sr. to serve as chairman.

The majority of committee members wanted a pastor very similar in education and theological beliefs to Dr. Harbuck, but I was one who desired a more fundamental conservative. The Southern Baptist Convention was deeply divided at the time, and the so-called "conservative resurgence" was in its early stages. All of the cooperating churches in the convention were deciding their future direction by their choices of pastoral leadership.

Our committee reviewed approximately a hundred resumes from pastoral candidates and narrowed the list to several men. We decided to pursue our primary candidate until a final decision was reached regarding him and move to the next one if needed. The man heading our list was Dr. Mark Coppenger, who had just completed his seminary training at Southwestern Baptist Theological Seminary in Fort Worth. He had no experience as a pastor, but had been a professor in the department of philosophy at Wheaton

College for six years prior to seminary. His doctorate in philosophy was from Vanderbilt University. His academic training and credentials seemed to indicate a man who would preach and lead in a fashion similar to Dr. Harbuck's. One of the committee members, Shad Medlin, said prophetically in one of our meetings, "I believe in just a few short years, Mark will be a well-known leader in the Southern Baptist Convention."

My initial opinion concerning Mark was not as enthusiastic as the others. I had met him two years earlier during a Christian Focus Week seminar at Ouachita Baptist University. We were part of a panel discussion with students regarding right to life issues, and we had a few issues on which we seemingly disagreed. I was convinced Mark was much more liberal in his theology than I desired in a new pastor, but I kept my opinion mostly to myself during our early committee discussions.

On a Sunday morning in September, we had a visiting speaker at church from Southwestern Seminary, Dr. Scott Tatum. It so happened that Cathy and I had invited him to join us for lunch at our home, and our family enjoyed a wonderful visit with him. There was no discussion about Mark Coppenger during the meal, but on driving him back to his motel, I asked privately if he knew Dr. Coppenger very well. For the next forty-five minutes, Dr. Tatum told me many things about him which I loved hearing. He said I was mistaken in thinking Mark was a theological liberal, saying, "Mark Coppenger may be to the right of Jerry Falwell." He told me other things about Mark's character and leadership qualities I had not suspected. When I returned home, I told Cathy I was a lot more excited about calling Mark as our pastor. I did not share my conversation with Dr. Tatum with the other committee members.

Our committee scheduled a trip to Stover, Missouri, on a Sunday morning in early October to hear Mark preach and interview him during a luncheon meeting. Mark was serving the small First Baptist Church of Stover as an interim pastor. We were to fly in a church member's large private plane and return home later that afternoon. In the early morning hours on the day of the trip, a surgical patient of mine developed a complication requiring admission to the ICU. The problems were such I was not able to make the trip with the committee. Cathy and I scheduled a trip for two weeks later for just the two of us to drive to Stover to meet with and interview Dr. Coppenger.

We met Mark and his wife Sharon at a restaurant in Jefferson City, Missouri, on October 15 for a two and a half hour meeting. I remember the date well because my birthday is October 12, and Sharon had delivered their third child, Chesed, on my birthday and was strong enough to meet with us just three days later! After our meeting with them and then hearing

Mark preach the following day in Stover, Cathy and I were convinced Mark Coppenger was the pastor our church needed.

The committee was unanimous in selecting Dr. Coppenger, and he was extended the call to our church with an overwhelming vote of affirmation by the members. He began his ministry as pastor of FBC El Dorado in December, 1983.

The five years Dr. Mark and Sharon served the church were the best years of ministry in any prior church for Cathy and me. Mark's preaching was solid and fundamental while being both challenging and encouraging. The church grew numerically and spiritually, and the emphases on personal soul-winning, discipleship, and personal involvement in missions were outstanding.

Cathy and I have maintained our relationship through the years with our wonderful friends, Mark and Sharon Coppenger. They still challenge and encourage us, and I am so very thankful my initial impression of Brother Mark was not correct and that Dr. Tatum's assessment of Mark was spot on. *Webster's* dictionary-definition of a fundamental, conservative Baptist just might accompany a photo of Dr. Mark Coppenger.

113. THE NAMING OF PISELM CIV

An Unusual Name Has a Biblical Origin

From earliest Biblical times, we are made aware of the significance of names, particularly the names we give our children. There are certain Biblical names thoughtful people should never give their children such as Ahab, Jezebel, Goliath, or even Lucifer. On the other hand, there are numerous inspirational names from scripture frequently given children such as Moses, Matthew, Rebecca, Ruth, and even John. In our culture parents label their children for life with unbelievable names because either the names are popular, politically-correct, or melodic.

When I was in medical school on the obstetrical service, a few of the older mothers had so many children they had run out of proper names and invited the staff doctors to supply names for their infants. I am aware of two instances in which insensitive and unbelieving doctors gave those mothers medical terms for their babies. The names I saw recorded on those birth certificates were "Alcaligenes" (*alcaligenes faecalis*, a colon bacterium) and "Escherichia" (*escherichia coli*, also a colon bacterium). It seemed humorous to medical students at the time, but those poor children probably still have those terrible names.

I was discussing unusual names one morning in the doctor's lounge at Warner Brown Hospital in El Dorado when one of the physicians related the following account of the most unusual name biblical name I'd ever heard. His mother had a position with the Bureau of Vital Statistics in a certain California city, and it was her job to verify the names entered on birth certificates in the local hospitals. This particular certificate had no name entered, and apparently the mother had left the hospital before completing the necessary paperwork. Because of this failure, this official was required to have a personal interview with the mother of the child and not only insert the chosen name, but also have the mother sign the document. She located the address and found the mother at home. After presenting her credentials and explaining the problem, she asked the mother if she had chosen a proper name.

The mother said she had decided to name her baby boy "Piselm Civ." My friend's mother asked her to please repeat the name, and this time she said the name more clearly. Then she asked politely, "I'm sorry but that is such an unusual name. Would you mind telling me where you got the name and spell it for me?" The mother replied, "I got the name from the Bible, but I don't rightly know how to spell it"—and so the request, "Would you mind getting me the Bible from which you got his beautiful name so I can spell it correctly?"

The mother disappeared into the rear of the house and a few moments later returned with a very large and what appeared to be the family Bible. They sat on the couch together while the mother turned the pages to the scripture verse where she had found the name. The Bible gave the chapter numbers in Roman numerals, which is seldom done today. The mother finally located the chapter heading in the book of Psalms and found her son's chosen name, "Psalm CIV" (Psalm 104). "There he is, Piselm Civ!" the mother excitedly indicated. The name was correctly spelled, entered in the birth certificate, which was signed by the mother.

I seriously doubt the gentleman in question is still being called Piselm Civ after at least fifty-five years. Perhaps he is known as "PC," "Dude," "Bud" or some other familiar moniker. Or perhaps he had his name officially changed to John.

114. REMEMBERING MARSH WHITE: GOD'S GENTLE GIANT

A Chance Meeting at a Summer Camp Forges a Lasting Friendship

Marsh White: Christ follower, Bible teacher, and evangelist

Cathy and I first met Marsh White in the early 1980s at Kanakuk Kamp in Branson, Missouri. We had heard there was a former, outstanding football player at the University of Arkansas working as a counselor at the summer camp our son John was attending. As we looked out across the athletic field that afternoon, someone pointed to a large black man with three or four, young, skinny campers who were either clinging to him or being carried by him. We were told, "That's Marsh White doing his thing." We were introduced to this shy, gentle man who would have an impact on our family in the years to come.

After we got to know Marsh on a personal level in the ensuing years, we learned he had been recruited by Coach Frank Broyles of the Arkansas Razorbacks to play football, and he was the second black football player for the school. Marsh was an outstanding high school football player in his hometown of Bonham, Texas. He said he was living with his grandmother in Bonham, and coaches from TCU were also heavily recruiting him. Two of the black coaches at TCU told his grandmother, "A white coach from

Arkansas is coming down here to steal your grandson and take him back to Arkansas, and you may not ever see him again." According to Marsh, when Coach Broyles arrived, she was waiting on the porch, and when she saw the Arkansas license plate, she ran him off with a broom. Coach Broyles probably had never received such an ungracious reception. Obviously, the coach returned, and Marsh went on to have a distinguished playing career as a Razorback. Following college, he was drafted into the NFL to play for several years for the New York Giants before retiring completely from football.

Marsh worked in the summers as counselor to young campers at Kanakuk Kamps while attending Bible college in Dallas. His heart for ministry involved personal evangelism, Bible teaching, and preaching, and the Dallas-Fort Worth area offered many opportunities. His teaching ministry included Southwest Bible Baptist Institute and Dallas Theological Seminary.

In the late 1980s, I received a telephone call from Bill Burnett, who was then a Christian counselor living with his family in Van Buren, Arkansas. He and Marsh had remained good friends since football days as Razorbacks. Bill said Marsh was very sick with a kidney disorder in Parkland Hospital in Dallas, and, with no medical insurance, he was in a bad place financially. Bill gave me Marsh's telephone number, and I connected with him to recommend he come to El Dorado, where I could arrange hospital care and consultation with our excellent urologist, Dr. Robert (Mickey) Murfee. Marsh came immediately and was found to require a kidney operation which Dr. Murfee did while I assisted him. Marsh was such a large man the operation was physically difficult for us, but Dr. Murfee did an excellent job, and Marsh began healing quickly.

He spent the next two weeks in our home with Cathy and our children providing loving post-op care, and all of us enjoying the sweet fellowship with him. It "just happened" our youth group at First Baptist Church had a mission trip planned to inner city Chicago, and when time for the trip arrived, Marsh was strong enough and agreed to go as one of the chaperones. All who made the trip said they never felt any sense of danger or threatening looks from any of the people in south Chicago because of the imposing presence of gentle Marsh White.

Marsh made many personal mission trips overseas including ministry into Russia, Africa, and England. He told me of episodes of smuggling Bibles behind the Iron Curtain into Russia when such an offence usually resulted in imprisonment. On one occasion when standing in the custom's line for inspection of his luggage in Moscow, Marsh had two huge suitcases full of Bibles. He related, "Here I am a large black man with two monstrous suitcases surrounded by white Russians, and I couldn't have been more conspicuous had I been waving an American flag. Just before I was to be checked, the customs agent who was to check me was called away and the man in the other line told me to go on without ever opening my suitcases. Only God could have done that," Marsh exclaimed.

In the ensuing years, Cathy and I would occasionally get ministry updates from Marsh and letters of encouragement for our own ministry in El Dorado. Marsh moved around so much he was hard to track, but we always knew he was ministering Jesus in whatever location he happened to be. We lost track of him for the past ten years while living in Branson, and were not aware of his final illness until we received word that he had departed this life. His obituary said that he died quietly on July 13, 2016, in the Baylor Scott-White Hospital in Rowlett, Texas. Our friend closed his eyes to this world and opened them in the physical presence of the Lord Jesus Christ.

My remembrance of Marsh White will always be of the gentle giant we first saw carrying a bunch of kids at Kanakuk Kamp and of later watching him as he engaged with people of all ages and ethnic backgrounds. Whether he was carrying or leading, he was always pointing people to Jesus Christ, and when he finally saw him on July 13, 2016, he heard him say, "Well done my good, gentle, and faithful servant. Now you may enter into your rest."

115. PREACHING AND SINGING AT THE MISSION

A Ministry at Home

Gary Hegi and John, 1983

The Good Samaritan Mission was founded in El Dorado in 1975. Brother W. O. Miller, along with the financial assistance of five committed Christian men, established the ministry in an economically-depressed area of town, and he faithfully preached the Word of God to those who came. His motto, which was printed on a sign displayed inside the mission, was, "Wanted, the Unwanted." Brother Miller was a wonderful encourager who made it known to the men involved with the start of the mission that he wanted them to have the freedom to preach at the mission any time they felt led. I was reluctant to ask if I could preach because those men were such spiritual giants in my eyes and able to deliver a much more powerful message. I never volunteered but always waited for Brother Miller to call and invite me. He would occasionally call and ask when I would be ready to preach again, and I would usually say I could be ready within the month. I had to coordinate the date for a weekend I was not on surgical call for our clinic. After I had preached a time or two, I told Brother Miller that I had a friend, Gary Hegi, who could join me in singing some special songs and help lead the worship music, and Brother Miller said it would be a blessing to have Brother Hegi join us.

Just a word about my preaching ability. I am confident God did not call me into a preaching ministry, but I had the heart and desire to faithfully teach the Word of God. At the time I was co-teaching with Robert Wike a Sunday school class of young couples at First Baptist Church. This was wonderful training experience for me as I spent many hours each week studying the Word in preparation. I was also receiving invitations from local area churches to give my testimony and to preach for special occasions such as Baptist Men's Day and Laymen's Emphasis Week. I have saved most of my sermon notes from those early years and in reading some of those notes, I am amazed anyone stayed awake listening to what I had to say. Perhaps they wanted to find out if I was able to finish what I started. I do take comfort in the conviction that God's Word does not return void, but will accomplish that for which he sent it! What also amazes me is that most of the small churches gave me a small honorarium for my efforts! Although I am still not accomplished at preaching, Cathy assures me I have improved (Praise the Lord!).

I don't remember how many times Gary and I sang special songs together at the Mission, but it was at least three times. The first time Gary joined me at the Mission, Brother Miller gave him a nickname, which has stuck with me ever since. I said, "This is Gary Hegi," to which Brother Miller said, "You mean like the prophet [Haggai]?" I said, "Just like the prophet!" After the initial meeting whenever Gary was joining me to sing, I would tell

Brother Miller The Prophet was coming also. Brother Miller never failed to say, "I can't wait!"

Our repertoire included such songs as "I'll Fly Away," "When the Roll Is Called Up Yonder," "Amazing Grace," "Fill My Cup Lord," and "Are You Washed in the Blood?" I played the guitar and sometimes also the harmonica, and Gary joined also on the guitar when I played my five-stringed banjo. Gary had sung with several groups in the past, had a much better singing voice, and had more songs committed to memory.

One of our more memorable experiences of singing for the folks at the mission involved the piano accompanist. There was an elderly gentleman whose name I can't remember who volunteered to play the piano for congregational singing whenever his health would permit. I had heard him on a prior occasion, and one could easily tell he played by ear and couldn't read music. He was in his late seventies, tall and slender in appearance, and absent most of his hair except the gray hair in the back and in his sideburns. He wore a hairpiece which was brownish in color and didn't match the color of his sideburns. He was neatly dressed with shirt and tie, and when he was vigorously playing and patting his feet, his long white socks were visible. His playing was similar to my preaching in that what he lacked in talent and ability, he made up for in desire and enthusiasm.

On this particular Sunday when Gary and I got to the mission just before the service was to begin, this gentleman said he would like to accompany us on our singing. I didn't have the heart to tell him we would rather not, so I told him the number we were playing was "The Old Rugged Cross" in the key of G. As I began playing the guitar introduction and Gary and I began singing in harmony the first verse of this beautiful song, I knew we were in serious trouble. Our accompanist was slowly playing with the proper rhythm, but not in the same key. As we came to the pause before the second verse, I whispered to our accompanist that we were in the key of G. The second verse was a repeat of his playing in a different key from us, but we again made it through and I nodded to Gary to close the song. Our friend looked like he was proud of himself to have joined us, and we thanked him for it. We did tell him the second number we had practiced a certain way and would prefer not to have a piano accompaniment. It didn't seem to offend him. Our performance was something like I have never experienced. Two instruments playing the same song in two different keys, and two hoot owls screeching to sing harmony in some unknown key. I don't remember what my sermon was that morning, but I imagine it was of about the same quality.

As we were preparing to leave the mission at the close of the service, Brother Miller in his typical fashion said, "Dr. Moore, you and the Prophet did a mighty fine job this morning and sure blessed all of us. We want you to come back any time you can!" What a mission and what a man! We did return again and both the singing and the preaching were slowly improving!

116. FRANK FISCHEL'S WORST MOMENT ON THE GRIDIRON

A Former High School Coach Recalls Meeting Bubba

Frank Fischel

While having lunch recently with a pastor whom I had just met, I mentioned to him that Cathy and I had moved to Branson from Fayetteville, Arkansas, and that I was an Arkansas native. Since I have been an Arkansas Razorback fan for life, he asked if I had ever heard of Frank Fischel, who was an All-Southwest Conference football player at Arkansas in the late 1940s and early 1950s. He said Frank had lived for over twenty years in Crane, Missouri, where he had known him, and Frank was a great Christian witness and his best deacon at the First Baptist Church of Crane. He wasn't too surprised I had heard of him, because he was such a great football player at Arkansas, but was shocked when I said I had known him pretty well.

Frank Fischel was an assistant football coach at El Dorado High School when I was a student from 1954 to 1957. He was never my coach since I only played basketball and tennis in high school. One day at a basketball practice, Coach Fischel was watching us scrimmage, and at the end of the practice, he asked if I was the younger brother of Berry Moore. When I said I was, he said he was a little surprised I wasn't playing football instead of basketball. He could see I was tall and skinny and not even close to the weight of Berry Lee (Bubba) when he was a high school All-American football player at El Dorado. Coach Fischel then told me about the day he first met Bubba on the Razorback practice field when he (Coach) was a freshman and Bubba was a sophomore.

Frank was born and raised in Helena, Arkansas, where he was known as a local hero. During the early years of America's involvement in World War II, he wanted to serve his country despite the fact he was underaged. He convinced the Army recruiter he was seventeen and enlisted when in fact he was only fifteen-and-a-half. He served in the Pacific Theater flying a torpedo bomber and was involved in the historic battle of Guadalcanal. Upon returning from the war to Helena as a high school student, he became a high school All-American football player. He was recruited by many major colleges but chose the University of Arkansas to begin his illustrious Razorback career in 1946.

Coach Fischel said that when he arrived in Fayetteville to play football, he considered himself to be the strongest, meanest, and simply the best football player on the campus. This was before he had seen the other players on the team or taken the first snap of the football. He didn't say it, but I assume his life-endangering experiences during World War II, which few if any other players shared, added to his inflated self-image.

On the very first play from scrimmage, he was on defense and lined up opposite the offensive tackle whom he heard was named Berry Moore. Coach remembered, "This guy didn't look like much of a player, especially since he was wearing plastic-rimmed glasses." He said I looked over at him and said, "I'm gonna run over you and kill you on this play." But, as Coach recounted, when the ball was snapped, he instantly lost consciousness, and the next thing he remembered was having the assistant coaches at his side trying to remove his helmet while mopping the sweat off his brow. When he groggily asked what had happened, he was told, "Moore caught you with an elbow!" Coach said my brother hit him with his right elbow so fast he never saw it coming, and the force was so great he sustained a concussion. He followed by saying he played football at Arkansas for four years and had a brief stint in the pros, but was never again hit with a blow like that. He also said from that point on, he gave Berry Moore a "lot of space."

I discovered Frank Fischel set aside a professional football career to re-enter the military as an Army officer to serve honorably in the Korean War. On returning from that conflict, he completed his training to begin work in various coaching positions throughout Arkansas. After he received a master's degree in administration, he moved his family to Missouri to continue his thirty-year career in teaching and administration. He finished his journey in Crane, where he is remembered as a wonderful man, a great teacher and encourager, and an exemplary husband, father, and grandfather. He died in Crane in 2013 having lived eighty-six years.

I wish I had known he was living in Crane since it is so close to Branson. We would have had a wonderful time reliving those times and experiences in El Dorado, and I could have gained so much from his wisdom and Christian fervor. I also wish he could have known Bubba as an adult and an equally-fervent believer. They would have instantly bonded again and been inspirations to each other. I feel confident despite Bubba's quiet and gentle nature, Frank would have kept his eye on Bubba's right elbow!

117. A GREAT COACH

A Respected Coach Trains a Walk-On Who Becomes an All-American

Several years ago, the long-awaited movie *Greater* was released, and Cathy and I had the privilege of watching the movie in a theater in Ozark, Missouri, a few miles north of Branson. The movie covered the life of Brandon Burlsworth, a young man born and raised in Harrison, Arkansas, about thirty miles south of Branson. This faith-based movie inspired and challenged us as we watched the life of this wonderful young man unfold, and as we saw him fulfill his dreams of becoming a phenomenal football player for the Arkansas Razorbacks from 1996 to1998.

Brandon's home life had been splintered by the absence of his father, who was an itinerant country-and-western musician, and who had a problem with alcohol abuse. Brandon's life was stabilized by the strong character of his mother Barbara and older brother Marty. By the time Brandon was in high school, he was an overweight kid with a love for football but with no personal discipline to train. Tommy Tice, his high school coach in Harrison, once told him if he wanted to play football, he had to be the "first to come to practice and the last to leave." He finished his high school days as a lineman with average abilities. He was offered a scholarship to play football at Arkansas Tech, but turned it down in order to try out as a walk-on for the Razorbacks.

In Fayetteville, Brandon encountered the offensive line coach Mike Bender, who initially saw no potential for him to ever play for the Razorbacks. Fortunately, Mike saw his gritty determination to succeed and allowed Brandon to continue to practice. He followed Coach Tice's advice and was always the first to arrive and the last to leave. At the end of year one, Brandon had developed his body into a strong six-foot three-inch, three-hundred-pounder, and had proved to Coach Bender he had the desire, discipline, and talent to play for the Razorbacks. He was offered a full scholarship at the end of his freshman year.

The movie depicted the relationship between Coach Bender and Brandon as almost one of a father to a son, and it helped me better appreciate the value of football coaches in general and more specifically Mike Bender.

Cathy and I became friends with Mike and Gayle Bender shortly after we moved to El Dorado in 1971. Mike was selected as head football coach of the El Dorado Wildcats in 1974, and I was the team physician. I watched him struggle with teams which didn't perform well in their conference and in fact lost most of their games. Mike was accustomed to winning, having been a great player himself for Strong High School (twelve miles east of El Dorado) and having become a standout at the University of Arkansas. He played on the 1964 squad, which was the only Razorback team to win the national championship. He was drafted into the NFL and played several years with the newly-franchised Atlanta Falcons.

Cathy and I were especially close to the Benders in those early years, because Mike and Gayle were members of our couples Sunday school class at First Baptist Church, and our daughter Ginny was best friends with their only daughter, Eden. Their other child, an older son Brent, had some physical challenges related to a birth incident, and because he was nearer in age to our son John, they occasionally spent time and played together.

On one occasion Cathy and I were at the Bender's home on a Friday night for a social event following a Wildcat football game, and we got to meet one of Mike's brothers, "Little Boy" Bender. When he stood up from the couch, he was at least six-feet-four, weighing over two hundred and fifty pounds. I said, "I'm not sure I want to meet 'Big Boy' Bender as huge as you are!" He laughed and said he was so-called because he was the youngest of the Bender boys.

Because of Coach Bender's belief in Brandon's abilities while instilling in him sound playing principles, Brandon became a starting offensive guard in his sophomore year. He performed so well the next year that he was selected as one of the team captains and named to to the All-SEC first-team offense. Before his senior year, a new head coach, Houston Nutt, was named to lead the Razorbacks replacing Head Coach Danny Ford. Coach Nutt was the one who coined the phrase, "Doing it the Burls [from Burlsworth] Way" when challenging the team to do the right thing in life or when playing football especially, when no one was watching.

As with all head coaching changes, many assistant coaches are re-placed by other coaches chosen by the new leader. Under Coach Nutt, Mike Bender was replaced as a Razorback coach, and he pursued other coach-ing opportunities. He was not present for Brandon's senior year when he excelled as a man and a player, receiving not only repeat, SEC, first-team honors, but also All-American first-team accolades. Academically, Brandon was named to the All-SEC academic honor roll for each year he was on the team and was the first Razorback ever to receive his masters degree before playing in his last game, the Citrus Bowl in Orlando in January, 1999.

To complete his unbelievable rise to football fame, Brandon was drafted by the Baltimore Colts in the third round, and following the initial training camp tryout, he was assured by the Colt's line coach he would be a starting guard on the team the following year. Tragically, Brandon died in an automobile accident just weeks before reporting to the team in Bal-timore. He was travelling from Fayetteville where he had worked out and was driving to Harrison in order to "take his mother to church." We recently learned he had a meal with his good friend Brent Bender just before leaving for Harrison.

As in life, where no individual achieves any measure of success apart from the influence of many people, so a football player does not become great without the instruction and encouragement of a great coach. Mike Bender was used of God in the athletic training of one of the greatest play-ers to don a Razorback uniform. Without knowing for sure, I believe that both coach and player helped mold each other's character and Christian witness and that they did so beautifully.

Note: On the day I posted this recollection, I read in the *Arkansas Democrat-Gazette* that Mike Bender stepped into eternity having died in his sleep the night before. I am very sad because I would have liked for him to read this tribute to him, but I do believe he is at peace with God and in the presence of his Savior.

118. A FUMBLING SHOT

Prescribing Treatment for a Common Condition

I doubt any doctor associated with sports medicine has ever heard of such a thing as a fumbling shot. If it were an effective medicine to prevent a foot-ball player from fumbling the football, every football coach in the country would insist his team doctor immediately administer the shot to every player on his team who handles the ball!

I was fortunate to be the team physician for the El Dorado Wildcat football team for most of the twenty-nine years I was a surgeon in the town. Shortly after Cathy and I arrived in town, I was contacted by Dr. Paul Henley, another surgeon, who had been in El Dorado for least twenty-five years. He was a member of the El Dorado school board and had been chairman of that board for the previous five years. His association with the school system had begun years earlier when he agreed to serve as the team physician, a role he played until I arrived. He convinced me I needed to serve as team physician until he retired from the school board, and then I should take his place as a board member. His exact words regarding the matter were, "The school board needs a doctor as a member, and you would be the perfect one." What I didn't realize at the time was that school board members were elected in a general election and not appointed.

I agreed to serve and was honored to have been asked. I wanted to begin community service as quickly as possible, and this was an open door to use my professional skills. Another motivational factor in my decision was our son John Aaron. He was four years old, and I wanted to involve him in as many sports activities as possible because I could see his potential. He was quick, fast, and with such excellent hand-eye coordination that he rarely dropped a ball when we played catch either with a football or baseball. I wanted him on the sidelines with me so we could spend the time at the games and travel together to the out-of-town games.

On our first away game, John and I rode the team bus which was exciting for both of us. He kept looking at the player one seat ahead of us, and, when the player happened to turn around, John asked him, "Are you really an Arkansas Razorback?" John hadn't quite made the distinction between the Wildcats and the Razorbacks since all he had heard about when we lived in Georgia were the great Razorbacks! When I learned our riding on the team bus prevented two lower-tier players from making the trip, I drove my car to all out-of-town games, which gave John and me additional time alone.

One of the major responsibilities of the team physician was to organize the pre-season physicals for the high school as well as the junior high school athletes. This required not only getting enough volunteer physicians to serve, but coordinating how it was accomplished. There were approximately three hundred physicals to be done annually for the sports teams and cheering squads of the two schools. Without a prearranged plan, such a task would have become utter chaos. We obviously had to separate the boys from the girls, and I assigned one doctor to be responsible for the girls' physicals, which were much less involved than the boys' physicals. This was prior to the institution of girls' competitive athletics in El Dorado. Most years, I was able to enlist at least eight doctors and four nurses to take vital signs and help with the paperwork, which fortunately was not complicated or extensive.

One of the doctors able to volunteer most years was Jim Sheppard, a family physician. He was born and raised in El Dorado, and I had known him and his family for many years. Jim was an excellent athlete who played high school football for the Wildcats and was skilled enough to play for the US Naval Academy for a couple of years. His familiarity with the football program and his wonderful sense of humor made the task of the physicals a lot more fun.

The location for the exams changed several times, but this particular year, we were doing the them in the chemistry lab of the high school. There was plenty of desk space on which to write our findings and the aisles seemed to make the flow of traffic more efficient. The young men had all stripped down to their underwear, and there were five lines of players, each going up to a doctor. Unknown to me, Jim had brought a fifty-cc syringe with a spinal needle attached, which made the injection unit approximately ten inches in length. He had filled the syringe with some unknown yellow liquid, which gave it an even more ominous appearance. He had it lying on the table behind him for just the right moment.

The right moment approached him in the form of a skinny, fifteen-year-old seventh grader who was experiencing his first football physical. He certainly had no expectation of what was next when his turn came to be examined by Dr. Sheppard. While the doctor was listening with his stethoscope to his heart and lungs and probing his abdomen for abnormal lumps, the young man was asked what position on the team he would be playing. The answer proudly given was "running back." Dr. Sheppard then slowly reached behind him and brought out the awesome syringe and held it up while squirting a small amount of the yellow liquid into the air. The promising, all-star running back's eyes widened greatly just before he asked, "What is that for?" Dr. Sheppard said, "This is a fumbling shot which we give to all running backs to keep them from fumbling the football for a whole year. You said you were a running back, didn't you?" "Naw sir! I play on the line. I don't carry the ball at all." To which Dr. Sheppard said, "Son, you're awfully skinny to be playing on the line. Maybe I need to get you a weight-gain shot." Feeling totally trapped and considering switching to track, the rising star was speechless. Dr. Sheppard finally confessed there would be no shots given this day. Had it not been so inappropriate, I believe the young man would have hugged the doctor right there.

Later when we learned that some of the "things the doctors said to a few students were causing them to be fearful," we changed our approach from being so jovial to conducting ourselves more seriously. After all, our doctors didn't want the reputation of creating fearful Wildcats even before the first hand-off of the season.

119. THE WITNESS AT THE SUGAR BOWL

Old Friends Reunite for a Football Game

I have been an Arkansas Razorback football fan since 1946, when my older brother Berry Lee (Bubba) received a full scholarship to play during his college days. He was only able to play one year, because he was disabled by a career-ending knee injury during his sophomore year. I never got to see him play in a Razorback uniform. My loyalty as a fan has never waned despite some very lean years and only one national championship, this in 1964.

Shortly after our family moved to Arkansas in 1971, I infected our son John Aaron with the same zeal for the Razorbacks, and we have attended a number of games together including three post-season bowl games. One of the most memorable games we attended was the Sugar Bowl in New Orleans in January 1980 when the Razorbacks played the University of Alabama Crimson Tide. It was not the game itself which was so memorable, because the Razorbacks lost the game 24–9, but the events in New Orleans which led up to the game. John Aaron, who was twelve years old at the time, and I decided to attend the game and enjoy a father-son get together with Dr. Joel Spragins and his son Mark, who was ten years old.

Dr. Spragins is a gastroenterologist who practiced medicine for many years in Shelby, North Carolina. We were classmates in medical school at the University of Arkansas in Little Rock and close friends during those years. He is the son of Dr. John Spragins, who formerly was a resident of Arkansas College in Batesville, Arkansas, (now Lyon College) where Joel had attended college. He was raised as a Presbyterian, but like me and by his admission during college and medical school days, he was nominal in his faith life. Between our sophomore and junior years, we spent two months together in Jacksonville, Florida, doing an externship at Baptist Medical Center. We had a fun summer in the sun with the beaches available while making lots of new friendships. In addition, we also learned some good medical principles from the staff physicians at the hospital.

While doing my four-year surgical training at Charity Hospital New Orleans, I became very good friends with Dr. Richard (Dick) Faust who was a staff physician and practicing surgeon at a large clinic in downtown New Orleans. He and I co-authored an article on tetanus which was published in a major surgical journal. In the interim between my medical training and my entering the US Air Force as a surgeon, I worked for two months in his clinic as a staff surgeon. He told me that when I finished my military responsibilities, if Cathy and I ever wanted to move back to New Orleans, I would have a position waiting for me in his clinic. He also said that whenever we visited the city, we had an open invitation to stay with him and wife Margaret in their beautiful home on Henry Clay Avenue in the Garden District, just off well-known St. Charles Avenue.

John Aaron and I invited Joel and Mark to join us as guests of the Fausts while enjoying all the Sugar Bowl festivities. It was a perfect place for us because the Fausts gave us their entire third floor with a large suite of rooms and complete privacy. They did take us to dinner one evening, but otherwise we seldom saw them. According to Dick, they wanted Joel and me to "give full time attention to our sons and not worry about them." That's the kind of friend Dick Faust was to me.

John Aaron and Mark made an immediate connection and really enjoyed talking and playing with each other. Their instant friendship made for an especially fun three days, because Joel and I already had a good relationship and conversation was always lively and sprinkled with lots of laughter.

I was able to tell Joel about the life-changing experience Cathy and I had in Dallas in 1977 when we attended the Bill Gothard seminar in the Dallas Convention Center. (See "A Shopping Trip to Dallas.") I didn't try to preach at Joel or even suggest he and his wife Jeanne should consider attending such a conference. Joel had lots of questions concerning our past and present lives and even asked John Aaron what he thought about his parents' new attitudes and life styles.

On the morning of the game which was played in the early afternoon, we all went down-town to the Riverfront Hilton, the team hotel for a huge pep rally. The Razorback band was there along with the entire pep squad and what appeared to be thousands of Razorback fans all decked out in red clothing, Hog hats, and Hog snouts. It was very exciting for all of us, and, had enthusiasm been the key to victory on the football field, we would have won the game hands down! Unfortunately, our beloved Hogs were beaten by an excellent and superior team from Alabama.

When we returned to the Faust's home for our final evening together before returning to our respective homes, Joel made this statement to me, "I've never seen such a change in a person since the last time we were together. I want you to tell me more about that conference in Dallas and how Jeanne and I might attend!" I told him there was also a conference held each year in Charlotte, North Carolina, only fifty miles from Shelby, and they could sign up for the early summer dates for that meeting. We also knew a couple we'd met at an earlier conference, Gary and Virginia Cooper from Charlotte, and they contacted Joel and Jeanne, inviting them to stay in their home during the four-day conference.

They did indeed sign up for the seminar, and Joel called me a few days prior to the start and asked, "Before we go over to Charlotte, are you sure this man Bill Gothard is not some sort of religious fanatic?"

I could hardly wait to hear their evaluation of the time spent in Charlotte, but Joel finally called to report that he and Jeanne had a very special week together. They connected with the Coopers and made a new friendship in the Lord with them. Overall God had helped them strengthen their faith and marriage, and they were very grateful to have made the sacrifice of their time. He thanked me multiple times for encouraging them.

John Aaron and I had a wonderful time in New Orleans with Joel and Mark, and we still talk about the weekend with fond remembrances when the subject is brought up. Despite the final score of the game at the Superdome, we believe we were part of a big win for the Lord at the Sugar Bowl in New Orleans on January 1, 1980!

120. TRAINING A HOME-CARE GIVER

A Patient Is Trained to Change Dressings

In a surgical practice, the treatment of certain types of wounds requires patience and the presence of a strong stomach in the care givers. As surgeons, we become accustomed to sights and smells which often are unpleasant at best and downright repulsive at worst. Infection in a surgical wound is a dreaded complication, and the treatment of such a wound can be unpleasant both to the patient and the care giver. This is just part of the job but thankfully does not represent the majority of the care giving experience.

One of my senior partners, Dr. C. E. Tommey, was one of the best surgeons I've known, and also one of the most beloved doctors in El Dorado. His surgical technique was superb, and his patients usually did very well and recovered quickly. In addition, he had a quiet and very kind demeanor which not only promoted confidence in his abilities but made his patients believe he always had their best interests in mind. I admired and respected him so much that when I had to have several operations, Dr. Tommey was my surgeon. Also, when I had a particularly complicated surgical case for which I needed a special assistant, it would usually be Dr. Tommey who

I would call to help. On one particular Fourth of July weekend when Dr. Tommey and I happened to be the only surgeons in town, we decided to assist each other on all the emergency cases. We did a total of twenty-three major operations from Friday evening to Monday morning and were both relieved when the weekend was over.

On one particular afternoon, Dr. Tommey was scheduled to see patients in the clinic as he had completed his operative surgical cases for the day. Clinic patients included new patients and doctor referrals for consultation. Also scheduled were post-operative patients for suture removal and patients seen and treated in the ER who needed more care.

One of the patients to be seen was Mr. Johnson, whom Dr. Tommey had seen and treated in the ER for an abscess in his groin area. He had never met Mr. Johnson prior to this ER visit and did not meet the patient's wife in the ER. Apparently, he had been brought by another family member. He was an elderly gentleman who had never had a serious infection problem because he was healthy for his age. In addition, he'd avoided doctors as much as possible. The abscess was quite large, but Dr. Tommey had drained it completely and left surgical packing in the wound to facilitate rapid and complete healing.

Dr. Tommey's nurse Reba called the patient into the treatment room and prepared him for the packing removal and wound cleansing. Because of the location of the wound and its size, the entire groin area had to be exposed but was done in such a way to protect his modesty as much as possible. When Dr. Tommey entered the room and inspected the wound, he told Reba that Mr. Johnson needed to have someone cleanse and pack the wound for him daily. He asked Mr. Johnson if he thought his wife would be able to do that, and he replied she could do it and not be bothered too much by the wound. Reba went to the waiting room and called for Mrs. Johnson to come back to the treatment room. Reba had never met either one of the Johnsons prior to this visit.

When the elderly, grey-haired lady entered the room, Dr. Tommey said he wanted to show her just how to cleanse and re-pack the groin wound, and it needed to be done each day. He gave her the surgical tools to do the job and guided her as she successfully removed the packing, cleansed the wound, and repacked it correctly. She applied a very neat outer dressing and then helped Mr. Johnson put on his underwear and trousers. As he walked out of the room, Dr. Tommey told him he needed to see him again in one week, and Mr. Johnson thanked him for his help.

The lady went to the corner of the room and sat down in the chair, and Reba told her the appointment was over. She told Reba she had an appointment, and Reba asked, "Oh, you have an appointment on the same day as your husband?" The lady said, "That was not my husband. I've never seen him before in my life." Reba said, "I called for Mrs. Johnson and you stood up and came into the room." She said, "I misunderstood. I don't hear very well. My name is Jackson and I thought you called for me!" Both Dr. Tommey and Reba were flabbergasted and apologized profusely to Mrs. Jackson for placing her in such an embarrassing situation. She said it was all right, and she was glad to help in any way she could. Apparently, she thought it was required for each patient to assist in the care of the patient ahead of them in order to speed up the treatment time and reduce the waiting time.

As a physician it is very gratifying to have a patient or family member follow our instructions to the letter, but in the case of Mrs. Jackson and Mr. Johnson, perhaps she should have been a little more suspicious of the wound care training she received. The positive aspect was that she was certainly prepared to provide good home care if her own husband ever developed a wound abscess.

121. SUDIE TEACHES A LESSON ON CHIVALRY

One Is Never Too Old to Learn

Sudie Garner is one of the dearest Christian witnesses Cathy and I have had the pleasure of knowing through the years. We were members together at First Baptist Church in El Dorado during the 1970s and 1980s, and in those years we shared many experiences of service together through the church. Her husband Hubert was a well-known barber in El Dorado for many years, and I was one of his customers for at least six years prior to his untimely death.

Sudie and Hubert like so many couples with strong marriages were quite different in their personalities. Sudie was quiet, introspective, kind, and known for her commitment to the Lord Jesus. She was especially fervent as a prayer warrior and intercessor, and all who knew her were confident that any prayer requests given her received serious and faithful attention. Hubert, on the other hand, was outgoing, fun-loving, and full of stories to tell. It was always fun to have Hubert cut my hair every two or three weeks because I relished his story-telling and would respond with several of my own.

I have previously told how impactful the Bill Gothard seminars were for Cathy and me, and in 1977 on attending our first seminar in Dallas, we gave our hearts and lives to the Lord Jesus. In the intervening seven or eight years, we attended other seminars, including not only the basic seminar but advanced seminars as well. We invited family members and various friends to attend with us, and the Garners were one couple who arranged to attend a basic seminar with us in the early 1980s.

I don't recall any specific events from our week together, but nearing the end of the week, Bill was teaching on how men should honor their wives. He pointed out that many of us have forgotten certain acts of courtesy to which we always paid attention during our courtship. One was simply opening the car door for our spouse either when she was entering or exiting the car. Bill encouraged the wives to help their husbands display this courtesy by remaining in the car until they remembered. I do recall that as we were leaving the conference center that day, Cathy and Sudie said to each other that this lesson might require some prolonged sitting time in the car on their part.

The next haircut I received from Hubert was about two weeks later, and we talked about the wonderful teaching we received at the conference. He said he had heard principles about life and marriage he had never before heard presented in such a practical way. I agreed and we both marveled that Bill Gothard could know so much about marriage having never himself been married. Hubert said Sudie was also helping him apply some of the principles, as we heard with the following account:

> We came home from church on Sunday night, and I pulled into our garage, parked the car, and entered the house through the garage. I closed the garage door before going inside. I sat down in my easy chair and turned on the television to relax before getting ready for bed. I called out to Sudie to fix me a glass of tea when she could. When I didn't hear her voice, I went to the bathroom, thinking she might be there, but she wasn't. I called out to her in a louder voice and heard nothing. I really began worrying and thinking she had passed out, so I looked all over the house going room to room. I thought the only place left was the garage and the thought struck me was she had had a heart attack and died in the car. I turned on the garage light, spotted her still in the car, and asked, "Sudie, are you all right?" She answered, "Yes, Hubert, I am all right." "Then why don't you come on in the house? Are you mad at me?" "No, I'm not mad. I'm just waiting for you to open the door!" As I walked over and opened the door I asked her, "How long were you going to wait?" "As long as it took. That's what Bill Gothard told us to do."

Hubert said he might be a slow learner, but he thought he had finally learned the lesson about being a gentleman and opening the door for Sudie while showing her in other ways how important she was to him. I've always wondered just how long Sudie really would have waited. Knowing her, I believe she would have waited in the car all night if that's what it took.

122. ME 'N SLEEPY

A Famous Singer Trusts Me to Operate on Him

I might not have met Sleepy LaBeef had he not had a medical problem which required an operation to correct. When I saw his name on my patient appointment list, I thought the first name might have been misspelled. That was in the late 1980s when I was a general surgeon in practice in El Dorado, Arkansas. During the initial consultation, I discovered his name was spelled correctly; it was a nickname given him as a child because he had a condition known as "lazy eye" causing his eyelids to droop making him to appear "sleepy" to his fellow students. I'm certain this was the source of lots of teasing, but because he was larger than most kids his age, the teasing eventually stopped.

Sleepy was born in Smackover, Arkansas, in 1935, the youngest of ten siblings. He was raised on his family's farm with kerosene lamps and a wood stove since they didn't have electricity until he was twelve years old. He learned to sing the Southern gospel style music in small country churches and constantly listened to the Grand Ole Opry and radio stations broadcasting rhythm and blues, bluegrass, and country music. Sleepy sold his .22-gauge hunting rifle to buy his first guitar and soon upgraded to a Sears & Roebuck model. His first quality guitar was a Gibson. He dropped out of school in the eighth grade and moved to Beaumont, Texas, where he worked as a bellhop and began performing publicly in many different venues.

During this period, Elvis recorded his first 45-rpm record, "That's All Right (Mama)," and he played often in the Houston area. Sleepy moved to Houston and began playing with a number of top-quality musicians such as Elvis, Glen Campbell, Roy Orbison, and George Jones. He often played in opening acts for Elvis concerts in 1954 and 1955, when Elvis was performing in the Houston area. Sleepy later moved to Tennessee and, along with his band, recorded for Columbia Records and Sun Records. The musical style he developed has been called "rockabilly," a cross between rock and roll and hillbilly. Sleepy refers to it as American roots music.

He has written and recorded a few original songs, but mostly has recorded songs of other writers. He has a phenomenal memory and is said to know the lyrics of well over a thousand songs. Sleepy's records have not made the top of the charts in the United States, but in Europe, he has been well-received, and at least two of his songs—"Good Rockin' Boogie" and "Hello Josephine"—have been chart toppers.

Throughout the years, he has given a number of young performers their first opportunity by allowing them to join his band. One of the musicians he helped who went on to achieve his own acclaim is El Dorado's Jason D. Williams, who joined Sleepy's band when he was only eighteen. Jason D. plays the piano in the musical style of Jerry Lee Lewis and, in the opinion of many, is more gifted musically than Jerry Lee. After a period of time, they separated to continue their own careers. Both Sleepy and Jason D. were inducted at the same time in the Rockabilly Hall of Fame in Jackson, Tennessee, in 2006.

At the time of his surgical procedure in El Dorado, Sleepy and his wife Linda had not moved back to Arkansas, but soon afterward moved to Springdale, Arkansas. Despite being in his sixties at the time, he continued travelling and performing in the United States and overseas in Europe. He was drawing very large crowds overseas where his albums were also doing much better than in the states.

When Cathy and I moved to Northwest Arkansas in 2000, I was not aware Sleepy and Linda were in Springdale until one morning I saw his name on my appointment list at the Wound Care Clinic of Washington Regional Medical Center. Before I saw him, he had told our receptionist, "I am one of Dr. Moore's former patients from El Dorado." I was really thrilled to become reacquainted with Sleepy, and because he had a problem which required regular visits over several months, we got to visit often. We talked about everything from faith to guitar playing to the difficult life of travel and playing concerts. I discovered Sleepy and Linda were deeply committed to the Lord Jesus and easily spoke about their faith. We prayed together during most of his clinic visits.

Following resolution of his wound problem, I didn't hear from them until one evening about a year later I received a call from Linda saying Sleepy was an inpatient at Washington Regional Hospital. He had been admitted following a cardiac catheterization and was scheduled to have coronary bypass surgery the following day. He told his heart surgeon, "I'm not having any operation until my surgeon, Dr. Moore, gives the ok." The surgeon asked Linda if she would have Dr. Moore, whom he did not know, come to the hospital to talk with Sleepy about the operation. I immediately went to the hospital and found Sleepy in amazingly good spirits. He told me about his symptoms which had caused him to seek an evaluation, and the results of the cardiac cath. I simply told him in my opinion, he had no chance of improvement until he had the planned procedure. I also told him his surgeon had a good reputation and was skilled in his ability to do the procedure well. When I told him if I had his problem, I would go ahead with the operation, and that in the final analysis God was in control of his life, he said, "That's good enough for me. Linda, tell the doctor to set the time for tomorrow." We had prayer for his healing and both Sleepy and Linda told me they were at peace.

I was in the waiting room the next day when the surgeon reported to Linda the operation was a success, and Sleepy would be home within a week. I was able to go to their home about ten days later to remove his sutures. That was the last time I ever saw him, because a short time later, Cathy and I moved to Branson where I began work at the Wound Care Clinic.

I spoke with Sleepy by phone on several occasions, and each time he would say, "Doc, why don't you buy one of those theaters in Branson, and I'll come over there and put on a show?" I told him if I could afford a theater, he would be the only performer I would have. He did continue doing limited performances after his heart procedure, but for the most part he stayed home enjoying his family and especially his grandkids.

He lived to the age of eighty-four and died at his home on December 26, 2019, probably from heart disease. I'm so thankful to have known and loved Sleepy over the years since his surgical procedure in El Dorado. He was a very kind, generous, and gentle giant of a man who seemed to have boundless energy. I wish I had been able to attend one of his performances. He could certainly sing and entertain like few others. Except for his eye condition, from which he derived his nickname, he was anything but sleepy.

123. THE CONSULTATION WITH A SPECIALIST

A Well-Known Consultant Is Presented with an Unexpected Challenge

Dr. Larkin Wilson was one of the best internists I had the privilege of knowing. Along with a number of other excellent, primary-care and specialty physicians, we served the medical needs of the people of El Dorado, Arkansas, and surrounding area for the twenty-nine years I practiced general surgery there. The other physicians in my family who served the people there from 1898 until my brother retired in 2001, included my grandfather, Dr. John Aaron Moore; my Pop, Dr. Berry L. Moore Sr; and my Bubba, Dr. Berry L. Moore Jr.

I met Dr. Wilson initially when I was a second-year surgical resident at Charity Hospital in New Orleans. I had the misfortune of developing serum hepatitis probably from a needle or scalpel puncture wound. As a busy surgical resident, I was often either the surgeon or assistant in as many as ten surgical procedures per day. Even a physician is hard pressed to diagnose himself with hepatitis because of the initial slow progression of the illness. I began feeling tired to the point of exhaustion and attributed those symptoms to my difficult work schedule. I developed a low-grade temperature after a few days and assumed I had the flu. When I finally agreed to "have a check-up" at Cathy's insistence, the doctor in Lake Charles, Louisiana asked me how long I had been jaundiced. Cathy and I were on a three-month rotation to the Charity Hospital in Lake Charles. When I carefully looked into my eyes in the mirror, I finally noticed I was deeply jaundiced, so the doctor admitted me to the hospital.

The disease became progressively worse, and there was some concern I would survive because my liver function tests were getting steadily worse. Cathy and I had only been married eleven months, and she was very frightened by the doctor's reports. When my mom heard the news, she insisted I be transferred by ambulance to El Dorado so Bubba could care for me. At that point I was too sick to object to such a plan. Cathy agreed with Mom to get me back to familiar surroundings, so the transfer back home was made. Bubba called in Dr. Larkin Wilson as a consultant, and he and Larkin agreed it was best for Larkin to assume my care in case I went into complete liver failure.

Larkin was very businesslike in his care of me, and there was not much frivolous conversation. After a few days, I began improving to the point I was beginning to worry about the cost of my hospital stay. Cathy and I were living on poverty-level wages, and we had no medical insurance. One morning I mentioned the fact to Dr. Wilson while he was checking my lab results for the morning. Without looking up he said, "I'm interested in your health and not your wealth." I said, "Yes sir, and I appreciate that very much. However, as my wealth sinks deeper into poverty, my health will quickly follow in a downward spiral." My logic did not move him. Years later, after I had been in private practice in El Dorado, I recognized that Larkin was indeed not only an excellent internist, but had a dry sense of humor which was beloved by his family, friends and patients.

After Cathy and I moved to El Dorado, and I was well-established in my surgical practice, I thoroughly appreciated the daily interactions I had with my medical colleagues. I was especially close friends with several internists, and they were the source of regular patient referrals. By this time, I had gotten to know Dr. Wilson much better, and we had regular and occasionally daily conversations about mutual patient concerns.

I was making my rounds at the hospital one morning, and, while sitting at the nurses station writing my notes on a patient chart, Larkin came out of another patient's room and agitatedly asked me, "Where is that brother of yours?" I knew he wasn't in the mood for levity so I answered, "I don't know. Is there a problem?" Bubba had one of his long-time patients in the hospital with a heart issue which required some additional care, so he had consulted Larkin who had a special interest and expertise in heart problems.

Larkin did not know the lady and was polite in his introduction and familiarization with her particular problem. He did a thorough evaluation which took about thirty minutes, and when completed, he told her he would present his findings to her doctor, and Dr. Moore would make the final decision on the best treatment. As he was about to leave the room, she gently held his sleeve and said, "You are not through yet." He said, "Yes ma'am, I have finished my exam and will now report to your doctor." She said again, "But you haven't finished. When Dr. Berry comes to see me, he always prays with me before he leaves." Larkin smiled at her and said, "I'll just let Dr. Moore take care of that for you today," thinking it would satisfy her. She responded to the startled Dr. Wilson, "Well, I'll tell you this: If you don't pray with me, I'm not going to pay you!" Larkin told me he was so shocked at her statement, he mumbled some brief prayer the content of which he couldn't remember. The patient must have been pleased with his effort and graciously thanked him.

Larkin said he was certain Bubba had "put the patient up to having him pray for her." I told him Bubba had done the exact thing to me all the time until I gave up and began praying with every patient. (He actually never put patients up to forcing either Larkin or me to pray with them, but I thought it sounded good at that moment.) Having been a patient myself on several occasions, I know how uplifting and encouraging it is to have one's doctor pray for your treatment and recovery.

I don't know whether Larkin used the incident to encourage him to begin ministering to his patients through prayer in their presence, but I do know that he continued serving his patients as an outstanding internist of excellence and integrity. I also know he would acknowledge it was God who had gifted him to serve and allowed him to continue his service for many more years. It certainly was my privilege to have known him and served with him.

PS: Several years after we moved from El Dorado in 1999, Dr. Wilson was in a serious traffic accident in Louisville, Kentucky, and he sustained injuries causing him to be quadriplegic. He lived for another year or so requiring total care, and finally died from other complications. The community mourned the loss of this beloved practitioner. A portion of the Medical Center of South Arkansas is named the Larkin Wilson Center.

124. "LOOKA HEAH, LOOKA HEAH"

Getting to Know the Blufords

The Bluford family all lived in South Arkansas and to the best of my knowledge never traveled much outside of Union County. There were two generations of Blufords who were faithful patients of my dad (Pop) and then switched over to my brother Berry Lee (Bubba) when he joined Pop in their general medical practice. The Blufords were by no means one of the prominent families in El Dorado, but were average, hard-working people who were intensely loyal to the Lord Jesus, to each other, and to their doctors. Usually when you saw a Bluford anywhere in town another member of the family was close by.

I was introduced to most of them at Bubba's office when I visited there, even before I became a doctor. There were so many of the Blufords that one of them was likely to be in the office with some complaint on any given day. I was always impressed by their humble and grateful attitude toward the doctors and the staff. One frequently heard all of them say, "Yas suh. No suh. Please, and thank yah!" depending upon the situation or the question. I don't think I ever met all of the Bufords, but was closely associated with four members of the family—Mittie, Major, Willie, and Sister Missionary Ruth Foster (as she was known within the family and her church).

After I returned home to establish a private practice in general surgery, Bubba was an immediate referral source and many of my surgical patients were referred by him to me. He called me late one afternoon to say he had admitted Mittie Bluford to the ICU at Warner Brown Hospital. She had suffered from severe abdominal pain for three or four days and now had nausea and vomiting with an extremely high temperature. Mittie was in her late sixties and had been treated for a number of years for hypertension associated with obesity. Bubba suspected gall bladder infection and needed me on stand-by in case the initial medical treatment was ineffective.

When I arrived, there were at least six members of the Bluford family in the waiting room, but the only ones I recognized were Major and Sister Missionary Ruth. She was easily recognizable because, in addition to her large size, she always had on a red Afro wig which never seemed to fit quite right. I didn't know the name of the church in which she was called as a missionary, but it must have been a Pentecostal church, because even in a conversation with her she would emphasize the things I would say to her by chanting such things as, "Yes, yes," or "Thank yah, Jesus" or "Amen, amen!" Her encouragement to my normal conversation almost made me feel like I was preaching, and it always spurred me to say more than I normally would. I'm sure if I had ever preached in her church, her encouragement alone would have caused me to preach with greater zeal and fire!

Mittie was indeed sick, and her initial tests confirmed gall bladder disease, but we wanted to wait another twenty-four hours to let the infection subside, if possible. The following day, she was getting worse, so the decision was much clearer—she needed an emergency operation. I told the nurse to call the family together at her bedside, and I would explain to Mittie and to them what needed to be done. The four members of the family whom I knew and several others I assumed were family gathered around her bed with Sister Missionary Ruth standing closest to me. I was sure they were all Blufords because they had their heads slightly bowed, and none of them had any questions which might indicate the slightest mistrust of me or of Bubba. Even Sister Missionary Ruth had her head turned more toward Mittie than toward me.

I directed my words toward Mittie so she could understand to the best of her present ability what was needed. She was very weak and not able to carry on much conversation. The only other voice beside mine which was heard over the next few minutes was not Mittie's but was her sister, Missionary Ruth, and she was emphasizing what I was saying. The conversation went something like this;

> "Mittie, you are sick; you are real sick."
> Sister Missionary Ruth: "Yas Lawd, Yas Lawd!"
> "Mittie, your gall bladder is infected and the infection is really
>   serious."
> Sister Missionary Ruth: "Dr. Mo, Dr. Mo!"
> "Mittie, you have to have surgery right away."
> Sister Missionary Ruth: "Looka heah, looka heah!" (translated:
>   Looky here, looky here).

Mittie had no questions for me concerning the operation; neither did any of the family members. I always knew this was a sign of total trust of the patient and family in the Lord's power to use me, and I never took the trust lightly. When I prayed at her bedside for her deliverance and healing from this illness, every one of the Blufords were also praying fervently out loud, so it was impossible to discern all of their words. I just know the Lord heard each one as clearly as if he or she were the only one praying, and it was a sweet offering to his ears.

At the operation, I discovered her problem was a diseased and abscessed gall bladder which could be removed for a cure. When I saw what was wrong, my response was, "Looka heah, looka heah!" not in jest, but in gratitude to the Lord for his healing, for Mittie's trust in Him and in me, and for all the Blufords. I knew where they all were at the moment. They were in the waiting room praying and thanking him for healing Mittie.

125. "HONEY, COME ON BOARD!"

Crowded Seating on an Airliner

During the years Cathy and I took mission trips with the International Congress on Revival (ICR), we met some of the most outstanding Christians we have ever known. The first trip overseas we made with ICR was to a conference in Salzburg, Austria in 1992. The team met in Atlanta and boarded a Delta L1011 for the non-stop flight to Munich. Cathy and I were seated in economy class along with most of the team. Several members of ICR were travelling in business class, including Bill and Sue Stafford, and I assumed it was because as president of the organization Bill scheduled all the trips overseas. The other couple in business class was Alton and Mabel Bean from Amity, Arkansas. They had been going overseas with ICR for at least three years before Cathy and I joined the team.

Alton Bean and his son Gary owned and operated Bean Trucking Company in Amity since 1969, and the company had grown into a very successful transport company. Alton and Mabel had met Bill Stafford in the 1980s when Bill preached a revival in their church, First Baptist of Amity. An immediate friendship began which continued until Alton and Mabel departed this life. Alton was selected to be on the Board of ICR from its inception, and I served on the same board with him.

Alton and Mabel were beloved by everyone who knew them. They were quiet, humble, generous servants of Christ who never sought the limelight. Alton was physically a large man who weighed in excess of three hundred and fifty pounds, but at his age of about 65 when we first met them, he was still very active and strong. One couldn't have a conversation with Alton for more than a few minutes without breaking into laughter. He could tell some of the funniest stories I ever heard and most of them related to some event or activity in which he and Mabel had been involved. I know Mabel not only experienced the events but had heard Alton recount them numerous times. Still, she would quietly smile and frequently laugh out loud as Alton relived each account. Alton's account of why he and Mabel always travelled business class was my favorite story, and, despite the fact I heard it many times, I usually laughed until I cried whenever he told it. The word pictures he painted and the gestures he used created a hilarious scene. Here's the account:

> The reason I started flying business class began when my brother Curt and I went on a bird hunting trip to West Texas around 1985. We drove from Amity down to Dallas to catch a Southwest Airlines flight to Amarillo, where we had hunted several times before. On Southwest, they only had economy class seats. We already had our tickets and had reserved two seats on the back row of the plane, which had three seats. We were hoping that third seat wouldn't be taken, which had been the case on our previous flights on Southwest. Curt is bigger than I am, and we not only filled our seats, but most of the third seat also. When we started getting on the plane, there were more people than usual waiting in line. They loaded us first, and when we got comfortable in our seats I told Curt, "You start praying nobody has this other seat, and I'll watch the door." When I saw the flight attendant finally close the door, I told Curt his prayers seemed to be working but keep on praying, and I'll keep watching. And then I saw her coming down the aisle!
>
> She was a younger woman than us, but she looked to be about our size. As she walked down the aisle, her hips were touching the seat arms on each side. "Keep praying Curt, maybe her seat is not this far back." When she got to our row she said, "Excuse me, but is this where seat 1B is located?" I said, "It sure is, honey. Come on board." She then said to me, "I can't get to my seat until you stand up." I told her, "I can't stand up until you back up!" We worked and worked and finally got her wedged in that seat between us. By the time we did, every person on the plane was laughing. I don't know how we were able to get her seated, because when the plane finally took off, I was having a hard time breathing. It seemed that when either she or Curt inhaled, I had to exhale, and that was the only way I could breath. We finally got to Amarillo, and the three of us laughed most of the way there. I told Curt when we got off the plane, I was always going to fly business class from now on.

He and Mabel kept his word regarding future flights.

Cathy and I loved our friendship with the Beans, and for at least five of the ten years that we travelled overseas with ICR, the Beans also made the trip. We had a special bond with them, since at the time, we were the only couples on the ICR team from Arkansas. They have now both departed this life, and we are confident we will see them again. I believe Alton's first words to us will be, "Glory be to God. Come on board!"

126. JASON D. AT GULLEY PARK

A Rock and Roll Singer Entertains a Crowd

Jason D. Williams

Cathy and I lived for thirty years in El Dorado, Arkansas, where I practiced medicine as a general surgeon, and where we raised our three children. In the spring of 1999, we began making plans to move to Florida. Leaving our home where we had family and many friends was a very difficult and emotional experience, but we felt led by the Lord to move to Clearwater, Florida, where I joined the staff of the First Baptist Church of Indian Rocks. I was to be the medical director of their new, church-sponsored medical clinic. Following opening of the clinic in February, 2000, I was able to work for two months before realizing this clinic concept was not the right fit for my skill set.

Again, with much prayer and agony we made a second move to Fayetteville, Arkansas, where I became a director of the Wound Care Clinic at Washington Regional Medical Center. This was not only a great fit medically for me, but Cathy and I were in the town where our daughter Ginny and husband John Luther lived, and that alone made the move exciting for us!

Soon after making the transition to Fayetteville, I received a call from Frank Luther, John's father, that Jason D. Williams was performing at Gulley Park during their annual summer concert series. It's a beautiful locale, which hosts six or seven artists each summer for free public concerts. The concerts are well-attended with perhaps as many as five hundred people taking advantage of the cool evenings to see and hear an array of outstanding performers.

Jason D. was well-known to Cathy and me because he was from El Dorado, and his parents, Hank and Marie Williams, were very good friends. We had been members together at the First Baptist Church and in the mid-1980s had gone with them on a church sponsored mission trip to Brazil.

We had known Jason D. since he was a young boy and had watched his musical career develop. He had an amazing talent for piano playing, which was similar in style to that of the well-known Jerry Lee Lewis. There were some who believed Jason D. was more musically gifted than Jerry Lee. On one occasion when Jason D. was between concerts he came to our home for a visit, and I asked him to give us a mini-concert. His wild piano playing style resulted at one point in his playing several bars with the heel of his boot. Cathy made him stop, thinking he might seriously damage our heirloom baby grand piano. He just smiled, stop playing, and continued with his visit.

Cathy and I were glad to join Frank and his wife Janice along with Ginny and John to Gulley Park for the concert that evening. In all the years we had known him, we had never heard Jason D. in a full program. The performing pavilion was surrounded by people seated on lawn chairs and with many sitting on blankets on the grassy slopes of the park. It was a pleasant, cool evening with lots of excitement and anticipation of a fun event.

Jason D. did not disappoint anyone expecting to see and hear robust and lively piano playing and singing. His style ranged from classical to rockabilly, from country to jazz, and finally rock and roll. He played sitting and standing on the stool, standing without the stool, and even with a few bars behind his back. I don't think he ever stood on his head while playing, but looked as if he wanted to. His songs included "Whole Lot of Shakin' Goin' On," "Great Balls of Fire," and "Drinkin Wine, Spo-Dee-O-Dee," all of which he had on several albums. There were so many songs, I can't remember their titles, but all were lively, raucous, and fun.

At the completion of the concert, he remained on stage for folks to come to the platform to ask questions about his life and playing style. I told Cathy and our group I was going to work my way through the crowd, and see if I could say a few words to him. By the time I got to the stage, he was almost finished with the Q&A session. I did hear one young lady who appeared to be in her early teens ask, "How much practice would I have to do to play like you?" His quick reply with tongue in cheek was, "Honey, you could practice a hundred years and not be able to play like this," as he ran his fingers up and down the keyboard several times. He then shouted,

"Thank y'all for coming out!" and ran off the platform to get in his motor home parked behind the stage.

Undaunted I walked over to the motor home and knocked on the door. The windows were tinted so I couldn't see inside. Some man whom I assume was his manager barely opened the door and asked, "What do you want?" I said, "Tell Jason D. that Dr. Moore is out here to see him." From the back of the vehicle, I heard him shout to the man, "Let Dr. Moore come in."

He hugged my neck while we exchanged greetings. He teasingly asked, "Were you out in the audience tonight?" "Of course, I was. Why would I be standing in your motor home right now, if not?" He said, "If I had known you were out there, I would have played more religious songs." I quickly said, "I'm already going to tell your mom about some of the bawdy songs you are singing these days." "Oh, please don't tell her. She already fusses at me about some of them." We had a good conversation about his current life and his career, and he asked about Cathy and our kids and why we were now living in Fayetteville. I asked him if he was taking his family to church, to which he replied, "Not as much as I ought to," so I didn't ask any more "religious" questions.

The last time we saw Jason D. was about ten years ago while we were visiting our son John, his wife Gina, and our three grandsons in El Dorado. We were walking downtown at lunch time and saw that a car had stopped in the middle of the street on the square. As we walked past the car, the driver's window was open and Jason D. was grinning widely waiting for us to stop and talk. He was home for a brief visit with other family. His parents had departed this life a few years earlier. Cathy and I sure loved the Williamses, and know they were proud of their talented son, despite some of his antics and a few of the bar room songs he played so well!

127. PIXIE VISITS THE NIGHT CLUB

A Brave Sunday School Member

Pixie Gordon, 2001

When Cathy and I finally made the decision and moved to Largo, Florida in 1999, we had mixed emotions weighing heavy on our hearts. On the one hand, we were leaving everything in El Dorado which was familiar and comfortable. Our life included our children and grandchildren, our many friendships, our church, a busy surgical practice, my mom, who was elderly and disabled, and the many intangibles of living in a small Southern town. On the other hand, we were moving to Cathy's home state where her brother, sister, and their families lived, and to a large and exciting metropolitan area with a beautiful beach. The area churches were growing rapidly, and the church to which we were going was one of the leading Baptist churches in the state. The one thing to which I believed God was calling me and the only motivating factor for the move, was the opportunity to direct the medical clinic ministry of the church. Cathy and I later discovered that there was a rumor circulating in El Dorado concerning our move that I had "lost my mind" and didn't understand the significance of this move to Florida. The rumor included Cathy's going along to protect me from making other serious mistakes in judgment.

Initially we had to rent an apartment until we could find the best house for us. It was located a few blocks from Starkey Road, which intersected Ulmerton Road, the main east-west road to the beach. Our church, First Baptist of Indian Rocks, was located on Ulmerton Road and the drive from our apartment to the church took about fifteen minutes. Located at the intersection of Starkey and Ulmerton Road was a gaudy purple building which housed a XXX-rated club which seemed to have some popularity in the area based on the number of cars in the parking lot. Whenever I passed that vile place, I would pray for the people who owned those cars that God would turn their hearts back to him and to their spouses.

Within a week of my arrival, Cathy was able to join me, and we began our ministry through the church. Throughout each week from August to December, I was studying and preparing to take the Florida Medical Board exam in order to obtain a medical license. The clinic doors could not be opened until I had the document in hand.

Together, Cathy and I started building the senior adult Sunday school class to which we were assigned. The first Sunday morning, there were five precious souls who came. One was confined to a wheel chair, one was using a walker, one needed a cane, and two were healthy—a couple who had agreed to help us build the class. They were near our age, were very active, and fortunately didn't need a device to stand or walk.

A special friend we made the first Sunday was Pixie Gordan, an eighty-something-year-old widow who, despite her age and the inconvenience of a walking cane, was very active and spry. Pixie had such an outgoing personality and a love for the Lord Jesus that she was just plain fun to be around. The first time we met her, she said she would be glad to help us build attendance since she had a number of friends who were looking for a "good Sunday school class." She assured us that her friends were not disabled, although that would not have made any difference. Cathy and I were excited to be part of a class which was growing and had a hunger for God's Word.

Pixie called one day and said she wanted to meet us for lunch and discuss something she believed the Lord was telling her to do. Pixie was one of the oldest members in the class and, despite her use of a cane, she was still driving and totally independent. We met at a favorite restaurant equidistant from Pixie and us. As we started on our appetizers, she began describing her thoughts about the declining morality of our nation and especially the area in which we lived. She said it was breaking her heart to drive by places where pornographic magazines and movies were being openly sold and how this type of business was corrupting the minds of young people as well as adults. Then she mentioned the name of the club at the junction of Starkey and Ulmerton where it was advertised there were women employed for lewd and immoral purposes. She said she knew those women had mothers and grandmothers who were also heartbroken over their employment and were praying for them just like Pixie and so many other Christians. She said, "God wants me to go and tell the people who own that club, as well as the people who work there, God loves them and wants them to close it down because of the harm it is causing." As we shook our heads in agreement that the club should be closed, I was thinking, I sure hope God didn't tell Pixie she was supposed to take her Sunday school teacher with her! She wanted us to pray for her, and, at the close of our meal, we did just that.

About two weeks later, Pixie called and asked us to meet her again for a report of her meeting at the club. We were anxious to hear all about it. She said she had gone to the club with her Bible, and the only person she encountered was a young man in his mid-twenties working at the front desk. She said he was very polite when she told him about the reason for her visit, but refused to allow her to go into "the back room" to talk to the employees or the owners. He also told her the owners would not permit people to talk to employees in that part of the building. Pixie said she asked him if his mother knew where he was working, and he said she did not. He agreed with Pixie on how disappointed his mother would be if she knew. Pixie then prayed for him and for the other employees that God would convict them of how wrong they were in this business. Pixie said she went back in another week and the young man she met was no longer working. She said the new man was "not very polite" and asked her to leave.

Cathy and I loved the heart and enthusiasm of Pixie and admired her courage to do what most of us would like to do. We are convinced she accomplished what God sent her to do, and the young man she encountered was removed from this place of moral corruption. Who knows, he might now be the very person leading the fight against similar clubs in Largo and central Florida? We do know God's ways are much higher than our ways and his thoughts higher than our thoughts.

128. "THESE TEETH NEVER HAVE FIT RIGHT"

How to Handle Poorly-Fitting Dentures

I have always enjoyed the interpersonal relationships I had with many of the men for whom I provided medical care. My dad (Pop) was a great story-teller, and I used to listen to his stories for hours at a time. Growing up and later having a medical practice in a relatively-rural area afforded me access to many men who enjoyed hearing and telling interesting life stories. I tried my best to not have any patients waiting in my office to see me while I was encouraging patients ahead of them to tell stories unrelated to their medical issues. Certainly not all of my story-telling friends were patients, but friends I had met along the way who were not looking for a doctor. Because most of the hours of each day were spent either in the hospital or in my office, most of my accounts come from those settings.

I had done a surgical procedure on a gentleman who was retired from a supervisory job at the local oil refinery and who was also a well-known fisherman. He had spent many years fishing the local lakes and rivers during his leisure time while employed, and now in retirement, he was able to fish three or more times a week. During the office visits he made during his surgical recovery period, I had the opportunity to ask him about any previous or current "fish stories." Probably the funniest fishing story I ever heard came during one of those post-operative visits.

"James" had a regular fishing partner named "Roy," with whom he fished every Saturday morning for years. James owned the flat bottom aluminum boat with a twenty-five horse power motor in which the two of them fished. They would choose the lake or river to fish during the week, and by 8:00 a.m. on Saturday morning, they would be at their favorite fishing spot for that particular body of water.

James said "ole Roy" had a habit when they arrived at their usual spot of taking out his upper false-teeth plate and placing it on the metal seat between them. He said he did that to "rest his mouth." He would then proceed to fish for an hour or so until there was a lull in activity. At this point he would say, "I guess it's time to have a snack" and would reach around to get his upper plate, secure it in place, and proceed to eat a candy bar, apple, or whatever snack he had brought. James said he had watched Roy go through this same routine for years when he decided one morning to pull a prank on him.

As they reached their designated spot, Roy took out his plate as usual and placed it on the seat. When he turned back around to start fishing, James took out his own upper plate, placed it on the seat and put Roy's dentures in his shirt pocket. They fished for a couple of hours until Roy said, "Let's have our snack. The fish don't seem to be biting right now." Roy took the plate, which he did not recognize as not his own, and placed it in his mouth. James said Roy rolled it around two or three times and even tried with his index finger to get the plate properly seated, all to no avail. Much to James's chagrin, he watched as Roy took the plate out of his mouth saying,

"My dentist has never gotten these teeth to fit right," and sailed the plate out into the lake. As he saw his own dentures sink, he said to Roy, "I guess we go to the same dentist, because these teeth of mine have never fit me right either," while throwing the plate in his pocket into about the same area of the lake! They both had a good laugh about their sorry-fitting teeth and were glad to finally do something about it.

James still chuckled about the expensive lesson he learned that morning and admitted it took him several years before he had the courage to tell Roy what he had done. He said it didn't matter to Roy because he had already made up his mind to get rid of those teeth. James said, "I wish I had known that sooner, I would have even thrown them for him and saved myself a whole lot of money!"

129. WAYNE BARBER AND HIS BUBBA TEETH

The Value of a Good Set of Teeth

Dr. Wayne Barber

Cathy and I had the privilege of knowing and hearing some of the best preachers in the world as a result of our involvement in the International Congress on Revival (ICR). We joined in the work of this particular ministry in the early 1990s as a result of our friendship with Brother Bill Stafford who was the President of ICR.

Brother Bill assumed the leadership of ICR upon the death of its founder, Brother Manley Beasley in 1990, and despite his demanding schedule as a Southern Baptist evangelist, he was fully involved in ICR. He invited me to join the board of ICR, which was meeting annually in Chattanooga,

Brother Bill's hometown. It was at the initial board meeting I attended that Cathy and I met Wayne Barber and his wife Diane. Wayne was Pastor of Woodland Park Baptist Church, a large and growing Southern Baptist church in which Brother Bill and wife Sue were members. Other members of this church which we later met were Kay and Jack Arthur, founders of Precepts Ministry; Costel and Mia Oglice, Romanian missionaries for Precepts Ministry; Dorie Van Stone, Precepts missionary; John Ankerberg, prominent Christian apologist; and Dr. Spiro Zodiates, one of the world's prominent Greek biblical scholars. There were many sweet and dedicated Christians who regularly attended Brother Wayne's church, and Cathy and I loved being in that atmosphere!

I was on the board for two years before Brother Bill convinced Cathy and me that we would have ministry opportunities by attending the overseas conferences which were primarily held in western and eastern Europe. There were also meetings in Australia and in South Africa. While I was on the board, we added Ireland, where conferences were held for two separate years.

Our initial ICR trip to Austria was in February, 1993, and we were able to take Mary Kay, our older daughter, and her new husband Dave Janke along with us and our younger daughter Ginny, who at the time was regularly dating her future husband John Luther. We all met in Innsbruck, Austria, for a three-day rest period before the conference in Salzburg, Austria began. It was in Salzburg that we first heard Brother Wayne preach, and he was on the schedule for at least four sessions. There were five other preachers present in addition to Brother Bill, and the quality of preaching and worship was outstanding. From our first conference in Austria, Cathy and I only rarely missed going overseas with the team and considered those meetings each February as spiritual highlights of the year.

Several years after our initial conference, Cathy and I were able to invite our good friends Brother Tommy Freeman and wife Sharon to accompany us to an ICR conference, again held in Salzburg. I have written elsewhere concerning my love and appreciation for Brother Tommy and the impact he has had on my spiritual growth ("Church Visitation with Brother Tommy," and "The Prairie Grove Revival"). Brother Tommy's personality is intense and focused, but he does have a good sense of humor. He had never met Wayne Barber or heard him preach prior to this meeting.

Although Brother Wayne was an outstanding preacher, he had a mischievous sense of humor which could sometimes catch people who didn't know him off guard. Wayne was a physically large, imposing man, six feet eight inches, weighing approximately two hundred and seventy-five pounds, so his size alone commanded attention. He always had a huge smile with beautiful white teeth, and always acted as if he had never met a stranger.

By this time, my brother-in-law and sister, George and Marilyn Berry from Austin, Texas had joined the ICR team, and we were all meeting at Hartsfield-Jackson International Airport in Atlanta for our overseas flight to Austria. We met George and Marilyn first and introduced them to Brother Tommy and Sharon, whom they had never met. Over the next ten to fifteen minutes, we had a lively conversation recounting stories of our children, mutual friends, and people from El Dorado, Arkansas with whom we had fellowship.

Coming down a long concourse, we spotted Brother Wayne and Diane walking toward us. All of us except Brother Tommy and Sharon recognized them. Wayne had a huge smile on his face revealing a hideous pair of Bubba teeth! He bear-hugged all of us, and when we introduced Brother Tommy and Sharon, he bear-hugged them as well! None of us mentioned the teeth, but as I hugged Wayne, I told him, "Brother Wayne you have never looked better!" After a few minutes Wayne and Diane excused themselves and moved back down the same concourse to greet other attendees.

When he had gotten out of hearing range, Brother Tommy asked, "John, did you say he was pastor of a large church in Chattanooga?" "Yes," I said, "one of the largest churches in the city." "Surely he must have a dentist in the church who would help him with his teeth problems." "What problem is that?" I asked, while keeping a straight face. "Oh John, did you see those teeth of his? They would be a huge distraction while he was preaching." "Brother Tommy, when he preaches, he doesn't open his mouth very wide and no one pays much attention to his teeth. Everyone in his church loves him and thinks he is a great preacher." Brother Tommy continued, "John, somebody needs to help him with those teeth because they are only going to get worse. I think as a member of the board you ought to try to help him." I didn't comment further and didn't say anything more about Wayne's teeth.

Later in the day before our flight departed, Brother Wayne visited with us again and had removed his fake teeth revealing his own perfectly white teeth. Nothing was said about the teeth, but Brother Tommy said privately to me, "John, I'm going to get you! You really got me on that one."

Brother Wayne served the Lord at Woodland Park Baptist Church for several more years after this and then moved to Albuquerque, New Mexico to pastor Hoffmantown Baptist Church until 2011, when he and Diane returned to Woodland Park.

Although we were no longer serving in the ministry of ICR, Cathy and I along with Marilyn and George Berry were privileged to hear Brother Wayne preach again in 2013 at the Cove, Billy Graham's Training Center in

Asheville, North Carolina. George and I each carried a set of Bubba teeth, and, at our initial reception with the Barbers, we grinned widely! He loved it.

Ironically Brother Wayne departed this life on August 29, 2016, at the Cove, where he was scheduled to be the conference speaker. He had developed a form of ALS a few months earlier, but was trying to finish his course well. Cathy and I, along with Marilyn and George, praise God we got to know and love Brother Wayne (Bubba teeth and all)!

130. "WOULD THE FATHER PLEASE STAND UP?"

Always Understand a Question Before Answering

Any fan of Arkansas Razorback basketball will quickly recognize the name Marvin Delph as one of the greatest players to ever don a Hog uniform. Marvin is from Conway, Arkansas and became a Razorback in 1974 following an outstanding high school career with the Wampus Cats. He joined two equally famous Arkansas-born players recruited by Coach Eddie Sutton, Sidney Moncrief and Ron Brewer, and the three of them came to be known as "The Triplets." Their playing time together became legendary and changed the entire basketball culture in Fayetteville, Arkansas from one of mediocrity to national prominence resulting in a Final Four appearance in 1978.

The road to a National Championship in basketball in 1994 began with the exploits of "The Triplets" in the late 1970s. What many may not know about Marvin Delph personally is what a strong and committed Christian he was (and is today). He could have played professionally in the NBA, but relinquished it in order to play for Athletes in Action following his college graduation.

Athletes in Action was founded in the mid 1960s by Campus Crusade for Christ. Outstanding Christian basketball players were recruited to play worldwide, and, among other things, to give their Christian testimonies at half-time to packed-out crowds of young and old alike. It was an excellent means of spreading the gospel in more unconventional ways, and gave young men like Marvin the opportunity to display their world-class basketball talent and personal devotion to Jesus Christ. Following is a true story told by Marvin when on an occasion in El Dorado, Arkansas I was invited to have lunch with him along with Buddy Hall and my son John Aaron. This was over thirty-five years ago, and the details of the story are exactly as I recall:

Whenever we played in a city, which was usually on a Saturday night, we would scout out a church near our hotel in which we could worship the following morning. On this particular occasion, we were playing in Madrid, Spain and the only church we could find close-by was a Catholic cathedral. The game was sold-out and we were enthusiastically received by all the Spanish fans. We stayed up late talking with fans and signing autographs, so were tired the next morning, but five of us walked together to attend the worship in the Catholic church. All of us were black and, at six feet and seven inches, I was the shortest man of the five. One of our players was six feet and eleven inches tall, so we stood out in a crowd just by our size alone.

As we were walking to church, we all acknowledged we had never worshiped in a Catholic church, and none of us either spoke or understood Spanish. We agreed to pick out one person sitting in front of us, and when he stood, we would stand, when he knelt, we would kneel, and when he would sit, we would sit and be quiet and reverent. The plan was working well, and we were blending in with the worship in which we understood not one word of what was being said. About half-way through the worship hour, the priest was speaking when he hesitated, and the man sitting in front of us whom we were following rose to his feet. As we had been previously doing, all five of us stood without noticing no one else was standing. All of a sudden, the entire congregation exploded in loud, boisterous laughter and we immediately sat down. I turned red with embarrassment, and it takes a lot to make a black man turn red! The remainder of the service we remained seated regardless of what the man in front of us did.

As we were leaving the church at the conclusion, the priest was at the door and spoke to us in perfect English. He recognized we were five of the basketball players he had watched the night before, and he thanked us for being present. I had to ask him why so many people thought it funny when we stood about half-way through the worship hour.

He said, "Oh that was very funny! I was giving church announcements, and I announced we had a new member of the church family. A little baby boy was born last night into the church family, and his mother couldn't be here, but would the father of the boy please stand up! It was quite a sight to have you five men stand in addition to the father." We all told him we don't speak Spanish, and didn't understand what we were doing. He said he already knew it and most in attendance also knew.

Marvin was honored by the state of Arkansas in 1998 when he was elected into the Arkansas Sports Hall of Fame. He and his wife live in Conway where they have raised their four children, and he is a successful businessman. He is a Christian role model, mentor, and frequent public speaker sharing his testimony around the state of Arkansas. I'm certain he has told of his Spanish Catholic Church experience many times.

131. THE WITNESS OF BROTHER BILL'S GOLF GAME

An Unskilled Golfer Can Witness for Christ

Brother Bill Stafford has made a significant spiritual impact on Cathy and me as a result of our friendship over the past thirty years. As president of the International Congress on Revival, he gave us the opportunity for involvement in this ministry for many of those years. The Congress (ICR) was established by evangelist Manley Beasley in the late 1970s in an effort to bring revival into the hearts of pastors and their wives in eastern Europe. This was several years before the lifting of the Iron Curtain. When Brother Manley departed this life in 1990, the leadership of the organization was passed to Brother Bill, and our prior friendship with him sparked our beginning involvement with ICR.

Brother Bill's personal ministry as an evangelist over a span of nearly sixty years was extensive and at times physically exhausting. He would preach as many as sixty evangelistic meetings per year, and most of these meetings lasted four days from Sunday morning through Wednesday evening. He often set aside several days every three or four months to rest and recuperate. He had very few hobbies outside of regular jogging each morning in the early hours, but occasionally would play a round of golf with one of his friends if the opportunity arose. Despite having some other athletic skills, golfing for Brother Bill was neither a priority nor a game he cared much about. It was all about emotional rest and sunshine.

Skeet May from Memphis had been a close friend of Brother Bill's for many years and occasionally he and his wife invited Bill and wife Sue to stay in their home when they were travelling in the Memphis area. Skeet was a very close friend of Brother Manley and was an original board member of ICR, so when Brother Bill assumed the leadership, Skeet helped him make the transition.

Brother Bill was in Memphis preaching a meeting, and when the meeting was over, Skeet invited him to stay over for a few days to just relax and unwind from his demanding schedule. One of those days, it was suggested they play a round of golf at a local municipal course. Both agreed they would not discuss ministry, preaching, or any problems related to either. They both committed to enjoying the sunshine, the beauty of the course, and the temporary freedom from their usual pressures.

After playing the first five holes, they noted there were two men close behind who were riding in a golf cart while Bill and Skeet were walking and pulling their carts. (Most golf courses now require players to use motorized carts to speed up play.) They also noted the two were laughing, telling off-color jokes, drinking beer, and obviously showing no interest in spiritual things. Bill and Skeet waited at the sixth tee box to allow the two men to play through since they were moving faster, but the two revelers insisted they play together as a foursome. They introduced themselves by only their first names and said nothing else about themselves personally. The two strangers continued their profane joke-telling and beer-drinking, and Brother Bill said the two, who were "pretty good golfers," were obviously enjoying their time on the course.

After playing several holes together, their conversation with each other centered only on the course and the difficulties the hazards presented. Brother Bill said he began really feeling guilty about not making any attempt to speak to the men about the Lord since they seemed spiritually lost with no apparent interest. Shortly, one of the men turned to Brother Bill and asked, "Are you a preacher?" Bill was taken aback since there had been no words spoken about their professions. Bill answered, "Well yes, as a matter of fact I am a preacher. Do I look like a preacher?" The man retorted, "No, not especially. I suspected you must be a preacher because anyone who plays golf as bad as you and doesn't cuss, just has to be a preacher!"

Bill said that during the remainder of the round, the conversation was quite different, and both he and Skeet had the opportunity to share their testimonies and give a good witness for the Lord Jesus. Neither of the other men were saved that day, but they certainly heard the good news of Jesus telling them he will save them if they would turn their hearts toward him! Jesus commands us as believers to be witnesses for him wherever we are, even on a golf course and especially when we are playing badly!

132. FREDDIE WILSON VISITS AFRICA

A Life-Long Dream Comes True

Freddie Wilson, South Africa, 1999

Freddie Wilson was a well-known personality in the medical community in El Dorado during the years of my medical practice there. I would run into him in various places in both hospitals, and, initially, I wasn't quite sure where he worked. But his primary employment was with Dr. Ken Duzan and Dr. Wayne Elliott, who were the pathologists. He had other jobs, including part-time work for the country club and assisting other physicians in various capacities.

Freddie had an outgoing personality with a continuous smile, and he was quick to express his love and devotion for the Lord Jesus. His cleanly-shaven head and his rapid walking pace made him easy to spot at a distance. I loved stopping and having a three-to-five-minute chat concerning things of the Lord and ministry opportunities. He seemed to always know what was currently happening in town because of his multiple jobs and his genuine love for people. At one point, I told him about the International Congress on Revival with which Cathy and I were involved and mentioned that the ministry included South Africa. He said, "Some day, I would love to go to Africa."

In the early spring of 1999, I began making plans to attend my first conference in Africa during the month of August and, without going into details of how it happened, Freddie obtained the necessary funding to join us. John Morgan, a local businessman and outstanding Bible teacher in El Dorado, felt led to go and the three of us traveled together. Early in our planning Freddie asked me, "Now just what am I going to do while I'm in Africa?" I jokingly said, "Freddie, it will be your job to go ahead of us with a machete and make a clear path for all of us white folks to walk." Freddie quickly said, "Doctor, I ain't going out in no woods!"

Upon arrival in Johannesburg after a grueling twenty-one hour flight, we boarded a van driven by an ICR team member for an additional five-hour trip southeast into the Drakensberg Mountains. This mountain range is in the South African province of Kwazulu-Natal and is the home of a large number of Zulu villagers. The contrast between the majesty and beauty of the mountains and the poverty of many Zulus is striking.

The conference was held annually in a beautiful lodge called the Drakensberg Sun and, upon arrival, we were thrilled to have a few hours to recover before the conference began. The purpose of the conference is to bring South African pastors and their wives to a retreat setting and give them five days of rest and encouragement in the Lord. All of their expenses are covered by the organization because most of these pastors are serving long hours without a great deal of compensation. By making investments in the spiritual enrichment of these pastors, the dividends are multiplied by the number of people they serve in their churches. The speakers for the conference included pastors and lay leaders from America and some of the South African pastors who also serve with ICR in other parts of the world. In addition to leaders from South Africa, there were present also pastors and wives from such surrounding countries as Zambia, Zimbabwe, and Botswana.

Freddie was an instant encourager for everyone at the conference because of his outgoing and winsome personality. During the preaching and singing, he was verbal and expressive in his hand clapping and amens. When there were breaks between the sessions, Freddie introduced himself to all the attendees and learned as much about them as he could.

Several afternoons were free for everyone to relax, rest, and visit some of the nearby Zulu villages. The photo above shows Freddie at the home of one of the villagers. The children had flocked to Freddie to get an up-close view of an African-American, and he didn't disappoint any of them by being aloof or unfriendly.

For the morning session on the third day of the conference, Brother Bill Stafford, the ICR president asked me to prepare a message. He notified me the afternoon before and in order to have the right word and have my heart prepared, I awakened at 2:30 a.m. to study and prepare. At approximately

3:30 while preparing my notes, I heard some muffled sounds from the adjacent room. I knew it was from Freddie's room and he was rooming alone. The sounds got a little louder and more animated and, because of the hour, I assumed Freddie was talking long distance by phone to his wife Verna. The conversation continued for at least thirty minutes, and I thought at the time a conversation for that long from South Africa was going to be very expensive for Freddie.

The next morning at breakfast, Freddy joined me at the table, and I asked him how everything was in El Dorado. He said, "I'm sure Verna is doing fine." "Didn't you talk to her on the phone last night?" I asked. He looked rather puzzled and said he had not spoken to her since we left. I said, "Freddie, I heard you talking to someone last night, and you were pretty loud." He laughed and said, "Doctor John, I was praying for your talk this morning and also thanking the Lord he let me come over here and meet all these wonderful people. I was especially glad so I got down and put my nose to the floor!" He told me that often at home when he can't sleep, he goes into his living room and has a "little talk with the Lord Jesus," and when he gets real happy, sometimes he talks pretty loud.

Freddie's prayer touched me so much I mentioned it to Brother Bill, and when I finished speaking, Brother Bill asked Freddie to give a short testimony of his prayer for the conference. I happened to record his testimony on video, and it still inspires me when I relive the moment. Praise God that "He does exceeding abundantly above anything we can ask or think" (Eph 3:20), and he allowed me to travel to South Africa with Freddie, John, and the ICR team. None of us will ever be the same for what he allowed us to experience so far from home.

133. MEETING DR. HAWKINS

A Chance Meeting at a Huge Convention

Dr. O. S. Hawkins

Dr. O. S. Hawkins is currently president and CEO of GuideStone Financial Resources for the Southern Baptist Convention, a position he has held since 1997. [John wrote this before Hawkins retired from this post in 2022.] GuideStone provides financial and retirement benefits for the many ministers of the SBC and is the largest Christian-based mutual fund in the world, with funds exceeding thirteen billion dollars. Dr. Hawkins has distinguished himself in his position by providing excellent leadership skills combined with loving, compassionate, financial advice for tens of thousands of ministers and their families. Dr. Hawkins has not spent all of his professional life in administrative work. The early part and perhaps the most productive and personally rewarding part of his ministry life was as pastor of various churches, both small and very large.

I first heard of Dr. Hawkins when he was the senior pastor of First Baptist Church of Fort Lauderdale, Florida. Cathy's mom (Gram Young) and her dad (Granddaddy Young) were from families who were pioneer settlers of this beautiful and famous south-Florida city. Gram Young served the city as a member of the city commission during the years 1971–1985 and was either mayor, vice-mayor, or mayor pro-tem during those years. Following her service as city commissioner, she was appointed to the Downtown Development Authority, a position she held from 1986 till 1993.

She and Dr. Hawkins became good friends despite the fact Gram and Granddaddy Young had been active members of Park Temple Methodist Church for years. Gram and Dr. Hawkins had breakfast together with several other prominent men every Sunday morning at the Riverside Hotel, a landmark hotel which was constructed in 1936 on East Las Olas Boulevard by the Young Construction Company. In the early 1980s, Cathy and I had visited First Baptist Church to hear Dr. Hawkins preach on two separate occasions while visiting her parents, but we'd never had the privilege of meeting him.

In June 1985, while serving as a deacon at First Baptist Church in El Dorado, I decided to attend the annual Southern Baptist Convention held that year in Dallas. It was to be a watershed year in terms of the struggle for leadership between the moderates and conservatives of the convention, and approximately forty-five thousand (messengers) were signed to attend. Cathy was not able to go with me because her parents were in El Dorado visiting with their grandchildren. Our pastor, Dr. Mark Coppenger was in attendance with his wife Sharon, and we were the three messengers from our church.

Dr. Hawkins was President of the Pastors' Conference that year, and all speakers of the preliminary conference were strong conservatives advocating a return to conservative leadership. Brother Mark and I were attending the final portion of the Pastors' Conference on Monday morning, and when it was over, we wanted to make our way to the front of the auditorium to meet Dr. Hawkins. There were at least two hundred people ahead of us, and we decided to forego meeting him at that time. I jokingly said (and perhaps a little haughtily), "I'm not worried. Before the day is over, Dr. Hawkins will come up and ask to meet me!!" Mark left to have lunch with his wife, and I milled around the convention center to just experience such a historic meeting. I had conversations with several messengers and asked them questions about their beliefs concerning the direction of the convention and how they might vote. The majority of people I polled were conservatives.

I noticed a small crowd gathering down near the street, and it appeared someone had fallen so I approached. An older woman had made a misstep off the curb and had fallen in an awkward manner. She could not stand, and after a brief exam, I was certain she had fractured her hip. I asked someone to summon an ambulance and stayed with her to bring her some comfort as a physician. As the ambulance approached, she asked me to send a message to her pastor who was there from Wichita Falls, so he could contact her family, where the ambulance was taking her.

I went directly to the press room to have her pastor notified by a message, which would appear on the screens in the main conference room. There were about twenty-five people in the bustling room, but I was standing next to a middle-aged man with the name on his official name tag— "Whiddon, Florida." I asked, "Excuse me, are you Gene Whiddon from Fort Lauderdale?" He was shocked I would know his name and said, "Yes, I am. Do I know you?" I said, "No, but you are good friends with my mother-in-law, Virginia Young." I heard her talk often about Gene Whiddon, who was President of Causeway Lumber Company, with whom they had done business for many years. Gene said, "I know you are from Arkansas because I talked with Virginia just this morning, and she said they were there visiting." Gene said he was in the press room with his pastor who was scheduled for an interview. "Is your pastor O.S. Hawkins?" I asked. "He sure is. Would you like for me to introduce you?" He brought Dr. Hawkins over, and I finally met him. We had a wonderful conversation about Gram Young and all the good things she had done and was doing for the city of Fort Lauderdale. I thought to myself, "I can't wait to tell Dr. Coppenger about Dr. Hawkins coming to meet me!"

In my current responsibility as a member of the Executive Committee of the Southern Baptist Convention, I get to fellowship with Dr. Hawkins whenever we meet and have introduced Cathy to him. He is always gracious and kind to us, and we remind him of the impact he once had on our beloved Gram Young. We never could get her to consider switching their membership from Park Temple Methodist to First Baptist because she said, "His preaching and invitations are too long." She might have been right, but Dr. Hawkins not only impacted her for Christ, but countless others in Fort Lauderdale and every other place he has served. I thank God for such a servant leader!

134. "I HAVE A CHECK FOR YOU"

A Severely-Disabled Friend Gives a Generous Gift

The Free Medical Clinic of the Ozarks was opened and became fully operational in November, 2008, as a medical ministry to people with no medical insurance in Taney and Stone Counties, Missouri. The Free Clinic (FMCO) has been a prominent part of my medical professional life since its founding. One of the more amazing things about the Free Clinic has been the funding.

In the initial planning phase of FMCO which began mid-2007, it was the founders' desire to provide free medical care, free medicines, and the free gospel to everyone who came. The planners had no idea what the annual expenses would be, but trusted God to provide. We were not presuming on God to supply that which was not in his sovereign will, but firmly believed the formation of this clinic was his will.

The funding for the clinic was to come from any churches who considered the ministry of the clinic an extension of their own ministry, from individuals who were led to make a charitable contribution, and from fees charged to legal offices for copying records. In the beginning, I contacted many church administrators and pastors to make our clinic known to them and to ask for support. Both the First Baptist Church of Branson and the First Baptist Church of Hollister agreed to be regular contributing partners, while other churches in the area promised their prayer support and financial help if possible. There was also a small but significant number of individual supporters who gave generously to the founding and maintenance of the clinic.

The clinic was initially located in a remodeled building owned and maintained by the Covenant Life Church in downtown Branson, Missouri. The pastor and ruling board of Covenant Life told us that, had they not invested significant funds in remodeling, we would have the use of the clinic space at no cost. The rent was to be fifteen hundred dollars per month, but from that amount, Covenant Life would give two hundred and fifty dollars back into our operating budget. We believed the rent was a good investment for a very nice and convenient office with good parking.

All of the workers at the Free Clinic were to be volunteers including the doctors and physician assistants, and most agreed to serve in at least one clinic evening per month. This kept our overhead expenses down greatly, and we were able to tell all potential donors at least 95 percent of every dollar donated would go directly to patient care.

Jerry Lilley, the executive director, and I were guests on two local radio stations, and Rick Beasley, a board member, and I, were invited to be guests on Mona Stafford's show on Bott Radio to explain the work and ministry of the clinic. Our goal was to make the work known and to solicit donations. I was twice invited as guest speaker at the Branson chapter of the Rotary Club, and was invited to speak at the Lion's Club in Branson and at a luncheon meeting of the chapter in Branson West. We were grateful to have the privilege of explaining the ministry and giving people the opportunity to partner with us. We were blessed by donors giving generously and were able to meet all the financial obligations with some to spare each month. We have never initiated a fund-raising event, although one Branson tribute artist, Keith Allyn, has voluntarily performed three separate benefit concerts over a three year span for the clinic, for which we are very grateful.

Approximately two years after the clinic opened, the local hospital Skaggs Community Hospital approached us with an offer for a new clinic space in Hollister, Missouri. The hospital had an existing clinic building which was not fully occupied, and they offered us one of the offices on the first floor. For us, the most amazing thing was that they offered the space for the lease price of one dollar per year. With their offer, our clinic's overhead expense was reduced by fifteen thousand dollars per year. In addition to providing ample clinic space there was more parking and easier access for our patients.

One of our original chaplains, Jerri Traister, told me one evening that the man for whom she had been providing personal home care wanted to make a contribution to the clinic. Her patient, Raymond B., had been quadriplegic for several years due to an accident, and Jerri had been providing general supportive care most of the time. When she was on duty as a chaplain, she would bring Raymond to the clinic where he had been interacting with the patients. Jerri said he "loved the clinic and wanted to help out with the finances." I told her how grateful I was for even his desire to be a part of the clinic.

About two weeks following our initial conversation I was at the clinic one evening while patients were being seen. I didn't realize Jerri was on duty this night, but when I saw her, she said Raymond was there with his check for me. She pushed his wheelchair into my office, and I noticed Raymond was holding a check between his index and long finger, and it was resting on his chest. I had known Raymond in prior years because he had been a patient of mine when I was director of the Wound Care Clinic in Branson. I told Raymond I was so glad to see him again, and he smilingly said, "I have a donation I would like to make to the clinic," as he lifted the check and placed it in my hand. At first, I didn't look at the amount, but I told him how grateful I was for his contribution, and how we would be faithful to use his gift wisely. I then looked at the check and it was for $10,000! This was the largest single gift ever made to our clinic, and I couldn't help shedding tears of gratitude. Who could have imagined a man with so many personal needs would give such a huge gift to help meet the needs of others!

God has demonstrated his faithfulness to the ministry of the Free Medical Clinic in so many ways, and, as we have seen him provide the needed finances at just the right time, our faith has grown. We have seen many demonstrations of his Word from Philippians 4:19, where he promises *to supply all our needs according to His riches in glory through Christ Jesus.* Raymond B. was used of God to fulfill God's promise to us, and I'm confident Raymond will be richly rewarded for his obedience.

135. THE ADMIRAL

A Lifelong Friendship Forged by a Ukulele

Captain Burt Renager, USS Farragut, 1991

I might not have been as close friends with Burton Whitmon (Burt) Renager Jr. had it not been for a ukulele. In the fall of 1960, I was a freshman in medical school at the University of Arkansas in Little Rock and had gone to the lobby of Jeff Banks Dormitory to take a short break from studies. Seated on a couch surrounded by several other students was this short, nice-looking, clean-cut guy playing his ukulele while singing a folk song with the group. The Kingston Trio was just becoming very popular, and they were singing "Tom Dooley," the signature song of the trio. His playing and singing, while not concert quality, was pretty good, so I joined them in singing. I told them I would get my Gibson guitar and join them if that was all right. This was the beginning of a friendship born in Kingston Trio-type folk music and nurtured through the years by many common interests including, most of all, love of God, family, country, and country music, especially Flatt and Scruggs bluegrass.

Burt was born and raised in West Memphis, Arkansas, the only child of B. W. and Elizabeth Crow Renager. His mom's roots had been planted in Eastern Arkansas in the town of Elaine where she was raised on a large cotton and soy bean farm. After moving to West Memphis following marriage, she and B. W. directed the operation and management of a farm which was subsequently passed on to Burt. We have joked often about the "current status of the soy beans in Elaine."

Among Burt's many talents during his formative years (apart from the ukulele) was flying private planes. After learning the skills of piloting, he continued flying small aircraft for many years until only recently. Never one to refuse a challenge as a young man, he told me he once flew a single engine plane under the large bridge at Memphis. For this act of bravery, he received a reprimand from the Federal Aviation Board and had his license temporarily suspended. He told me he suspected he had been reported by the one who challenged him and was angry he had lost the bet over the stunt.

Burt was focused on his pre-medical studies in college and graduated with honors from Memphis State University before entering medical school in the fall of 1960. His initial goal was to become a family physician like his own doctor whom he admired. In those early days none of us really knew what rigorous training lay ahead and where our paths would lead. It was important to have an outlet to help relieve the stress of the academic world, and music was a good one for us.

Our playing and singing gigs during the first year in medical school were lots of fun, and we probably spent too much time honing our musical skills in various ways. We made a memorable trip one weekend to Mountain View, Arkansas to the Jimmy Driftwood Folk Festival and even played a few of our songs on the square while surrounded by ten to fifteen mountain folks. They seemed curious to hear what these "city slickers" could do, but I don't remember their being very impressed with our style of folk music. We were not invited to perform on-stage that evening, but loved the people and enjoyed the music which was everywhere on this weekend in Mountain View. Elsewhere, I've written about one of our more unusual performances ("One Night at the Rackensack").

Burt had a gift for generating a background story for the songs we performed when in reality the songs we played and sang were mostly learned from albums of Flatt and Scruggs and recordings of Bob Dylan and others. We thought we were the only ones who really knew the truth concerning those stories.

Burt's professional trajectories took a turn following our freshman year, and he dropped out of medical school to pursue a military career. I'm not sure his initial intentions were career-military, but the war in Vietnam was beginning to escalate in the mid 1960s, and all young men in those days were subject to being drafted into the war effort. Burt became a junior officer in the United States Navy via Officers Candidate School in Newport, Rhode Island in 1965. About this time, he married his longtime sweetheart, Paula Kalder also of West Memphis, and they started building their family and life together in Virginia Beach, Virginia.

Early on, Burt spent a tour of duty in Vietnam commanding a Swift Boat, the modern analog of the PT Boat of World War II. Some of his exploits were recorded in a book written by Jim Guy Tucker (*Arkansas Men of War, Penguin Press, 1968*). Tucker was a war correspondent when he wrote and published the book. He was later elected Governor of Arkansas and subsequently resigned following conviction for fraud in the Whitewater Affair.

Burt had a distinguished naval career and rose in the ranks to captain before retiring in 1991. His last command was aboard the *USS Farragut*, in a modern class of missile destroyers. Under his command were over four hundred enlisted men and twenty-five officers. I thought he would stay on active duty in the Navy until achieving the rank of admiral, but it was best for him and his family to retire when he did. Regardless, I have always addressed him by this rank when calling and speaking to him by phone.

Burt and Paula have spent their years in Virginia Beach raising their sons Jason and Joshua, who are grown now with their own families. There are five grandchildren to spoil and enjoy whenever they can be together. I don't know if he has taught any of them to play a ukulele, but I'm quite certain he can still remember the chords to play and the lyrics to many of the songs we knew so well. Just like two old retirees, most of our songs are outdated.

It has been many years since Burt and I have been together, but we regularly stay in touch by phone, occasional letters, and text messages. I've learned quite a few life lessons from him and even a few medical tips I have used which hearken back to our medical school days (e.g., Schoettle's Rule of X-Ray Diagnosis). I still believe he would have been an excellent family physician, but God had another career path for him, and he excelled in it. I thank God for that evening sixty-five years ago playing and singing "Tom Dooley," and I remember it as if it were only yesterday.

136. MY SURGICAL MENTOR

A Trusted Colleague and Outstanding Surgeon

Dr. C.E. Tommey

Throughout my surgical career of thirty-five years, I had the privilege of observing and operating with some of the finest surgeons in the South. My initial experience in the operating room was as a teen assisting my dad (Pop) with a few of his operative procedures. Those were the days prior to the explosion of lawsuits for medical malpractice. Although Pop was careful to not allow me to do anything which exceeded my skill set, I was unlicensed and by today's standard unqualified to participate in any procedure. Pop's permission extended through my high school and college years, and, by the time I enrolled in medical school, I was far more skilled in OR techniques than most interns and many junior surgical residents. I was certain of my career path from the first day Pop allowed me to assist him.

For the last two years of medical school, each student rotated through the surgical service for three months of every year. We were taught the skills of sterile technique in the OR and were allowed to scrub, gown, and glove to stand at the operating table while only observing the surgeons and their assistants at work. I saw all the surgical residents and many of the interns operating while quietly longing to have an active role in certain procedures with which I had personal experience. I remained quiet about my skills until on one occasion I was asked to assist an intern on an appendectomy while the resident only watched. I was placing sutures and tying knots faster than the intern, and the anesthesiologist, Dr. Ronnie Lewis, sarcastically asked me, "Hey you, where did you learn to do all that?" When I told him my dad, Dr. Berry Moore, had been teaching me for years, the doctor was astounded. The reason was because he was preparing to enter private practice in El Dorado, and he wanted me to give a good report on him to Pop. (Even though he had previously been pretty rough on me!) In the intervening years, while I was working with Dr. Lewis, I would occasionally remind him of the account. His only response was, "I was just young and too cocky for my own good."

During my four years of surgical training at Charity Hospital in New Orleans, I participated in or performed several thousand procedures. I worked with at least eight surgeons who were in private practice in New Orleans and countless other men and women who were in training. A few of them stand out in my mind concerning their diagnostic and technical skills. One of the best surgeons I worked with was Dr. Lewis Crow, who was two years ahead of me in training. I assisted him on at least ten procedures which were of such magnitude I never forgot his speed and accuracy of performance. He later had a surgical practice in Little Rock, and I was able to refer a number of very difficult cases to him, which he handled extremely well.

When I began my practice in El Dorado in 1971, I was in the office of my brother Berry Lee (Bubba). I continued with him for two years, although for the referral practice I desired to have with him, this was not ideal. He was a general medical doctor, and it was not best for him to take time away from his practice to assist me in the OR. In 1974, I was invited to join with three other surgeons, Dr. David Yocum, Dr. C.E. Tommey, and Dr. Bill Scurlock to form the Surgical Clinic of South Arkansas. This was one of my best professional decisions. In the following years we added Dr. Moises Menendez and Dr. Robert Tommey (son of Dr. C.E.) to our surgical staff.

Over the next twenty-five years, I had the privilege of working in the Surgical Clinic with these surgeons who were not only accomplished physicians but were men of outstanding character. I was able to either assist each one in the OR at one time or another or have them assist me on difficult surgical cases. The one who had the greatest influence on me regarding my skill development and my interaction with patients apart from my brother Berry Lee was Dr. C.E. Tommey.

Dr. Tommey moved to El Dorado in the early 1950s with his wife Clara and their children. He immediately joined with Dr. Yocum to begin their long career together. Dr. Tommey had trained in the Cleveland Clinic prior to entering military service for two years in the United States Army. He had no family ties to El Dorado but had connected with Dr. Yocum as a result of an earlier friendship in medical school. Dr. Scurlock joined them in the mid-1960s after he'd completed his military obligation.

Dr. Tommey (Dr. Eldon) was a quiet man of few words. When you could engage him in a lengthy conversation, he had a witty personality with an infectious laugh. One of the funniest professional stories I love telling involved him and his nurse Reba McDuffie (see "Training A Home Care Giver"). I never heard him being critical of any person and, in particular, of another physician. Over the course of twenty-five years, we certainly were eye-witnesses to situations and heard conversations which could have led to judgment and condemnation, but one never heard anything like that from him.

He was a tireless worker who was never late nor absent from a responsibility. One particular Fourth of July weekend, he and I were the only surgeons in town, and he was on ER call on Friday and I on Saturday. We agreed to assist each other on those days, and it was the busiest weekend of my thirty-five year career. We did eleven emergency cases on Friday and twelve on Saturday. As I write this, I am still amazed at our endurance. To my remembrance all of the twenty-three patients recovered from their problems.

His diagnostic skills were superb, and I frequently consulted with him when I had a puzzling or difficult diagnostic case. Often, just his presence in a patient's room would bring them comfort and peace because of his reputation. By far, he was the best-known surgeon in El Dorado during those years.

His dress and appearance were always professional and elegant. When we learned about tailor-made, Tom James suits, he and I began purchasing them at the same time, and I always knew when he had a new one. Only a very few times did I ever see him in casual dress, and it just didn't quite seem natural.

Dr. Eldon was a strong Christian witness, and he and Clara were faithful members of First Baptist Church. He was active in Sunday school as a member of the Men's Bible Class and participated in many other activities of the church as he was able. He was appointed and served as a deacon of the church for many years and was elected chairman of deacons on more than one occasion.

His humility was characterized by a conversation I heard in the operating room while assisting him on a particularly difficult case. One of the experienced scrub nurses, Mrs. Gunter, asked him, "Dr. Tommey, how do you keep from making mistakes in the operating room?" He replied, "By gaining experience." Mrs. Gunter continued, "And how do you gain experience?" to which he replied, "By making mistakes!"

Dr. Tommey lived a long life and served the people of El Dorado with skill and loving kindness. He retired from his surgical practice in the late 1990s but continued working in the wound care clinic for another ten plus years. He completely retired from medicine around 2010 because of health reasons. After we moved away from El Dorado in 1999, I was able to visit him in his home on several occasions when Cathy and I were in town to see our children and grandchildren.

This past January 13, I decided to call him on his ninety-eighth birthday, and his care giver gave him the phone. Although it was obvious that he was weak, we were able to have about a ten-minute conversation which included recounting some interesting and funny experiences we shared for those twenty-five years. At the close of the conversation, I said to him, "Dr. Tommey, I love you and have counted it a great honor to have worked with and learned from you all those many years!" His reply was typical and brief, "John, I loved working with you." The next morning, I received a surprising call from his son, Dr. Robert, who asked, "Did you call and talk with my dad yesterday?" When I replied that I had, Robert said, "He passed away and entered heaven early this morning."

I have frequently written about the tremendous temporal and eternal impact that my brother Berry Lee (Bubba) had on me and my family. There has never been another one comparable to him. But in the field of surgery Dr. Charles Eldon Tommey was my greatest mentor in regards to surgical technique, and in the way to live life while treating others as Jesus would (Matt 5:16).

137. MY FOREVER FRIEND, PASTOR TYRONE

God Sends a Great Friend at Just the Right Time

Pastor Tyrone and Alisha

There are some men whom you meet for the first time whom you know will become a great and forever friend. Such was our introduction to Pastor Tyrone Thorpe and his wife Alisha in 2014 at a marriage seminar in East St. Louis, Illinois.

Cathy and I were invited along with our wonderful friend, Carolyn Lilley, to assist in a marriage seminar to strengthen believers at 15th Street Baptist Church in East St. Louis. Carolyn, Cathy, and I are members of First Baptist Church, Branson, Missouri, and our church has had a missions relationship with 15th Street Baptist and their pastor Andrew Prowell for at least fifteen years. We had done two marriage seminars in previous years in their church and were purposing to make this teaching seminar an annual event. At this particular seminar, Pastor Prowell's brother, Tyrone Thorpe and wife Alisha were in attendance, and we were introduced to them. At the time Tyrone was serving as a deacon in another church, and he and Alisha were not regular attenders at 15th Street Baptist.

Several personal qualities Cathy and I immediately noticed in Tyrone were his infectious smile and his exuberant joy in the Lord. He seemed to be continuously smiling and praising God for everything to the extent it seemed disingenuous. The more we were with them convinced us he was for real. His obvious love for his bride Alisha was genuine, and we were thrilled having them at our marriage conference.

Before the conference was over, the Thorpes spoke with us about the possibility of returning the following year to participate in a conference they would organize and manage. We were thrilled with their initiative and readily agreed. We believed their enthusiasm and energy were just the sparks needed for a very special meeting.

Throughout the following summer and fall months, we stayed in touch with the Thorpes, anticipating either a spring or early summer marriage retreat. They set a date compatible with our schedule and made more complete preparations for the seminar, which included several other couples who also would be in leadership roles. We agreed to be in prayer together for God's hand to be on the conference, and because we were separated by such a distance, a conference-call prayer meeting was scheduled for every two weeks for two months.

What an experience the conference calls were for Cathy and me since we had never been part of anything similar. There were at least six people on-line each time, and each was respectful of the one who was praying. It was exciting for Cathy and me to be part of such a diversified group of believers whose sole purpose was to ask for God's blessings on the seminar.

The seminar was so well-planned by Pastor Tyrone and Alisha that it was by far the best marriage enrichment event we have ever attended. A highlight for us occurred on the evening prior to the start of the meeting, when Cathy, Carolyn Lilley, and I joined Pastor Tyrone and Alisha for supper at the Golden Corral in Belleville, Illinois near the Thorpe's home. Our enthusiasm for the restaurant was fueled by the Thorpes, and especially Tyrone who seemed to witness to everyone present in the place. It was there I was especially drawn to Tyrone's love for Jesus and his sincere desire to share the gospel with everyone.

Tyrone had been delivered years before from the deadly trap of alcohol, drugs, and the life-style they create. His life was a total wreck, including breakup of his marriage and family and a prison sentence. By his testimony of hitting rock bottom and being homeless, his deliverance by the Lord Jesus was dramatic and complete. He had an intense and abiding heart interest for men and women, who like himself were trapped by their sin and circumstances.

In addition to his deliverance from the trap of sin, he was delivered from the initial effects of a head and neck cancer, which had possibly resulted from his life-style choices. He received multiple irradiation treatments followed by chemotherapy and for more than five years seemed to have been cured.

At some point following all of this, he met Alisha who was working as a nurse at the VA Hospital in St. Louis, where he also worked. They began dating and decided it was God's will for them to be joined in marriage. Alisha had endured harm from an abusive husband in her first marriage and through her faith and trust in the Lord Jesus had become a strong and faithful witness for him. Tyrone and Alisha were made for each other and were married in 2011. Together they developed a ministry of hope and encouragement for any person who had been damaged by sin and poor life-style choices. It was three years after their marriage we first met them.

The final chapter in Tyrone's earthly life began in mid-2016 when he developed increasing symptoms of severe throat pain and difficulty in swallowing. He phoned me on several occasions, and we prayed together for each other. I was having increasing symptoms of heart disease and growing progressively weaker. Our times of prayer by phone encouraged me and drew me closer to the Lord Jesus, whose voice I seemed to hear in Tyrone's voice.

He began the testing process which resulted in recommendation of a major surgical procedure to remove the recurrent head and neck cancer. Near the same time, I was recommended to have open-heart surgery. It was not coincidence that our surgical procedures were on the exact same day, December 1, 2016. Tyrone was operated on at St. Louis University Hospital, and my procedure was done at Washington Regional Medical Center in Fayetteville, Arkansas. Had they not been on the same day, we each would have been present at the other's hospital.

Tyrone's operation for complete cancer removal was not successful, and he grew increasingly worse from the cancer. Alisha faithfully cared for him day and night using her nursing skills and doing many things which would normally be done by other health care providers. We stayed in touch as much as possible, and I gained enough strength for Cathy and me to travel to St. Louis to see him in the hospital in mid-April. He was so weak and couldn't talk because of his tracheostomy, but we saw the special twinkle in his eye and felt the mutual love in the handshake and ever-present smile. He was surrounded by family members, but we were able to stay for several hours, especially giving time for Cathy to spend together with Alisha. I was fortunate to have about thirty minutes alone with Tyrone and Veronica, his lovely daughter from his first marriage. Veronica lives with her husband and children in Tampa, Florida, and she is a wonderful example of a Christian witness similar to her father. As I was leaving, I kissed him on his forehead and whispered in his ear, "I love you Tyrone, and I will see you again at the feet of Jesus."

My brother Tyrone departed this life on April 26, 2017 at age sixty, and his spirit was immediately taken into the presence of his Savior, the Lord Jesus Christ. I can only imagine the reverence and awe he experienced and can also visualize the enormous joy and gigantic smile which is now continually on his face. I miss him very much but am confident I will see that smile and sparkle in his eye once again (1 Thess.4:13–18).

IV. Spiritual Lessons
Along the Journey

God will use every relationship and every event in our lives to teach us more about himself and conforms us more into his image. The more alert we are to his working, the more teachable we become and the more thankful we are for his unchanging love.

138. DIAGNOSING SMILING MIGHTY JESUS

Learning a New Diagnostic Term

Following completion of medical school at the University of Arkansas in Little Rock, I wanted to continue my training in a large inner-city hospital, preferably located in the South. The teaching hospital associated with the medical school in Little Rock was relatively small in terms of the number of patients treated daily, and I wanted a larger facility with a wider variety of medical problems. Grady Memorial Hospital in Atlanta fit all of the criteria I had set, and I was thrilled when I received word from them that I had been accepted into their program along with two medical school classmates. With my new title "MD," and a false sense of my own importance to the medical community and the world at large, I set out for Atlanta fully expecting a hero's welcome at Grady. I quickly discovered I was one of sixty new interns and over a hundred resident physicians training in various medical specialties. Because we all had to wear white uniforms, I blended into a large crowd of young doctors and immediately lost my unique status. My humbling process was just beginning.

My first service rotation at Grady (affectionately known locally as "the Gradies") was on the pediatric service. Part of my responsibility was to work in the out-patient clinic. There were hundreds of sick children treated daily, and they were divided among four to six interns, so the patient load per physician was huge. With my relative inexperience in patient care, I was very slow and meticulous in asking the right questions of the mothers concerning their children's problems. Because of the patient mix at Grady, many of the mothers had deep southern accents and used terms which were not common in medicine. In my limited medical school experience, I had heard most of the commonly used slang terms and was confident in my ability to understand what was said and to communicate appropriately.

On this particular morning, I was questioning a mother about her four-year-old's past medical history and previous hospitalizations. She said proudly that her child had been admitted a year ago to "the Gradies" and had now fully recovered from the problem, with no after-effects. I asked her what was the illness for which he was treated, and she said it was "smilin' mightyjesus." Believing I had misunderstood what she said, I asked her to repeat the diagnosis, and she said exactly those words: "smilin' mightyjesus." I told her I needed to consult with one of the senior physicians and quickly excused myself from the exam room. I found a resident physician with several more years of experience, and asked him if he had ever heard of an illness called "smilin' mightyjesus"? "Of course, and so have you," he said.

"You were taught all about the illness in med school, how to diagnosis it, how to treat it, and what complications to expect. I'm surprised you didn't immediately recognize what she said," he teasingly rebuked me. "Please tell me what in the world did her son have?" He proudly informed me that the diagnosis I couldn't make that morning was "spinal meningitis!" My learning process took another giant step forward.

In remembering this amusing episode from my past, I am more convinced our Savior, the Lord Jesus Christ is truly mighty. He is mighty to save and mighty in his love and patience toward us as we are growing more into his image daily. I can only imagine our mighty Jesus smiling broadly watching his children struggle and grow, including a young and proud intern beginning to learn how much he doesn't know and how far he has to go.

139. DOES GOD HEAL TODAY?

A Significant Question for All Who Are Sick

This may seem like a strange question coming from a physician who for many years has dedicated his medical practice to the healing ministry of the Lord Jesus Christ. The question, however, is valid in light of certain applications of biblical principles regarding healing which are made by many sincere Christians. All Christians today would resoundingly agree that God does heal all manner of diseases, but does he heal today in the same way Jesus Christ and his disciples healed when he walked upon the earth? The larger question to consider is whether Christ died for our sicknesses as well as our sins? Was physical healing from diseases made available to all Christians as a result of Christ's atoning death on the cross? Should I expect to be healed from any illness on the same basis I am forgiven of sins whenever I earnestly pray?

There are some who believe it is not only a Christian's privilege, but also his right to be healed from any disease. The scriptural justification for this belief is from Isaiah 53:5 where the prophet Isaiah foretells the Messiah would be "wounded for our transgressions, bruised for our iniquities, chastised for our peace, and with His stripes we are healed." Another passage for the belief in atonement-healing concerns praying in faith in Mark 11:24. Therein, Jesus told his disciples that whatever they asked in faith believing, they would be given. To bolster the conviction of some that healing is available today to believers as it was in Jesus's ministry, they turn to Hebrews 13:8, which states, "Jesus Christ, the same yesterday, and today, and forever."

It is easier to think and write about the availability of God's healing when the problem exists in another person, but quite another thing when I am the one who is sick and conventional methods of healing have not worked. As a surgeon who's operated on hundreds of patients with hernias, I am well aware that hernia recurrences unfortunately do occur, and some are very difficult if not impossible to repair.

While dealing with my own problem of a twice-recurrent hernia, I was lying on our couch at home in pain one evening while listening to a well-known television healer. At one point in the program the evangelist said, "I perceive there is a professional individual watching this show, and he is in great pain suffering with a recurrent hernia. I am claiming in the name of Jesus, he is now healed!" I was absolutely convinced he was speaking to me, and I claimed his word of faith in healing as my own. When I stood to tell Cathy God had healed me by faith, I discovered to my great disappointment the hernia was still present and healing had not occurred. What was wrong? Was the televangelist wrong in his word of faith, or was my faith so weak God chose not to heal me? Should I discount as bogus anyone who says God is still in the business of healing by faith? Was it wrong for me to presume upon God and to ask for such a miraculous healing? I was filled with many questions and no answers.

In my professional career as a surgeon for thirty-nine years, the patients I served did not come seeking miraculous healing. They wanted to be cured of their hernias, their gallstones, their cancers, and their internal infections through particular surgical procedures which I was trained to employ. Did I think I was the one who could or would heal them? I told most of my patients, "I am the one who puts in the sutures, but it is God who heals you." How was I to advise someone for whom conventional methods of medical practice had failed? Should I have advised that they pray for healing before consulting a physician? Is prayer always the answer for healing? There were more questions than answers.

In this piece on healing, I'll try to answer some of these perplexing questions, drawing on God's Word and my personal experience in the healing ministry over the past forty-eight years. First, I will address the question of atonement-healing and the Christian's response to illness. Then I will explore the dilemma of when a person should pray for healing and when he should consult a physician. Finally, I will attempt to answer the oft-asked question, "What should I do when I have tried everything I know, and I am still not healed?" When faced honestly, these questions do not call for glib or quick answers, for they are personal, usually painful, and potentially life-changing. We can be comforted in knowing our heavenly Father is aware of our concerns and will direct our paths when we seek him with all our hearts.

Atonement-Healing

As a Christian do I believe I have the right to be healed from any disease? Can I claim this right by praying in faith and believing I will be healed in order to receive what God intends for me in the first place? There are loud voices telling us this is true, and we have viewed on television the proponents of faith healing as they appeared to have healed some who have come seeking healing.

Who among us has not suffered from an illness or had a loved one with a problem, and we earnestly desired to have the burden removed by healing? When weakened by an illness, we will seek God's hand, but when healing does not occur we are susceptible to hearing voices other than his. We are told things like, "It is not God's will you are sick" or "You don't have to endure something which has already been secured for you by his stripes." This dilemma regarding healing has caused many devout Christians to doubt their own salvation while adding guilt to their grief.

Atonement-healing, a doctrine which is believed and taught by many, claims that Christians can be healed from all their diseases, and that the healing was secured when Christ died on the cross. Stated another way, Christ died for our sicknesses as well as our sins. The scripture often quoted for this doctrine includes Isaiah 53:5, Matthew 8:16–17, and I Peter 2:24. The passages in Matthew's gospel and Peter's epistle refer to the Isaiah prophecy which states the coming Messiah would be "wounded for our transgressions, bruised for our iniquities, chastised for our peace and with his stripes we are healed." The Matthew account records Jesus's early ministry in Galilee, in which he healed all who were sick who were brought to him in fulfillment of Isaiah's prophecy. This was three years before the cross and, therefore, did not fall under Christ's atoning work at Calvary. When Peter wrote the following, "Christ bore our sins in His own body, that having died to sins, we might live to righteousness—for by whose stripes we are healed," he was describing spiritual healing and not physical healing.

If physical healing like sin was atoned for at the cross, then one should be able to be healed on the same basis as forgiveness of sins. When one comes to Christ for salvation, repents, and is born again, we believe he receives forgiveness and salvation at that moment. Our experiences with sickness however, are very different. We are frequently left unhealed when we have prayed earnestly for healing. Forgiveness is immediate, but even the advocates for atonement-healing tell us that healing in some cases is gradual and progressive. The reason usually given for failures in healing is, "You simply didn't have enough faith." My response to this reasoning is to ask "How much faith does it take to be healed? I prayed once at an altar and believe I was saved, but I have prayed without ceasing, and am still sick. Does it take more faith to receive something which is temporal as opposed to something which is eternal? This doctrine can lead to self-condemnation at the least, and disbelief in scriptures at worst."

While it is true that Christ's atoning death paid the full price for sin and its consequences, Christians have not and will not receive in this life all his death has secured for us. Men will continue to have to work, women will travail in childbirth, marital relationships will suffer, and both men and women will die. One day, however, at the final trumpet of God, Christians will all be changed and will receive everything which was paid for in full at Calvary. Unfortunately for some, they will have to wait until that time for their physical healing to be complete. There will then be no more suffering or sorrow; there will be no more diseases or death; and all tears will be wiped away.

Our understanding of scriptures and our personal experiences lead us to conclude that there is healing in the atonement, but the healing we received immediately at salvation was spiritual in nature and not physical. We may have to wait on the physical healing we are currently praying for but have not yet received. We must not be discouraged nor led to believe that God does not love us, or that he has left us without hope. His promises in Romans 8:28 assure us that he will work everything out in his time, for our good and his glory. To quote Charles Spurgeon, "God is too good to be unkind, and he is too wise to be mistaken. And when we cannot trace his hand, we must trust his heart."

Praying for Healing

Attend any prayer meeting and notice that when prayer requests are asked, the first and the largest number of requests will be related to physical illnesses. Listen carefully to the prayers offered for the sick and dying, and observe whether those praying seem to have the conviction their prayers for healing will be answered. I would not be so callus nor foolish to believe I can discern the intent of one's heart, but I sense we have become routine in our intercessions, and have lost some vitality and fervor in our prayers for healing. When we pray for healing, are we convinced God hears our prayers and answers them according to our needs? Is God concerned about our sicknesses, and if so, why do my prayers seem so ineffectual? When medical science has failed and we have been told to expect the worst, can we confidently come to Christ in prayer and expect Him to perform a miracle? Should I pray for healing even before I seek medical treatment? There are so many questions, so many opinions, so much confusion, and so much heart-ache related to this subject. I'm certain, however, our heavenly Father does not want us to be anxious, and he has provided direction for us in his Word.

A scriptural truth we can claim is this: When healing is truly a need for us, God will meet the need every time (Phil 4:19). Our struggle is to understand just what is a legitimate need and what is an imagined need? I can already hear the next question: "When I am sick, how can it only be an imagined need for me to be made well?" God has shown us some sicknesses are for chastisement (1 Cor 11:28–30), some are for the glory of God (John 9:1–3), while other sicknesses are unto death (Eccl 3:1–2). Our desires must be what God desires, and when it is his desire to heal us, it will happen.

Have I ever stopped to consider that this present malady may be God's means not only to get my attention but to teach me an eternal truth which can only be learned while I am sick? If it is God's will to heal everyone, then why did the Apostle Paul remain sick despite praying three times to have the thorn in the flesh removed (2 Cor 12:7–9)? Why did Trophimus remain sick in Miletus when he might have come to Rome to speak in Paul's defense (2 Tim 4:20)? Did they not have enough faith to be healed? It is simply not God's will to heal every believer of every illness every time. God is definitely concerned about our health, but his primary concern is our holiness, and holiness is strengthened in the crucible of pain and suffering (Jas 1:2–4).

It is within God's will, however, when one is sick to call for the elders to pray for healing (Jas 5:13–16). The mental picture most of us have concerning this passage is of a church service in which sick people come to an altar for anointing with oil and receive prayer for healing. There have been some who needed healing who came to such services and were healed, but I believe far more have come and left sick, disappointed and dejected. The command of these verses in James's epistle is that the one who is sick should call for the elders to come to him and not that he go to a mass meeting for healing. What we are observing in such healing services today in no way resembles what the Lord commanded in these passages.

The prayer of faith mentioned in James 5:15 is not the prayer of a be-liever, although it is prayed by a believer. It is a special God-initiated and God-directed prayer into the life of the sick one. The definite article "the" indicates this prayer is different from believing faith. I may believe God will heal everyone, but, in reality, not everyone is healed. The prayer of faith however, is born from above and accomplishes its purpose to save the sick.

In verse 16, we see that the ones present are commanded to confess their sins to the Lord, and healing, which results from those confessions, are spiritual in nature and not necessarily physical.

When is it appropriate to pray for healing? The Bible urges us to pray without ceasing (1 Thess 5:17), and this is how often to pray. There are times when God elects to heal in a supernatural fashion, but more often, our experience is either a natural healing, an assisted-healing using some form of treatment, or non-healing. It is never wrong to call for the elders for confession, prayer, and healing, particularly when one remains sick despite standard treatment. I do not believe it is God's will, however, to withhold standard medical care while waiting on a supernatural healing through prayer. I am even more adamant about this when one is deciding on the plan of care for a child or a dependent person. God is able to heal in an instant, but much more often, God uses people trained in the healing arts to assist in that process.

The final area I want to cover concerns failures of healing. What should be the response of a Christian who has done all he knows to do and still remains sick? What is God trying to teach about his love and concern for us regarding our illnesses? How can we know what He wants us to do and how he wants us to act? The Bible must be our guide for faith and practice, and the Lord will direct our path according to his Word when we diligently seek Him (Prov 3: 5, 6).

What If I Am Not Healed?

As a physician with years of experience in the healing ministry, I have witnessed the healing of thousands of grateful patients. The vast majority of these would be classified as assisted-healings resulting from medications given or surgical procedures done by me or one of my colleagues. A small number of patients whom I observed were supernaturally healed in such a way in which no scientific explanation for their healing could be given. There were some who remained sick, however, despite the best efforts of the physicians involved and the fervent prayers offered by spiritual friends and pastors.

The overriding question is this: "Why does God choose to heal some while others remain sick?" The question becomes intensely personal when I am the one who is ill or if it is a loved one who remains sick. I can become bitter and angry toward God who appears to have abandoned me, or I can trust in His love for me and seek to allow Him to teach me through this sickness. This is a critical crossroads of faith, and the lessons to be learned are better received in the light of good health rather than the dark shadows of an illness. How can I be so certain my Savior, the Lord Jesus Christ, loves me? He knows how badly I am hurting, and he wants the best for me. I must be prepared to take a stand on his unfailing Word and trust that what he says in his Word he will do.

The rapid advances in medical science particularly over the past ten years have caused many to believe there is a scientific explanation for every illness. We are confident a cure will result when the correct diagnosis is made and the proper treatment given. There is little credibility given to the sovereignty of God over our health, at least not until there is a treatment failure. In prolonged illness, some say, "Where is God now when I need him?" There are passages in the Word, such as Jeremiah 29:11–13 and Hebrews 4: 5–16, in which God plainly declares His never-failing love and concern for His children who are ill. He tells us to come boldly to his throne of grace for help when all else has seemingly failed. Regarding his presence, he promises in Hebrews 13: 5 that he is always there, and he never forsakes us. When we are caught in the despair of failing health and the uncertainty of our future, it is comforting to know our God is not only present but is in control.

There are truths about our lives and health which we will never fully understand. For example, I might ask, "Why am I being afflicted with an intolerable illness when I have purposed to love and serve God? There are people around me who seem to mock God and are perfectly healthy. Why do I seem to be facing so many closed doors when an open door to good health would bring me such happiness? Do I have so much sin in my life that God is punishing me to teach me a lesson, and he simply doesn't want me to be happy? It is here I must trust in Romans 8:28–29 with confidence—that God is at work in my illness. He will work it out for my good, and what seems like a closed door is really an open door for him to work in and through me.

It is possible to have a rejoicing spirit toward God and an attitude of praise in difficult places. In Second Corinthians 12:7–10, the Apostle Paul writes that the "thorn in the flesh given to him" was an opportunity to glory in God's goodness to him, because the strength of Christ could then work through his own weakness. God's promise is that he uses every event in our lives to help us grow stronger and have more of the character of Christ. He further reinforces this truth in Second Corinthians 4:17–18, noting that "our light affliction which is but for a moment" is working an eternal purpose in us. We are challenged to keep our eyes on the eternal purposes of God and not on the temporal afflictions which have happened.

It is not an easy thing to be sick and to suffer heartache with no apparent relief in sight, but our God, who lives in us and loves us more than we can imagine, will bring comfort and peace to our weary minds. At the same time, with no extra charge, "He will put a new song in our heart and on our lips, and many will hear it and give glory to Him who desires the very best for us!" (Ps 40:3).

140. A PANHANDLER AT THE COTTON BOWL

God Begins His Teaching to Me on Giving

As a young teen from a small Southern town, I had no experience with life on the street in a large city such as Dallas and knew absolutely nothing about panhandlers, those who accost passersby on the street to beg money from them. I met my first panhandler on January 1, 1955, on a Dallas street corner. The incident impacted me for years, and I still deal with attitudes toward the poor and homeless which were formulated in my heart as a result.

I have written of my love for the Arkansas Razorbacks, which dates back to my Bubba's playing football for the Razorbacks from 1946 to 1948. He was a high school All-American tackle for the El Dorado Wildcats, which resulted in a full scholarship to play tackle for the Razorbacks in the late 1940s. He sustained a career-ending knee injury during his sophomore year and was able to play in only two or three varsity games. Unfortunately, I was never able to see him play in a Razorback uniform, but that did not dull my love for the team.

I was thrilled beyond words during the Christmas holidays in 1954 when the parents of a friend invited me to join them for a trip to the Cotton Bowl on New Year's Day. For the first time in years, the Razorbacks had won the Southwest Conference title in football and received the automatic bid to play in the Cotton Bowl against Georgia Tech, the Southeast Conference champions. The invitation to see my team play in this huge game was a dream come true. We were to spend one night in a downtown hotel, attend the game, which began at 1:00 p.m., and return to El Dorado the same day. The events which took place on the morning of the game have overshadowed in my memory everything else that happened.

Following the six-hour drive to Dallas on the eve of the game, it was difficult for me to sleep in a strange hotel, on a bed with a sagging mattress, with the excitement of my first Cotton Bowl streaming through my mind. I don't remember sleeping at all, but arose completely refreshed and energized. After breakfast, I wanted to walk outside in front of the hotel and enjoy the noise of the crowd while joining in the standard Razorback cheer, "Wooo Pig Sooie!!" I didn't stray far from the hotel entrance for fear of getting turned around in this unfamiliar setting and perhaps not being able to find my way back to the hotel before leaving for the stadium. There were no cell phones then.

All of a sudden, a bedraggled street person approached me and began speaking. He appeared to be in his fifties with a two-to-three-day-old beard and reeking of body odor, tobacco, and cheap wine. He said, "Sonny, is there any way you can help me?" I felt compassion for him since I had seen Pop help and treat men like this in his medical practice in El Dorado. I meekly said, "I will if I can." He said, "I haven't eaten in two days and am so hungry. Could you give me some money for food?" I thought this was something I could do because Pop had given me ten dollars for extra-spending money. In today's economy, ten dollars would be equivalent to fifty dollars.

I reached into my pocket and pulled out one of the two five-dollar bills and handed it to this supposedly hungry man, and he grabbed my hand to shake it and thanked me three or four times. As I watched him disappear into the growing crowd, I assumed he was headed to some near-by restaurant to have his first meal in days. For the first time in my life, I had actually been the agent of help for a hurting man, and the feelings I had deep within me were so gratifying. I kept thinking, "How great is this to feed a hungry man and see a Razorback game the same day!"

Within fifteen minutes the crowd within several blocks of the hotel was filling the sidewalks, and I was preparing to go back to the hotel when I spotted a scene which stunned me. Less than twenty feet away, I saw the same man talking with three of four men, and I thought he must be asking them for money also. I got close enough to see that he was holding a huge wad of money which looked like several hundred dollars. I heard him ask the men how many points they would give him on the upcoming game. He was placing bets on the Cotton Bowl game and a very small part of the money he was betting was one half of all the money I possessed. In trying to provide food for him, I gave him money to gamble. I did not have the courage to confront him for fear he might hurt me. If he would rob a kid like me, he probably would have no qualms about beating me up.

I went around the corner where I couldn't be seen and cried for several minutes. My tears and broken heart turned to anger and resentment, and I told God I would never again in my life give so much as a penny to a street bum. The incident so wounded me toward the homeless and street-people that I kept the promise for years.

Cathy has helped me immensely in this area because she has such a loving and generous heart for the disadvantaged. I am not as stingy as I once was, but still not as generous as I should be. In thinking what Jesus said about helping the helpless, I recalled that he said, "As you have done it to the least of these, you have done it to me." Because my heart was pure that day in Dallas in my intent to give, I believe Jesus credited it to my account of giving. What the panhandler did with it was his responsibility and not mine. The Lord Jesus has been patient in making me a more cheerful giver.

141. THE THREE CREEKS REVIVAL, 1864

A Significant Revival During the Civil War

Three Creeks is a small community in southern Arkansas located on Highway 15 approximately fifteen miles west of El Dorado. On the scale of national or international importance, Three Creeks would go unnoticed. But to our branch of the Moore family tree, it holds great significance. I have never lived there, and my immediate family has spent very little time exploring the surroundings, but ask any member of our family how and why Three Creeks is important, and you will get an instant and positive response.

In 1846, my great-great-grandfather Alexander Moore brought his family west from Perry County in Alabama to settle and farm in Three Creeks, Arkansas. Some of the migrant Moore family members didn't stop in Arkansas but traveled to and settled in southeast Texas. At an early family reunion of the entire Moore clan, the question was posed, "Why did some stop in Arkansas while others moved on to Texas?" The answer given by the Texas branch was, "When the travelers came to a road sign pointing to Arkansas, those who could read kept going to Texas while the others proceeded towards Three Creeks."

Alexander and wife Lydia purchased several thousand acres of Three Creeks land for farming, because the land there was very fertile with an excellent water supply and abundant wildlife. I have one of the original deeds of his purchase of land which was available as the result of a land grant from the Treaty of Dancing Rabbit Creek by the Choctaw Indians. The Choctaw Nation agreed to deed their territory in Mississippi and Arkansas to the United States in exchange for cash settlements along with safe passage and resettlement lands which were guaranteed in Oklahoma.

Alexander and Lydia's son Richard Andrew Jackson (RAJ), who was my great grandfather, continued farming the land at Three Creeks and had a very successful career in his profession. During the War Between the States, RAJ served in the Confederate Army, and fought in several encounters in Mississippi and northern Louisiana against the Northern Army. He survived the war, but had a bullet wound injury to his right leg, which caused him to have a permanent limp the remainder of his life.

The land owned by Alexander and RAJ Moore was passed down through the generations of the family. My grandfather, John Aaron (JA) was the recipient of a significant portion of the original land and passed the land to his three children, Walter, Lillie Mae and Berry Lee (Pop). Because Walter and Lillie Mae had no heirs, the land was passed on and inherited by my brother, my sister, and me. For generations, the land has produced income to the family, not from farming as in the beginning, but from pine and hardwood harvesting, from oil leases, and currently from brine leases. It has been discovered the brine (salt water) in South Arkansas is extremely high in bromine content, and bromine is widely sought for industrial purposes. The latest discovery concerning the Three Creeks land is that the brine located throughout the region is extremely high in lithium, and with the advent of cell phones and electric cars, lithium has become very valuable.

Perhaps the greatest value of the land in the Three Creeks area is spiritual in nature, and it began near the close of the War Between the States. One of the largest revivals concerning salvation decisions in the state of Arkansas occurred at Three Creeks during the summer and early fall months of 1864. The information concerning this revival is from a monograph entitled *Arkansas Baptist Revivals,* written in 1988 by Dr. Mark T. Coppenger, a former pastor at First Baptist Church, El Dorado, and a continuing great friend:

> A Confederate chaplain named Kavanaugh reported after battles of Mansfield and Pleasant Hill in Louisiana, the soldiers of the Confederacy moved to the Three Creeks area of Arkansas to rest and be restored to fighting strength. While there an unnamed chaplain began having revival meetings among the troops with preaching, prayers, and singing every evening around the camp fires. When the preaching and singing stopped around 10:00 p.m., the men began gathering in groups of tens and twenties for individual prayers and testimonies of faith. It was reported shouts of praise and thanksgiving from newly converted men could be heard night after night as a result of these smaller camp fire gatherings. The prayer meetings continued in the same fashion for several weeks resulting in the spiritual conversion of the majority of the two brigades encamped in the Three Creeks area.
>
> Chaplain Kavanaugh further reported a conversation with General Parsons, the Division Commander in which the General not only was in favor of the revival meetings but was pleased with the general conduct of the men under his command. He

had not had one complaint of the civilians living in the Three Creeks community against any soldier. He further stated a number of the civilians were attending the meetings and were among the ones also being converted to faith. The total number of conversions at Three Creeks was estimated at five hundred. Similar revival meetings of Confederate soldiers and civilians were held in the Camden (Arkansas) area approximately fifty miles away, and the number of converted men there also approached five hundred bringing the total to near one thousand in South Arkansas alone.

I have no record of any of the Moore family attending those military prayer meetings in Three Creeks, but I believe given the immensity and intensity of the meetings many in the family were there and were converted and strengthened in their faith. God will use every circumstance in our lives to drive us to Him when our eyes and our hearts are open to his grace. Times of stress and the surrounding danger of wars are fertile gospel grounds. Thank God for the Lord Jesus and his redeeming works, especially at Three Creeks, Arkansas. I am thankful Alexander chose to move there instead of going on to Texas, whatever the reason. As far as I know he could read!

142. OPERATING WITH DR. PAUL BRAND

One of the World's Greatest Hand Surgeons Teaches Me

Dr. Paul Brand

One of the highlights of my four years of surgical training at Charity Hospital in New Orleans was the privilege of operating on two separate occasions with Dr. Paul Brand. The LSU General Surgery Department had a separate orthopedic division apart from the LSU orthopedic department, and the general surgery residents spent three months on our own orthopedic service caring for major fractures, repairing broken tibiae and hips, and performing tendon repairs on injured hands. It was a very busy rotation because there was only one resident and an intern on the service caring for a large number of patients.

One evening while on the orthopedic service, our chief resident announced I would have a visiting staff surgeon assisting me the following morning on a patient needing a major tendon repair on his hand. I asked who would be staffing me and was told it was Dr. Paul Brand, a hand surgeon who worked at Carville Hospital near Baton Rouge. I knew Carville was the only hospital in the continental United States which treated patients with leprosy, but I had never heard of Dr. Brand. I had no idea he was recognized at the time as one of the greatest hand surgeons in the world!

For many years previously, Dr. Brand was a missionary surgeon to India, working with the Leprosy Mission Trust in Vellore. As a pioneer hand surgeon working to reconstruct diseased and crippled hands and feet, he had devised a number of unique tendon transfer procedures, all of which bore his name. His experience and expertise were vast, and surgeons all over the world learned from him. Some even traveled to India for the privilege of working with this legend. I knew none of this when he arrived that morning at Charity and introduced himself as we scrubbed our hands to go into the operating room to don our sterile gown and gloves.

As he began asking questions about this particular patient and then described the condition of his hand, I immediately knew I was in the presence of a phenomenal man and surgeon. I was not a Christian at the time, but, as he spoke, he interwove the spiritual relationship an injured body part plays to prevent the body from functioning as God intended. He was the first physician I'd ever heard speaking about the importance of the power of God in the healing process, and how necessary it was for a physician to know and cooperate with the Lord Jesus in the process. He allowed me to do the procedure but showed me certain techniques which improved the quality of my work and lessen the trauma to the tissue which always occurs when it's handled too roughly.

At the conclusion of the procedure, he said he was very pleased to have been with me. (I never had a staff surgeon speak those words!) Had I not had on a mask he would have seen my mouth remain open in awe of him the entire time. I couldn't wait for him to return, and we scheduled another case for about two weeks later. It was interesting when I discovered that the staff of the LSU orthopedic department was angry that Dr. Brand had joined the general surgery staff instead of their orthopedic staff. He had trained as a general surgeon in London during the Battle of Britain and always considered himself a general surgeon who worked on the hand.

Years later in the mid 1980s, our pastor at First Baptist Church El Dorado, Dr. Mark Coppenger, invited Dr. Brand to speak at our Sunday morning worship service. Since those days in 1967 at Charity Hospital, I had become a believer and had read Dr. Brand's biography, *Ten Fingers for God*, so I was very excited he was coming. By this time, he had collaborated with Phillip Yancey and authored 2 magnificent books, *Fearfully and Wonderfully Made* and *In His Image*.

At the time of his visit to El Dorado, he was still living in his home on the grounds of Carville Hospital (US Public Service Hospital in Louisiana) and had retired from his surgical practice. He continued working as the chief of rehabilitation services. His wife Margaret, whom I never met, was a distinguished eye surgeon and had a wonderful career of her own.

We made arrangements for him to speak to the doctors at South Arkansas Medical Center on Saturday prior to his talk at First Baptist on Sunday. He spoke on the topic "The Insensate Foot," which is a common problem for patients with diabetes. I took notes of that talk which I still have because the things he taught were so informative and practical.

Later the same day he came to our home for a short visit and to enjoy a piece of Cathy's famous key lime pie. While there, he demolished my years of reasoning to Cathy that she should not go barefoot in our home for fear of stepping on a foreign object such as a pin. As he entered the house Cathy had her shoes off and said to Dr. Brand, "Excuse me while I slip on my shoes. John has fussed for years I should always wear shoes." He looked at me and said in his deeply British accent, "Oh no, you mustn't fuss at Mrs. Moore for doing something very healthy for her feet! Walking barefoot strengthens her feet and makes them more sensitive to foreign objects." So much for my endless arguments.

Several years later Dr. Brand wrote his last book with Phillip Yancey, *Pain, The Gift Nobody Wants,* which was very practical for me in my practice as a wound-care physician. One of the truths he taught in the book was that people in America spend billions of dollars each year to free themselves from pain, while there are millions of others suffering from neuropathy (numbness) who would pay any amount of money to experience a return of feeling to their feet, even if it was pain. What most don't realize is that pain in most situations is a God-given mechanism to protect us from further injury.

My experience of having Dr. Paul Brand assist me with the two orthopedic hand procedures years ago was worth a year's added knowledge in surgical technique. But the spiritual lessons I learned from his Christian wisdom and witness in providing loving care for my patients are priceless and eternal.

PS: Because of Dr. Brand's recommendation Cathy continues to walk barefoot in our home.

143. THE SAVING LOVE OF A FATHER

A Letter from a Dad Begins a New Life

Dr. John F. Redman was chairman and head of the Department of Urology at the University of Arkansas for Medical Sciences for many years and has had a distinguished career in the field. When he was appointed to the position at age twenty-nine, he was the youngest department head in the history of the medical center. During his long career he trained many of the current physicians of the state in his field and received numerous awards for his accomplishments. I knew "Johnny" Redman in medical school. He was in the 1963 graduating class, a year ahead of me. I don't believe anyone who knew Johnny in those days predicted what lay ahead for him, although he was a gifted and precocious student, who graduated from high school at age sixteen and finished college in two years.

If one were looking for a wild party, it entailed only that you find Johnny Redman; he would be front and center of the action. Because he was a year ahead of me and I wasn't seeking an association with this crowd, I didn't have much personal contact with him. I lost contact with him during my training years, but when I began my practice in general surgery in El Dorado in the early 1970s, I knew Dr. John Redman was now head of urology at the U of A med center. And over the next twenty years or so, I was pleased to refer some patients to him. All of them did well and reported they were treated very well by him. I had an occasional phone conversation with him during the time, but it was always concerning the patients.

In the mid 1990s after Cathy and I had become believers and were very active at Immanuel Baptist Church, I was invited to give my personal salvation testimony at the Arkansas Baptist State Convention. Our pastor David Uth, was president of the convention, and he made the arrangements for me to speak at the First Baptist Church in Little Rock. While sitting on the front row of the church awaiting my turn to speak, Bill Elliff, the pastor of First Baptist leaned over to me and quietly said, "The best soul winner by far in our church is Dr. John Redman." I said, "You mean the Dr. Redman who is the head of urology at the medical school?" I was shocked at such a change in an individual. "How did that come about?" I asked. He briefly told me of Dr. John's conversion experience, and in that quiet, two-minute conversation, I was brought to tears and wasn't sure I could stand and speak. Here is the story I later confirmed from John himself when I called him that same week:

I lived a wild life from the time I finished high school, and it continued through the years I became department chairman of urology at the U of A Medical Center. I cared nothing about spiritual things, had several failed marriages, and was less than exemplary in my personal life. I hated the fact that both my parents were committed Christians and were constantly telling me I needed to change my way of living and follow Jesus. My Dad was a physician in Fort Smith and understood the pressures of our profession, and he seemed more urgent in his witness to me. He was always kind but very persistent. I came to a point of frustration and anger and finally told both parents since all they wanted to talk with me about was religion, I wanted nothing more to do with them. I cut off all communication and refused speaking with them or writing and never read any of their letters to me. It was not long after I had done this that my Father died unexpectedly. I felt terrible about his death, but at least I didn't have to hear any more about changing my life.

About four years later, I was moving into a new office at the medical center and was alone one evening arranging my desk. I was placing items from my previous desk into the new one, and I saw a letter from my dad written four years earlier but left unopened. I decided to read the last communication I ever received from him, knowing all the while the substance of the letter. Sure enough, in the letter he told me how much he loved me, how much he missed me, and how badly he wanted me to get myself straightened out. In the lower corner of the letter, he wrote a scripture verse, drew a circle around it, and wrote "Do what this says!" The verses were Romans 10:9–10. I didn't know where to even find a Bible, but in the same drawer containing the letter, I spotted a New Testament which I'd been issued by the Air Force about fifteen years earlier. I looked in the table of contents to see where Romans was located. Finding the passage, I read, "If you will confess with your mouth the Lord Jesus and believe in your heart God raised Him from the dead, you will be saved. For with the heart man believes unto righteousness and with the mouth confession is made unto salvation."

I sat there for a very long time thinking about the verse and finally, in desperation, called out, "God if you are really out there, I do want you to save me, and I confess you as my Savior."

I didn't see lightning flashing or hear thunder rolling, but at that moment, I knew I had been changed.

I went home and told my live-in girlfriend Anna (also a physician) that we could no longer live together without being married. She didn't understand this sudden change, but moved out. She was very mad at this drastic change in my attitude, but in the months following, I witnessed the Lord Jesus to Anna, and she also was saved. We subsequently married and joined First Baptist Church in Little Rock and were baptized.

Hearing the condensed version of this testimony while seated on the front row of First Baptist Church in Little Rock moved me greatly. It is more evidence that no one is so far from God he cannot be saved from destruction, and God will transform the heart of the worst sinner and make it brand new. It also challenges us to never give up on a loved one. The love of a father and mother can powerfully lead a prodigal back to our saving Lord, even years after they have departed!

144. "THE ONLY ONE WHO CAN HELP YOU"

A Total Stranger Offers Saving Help at a Swimming Pool

Perhaps the greatest joy a Christian can experience is leading someone to confess faith in the saving grace of the Lord Jesus. I believe this is not just a good option for a Christian but also a command given to all believers by Christ himself when he issued the Great Commission at his ascension (Matt 28:18–20). I love hearing stories of salvation experiences and will ask someone whom I believe is saved to relate their journey of faith. Every story is different just as we are all different, and every story is important because our Savior is the central figure of each story. One of the most unique accounts was part of the testimony of Herb Hodges, an evangelist from Memphis, Tennessee.

I had never met Herb prior to hearing him speak to the Kaleos at Kids Across America in Branson, Missouri. It's an urban sports camp which has been ministering for the past thirty years, and each year, as many as nine thousand kids get a one-week, fun-filled camp experience at no cost to them. One of the primary reasons Cathy and I moved to Branson in 2005 was to be close to our daughter Mary Kay, her husband Dave Janke, and their two daughters Rebecca and Sara Beth. Dave has been on the staff at Kids Across America since its inception in the early 1990s. This brilliant camp concept was born out of the ministry and hearts of Spike White and his son Joe, who were the leaders of Kanakuk Kamps, which had operated in Branson for over seventy years. These camps give kids from ages six through eighteen the opportunity to have a fantastic experience combined with a major emphasis on Christian living. Because inner-city kids could not afford the cost of a week at camp, Kids Across America (KAA) provides the means and the beautiful camp grounds on Table Rock Lake in Golden, Missouri.

Many of the kids from cities like Kansas City, Dallas, St. Louis, and Chicago come to the camp in the Missouri Ozarks having never seen a tree growing in the woods nor experienced such a loving environment as they find at KAA. From the moment they set foot on the camp grounds, they are loved, hugged, encouraged, and challenged to be the kind of kids God wants them to be. The total atmosphere is so unreal to the first-time campers they are speechless, but they soon understand they are among friends who love Jesus and love them as well. It is not uncommon for the kids to receive the gift of life that Jesus Christ offers before the week is over.

The counselors who accompany the kids from their individual cities and stay with them the entire week are called "kaleos" (Greek for "called or invited"). During the week kaleos attend talks and training sessions by camp leaders intended to challenge and encourage them in their Christian walk. Guest speakers are invited from various places to add to their total experience. Herb Hodges was a frequent guest speaker, and I happened to be present when he was speaking one morning. Herb gave the following account of his spiritual journey:

> When I was a young man in my late teens living in Memphis, I was a rough kid with no thoughts about Jesus Christ or any interest whatsoever in living for anything or anyone except myself. I wanted to emulate the people I admired, except I wanted to be bigger, stronger, and meaner than the worst of them. I believed a real man spoke roughly and used curse words regularly to enhance his image as being a tough guy. I cursed often and frequently used the Lord's name in vain. Anyone in my presence saw and heard what I considered to be a "real man."
>
> One afternoon while swimming in a popular public pool, I decided to get out of the pool by climbing out the side rather than at the steps which everyone else used. As I was looking down while getting out, I noticed a hand being extended to assist me. I looked up into the face of someone I had never seen before, and while he was helping me up, he said, "Son, the One whose name you use as a curse word is the only One who can help you." This was all he said, and he turned and walked away. I didn't make any comment to him and never saw him again. Those words kept resonating in my thoughts over the next seven to ten days, and I couldn't stop thinking about what he

said and what it might mean to me. About a week later I just "happened to walk past a church having a revival meeting" and entered the church out of curiosity. I was strangely moved by what I saw and heard, and when the invitation for salvation was given, I responded by giving my life to the Lord Jesus Christ!

One can never know the eternal impact he has through his life style or the words he might speak or even the extending of a helping hand to a stranger. The point Herb Hodges made so well that morning at KAA was that our responsibility as believers is to sow seeds of God's loving grace regularly and often wherever we might be. We never know when one tiny seed might fall on the fertile soil prepared by others. It could even happen at a public swimming pool!

145. "WE'VE DONE EVERYTHING EXCEPT PRAY"

My First Experience in Praying for a Seriously-Ill Patient

When I began private practice in general surgery in my hometown, a large part of the decision to return home was based on the fact that my older brother Berry Lee (Bubba) was in a family medicine practice there. I was excited to have his fourteen-year-practice experience to lean on. I also loved just being around him because of my love and respect of his wonderful character. One aspect of Bubba's personality which made both Cathy and me very uneasy was his spiritual life. According to him, he'd had a spiritual conversion four years earlier, and we couldn't relate to the changes which occurred in him. Although we were moral in our character and religious in nature, neither of us had experienced life changes like the ones he described. Whenever the topic of faith arose in our conversation, we changed the subject as quickly as possible. His zealous attitude towards everything related to faith did not affect our professional relationship, and he referred every one of his surgical patients to me.

Barbara H. was a woman well-known in our community because of her father's excellent reputation as a businessman, and she herself was married to a prominent businessman. Although she was several years older, I had known her and her siblings since childhood. She suffered with childhood diabetes and, even at her young age, was beginning to have major complications because she was not managing the disease well. She had been admitted by Bubba to the hospital with severe abdominal pains and fever and was getting worse despite large doses of intravenous antibiotics. Her tests showed gall stones and her symptoms indicated an acute infection. We were hoping the infection would subside so the gall bladder could be removed at a later time instead of as an emergency. She grew worse on good treatment, and an immediate operation was necessary. Both she and her husband were made aware of the dangers and complications of surgery under these dire conditions.

The operation was more difficult than anticipated because she had pancreatic infection in addition to the abscessed gall bladder with gall stones. The combination of these two problems in a diabetic patient made her condition critical, so she was admitted to the intensive-care unit. Unfortunately, she did not awaken from the general anesthetic, but was breathing on her own, so she didn't require the use of a ventilator.

Bubba consulted an internist and a pulmonary specialist to get their best thoughts and recommendations regarding her management. Despite our best efforts, she steadily worsened over the next three days and didn't awaken from the coma. Her temperature reached a level I had never seen. It was so high that our current thermometer couldn't accurately measure it, but we extrapolated it to 108 degrees F. We placed her on an ice blanket to try to bring it down.

On the evening of the third post-operative day, her vital signs were beginning to worsen while her temperature remained off the chart. Bubba and I went to the waiting room to give her husband Bill this new and dreaded report. Bubba said, "Bill, it looks like Barbara won't make it through the night unless a miracle occurs." Bill began to cry and said, "She has been a wonderful wife and mother to our children, and I don't know how I will get along without her. I am going to miss her so much." We assured him we were doing everything possible, and he said he was confident she was getting the best care possible.

Bubba went back to her bedside while I went to the nurse's desk to write my progress note for the evening. I heard Bubba say, "We have done everything for her except pray, so I want all of us to gather around her bed and pray." I had never done anything like that in my professional or personal life, and I was not interested in any public display of religion. Bubba was insistent I join them, and to keep from making a further scene in the ICU, I reluctantly went to her bedside. There were two nurses and a nurses aid, and he had us hold hands while he prayed. I was very embarrassed with all of this, so I don't remember exactly what he prayed. It was something like, "Lord, we've done all we know to do, and it hasn't worked, so would You take over and heal Barbara." I was glad when he finished, and I went back to the desk to finish my charting. Before I got to the desk, I heard a stirring from the direction of her bedside and turned in time to hear her voice as she said weakly, "I am so cold. Could I have another blanket?"

I was shaken to the core, because not only had I never been part of a bed-side prayer by a physician, but I had never witnessed such a dramatic physical change in a patient so near death. Although we were all very excited for Barbara and for her family, Bubba acted like he had expected this result from his prayer. His confidence only added to my amazement.

When I arrived home, Cathy was standing at our kitchen sink, and she told me she had been praying for Barbara since I left for the hospital earlier in the evening. When I told her what had happened, we rejoiced and were beginning to reconsider our belief in the power of prayer.

Barbara fully recovered from this problem and lived another fifteen years. As a result of this experience and a number of other things, both Cathy and I had a spiritual conversion two years later. Everything changed for us, and, among other things, I began praying with and witnessing to my patients.

Subsequently, when I saw Barbara as a patient or in a social setting, we discussed how God used her illness and near-death experience to teach me the power of believing prayer. I also learned that prayer should be primary in my care of every patient, not held in reserve until all medical efforts failed. Christ alone has the power to heal all our illnesses (Ps 103:3).

146. CONFIDENTLY PLACING SUTURES

Acknowledging God as Healer

I was recently watching Cathy quickly sew a button on one of my shirts and made the comment, "I guess I should be sewing my own buttons with all the experience I have with needle and thread." I quickly told her, however, she did a much better job, which is true. I believe the average seamstress is more gifted in sewing than the most skilled surgeon, and Cathy is far above average. The difference lies in what one is sewing. Accurately placing sutures in wounds with skill and speed are basic to the work of a surgeon. Over the course of forty-five years as a surgeon, I placed multiple thousands of sutures in untold types of wounds, and in some respects, I miss exercising the skill now that I am retired.

My dad (Pop) taught me how to place sutures when I was in high school. I would go with him on house calls or accompany him to the emergency room to treat people who had sustained an injury requiring sutures. He would allow me to suture relatively minor wounds while explaining to the patients I was in training under his watch care. I don't ever remember a patient objecting to my work since Pop was there in the room making certain I did it correctly. This was at a time when malpractice litigation was almost non-existent, and most people were thankful to get medical care even from a non-licensed trainee. By the time I entered medical school, I could place sutures more quickly and accurately than the majority of interns.

During my surgical residency at Charity Hospital in New Orleans, I spent four years learning all the intricate techniques necessary for a general surgeon. Early in my first year of training, when Cathy and I were newly-weds, I would bring home needle holders, sutures, and scissors to practice all forms of suturing. I would sew the neck of socks together to simulate the technique of sewing intestine end to end. I don't remember how many pair of socks I owned, but at one time or another, they all were stitched to each other. I would cut them apart and sew them back together again. I think Cathy got pretty tired of examining my handy work. I tried my best to convince her that I was able to place some of the most beautiful stitches ever done at the "Big Charity." I know she thought I was great, but I don't believe I ever impressed her with my surgical skills. I also practiced sewing in tight places by sewing objects together within a match box. It was certainly better to hone those skills at home with inanimate objects rather than in the operating room on a patient in need of immediate help. I wasn't able to simulate the stress of the OR in our tiny apartment.

When I began my private surgical practice in El Dorado, I was sharing office space with Bubba, even though his practice was family medicine. Initially, he assisted me in the operating room until I became familiar with the other surgeons in town and could confidently ask them to assist. I did not do many procedures the first year, but I was sure grateful to have him in the OR. He had assisted Pop for twelve years prior to my arrival, so he was very familiar with good surgical technique. This was when I learned that Bubba wanted to become a general surgeon, but by the time he completed his obligation of two years in the US Air Force, he and La Nell had two children (Lydia and Andy). They believed they could not afford the huge expense of an additional four years of training at a medical center.

Elsewhere, I've written about the spiritual conversion Cathy and I experienced when we attended the Bill Gothard seminar in Dallas in August, 1977. We had been married twelve years and had been living in El Dorado for six. God transformed us and made us new as promised in his Word (2 Cor 5:17). Bubba was one of the first to know about the change, and he began slowly to mentor me not as a doctor who also was a Christian, but as a Christian who also was a surgeon.

One day while assisting me in the OR, Bubba asked, "Do you know how a wound is held together and heals following placement of sutures?" He was always very precise in his approach to life and medicine, and I thought he was quizzing me on the exact physiology of wound healing to see if I remembered what we had been taught in medical school. I began by saying that with the injury, there is coagulation of platelets in blood at the wound edges which leads to the formation of fibrin. He interrupted me by saying, "You are giving the scientific explanation, but God gave us the Biblical explanation of wound healing." I said, "All right; you have my attention." He said the wound-healing passage is in Colossians, chapter one, verses sixteen and seventeen. He continued, "It says that the Lord Jesus created all things in heaven and earth, visible and invisible including principalities, powers, kings, and queens. It further says all things are under his control and by him all things consist." Bubba stopped and asked, "Do you know the definition of the word *consist*? It means "held together." Jesus is the one who holds all the universe together and keeps it from falling apart. That includes the edges of this surgical wound you have just caused. Jesus himself will be holding this wound together! You can put the sutures in place, remove them in seven days, and assume all the invisible physiological processes have occurred. If Jesus isn't holding it together, it will break open."

I have never forgotten Bubba's explanation of this particular passage. Every time I counseled with a surgical patient before their procedure, I could confidently say I would be placing the sutures, but it would be Jesus who would be holding the work together and healing the site. As my preacher friend, Luther Price, would say after explaining a particularly difficult Bible passage, "My, what a God!"

147. THE MAN WHO GAVE ME THE MOST TROUBLE

A Serious Evaluation of Life

Ron Dunn, Evangelist

Through the years I have had the privilege of meeting and hearing some of the greatest preachers of the gospel, and I have been stirred and moved by all of them. One particular, favorite evangelist is Ron Dunn, whom I only met once, but I've have read most of his books and listened to many of his audio tapes.

Ron, who is in glory now, was raised in Fort Smith, Arkansas, and in his adult years while living in the Dallas area, he maintained the family farm near Fort Smith. When time permitted, he, his wife Kaye, and their three children often spent vacation time on the farm relaxing by hunting, fishing, and spending quality family time together.

He surrendered to vocational ministry at a young age following his spiritual conversion at First Baptist Church Fort Smith and attended seminary at Southwestern Baptist Theological Seminary in the late 1950s. He began his preaching as pastor of a number of smaller churches where he also developed administrative skills. His largest and most significant pastorate was at MacArthur Boulevard Baptist Church in Irving, Texas, where he began in 1966. It was there the church experienced a Spirit-led revival in 1972, one which continued until 1975 when Ron was called into vocational evangelism. He served in itinerant evangelism for the next twenty-six years until his untimely death from pulmonary fibrosis in 2001.

I have learned many spiritual truths from Ron Dunn although I was only in the congregation where he preached on seven occasions. Five of those experiences were in El Dorado, Arkansas, where he preached a revival meeting at First Baptist Church at just the time Dr. Mark Coppenger was leaving the church to move with his family to Indiana.

On Wednesday of that week, I had a free morning from my surgical schedule, and I invited Ron to have breakfast at our home. There I was able to spend several hours with him discussing life situations and what it means to walk with Christ. The time spent with him that morning was both rich and rewarding. During the visit, Ron told me a story related to his formative years in Fort Smith as a young man under the spiritual influence of his pastor, Dr. J. Harold Smith. Ron had his spiritual conversion during Dr. Smith's tenure, and, while he was pastor, surrendered to the ministry and was ordained by the church.

Dr. Smith became pastor of the relatively large First Baptist Church of Fort Smith in the 1950s and remained there approximately ten years while leading the church successfully in evangelism and discipleship. At times, his pastorate was marked by turmoil and dissent, because Dr. Smith was a biblical inerrantist and the moderates in the Southern Baptist Convention in those days were strong and challenged his biblical interpretations at every opportunity. He had the reputation of being strong in his opinions and firm in his convictions concerning the Bible and its relevance. His stance was affirmed by the vast majority of members of this prestigious church, but not by all of them.

On the occasion of Dr. Smith's five-year anniversary as pastor, he announced in the Sunday morning service, "Tonight in keeping with my five years as pastor of this church, I will name the man who has given me the most trouble as pastor." Ron said he was sitting in his seat in the choir loft and was able to observe the congregation's response to this startling announcement. He said there was stunned silence with looks of anxiety and certainly no "Amens" spoken to encourage the pastor. Everyone in the congregation knew Dr. Smith well enough to know he would keep his word in revealing the troubling culprit.

Ron said that by the time the 6:00 p.m. worship service began, the church was packed with more people present than had ever attended a Sunday evening service. People lined the aisles in folding chairs, and some were standing in the foyer in anticipation of his announcement. From his seat in the choir, Ron had a perfect view of everything taking place in the auditorium that night. He said that several of the deacons had brought their lawyers with them to hear what was to be said!

Dr. Smith said nothing concerning the matter during his spiritual message or during the invitation hymn or the altar call. It seemed for the first time in his ministry, he might have changed his mind and decided not to mention the name of the troubling man who had plagued him for five years. But just before closing the service, he stepped back to the pulpit and said to an absolutely hushed and anxious congregation, "I told you this morning I was going to announce the name of the *man* who for the past five years of my ministry has consistently given me the most trouble here at First Baptist, and I am going to keep my word." Ron said the auditorium was so quiet at that moment, one could have heard folks breathing, but everyone was holding their breath! "The name of that man is . . . J. Harold Smith!!" Ron said there was an obvious release of anxiety in the auditorium, and at least one of the deacons appeared he might faint.

What a great object-lesson the folks at First Baptist Fort Smith gained from their pastor that entire day. Each of us must make certain we are not the source of any quarrelsome attitude or the driving force behind any dissension of the brothers within the body of Christ. God clearly states in his Word in Proverbs 6:16–19 that there are seven things He hates and the seventh one on the list is "he that soweth discord among brethren." May this never be said of me.

148. THE DIFFERENCE BETWEEN DOING WELL AND WELL-DOING

Everyone Wants to Do Well

As a result of recent heart issues and a series of hospital admissions with tests and procedures, I have repeatedly been asked the question by loving, concerned family and friends, "How are you doing?" The context of the question is health, but in a larger sense I have been pondering just how am I really doing? My general response to almost every health-issue query has been, "I am doing well" when in the back of my mind I'm thinking that I'm not doing well at all. Is it possible for me to be doing well when all around me seems to indicate just the opposite?

An evangelist friend, Junior Hill from Hartselle, Alabama, has a 2002 paperback book entitled *Out of Season*, which Cathy and I have been reading together. The overall theme of his book is for all Christian workers and especially pastors and teachers to remain faithful to their call to love and serve God in whatever situation they find themselves. This beautiful book has come to Cathy and me at an especially critical time to help us focus on the really important issues of life and service to God through others. Even when health was good, how many of us have not thought how poorly we seemed to be doing when our external circumstances seem to indicate it? Brother Junior helps clarify and refocus such a negative self-analysis by referring often to the passage from the Bible in Galatians 6:9–10 in which the Apostle Paul admonishes all believers with these words: "And let us not be weary in well doing for in due season we shall reap if we faint not. As we have therefore opportunity, let us do good unto all men, especially unto them who are of the household of faith."

There is a clear distinction between doing well and well-doing, and the distinction has to do with our focus. A person who has tremendous wealth, reflected in living in a luxurious home, wearing the latest designer clothes, and driving a Mercedes-Benz sports car may think he is doing well. Another individual living in a rented, one-bedroom shack, wearing second-hand clothes, and driving a broken-down Model A may not think he is doing very well at all. A deeper focus for each of these individuals to see just what they are giving their lives to might reverse their answers.

Doing well tends to focus on the externals of life, the worldly pleasures and treasures which at best are temporary. Well-doing focuses on matters of faith, concern for others, and a deep desire to know and obey God's Word, which is eternal. The former passes away while the latter is forever. Discouragement is always at the doorstep of the one whose external circumstances are poor. Although never intended, all of us are guilty of nurturing our disappointments in order to obtain the maximum in attention and sympathy. It takes intentionality and resolve for the enemy of discouragement to be thrown out and kept out of our thoughts and lives. Our #1 enemy, Satan, loves to constantly whisper in our ear that we are getting just what we deserve when we look around and don't find many of the attractive and shiny things our neighbors are enjoying. His constant harping may sound like this: "See how poor you are? This is the result of your trying to be a so-called good Christian! Give up all this nonsense, and I will make you more comfortable like your neighbors."

When recently I was a hospital in-patient for several days, I was able to share the principle of well-doing with a hospital employee who was in my room more often than I would have desired. He was a phlebotomist (blood drawer) named Chris and was taking samples of my blood every six hours to help regulate my blood clotting mechanism. I began asking him about his goals in life, and he said he was considering becoming a doctor such as an orthopedic surgeon. He said he wasn't sure he could afford the time and the cost required to achieve such a goal, but wanted to be a doctor so he could do "a lot of good for people." I reassured him he was already doing a lot of good for people by being the very best phlebotomist. God had gifted him to be very steady and confident in his skills, and he really was the best phlebotomist I ever had. (I had lots of others over the past two years!) I further encouraged him to not compare what he had in terms of houses, clothes, and cars to what an orthopedic surgeon might have. They would seem to be *doing well* while he would seem to not be doing so well. The truth is, he was *well-doing* because he was using his God-given skills to help lots of people, and this was well-pleasing to God! I was able to further explain to him the passage from Galatians 6, where God promises that, as he continues well-doing, he will reap much greater rewards from his God and his Savior. He had told me he was a Christian. When he left my room for the last time he said, "Thank you Dr. Moore. You helped me a lot." I said, "Thank you Chris. You helped me a lot!"

As a result of carefully examining the real issues of my heart (the intent of my heart instead of the heart rate) I am resolving to focus entirely on well-doing instead of doing well. I would certainly enjoy doing well, which I know won't last, but I will continually reap the greater rewards of well-doing which will last forever!

149. PRAYING WITH PATIENTS

Challenged by a Godly Brother

I had completed all of my medical training, had spent two years serving in the medical corps of the Air Force, and had been in private medical practice for two years before I witnessed a physician praying with a patient—a total of fourteen years of training and practice time. What an indictment on the spiritual poverty of the medical profession during my training era. My brother Berry Lee (Bubba) was the first doctor I ever saw praying at the bedside of a critically-ill patient, and I remember at the time feeling embarrassed because it was such a strange experience. (I documented the account in *We've Done Everything Except Pray*.) It was several years later in 1977 when Cathy and I had a spiritual conversion where I gave my life and medical practice to the lordship of Jesus Christ. That bedside prayer of Bubba in the ICU at the Medical Center of South Arkansas played a role in the conversion of my heart and life and definitely impacted Cathy and me at the time.

I am so very grateful to Bubba for the kind of man and role model he was for me, our sister Marilyn, my Cathy, his family, and countless others. I am also very thankful for the thirty-three years from my conversion until Bubba departed this life that he was a Christian mentor for me in my practice. Early on he suggested I begin praying with my patients prior to their operations. Having watched him pray and spiritually minister to his patients, I saw in them a certain peace and comfort other patients didn't seem to have. In the beginning, there were so many negative thoughts which were not of God. I suspected my patients might think I did not have confidence in my own surgical skills, so I was having to resort to prayer. I was concerned that I would alarm my patients to fear since, by praying, I might signal to them that I was thinking they were going to die. I also worried that if I stumbled and stammered in my prayer, they would think this was the way I operated—stumbling and fumbling. These were all foolish fears and unfounded.

My initial efforts in prayer with patients were certainly awkward, but I persisted with every hospitalized surgical patient. Within a few months, I was more at ease. I don't know if other doctors in El Dorado apart from Bubba and me were praying with patients, but I believe some were. There were definitely some committed Christian doctors in town. At the time I didn't want to ask any of them about praying with patients for fear of embarrassing them if they weren't, or not wanting to seem proud and puffed up since I was. I am certain of the impact prayer had on me spiritually and the countless opportunities for ministry with my patients which opened. I became convinced every patient encounter was a divine appointment, and the more faithful I was in seeking the eternal perspective of that encounter, the more likely I was to discover it.

I never tried to force my faith perspective on any patients, and always asked their permission for me to pray. In the twenty-nine years of surgical practice in El Dorado, I can recall only two patients who refused my offer to pray for them. One was a woman scheduled for a relatively minor operation. On the evening prior to the procedure, her husband was in the room. After I answered their few questions regarding the operation, I asked if I could pray for her safety and healing. Her husband graciously thanked me but said, "We are Witnesses and we will take care of our prayers." Following a brief exchange on the core beliefs of Jehovah's Witnesses, I understood that they believed the prayers of evangelical Christians were ineffective and unnecessary. He handed me a copy of their "Green Book," which I accepted from him, but I never read it. In fact, I placed it in the trash on my way out of the hospital. She healed nicely from the procedure, and I believe my ongoing relationship with her and her husband was cordial and respectful.

The other person who refused my prayer was a locally-well-known-pastor's wife who had suffered the death of her unborn child at the fourth-to-fifth month of her pregnancy. I was visiting her in the hospital to offer my condolences, and, at the end of a brief visit, asked if I might pray for her and her husband. She said, "I would rather you would not pray." I was surprised at her answer and looked toward her husband who was standing at the foot of her bed. He nodded for me to go ahead because he wanted me to pray. I don't remember what I prayed but briefly asked God to bring healing and comfort to their broken hearts. As I left her room, I understood she was dealing with great hurt and sorrowful disappointment, and, at this particular time, was angry with God. In the months ahead her heart was healed, and her faith in her sovereign Lord was restored.

Through the years of my practice in the same town with Bubba, we were able to encourage and challenge one another in the application of faith and witness with our patients. I loved hearing him tell one account after another of God's hand at work in the lives of his patients, and it challenged me to remain faithful not only in prayer but in witness. Those conversations I recall are cherished memories of an older brother who for me was a hero of the faith. I was challenged by his example, and I purposed to encourage younger doctors I encountered who I knew were believers in Jesus Christ. "As ye have therefore received Christ Jesus the Lord, so walk ye in Him" (Col 2:6).

150. "I NEVER WANT FIRE ON ME AGAIN"

Understanding the Eternal Significance of Fire

I was on ER surgical call the weekend Fred was admitted to the hospital for second-and-third-degree burns to about 40 percent of his body. Although the burns were severe, we were confident in our ability to treat him in our hospital and not have to transfer him to a larger hospital with a special burn unit. His major problems were fluid loss and pain relief, and we could handle those very well in our regional hospital.

Fred's life over the previous six months was a continuing series of reversals and poor choices. Although he was thirty-five, he had not married and had chosen to live out of wedlock with a number of different women over the past ten years. Understanding his current lifestyle was not conducive to a long-term relationship, he had chosen the friendship of several like-minded men, and confined his heterosexual relationships to multiple, one-night stands. Fred was not very good husband-material to say the least. The friends whose company he enjoyed all loved drinking alcohol to excess and partying until early morning hours, and this was the source of many of Fred's problems. If he made it to work at all, he was usually sleepy and shaky, and he was fired from at least three good jobs over the previous six months because of his unreliability. With his savings depleted he was able to afford only the bare necessities, but this didn't prevent him from purchasing all the alcohol and cigarettes he wanted. He had a dilapidated car but seldom drove because he couldn't afford the gasoline.

On the fateful Saturday afternoon of the accident, Fred and two of his buddies were in the oilfield at a producing well-site "just drinking and having fun." They were also stealing casing-head gasoline from the oil company, so that they could each fill their car tanks, as well as four five-gallon cans they had brought along. In the course of their fun, Fred was accidentally sprayed with the gasoline and soaked from the waist up. One of his buddies jokingly said, "I think I'll just set you on fire," and pulled out his Zippo lighter. With the lighter in his hand his thumb instinctively pushed the wheel, and a spark accidentally ignited the gasoline. With Fred running and screaming it took longer than necessary to extinguish the flames, and he was severely burned.

Following hospital admission, he was given the necessary burn treatment, which included heavy sedation with IV morphine. So, for about forty-eight hours, he was incoherent in his thoughts and speech. When I believed he could understand what I was about to say, I pulled my chair up to his bed and asked his permission to ask him a few questions. "Fred, you know you could have been burned to death out there in the oil field two days ago," I said. He replied, "I know that is true," without even hesitating. "Where do you think you would be right now if you had died out there?" Without the slightest hesitation, he said, "In hell!" "Is that where you would want to be?" I continued. "The Bible describes hell as a lake of fire, and the fire is never quenched." Without waiting for the sentence to be complete, Fred said, "I never want fire on me again!"

I said that if he would allow me the privilege, I would show him from the Bible how he could receive Christ's free gift of eternal life, and he would never have to fear being cast into the lake of fire. After showing him several passages from the Bible regarding personal salvation and assurances of those promises, Fred quietly and humbly bowed his head, confessed his sins to the Lord, and asked Him to save him. I believe Fred's eternal future in heaven was secured that morning in the hospital room, which for him was transformed into a delivery room! Several months later when Fred's body had healed from the burns, he was baptized in a local church as a new believer in Christ. To the best of my knowledge, he remains a faithful follower, and started making changes in his life and lifestyle.

Some might say I took advantage of a helpless patient, and he couldn't refuse to do what I said because he was afraid that he might die. My response is that he certainly was in danger of death, but his greatest danger was not his physical death but his spiritual death. By his own belief and admission, he was headed for an eternity in hell. Second, I didn't take advantage of a helpless patient. I believe God allowed the accident to happen in order to show Fred the reality of his fragile mortality and his ultimate future. I was simply the agent to tell him the good news that Jesus saves, and to show him from the Bible how to receive his free gift of salvation. When one is saved by God's grace, he will never have to worry about the fire which Fred feared! Have you considered your future in the same way Fred did that morning? My prayer is that you will, and that you will make the same wise decision he made. Your future depends on it.

151. THE VALUE OF A SOUL

The Value of a Man Was Learned at a Late-Night ER Visit

Psalm 142:4 came alive to me very early one morning in the emergency room at Warner Brown Hospital. I was the surgeon on call to the ER this particular night and was soundly sleeping until the telephone rang at our home at 3:00 a.m. These were the days before ER physicians were hired to stay on-site and treat most every emergency including lacerations. My responsibilities as the surgeon on-call were to treat every surgical emergency from simple lacerations to major traumatic wounds.

The ER nurse informed me she had just admitted a patient who had been drinking alcohol in a local bar, had gotten into an argument, and sustained multiple facial lacerations which needed repair. I knew this was going to take about two hours, so my sleep for the night was essentially over. While driving to the hospital, I had a major struggle in my heart with a wicked attitude toward this person whom I did not know. My thinking was something like this: "Why in the world would a person be drinking whiskey in a bar at this hour and then have the ignorance to get into a fight? He doesn't have the slightest concern for the doctor who has to come and sew him. He couldn't care less that the one to sew him up has major surgical cases scheduled at 7:00 a.m. and needs his rest!" By the time I got to the ER, I had worked myself into a state of anger toward this man whom I had never met.

I half-heartedly introduced myself to Tony, a sixty-year-old man, unshaven with a three-day-old beard. He reeked of whiskey or cheap wine and was barely coherent in speech. I discovered he was unemployed and had no insurance to cover the large hospital charges he would incur, and he was certainly unable to pay my much smaller fee for this service. So here I was in the early morning hours, stuck in the emergency room, with no prospect of further rest and no possibility of any financial reimbursement. The more I thought about it, the less I liked Tony and the more resentful I was of him and people like him. I would describe my attitude as civil but certainly not kind or compassionate. I sutured his multiple lacerations as quickly as I could, without taking much time with the cosmetics and engaging him in as little conversation as possible. If Tony had gauged my Christian witness to him on a scale of one to ten, I am certain I would have received a one. In his present state, however, he wasn't able to gauge much of anything.

When I finished and Tony was bandaged and ready to be released, I went into the small adjacent staff room where coffee was available in a quiet place where I could write on the medical record. A good friend and medical colleague was there also. He had been treating a young patient with a severe nose bleed and had finally gotten the bleeding stopped. He asked me why I was there, to which I responded as I was sipping the hot coffee, "I've been sewing up a character named Tony who is so drunk he can hardly speak. I don't know why we have to keep treating such sorry excuses of humanity like him, and especially in the middle of the night!" I seemed to have felt better by getting all of that out. My friend listened quietly to my tirade and then softly said, "Isn't it a wonderful thing our Savior died for characters like

Tony just like he died for you and me." I suddenly didn't feel so well and was ashamed my flesh had so ruled my thoughts, my words, and my actions. I failed to see just how much value the Lord Jesus had placed on Tony, and what little value I had placed on him.

Psalm 142:4 is a cry from David at a time he was hiding in a cave and could not tell whether anyone cared for his safety or his soul. The world is full of desperate people who have lost hope that there is anyone who has the slightest concern for them whether they live or die. My experience with Tony in the emergency room that night combined with the gentle rebuke from my Christian colleague changed my heart. I saw my role as a Christian physician more clearly. God called me to serve others with gladness, to consider every appointment as divine, and to value everyone's soul as much as he does. Thank you, Tony, for allowing me the privilege to serve you. God loves you, and so do I.

152. SHARING JESUS WITH RABBI NORMAN

The Rabbi Becomes a Captive Audience

Rabbi Norman M. Goldburg

The Arkansas Razorbacks have always been my favorite college football team, and especially after Bubba received a full scholarship to play tackle for them in 1945. While attending college in Fayetteville in the late 1950s and medical school in Little Rock in the early 1960s, I was able to see the

Razorbacks play numerous times. The team had few winning seasons until Frank Broyles coached them to much success in the 1960s and into the 1970s. Lou Holtz took over as head coach in 1977 when Coach Broyles retired after coaching the Razorbacks for twenty years.

In his first year at Arkansas, Coach Holtz led the team to a 10–1 season, losing only to the Texas Longhorns. The prize was a trip to the Orange Bowl to play the University of Oklahoma Sooners. Cathy and I decided to travel to Fort Lauderdale to spend Christmas there with her parents, and John Aaron and I were excited at the prospect of attending the Orange Bowl with George, Cathy's brother.

Making plane reservations for Fort Lauderdale relatively late during the Christmas season was difficult, and we were fortunate to get five seats on a Delta jet out of West Monroe, Louisiana. On the flight to Atlanta, our seats were together, but on the connecting flight to Fort Lauderdale, we were not so fortunate. Four of the seats were together, but the other seat was four or five rows away. This was to be my seat, and I didn't much like being separated from them.

After making sure everyone was seated properly and knowing exactly where they were located on the plane, I found my assigned seat easily. It was between two adult men. As I began sitting, I asked the balding, elderly gentleman on the aisle, "Is this seat taken?" He quickly responded with a smile, "Yes, we were saving it for you!" I knew he would be a friendly travel companion so, as I buckled in, I said, "I'm John," to which he responded, "Good morning, I'm Norman."

While the plane was taxiing to the runway, Norman began asking where I was from, what my occupation was, and why was I going to Fort Lauderdale. He told me he was the rabbi of the only Jewish synagogue in Augusta, Georgia and had lived there for many years. He was on his way to work as chaplain on a cruise ship out of Fort Lauderdale, one of several times he had made such a cruise. He obviously enjoyed meeting people and establishing relationships.

I had never met a rabbi, much less anyone who was so friendly and open to conversation. My heart rate began to speed as I contemplated sharing Christ with him, and I wondered how I might direct the conversation toward faith. I had been reading recently about the Jewish Feast Days, so I thought this would be a good starting point. He began answering specific questions, and I was learning more practical information about Judaism than ever before. Then I asked him the most important question, "Rabbi, what do you think about Jesus of Nazareth?"

I can still hear his answer, "Doctor, Jesus of Nazareth was the greatest prophet who ever lived." I said, "But Rabbi, the one you say was the greatest prophet told many people he was the Messiah, the fulfillment of all the prophesies of the Old Testament." Rabbi Norman's response was just as quick, "Jesus never claimed to be the Messiah." I told him it was recorded by all the Gospel writers that he did indeed claim to be the Promised One. I quoted several specific passages from the Gospel of John, particularly John 8:58 in which Jesus told the Pharisees he was the great "I Am."

I said, "If Jesus knew he wasn't Messiah and claimed to be, he was the world's greatest liar. If he claimed to be God and wasn't and didn't know he wasn't, he would be the world's greatest lunatic. The only conclusion one can draw about the man Jesus is he is either a liar, a lunatic, or, indeed, Lord!"

I thought I had the Rabbi trapped into believing and confessing Jesus was the Messiah and he would confess him now as his own Savior. The Rabbi smiled and said, "Doctor, if we lived in the same town, we would be best friends. I know what you have tried to do, and I am not offended. The error in your logic is this: Jesus's disciples wanted him to be Messiah so badly, they claimed he was Messiah, but Jesus himself never claimed it." I stated I believed every word in the New Testament as well as the Old Testament, and I was staking my future on that belief. His final comment regarding the matter was, "We shall see."

Within a week or two after we returned home, I received a copy of the rabbi's book, *Patrick J. McGillicuddy and The Rabbi,* which is a tongue-in-cheek account of the life of a rabbi. I sent him a copy of Josh McDowell's book, *Evidence That Demands a Verdict.* I never heard again from the rabbi, so I don't know if he embraced Jesus of Nazareth as the Messiah whom he was seeking.

PS: The Razorback defeated the Oklahoma Sooners 31–6 in what the Sooners considered an upset!

153. LIGHTING THE ORANGE BOWL STADIUM

Jesus Is the Light of the World

In 1977, a number of exciting things happened in my life, in Cathy's life, and in the lives of our children. The most life-changing event happened for Cathy and me in August in Dallas when we were saved and born into the Kingdom of God. I have recounted the story of our conversion in "A Shopping Trip to Dallas." Everything in us was transformed when Christ entered our lives (2 Cor. 5:17).

Another exciting thing happened the same year when the Arkansas Razorback football team coached by Lou Holtz was invited to play in the

Orange Bowl against the Oklahoma Sooners. Because the Orange Bowl is played in Miami, it was a great opportunity for us to visit Cathy's family for the Christmas season in Fort Lauderdale. The game was to be played on January 2. I called Cathy's brother, George, asking him to try to get us tickets to the game because he had good connections through his college. He was the dean of students at Broward Community College in Fort Lauderdale and knew the right people to get good seats. He was able to purchase a ticket for son, John Aaron, for himself, and for me.

Our flight to Fort Lauderdale was memorable, and I have written about my encounter with Rabbi Norman on the flight from Atlanta to Fort Lauderdale ("Sharing Jesus With Rabbi Norman"). As a result of our meeting, he sent me a signed copy of his book, *Patrick J. Magillicuddy and The Rabbi*.

The Orange Bowl is one of the premier bowl games every year, and this was the first time the Razorbacks had ever been invited to play in it. No one in the sports world apart from ardent Arkansas fans gave the Hogs even the slightest chance against the mighty Sooners from Oklahoma. They were ranked number two in the nation in all the polls with the undefeated Texas Longhorns ranked number one.

George, John, and I were excited (especially me) as we drove the thirty-plus miles from Cathy's parents' home in Fort Lauderdale to the stadium in Miami. The game was played at night, so the closer we got to our destination, the better we could see the bright lights of the stadium in the clear, crisp evening. We also saw many cars carrying OU fans with their signs and streamers proclaiming their Sooners as national champions. Notre Dame had defeated the Texas Longhorns in the Cotton Bowl earlier in the day, so all Oklahoma had to do was defeat the lowly Razorbacks to claim their national prize. As we walked into the stadium with our red shirts and hats, several OU fans told us we had wasted our time driving such a distance to witness an ugly slaughter!

At the gate each of us was handed a tiny flashlight in the form of a candle and were told to leave the light off until the halftime show, at which time we would be instructed what to do with it. Disney Productions was in charge of the half-time show, and it had been promoted as a typical Disney extravaganza. I noticed one fan after another turning their candle on with many of the children leaving theirs on as they took their seats. Although our seats were good with an excellent view of the field, we were seated high in the lower deck. There were many more OU fans present than Arkansas fans, and seated directly in front of us was a husband, his wife, and two children with OU shirts, hats, and pom poms. They were very animated and vocal prior to kick-off, so we remained pretty subdued.

George had given John a battery-powered fog horn, which he normally used on his boat. He told John to use it sparingly because it was very loud. (Wrong thing to tell a 10-year-old!) The Razorbacks jumped to an early lead in the game, and our nearby OU fans became more subdued. As the margin of our lead increased our cheering with the fog-horn emphasis also increased. The folks in front of us particularly cringed when John blew the horn, which he did every time our team made a first down.

Something happened at halftime which I have never forgotten. When the Disney people took charge of the program, we were all reminded to turn off our candles if we hadn't already done so. We were told that at the appropriate time we would be instructed to turn on the light. The announcer then said very loudly, "Let's begin the show," and all the stadium lights were turned off.

I was struck by the extreme darkness which enveloped the stadium. As I looked around, I noted I would have had difficulty leaving my seat and walking down the long flight of stairs if we were to have an emergency requiring an immediate exit. It was impossible to see much beyond one or two rows ahead in the darkness. Then something happened which impressed me greatly. Across the stadium in about row twenty-five, one person turned on their light long before the announcer instructed us to do so. It was a young man I estimated to be a teenager. I could almost see his face clearly even though moments before I could not see anything beyond eight to ten feet.

Later, I thought of the spiritual significance of one single light in a totally dark stadium of sixty thousand people. In Matthew's gospel, Jesus commanded us when he said, "You are the light of the world. Let your light shine before men that they may see your good works and glorify your Father who is in heaven."

I have wondered what my meager light could possibly accomplish in a very dark and sinful world. Now I am reminded of the halftime show at the Orange Bowl in 1978, and the teen-aged boy who failed to follow instructions. He taught me that one tiny and seemingly-insignificant light can illuminate a dark place when it is empowered by the Father of Lights! (Matt 5:14–16).

PS: For those who don't remember, the Razorbacks trounced the Sooners 31–6 that night at the Orange Bowl. After the game we couldn't find any of those Oklahoma fans who questioned our intelligence for even attending.

154. SEEING THE UNSEEN

God Pulls Back the Curtain to Heaven

As a physician and surgeon for many years, I was trained in the art and skill of observation. From the time I entered the third year of medical school and left the classrooms to enter the patients' rooms, I was taught how to look at a patient from the top of his head to the soles of his feet. I was taught to look for tell-tale signs of impending or actual health problems in order to begin prescribing the needed remedies. It is a reflex pattern of observation which I learned early to use and since have painfully discovered by experience this skill is only appropriate in medical settings. The Bible speaks about things which are seen and things which are not seen (2 Cor. 4:17–18). The things we see are temporary while the things we cannot see are eternal. We are challenged to look for the latter things rather than the former.

My brother Berry Lee was a family physician who practiced for fifty years in our hometown of El Dorado, Arkansas. I began my surgical practice there fourteen years following his start and was very grateful to have his expertise and encouragement, particularly in the early years of my practice. He referred all of his patients who needed operations to me, and that was an added incentive and blessing to live and work in the same town with him.

George was a ninety-three-year-old gentleman who had been one of Berry Lee's patients for many years and had been in relatively good health until six months prior to our introduction. He had been having vague stomach pains, particularly after meals with foods having a high-fat content such as pork chops, barbecued meats, and turnip greens, all of which he loved. Following a severe bout of pain associated with fever he was admitted to our hospital ICU in a very serious condition. I saw him in consultation, and the diagnosis of acute gall bladder infection with abscess was made. In spite of his age, I recommended surgical removal rather than medical treatment because his condition was worsening despite aggressive medical treatment with antibiotics. My brother was reluctant to allow him to undergo such a dangerous procedure considering his age and weakened state, but he agreed that if the operation was not done quickly, George was not going to live.

I went to George's bedside to give him our decision and to get his permission to proceed. I explained all the facts we understood and tried to help him understand the risks and consequences both with and without an operation. He agreed to accept our recommendation, and said he knew he might die either way. I said to him, "George, I am going to do everything in my power to get you through this, but I need to know if you are certain you will go to heaven if you don't make it." "O, yes suh," George said in his deep southern accent, "I have loved Jesus mos' of my life, and I'm a lookin' forward to seein' Him." I prayed with George and asked for deliverance for him from this disease, and then thanked God George was certain of his eternal future.

The operation was very difficult, and the findings confirmed the diagnosis of gall bladder abscess along with perforation and a rapidly spreading intra-abdominal infection. Post-operatively George's condition worsened, and he became comatose never awakening from the effects of the anesthetic. He lingered near death for the next thirty hours while his family and his physicians prepared for the inevitable. I went to see him shortly after lunch the following day, and, while reading his chart at the nurse's station, his assigned nurse said to me with alarm, "Look, he is trying to get out of bed!" For the first time since the operation, he had his eyes open and had lifted his head and shoulders slightly from the bed while extending his arms toward the opposite wall. His palms were turned upward as if he were welcoming someone into the room. I told the nurse, "Don't disturb him, he is seeing something or someone we can't see, and he is not going to fall out of bed." We watched him for at least a minute, and then he closed his eyes and lay back on the bed with a look of total peace on his face. Within the hour George's spirit left his body, and we pronounced him dead.

What or whom did George see that afternoon? I don't know for sure, but I told the nurse I believed God had pulled back the curtain for George, and the Lord Jesus Christ himself had entered his ICU room. I believe he came to welcome and to take home one of his children from his long and faithful service for him. I also believe God allowed the nurse and me to witness what it will be like for us on the day when our earthly service is completed. Right now, most of us can only see the temporary things with our physical eyes while the eternal things are only imagined. As believers in Christ as Savior, we do have spiritual eyes and are commanded to look upon eternal things with them. I cannot state exactly how to do it, but the Spirit of God always empowers us to do what he commands.

I learned a lesson that day from George. In spite of the seemingly-painful process of death, it is not to be dreaded by any believer in Christ Jesus. When the time comes, my Savior will come for me to take me home, and he will no longer be imagined. My eyes will see him for the first time, and his beauty, his glory, and his majesty will be so great that everything else will be insignificant. He has promised to do this for me and for everyone who loves and trusts him and believes on him as their Savior.

As Helen Howarth Lemmel put it in the form of a hymn, "Turn your eyes upon Jesus, look full in His wonderful face. And the things of earth will grow strangely dim. In the light of His glory and grace."

155. GOD'S ARROW PIERCES THE HEART

A Near-Death Experience Leads to New Life

I spent many hours of my surgical career treating patients who were admitted through the emergency room, and I treated them for a multitude of acute and serious problems. It has been more than twenty years since I retired from my surgical practice, but I still experience some anxiety when a hear an ambulance siren and reflexively think that I might soon be getting a call to the ER. Some of my angst in those days was thinking that I would have to provide emergency care to a family member or a close friend, which occasionally happened. That is the reality of practicing medicine in a small community.

I received a call from the ER early in a mid-week evening when emergency calls are usually fewer in number. The nurse informed me that I needed to come to the ER to see a man who was stabbed in the neck. Frequently a stab injury to the neck requires an emergency operation to determine if a vital organ is injured, but I was hoping this wound was superficial, and the patient could be observed for a few hours and sent home. The nurse simply told me the wound "was pretty deep and there is a lot of blood," so I got into my vehicle and drove quickly. It was a five-minute drive to the hospital, but when I walked into the trauma room I discovered the injury was very severe.

Four emergency personnel were attending the injured man, starting IV's, monitoring vital signs, and obtaining essential information about the accident, while one person was doing nothing but holding tight pressure on the man's neck using four, large, blood-soaked towels. There was a lot of blood on the floor, so I told them, "Type and cross match four units of blood as quickly as possible! What happened to him?" "He was stabbed in the neck by his ex-wife's boy-friend following a heated argument," stated one of the nurses. "Let me see the extent of the injury," I said as I began to slowly remove the bloody towels. As I very carefully began lifting the final towel, I could see blood beginning to escape very slowly from the wound. Upon complete removal of the towel, there was a sudden and cataclysmic gush of blood which seemed to reach a height of two to three feet, and I quickly replaced the final towel and held the life-saving pressure myself.

"We're taking him immediately to the OR without any more tests!" I commanded. I was told the OR crew was enroute, so we started the move to the OR while I continued holding the critical pressure. I asked the patient how he was doing and he said, "I'm scared to death." "We've got it all under control Jim, and you are going to be alright," I tried to reassure him.

Jim was a thirty-year-old man with a husky physique and a bull-like neck, which made our work a lot harder. I was thankful he was alert and able to communicate, because his injury was obviously to the left carotid artery, and he was not getting any blood flow to the left side of his brain from that artery, which I had occluded.

Once we had him asleep under anesthesia and could get two occluding clamps on the proximal and distal ends of the severed artery, we could proceed at a more relaxed pace. I discovered he had been stabbed with a fixed-blade, broad-head arrow, well known to local deer hunters. We discovered that the external wound was quite scary once we had time to fully inspect the injury. We repaired the artery and re-established blood flow to his brain within thirty minutes. We waited to see if he had any significant brain damage, and fortunately, within an hour or two after awakening from the anesthetic, he was talking coherently and his cognition was excellent.

The following morning as I made my rounds, I found Jim willing to discuss the details leading up to the conflict. We both agreed it was a miracle of God we were able to have a conversation that morning. Then I asked him a key question: "Jim, if you had bled to death yesterday in that yard, where would you be this morning?" "I guess I would be in hell, considering the life I have been living," he slowly confessed. "Jim, would you like to ask God to save you from hell and make you a new man?" I asked. "Yes sir, I sure would," he quickly replied. I opened my pocket Bible, and showed him the scriptures which explained biblical salvation, and how one asks for and receives the free gift of salvation from Christ. Jim received the gift from his Savior that morning, and I believe there was a great celebration in heaven. I know there was a celebration with tears of joy in his hospital room that morning.

Before I left his room, I gave Jim my final thoughts on what had happened: "Jim, yesterday that man pierced your neck with an arrow and nearly ended your life, but this morning God pierced your heart with his forgiveness, and now you have life forever. That is some kind of great deal, isn't it?" Jim quietly said, "I know you are right!"

Three weeks later when his wound was healed and water-tight, he followed with baptism in a local church. I do not know where Jim is today, but I am confident wherever he lives, he has told this life-saving and life-giving story many times to his friends. I feel confident his bow-hunting buddies related to the deadly potential of such an arrow. Perhaps some of them have even had their lives changed by his story.

156. THE MEN'S THEATER BIBLE CLASS

A Unique Assembly

Men's Theater Bible Class officers, 1981

The most unique Sunday School class I have ever been a member of was the Men's Theater Bible Class at First Baptist Church in El Dorado. The path God took me from being a religious agnostic to becoming a co-teacher of this prestigious class was unusual to say the least and, at best, not without major struggles.

Cathy and I moved to El Dorado in 1971 to begin raising our family and for me to begin my surgical practice. The decision to return to my home was difficult for me because I had once made the statement I would "never live in such a small town." It was difficult for Cathy, because she was from Fort Lauderdale, Florida, and the idea of living in a small Southern town was a huge cultural shift. Having family there and having a ready surgical referral source in my brother (Bubba) overcame most but not all of our objections.

Shortly after our move, we joined the First Baptist Church without visiting any other church. Mom and Bubba and his family were longtime members, and it only made sense to have our membership where our family belonged. At this point in our lives, Cathy and I were not even faithful church attenders. We seldom attended church during the four years we lived in New Orleans, and for the two years we were in the US Air Force in Valdosta, Georgia, our only attendance was in a Methodist church. We quickly made new friends at First Baptist, and because we wanted our children to have good spiritual training, we became regular in attendance. We were members of a young adult couples class which was taught very well by Robert Wike, a friend who was in charge of the physical therapy department at Union Medical Center (now Medical Center of South Arkansas).

In 1975, Robert told the church nominating committee he would only continue teaching the couples class "if John Moore will agree to co-teach the class with me." I was reluctant to accept the appointment because I had no prior experience in teaching and the class was quite large, with some individuals who had more Bible knowledge than I. But I said yes. There was a long learning-curve for me, but I remained faithful in study and preparation, and my teaching skills slowly improved according to Cathy who was my greatest encourager.

As a result of a number of factors, especially the faithful witness of Bubba and others, Cathy and I attended the Bill Gothard seminar in Dallas in August, 1977, and we had a major spiritual change in our lives. We finally understood that being born again meant having a personal relationship with the Lord Jesus Christ through repentance and by faith receiving his salvation by grace.

We received the free gift from him on August 6, 1977, and everything about us changed. Among other things, the scriptures had a more personal significance, and I had a fresh and greater desire to learn his Word and become a more effective teacher. We continued in the couples class until 1980, when I accepted a new appointment and the challenge to co-teach the Men's Theater Bible Class.

This class had a long and significant history in the life of First Baptist Church. Started in the 1920s when El Dorado had a meteoric increase in population due to the discovery of oil, the class reached out to men of all denominations. They met in the Rialto Theater, which had the largest seating capacity of any downtown building apart from the church itself. At its peak, the weekly attendance exceeded three hundred men and was taught by Judge John Ragsdale, who was an active member and deacon at First Baptist. By the late 1970s, Judge Ragsdale had departed and the class was being taught by Judge Oren Harris. He was a long-time member of the US Congress from the Fourth Congressional District of Arkansas and was then serving as a Federal Judge on the bench at El Dorado. The class had dwindled to a small handful of men, perhaps twenty-five to thirty.

A group of men from the class approached me in 1980 and asked if I would consider assuming the teaching position of the class. I assumed Judge Harris had decided to relinquish his responsibilities as the sole teacher, and he and the class were all in agreement with the change. After consideration and prayer, I told the committee I would accept the position if my friend Bob Watson would agree to co-teach with me. In my surgical practice I was responsible for weekend ER call once each month and wanted to make certain the teaching was covered in case I got called to the emergency room.

On the Sunday morning we agreed to be presented to the class and receive a vote of affirmation, both Bob and I were present, and prior to the class opening, we shook hands with all the members including Judge Harris. When Judge Harris spoke to us, he said, "I understand you two men have been asked to take my place and teach this class next year," to which we responded, "If the class is in agreement." I thought his question was unusual since I thought he knew about the committee's approaching us. We discovered when the class began, Judge Harris was not interested in stepping down as class teacher and was not in agreement with the actions of the apparent self-appointed committee. After the opening prayer the judge stood and said, "I would like a vote of confidence from this class for me to continue as your teacher next year and have all those in favor to stand." Every man present stood while the men who had approached us remained in the back of the class, out of sight of the rest. It was an extremely embarrassing moment for Bob and me, and, when the class was over, we spoke to Judge Harris and explained our dilemma, and why we were even there. He said he understood our situation and made an appointment for us to have lunch the following week to determine if we could reach a mutually agreeable plan. The lunch meeting was set for Wednesday noon.

The Wednesday lunch meeting with Judge Harris was a little tense at first, because Bob Watson and I didn't know what to expect from the man who might have thought the two of us were part of a plot to have him ousted as teacher. Bob and I knew we were totally innocent of any deception. The Judge couldn't have been more gracious and forgiving, and assured us he understood there were "a few men who wanted some younger blood as teachers for the class." During the meeting he said he would appreciate some help with the teaching, and offered to share the responsibility with each of us taking one Sunday each month. This was perfectly acceptable with us, and we shook hands on the new arrangement.

The Rialto Theater at the time was a dreadful place to have a Sunday school class, or any other kind of meeting for that matter. The lighting was poor and it made the atmosphere dark and eerie with its decor and especially the thick red curtains on the stage. Fifty years earlier, the theater was a picture of elegance, but time and deterioration had taken a huge toll. When one walked down the aisle, there was a film of sticky substance, probably spilled soda which lightly adhered to the sole of your shoes and caused a squeaking sound when walking. If you were positioned behind the speaker's stand, the lighting was so dim you couldn't see the audience very well. This was an advantage for some of the men who used the comfortable theater chairs and the dim lights for a little nap during the lesson!

It wasn't long before a group of us began a campaign to move the class to a location more conducive to fellowship in the light, with less of dark, nightclub atmosphere. The preference of a few of us was to move the class to the church since most of the members of the class were also members of the church. In its long history, the class had never met at the church, and the general attitude was one of independence from the authority of the pastor and church staff.

Judge Harris was the key to making such a radical change in location, and when he became convinced of the need for a move, a unanimous decision was reached. The new location for the class was to be the main courtroom in the Union County Court House. The class name was also changed to the Men's Bible Class. I would have preferred having the name indicate that the class was a part of First Baptist Church, but that was too much change for some of the long-time members.

It was indeed strange to have a Bible class in a courtroom, but for me the Word was being faithfully taught, and the location was secondary. I was happy we were no longer meeting in the dreadfully dark atmosphere of the Rialto Theater. The photograph above was taken of the officers of the class in 1981. I am seated on the front row with Dr. Don Harbuck, the pastor of First Baptist, on my right and Judge Oren Harris on my left. I don't remember why Bob Watson was not in the picture, but he must have had other responsibilities for this day. Bob was the principal of El Dorado High School at the time. It was a big step forward in class thinking to allow Dr. Harbuck to be in the photo since independence from the church had always been a hallmark of the class.

An interesting and potentially hazardous thing happened one Sunday morning while I was at the hospital and not present. This incident caused the men of the class to begin thinking a courtroom might not be an ideal place for a Sunday school class. The county jail was on the top floor of the building, and, through some strange circumstances, there was a breakout of several prisoners from the jail. During the fellowship time prior to the class opening, one of the escapees came into the room and for a short time held the class hostage while brandishing a knife or some type of weapon. He apparently realized a hostage situation with old men was futile, and he quickly fled with no harm done to anyone. Within a few hours, the escapees were caught and arrested. It made for an interesting morning of Bible study, and I was sorry I missed the action. I believe this planted the seed for yet another move for the class.

Within this time frame, the church had completed and moved into a beautiful family life center, and the fellowship hall was a perfect location for our class. Dr. Harbuck was totally in favor of the move but didn't want to appear he was requiring such an action, so he took a low profile in the discussions. The majority of men in the class were in favor, but there were some who just weren't going to move into the church building regardless of the vote. There were perhaps ten or twelve who voted to stay in the court-house and said they would obtain their own teacher since the judge, Bob, and I voted to move. It was an excellent decision, and now for the first time in sixty years, the Men's Bible Class was truly a part of the church and was submissive to church leadership.

Following the move, Bob Merkle, a retired businessman and long-time resident of El Dorado agreed to teach along with the other three teachers, so each one of us was responsible for one Sunday per month. A significant innovation was begun which revolutionized the outreach of the class. We started a conference call ministry by which the telephone company patched into our audio system and people could join the class each Sunday on an 800-number conference call. Seventy-five spaces were available for one price.

A significant member of our conference-call class was my Uncle Harry Gosling from St. Louis, Missouri. I had led him to faith in the Lord Jesus while he was on vacation in El Dorado and offered him this option for a Sunday school class. I was glad to keep him supplied with Sunday school material, so he could follow along with the teaching. He continued calling in each Sunday for the next six months before his final sickness and death from Lou Gehrig's Disease.

Within the next year, we switched from a conference-call class to a ra-dio Bible class. A local FM station offered to broadcast the class at a charge which was lower than we were paying the phone company. The availability and quality of the transmission was so much better. To this day, this unique class is still broadcast throughout Union County each Sunday for an hour. The total outreach and effect of the ministry of this class is not known, but I am confident the Lord is blessing their efforts to reach others with the gospel. I have nothing but great memories and respect for the men I was privileged to know and serve alongside in that Men's Bible Class and am grateful to the Lord He opened this door of ministry.

157. A DIVINE APPOINTMENT

Lifelong Friendships Never Occur by Chance

Brother Bill Stafford

Years ago at a weekly Bible study I was attending one of my good friends, Dr. Jim Weedman handed me an audio tape and said he thought I would enjoy it. It was a monthly tape sent to him by an evangelist of whom I had never heard—Bill Stafford from Chattanooga, Tennessee. The message delivered in Brother Bill's unique preaching style was loud, compelling, and convicting. I had never heard a preacher say "Amen" more times in one message. He interlaced biblical truths with such force and humor that I replayed the tape three or four times to make sure I hadn't missed anything. I asked Jim to allow me to listen to the tapes each month after he was finished with them, and I looked forward with great anticipation to receiving each one. I listened to each tape multiple times and practically had them memorized by the time I returned them.

Months later on one of the tapes, Brother Bill said that he would be preaching a revival meeting in a local Baptist church in El Dorado within the next six weeks, and I was very excited to finally hear him in person. I also anticipated joining his monthly tape club, so I wouldn't always have to depend on Jim's giving me his tape each month. I planned to attend the Monday evening service because I had commitments at my own church for both the morning and evening Sunday services.

On the Monday afternoon clinic schedule in my surgical office, a good friend Johnny Beebe had a minor procedure scheduled for 3:00 p.m. As I was prepping the surgical site, I asked him if he was going to hear Brother

Bill preach in the evening since I knew they were good friends. He said, "Yes, I'll be there tonight. In fact, Brother Bill is staying at our home, and he came with me for this appointment!" I said, "Johnny, you mean he is in my waiting room?" "He sure is," he said. "Would you mind waiting a few minutes while I go out to meet him?" Johnny was lying on his stomach with a sterile surgical drape over the operative site on his back and he said, "I'm comfortable, so go ahead and meet him."

I walked to the waiting room and called Brother Bill back to my office suite. Following the usual introductory remarks, I told him how I had heard about him, and how much I had been blessed by his tapes each month. We had a lively conversation which lasted at least twenty minutes, and it seemed as if we had known each other for years. I lost track of time and had completely forgotten Johnny had been lying on my exam table for all this time. At that moment, I was thankful he was a very good friend who would be forgiving for such an extended delay.

As Brother Bill and I walked to the door of the procedure room, I jokingly said to Johnny, "The reason it has taken so long, there has been an anointing, and the gift of healing has been transferred to Brother Bill. He is going to perform your procedure as his first act of service for the Lord!" Johnny said, "No sir; the only one doing this procedure is you, no matter how much anointing he has received!" Fortunately, despite the unusual delay, the procedure went well, and Johnny healed quickly.

A significant reason for the appointment that day was to allow me to meet Brother Bill and begin a life-long friendship. Over the next several years, our relationship grew to the extent that he invited me to become a member of the governing board of the International Congress on Revival, which he headed as president. This worldwide ministry to pastors and their wives afforded my wife Cathy and me the privilege of travelling overseas for fifteen years with Brother Bill, his wife Sue, and the entire ministry team.

We were able to invest ourselves into the lives of hundreds of pastors and their wives and to encourage them to remain faithful to the ministry to which God had called them. The pastors attending those meetings represented at least twenty countries, including those in Western and Eastern Europe, England, Ireland, Scotland, Australia, South Africa, and several of the countries of the former Russian Republic. Our investment into those pastors' lives was multiplied many times over through their ministry to the members of their congregations.

As a result of Johnny Beebe's introduction of Brother Bill to me, Johnny and his wife Martha Sue accompanied Cathy and me twelve years later to an ICR meeting in Newcastle, Ireland. It was a lively Spirit-filled conference, which ministered to seventy-five pastors and their wives, and gave the four of us the opportunity to spend a wonderful two weeks together. In addition to Ireland, we also travelled to London and spent time touring the city and a portion of the English countryside.

Brother Bill had a profound impact on Cathy and me since the first meeting. He has encouraged and challenged us, and even rebuked me a few times when needed. On more than one occasion when there was a crisis situation in our family, Brother Bill was one of the first to respond with counsel, prayers, and tears. Next to my brother, who was my professional and spiritual mentor, Brother Bill has meant as much to me as any other man, and I thank God for him.

I am so glad for those initial audio tapes from my friend Dr. Jim, which stirred my interest in a preacher known then as "Wild Bill." And I was equally thankful for the appointment Johnny Beebe had that afternoon in my clinic. God used those two men to arrange my meeting Brother Bill. Divine appointments are always perfect and never disappoint (Jer 29:11).

158. THE COUNSEL OF TEARS

Tears Can Speak Louder than Words

Throughout the years of my medical practice, I experienced the pain and anguish of many patients and their families when an operative report was not good or when a person with a terminal illness departed this earth. I always had good intentions to bring peace and comfort where there was suffering, but, like so many, I was at a loss for words. I discovered early that the best comfort was in just having loving and caring friends present. A heartfelt handshake or hug says volumes to the anguished and the distraught. The Bible teaches us that we are "to rejoice with those who rejoice, and weep with those who weep." As a surgeon with lots of experience, I trained myself to keep my personal feelings and emotions in check, which strengthened my objectivity in stressful situations. Some of this attitude was also present in my personal life and may have been interpreted as a lack of compassion.

For most of our married life, Cathy and I have had a desire to help strengthen homes and marriages. We had our own struggles early, and as our own marriage was made stronger by the love of Christ, we wanted to help others with similar problems. We have taught young adult Sunday school classes for a long time. This was where we met one particular couple who were a few years younger. We had lots in common besides the Sunday school class. We were strongly committed to our marriages, our children were approximately the same ages, we desired to grow stronger in our spiritual lives, and we wanted our church to grow stronger in its ministries.

He and I bonded quickly and soon became running mates as we began jogging together in the early morning hours before work. We stuck with our daily exercise schedule and continued jogging together for several years. As we huffed and puffed into better health, we shared a number of common things such as sports, church-related issues, spiritual truths we were learning, and even advice to each other concerning common marital struggles. Our conversations were many but were never so deep or heavy that we didn't enjoy our morning jog. The relationship was one like brothers, and I always looked forward to awakening an hour earlier than normal to spend time with him.

Unfortunately, his work responsibilities began requiring him to be out of town more often, and the days he was in town he needed to be at home. Our jogging times together came to a halt, so I continued exercising solo. I began teaching a senior adult men's Sunday school class so I didn't see my friend for weeks if not months at a time.

One morning when I happened to be home with no surgical cases scheduled, we received a phone call from my friend's wife asking if she could come over right away and speak with both Cathy and me. She was tearful over the phone saying their marriage was in a very difficult place, and she needed counsel from both of us. We prepared ourselves with prayer while she was driving over.

She sat at our breakfast room table and poured out her heart to us with tears, telling us their marriage was in great danger of breaking up. There were some issues which seemed insurmountable, and the separation his work required had made the entire situation worse. The more she talked and wept, the more we were convinced the problem was very serious.

As she was trying her best to tell us their problems, I was thinking about our relationship with them as a couple and my close friendship with him over the previous several years. It was as if a brother and sister-in-law were having such a problem, and the longer I thought about my response the less objective I was becoming in my heart. When she then paused and asked the question, "What do you think I should do?" I began to respond with carefully chosen words and as much wisdom as I had for the moment. In the middle of a sentence my emotions spilled out and I began crying. The more I tried to speak, the less able I was to put sentences together. I finally said, "I am so sorry for these tears and my lack of ability to say very much at all." She said quietly, "That's okay, they seem to be helping."

I don't remember any advice I was able to give her, but we did assure her of our love for them. I said we would be praying that God would give her wisdom in moving toward healing. I do remember telling her not to cross any bridges she could not get back over. We prayed for her and told her we would be available for any help we might give.

We learned several lessons with our friend. Always be available for family or friends whenever difficult problems or tragedies occur. Before you counsel, prepare your heart with prayer and with fasting if there is enough time. Be aware it is more important to listen than it is to talk. Avoid using clichés like "time will heal all wounds" or "everything is going to be okay" or even "God never puts on us more than we can bear."

These are biblical truths which are best left unspoken at times of great emotional distress. The most endearing help and comfort from God comes when loving family and friends come with a hug or a handshake, and often the best advice is expressed through tears and not words. This couple I am delighted to report was able to work through their problems to a resolution, and now, forty years later, they are still happily married with grandchildren. It is all to the glory of God!

159. MINISTERING IN THE EL DORADO JAIL

A Vicious Attack Opens a Jail Door

Jail ministries are tough because the ones incarcerated in jails and prisons are tough. Very few prisoners are willing to admit their guilt for the crimes which caused their imprisonment, and many will say or do whatever is necessary to be released immediately. I have not been involved in an ongoing prison ministry except when Cathy and I provided support and encouragement for a young man who was an inmate in our county jail. There was not a designated jail or prison ministry of which I was aware sponsored by a church in El Dorado, Arkansas during the thirty years we lived there. My initial experience of visiting the local county jail for the express purpose of witnessing Christ occurred as a result of an emergency surgical procedure.

As a surgeon with the Surgical Clinic of South Arkansas, my responsibilities included taking weekend ER surgical calls one weekend per month. There were some weekends which were extremely quiet with no emergency surgeries required, but those weekends were rare. In a small town like El Dorado, it was possible to hear the siren of most of the emergency vehicles as they travelled to the hospitals. Whenever I heard a siren while on call, I wondered if a close friend or even a family member was being transported to the ER, and it would create in me a level of anxiety. For at least ten years after I stopped taking emergency room calls, I felt the same anxiety upon hearing a siren.

On one particular weekend late on a Saturday night I received a call from the Warner Brown Hospital emergency room. A forty-year-old woman had been admitted with multiple, severe, knife wounds to the face, neck, and shoulders. They reported she had lost a lot of blood but was conscious and alert. I arose from bed, dressed quickly, and was in the ER in less than ten minutes. The nursing staff had done all the preliminary lab work and had called the OR team to come to the hospital in preparation for an emergency operation.

Without being too graphic, I'll say she sustained major disfiguring lacerations to her face and multiple stab wounds to the neck, right shoulder, and upper abdomen. Her right arm was totally paralyzed. When I asked her how all this happened, she answered, "My husband had been drinking heavily tonight, and when we began arguing about it, he went completely berserk and attacked me with his hunting knife. While he was hurting me, his eyes were fiery red, and he looked just like Satan." In all of my years as a trauma surgeon, I had never seen such extensive knife wounds, and, along with the entire emergency team, I had great compassion and sadness for this innocent woman. We gathered around her and prayed for her before taking her to the OR.

My surgical team had the reputation for the ability to operate quickly and efficiently, but for this particular patient, with the nature and severity of her wounds, it took us in excess of six hours to complete the repairs. Throughout much of our time in the operating room, many comments were made such as, "How could anyone do such a thing?" and "I hope he has to go to jail for a long time." One person even said, "If he looked and acted like Satan, I hope he joins him in hell!" The comments were made by the women present in the OR, and I could understand their indignation on behalf of this poor woman who would be forever scarred and disabled. I remained quiet most of the time, but did say, "Since they have arrested him, I wonder what he is thinking now that he has sobered up?"

I finished all of my hospital responsibilities by 6:30 a.m. and decided to go to the jail before returning home to shower and shave in preparation for church. Usually, one had to have special permission from the sheriff to visit an inmate in the county jail, but I thought the jailer on duty might be sympathetic to my request and not require prior authorization. When I told him I had a report for this inmate on his wife's medical condition, he consented to my unauthorized visit. I was not allowed into the cell, which contained at least five other inmates, but I stood outside the bars speaking as quietly and privately to the man as possible.

He had mostly sobered up from the previous night's bout of excessive alcohol consumption, and, as far as I could tell, he was lucid and very sorrowful. I told him I had spent the night in the operating room repairing the damage he had inflicted on his wife, and her life had been spared. He immediately fell on his knees crying out, "I'm so sorry. I'm so sorry!" I did tell him the injury to her right arm resulted in complete paralysis, and it could be months or even years before she could use her arm again, if ever.

In the midst of his sorrowful weeping, he asked the question, "What can I do to make up for this?" I responded by saying, "There's a lot which needs to be done, but the best starting place is for you to repent of the shameful life you have been living and invite the Lord Jesus into your heart." "I'll do whatever you say I need to do," he cried. "If you are serious and you really want to change and have a new life, you must confess, repent, and ask the Lord Jesus to save you," I told him. I helped him pray a tearful prayer of repentance while still on his knees. When he stood, I could only shake his hands through the bars and tell him I would be praying for him and would continue to medically assist in his wife's healing process.

The following day I contacted the pastor of a sister church in El Dorado whom I knew would follow up on this man and his decision. There is no way I could discern this prisoner's heart motives, but I witnessed and heard his prayer. I also know that our Savior told us in his Word that he came to set the prisoner free, and from the moment this prisoner asked for mercy, he received it in full measure. It is wonderful to know we can never fall so far down that we are out of reach of our Father's hand.

160. PINNED TO HIS WORK

A Tragic Accident Leads to Greater Service

A large and significant portion of the practice life of a general surgeon involves taking emergency room calls and treating patients involved in trauma. I treated injuries from automobile accidents, gunshot and knife wounds, industrial accidents, domestic and workplace violence, and injuries sustained in the home, such as lacerations and puncture wounds. Over the years, I thought I had seen and treated patients with every type of injury until I received a call from the ER one Saturday in mid-afternoon.

The ER nurse said there was a forty-five-year-old man who had sustained a large puncture wound to his left thigh while working on a tractor earlier in the day. "How large is the puncture wound?" I asked. She responded, "It is really big!" Not knowing what I might find I didn't waste any time getting to the ER. I had gotten some other information from her such as his vital signs, whether he was actively bleeding, whether he was conscious and alert, and how much pain he was experiencing.

When I entered the ER, the excellent staff at the South Arkansas Medical Center had an intravenous line well placed, and Robert was receiving fluids and pain medicines while his lab work was being processed. He was conscious but groggy from the sedation when I told him I wanted to inspect the wound. As I lifted the sheet to inspect his left groin area, I saw an eight-inch limb from an oak tree protruding from a puncture wound to his upper, inner left thigh. The limb was approximately two inches in diameter, and I could tell by slightly moving it that it was deeply imbedded. The wound was very close to the femoral artery and vein which are the main blood supply to the leg, and, because there was no active bleeding, I was fairly certain those essential vessels were not injured. "How in the world did this happen?" Here's what he told me:

> I was driving a big tractor this morning clearing land and up-rooting very large trees and stumps. There was another man about a quarter of a mile away on a similar tractor clearing this land along with me, but we were not in contact with each other. I saw an oak sapling ahead which I thought I could run over, and it would break to the ground. What I didn't know was that the sapling bent over, and when it did snap, the lower end sprang back into the cab of my tractor. It penetrated my leg and lifted me off the seat and pinned me to the top of the cab.
>
> For some reason when I was lifted off the seat, the tractor stopped running or the tree in my leg would have torn me in two. Normally, a D2 tractor will keep running until it runs out of gas. I was pinned so high in the cab I couldn't reach anything to help me free myself. I reached in my pocket to get my pocket knife and began cutting the limb. Because of the intense pain, I kept passing out but was able to hold onto the knife. I was screaming for my friend to come help me, but he was too far away to hear me. After at least fifteen minutes, I was able to cut through the limb, and I dropped to the seat of the cab. At about the same time, help arrived because my friend could see the tractor was not moving, and he came to check on me. I'm sure glad he did.

Following the necessary tests and x-rays to determine the extent of internal injury, Robert was taken to the OR for the exploratory operation. Before we prepped the operative site, I firmly grasped the protruding tree and pulled it out. The internal portion was another ten inches, so the total length was about eighteen inches. Given the extent of the injuries, it was miraculous he sustained no major blood vessel injury, which he probably would not have survived. We were able to repair the massive internal damage.

During his prolonged recovery, I discovered Robert was a bi-vocational pastor, and we both agreed he would now have many sermon illustrations as a result of his experiences this day. We also agreed that in God's plan for each of us, we are indestructible until God's purposes are completed. Robert returned to his responsibilities as pastor and continued his teaching ministry. I'm not certain of this, but I believe he gave up his tractor driving job.

161. THE GOOD SAMARITAN MISSION

A Ministry Has Its Origin in an ER Visit

Uncle Paul West seemed to know everyone in El Dorado, and he introduced many of his special friends to me. He and Uncle Ed were brothers of my mom, and both were special, favorite uncles. When Pop and Mom married in 1944, her brothers were serving on active duty in the army, and when they returned home in their uniforms as privates first class at the end of World War II, they were heroes to me. To an impressionable six-year-old, anyone in uniform automatically becomes a revered hero. Just to have the chance to talk with them would have been enough, but they loved to tell me about their experiences while serving overseas and fighting the Germans. Uncle Ed fought in the Battle of the Bulge, and when he told stories of bullets flying, grenades exploding, and mortar shells coming in, I sat with rapt attention.

When they returned home, both men had families to support, and there was not an abundance of job opportunities in El Dorado. Mom and her wealthy sister from St. Louis, Aunt Tooky (Thelma Manne), purchased a small grocery store on Jackson Street to give their brothers steady jobs. Both men were personable and able salesmen, and the Quality Grocery was moderately successful with their work in the meat and produce sections.

Uncle Paul was by far the best in the family at sales, and the other jobs and positions he held in later years were enhanced by his ability to meet people and establish close relationships. He seemed to know people from all walks of life and could usually tell a funny story about everyone he knew. I was always fascinated to hear his stories but was never quite sure they were all true.

After I entered my surgical practice in El Dorado, Uncle Paul was a very good referral source for me. I have been present when he would tell someone with whom he was having a conversation, "When you get ready to have surgery, you need to let John Henry operate on you. I taught him how to cut meat down at the Quality Grocery!" Depending on who heard the story, I would usually smile and say something like, "Uncle Paul is a great surgical teacher, and he never had a patient complain."

One evening when I arrived home for supper after a particularly hard day, the phone rang and it was Uncle Paul. I was pretty sure he had another referral when he said, "I have this good friend named Brother W. O. Miller, a retired Baptist minister, and he needs some help. He is bleeding and had to go to the emergency room. Can you go out there and take care of him?" My initial impression was to let the ER doctor take care of him, but I would have disappointed Uncle Paul and made him look bad when he told Brother Miller he would call me to help him. I'm glad I did without supper this particular night and went to the ER to offer my services. Brother Miller needed an operation which I was able to do for him, and he recovered from a serious malignant condition.

Brother Miller and I became good friends and spent lots of time talking about the Lord Jesus and how he had changed both of our lives. He had a passion for serving people, and he demonstrated it daily through his fifty-plus years in the ministry. His pastorates had been mostly with small congregations who struggled financially. Consequently, Brother Miller and his wife had lived on a meager income and had no significant retirement funds apart from Social Security.

About a year following his recovery from the operation, Brother Miller called and said he had a group of like-minded men who were meeting to discuss the formation and opening of a mission church. The church would be in a very economically depressed area of El Dorado and would minister to the poor and needy. He wanted me to meet with them. The meeting culminated in the establishment of the Good Samaritan Mission, which opened its doors within three months of the initial meeting.

Brother Miller was the pastor, and Uncle Paul was the Administrator. My brother Berry Lee (Bubba) was on the original administrative board along with three other committed Christian men and me. Brother Miller had our motto printed on one of the signs for the Mission, "Wanted, the Unwanted."

The photograph above was taken on the official opening Sunday morning in 1975. Brother Miller is seated on the front row and to his right is his wife with a small child between them. On the end of the front row to Brother Miller's left is our son John Aaron and to his right is Mom in her elegant fur coat, which seemed a little out of place at the mission. To her right is Aunt Helen, Uncle Paul's wife. I am on the back row directly behind Brother Miller. Bubba is to my right, and he was one of the speakers that morning. Uncle Paul is to Bubba's right. Bubba's wife, LaNell, is seated in front of Uncle Paul.

The Mission served God's purposes in this area of town for a number of years. Most of the people in the photograph apart from Bubba, Mom, John Aaron, and me were regular attenders of services at the mission. We were active in our own church and couldn't attend most Sundays. On this particular Sunday, my wife Cathy and our daughters Mark Kay and Ginny were not present because of prior commitments at our church.

Brother Miller invited Bubba and me to preach as often as we were available, and those were some of my earliest experiences at preaching. In looking at my notes from those days, my preaching was pitiful but never lacked for personal enthusiasm. I would study for hours and based on my notes, the messages were deep on historical information, and very shallow on practical spiritual information which would have ministered better to the listeners at the mission. Everyone present endured my messages patiently and many even complimented me on a "fine job." I now understand that the effectiveness of sound biblical preaching is not related to how well the preacher does, but how effective the Word of God penetrates the hearts of the preacher and the hearers.

Brother W. O. Miller completed his earthly service for the Lord at the Good Samaritan Mission, and his work there might have been his greatest. I do know he was faithful to the finish, and I am so thankful my Uncle Paul knew such a spiritual giant who served as an ordinary preacher. I'm equally glad Uncle Paul introduced me to him, because I am a much better man for knowing both of them.

162. MISTAKEN FOR AN EVANGELIST

Being in the Right Place at the Wrong Time

In the mid-1980s, large evangelism conferences across the South were beginning to achieve popularity. It was not uncommon to see advertisements each week in the *Arkansas Baptist*, the Baptist state convention paper, inviting people to attend such conferences in nearby cities such as Little Rock, Shreveport, or Dallas. These meetings would feature some of the best-known preachers in the area and, not infrequently, outstanding, nationally-known preachers.

Cathy and I had become friends with evangelist Bill Stafford from Chattanooga as a result of some circumstances I've covered elsewhere. I was a member of his audio-tape-of-the-month club, and, at the end of each tape, he always gave his preaching schedule for the following two months. I loved his preaching and enjoyed his friendship so much that whenever he was preaching within a few hours of El Dorado, I would try to arrange my schedule to attend an evening meeting. On this particular occasion, he announced he had been invited to preach in a Bible conference in Euless, Texas at the First Baptist Church. The conference was to begin on a Friday night and continue through most of the day on Saturday. I was definitely interested when I heard his announcement.

Shortly thereafter, I read more details concerning the conference in the *Arkansas Baptist* and was able to not only register for the meeting, but get the names of several prospective motels to call for reservations. Two other men expressed interest in the conference, so my good friend and co-Sunday-school-teacher Bob Watson and our pastor Mark Coppenger made plans to attend together. I called Brother Bill to tell him we were coming, and we made arrangements to have breakfast together on Saturday morning.

In addition to Brother Bill's preaching, which would have been enough for me, several other well-known preachers I recall were Charles Stanley, Jerry Falwell, Ron Dunn, Bailey Smith, and Jimmy Draper, the pastor of First Baptist Euless. That was an all-star lineup of preachers, and there were several others whom I don't recall.

Pastor Mark, Bob, and I drove the six-and-a-half hours from El Dorado to Euless and arrived in time to attend the evening meeting. The atmosphere was more exciting than I had anticipated, and the church was packed. Brother Bill was scheduled to preach, preceding Charles Stanley. I don't recall any details of their sermons, but they were outstanding and were punctuated with large numbers of amens and occasional, appropriate applause. There was at least one other speaker the first evening, Ron Dunn.

The following morning the three of us were able to meet Brother Bill for breakfast at a nearby restaurant, and he was accompanied by his son, Bill III, who was a student at Criswell Bible College in Dallas. I had heard about young Bill from his dad but had never met him. His personal testimony of deliverance from a life of drug and alcohol abuse to surrender to the ministry was very inspiring, and I had heard Brother Bill tearfully recount some of the details on several occasions. We were not able spend much time with the Staffords because the conference was to begin at 9:00 a.m., and Brother Bill was scheduled to speak again before the lunch break.

We arrived at the church about twenty minutes before the opening of the Saturday session, and, for a short period, I was separated from Mark and Bob. I wanted to walk around the beautiful church facility, and see if anyone I knew was attending the conference. An older gentleman approached me in a manner which made me suspect I might have met him before. He reached out to shake my hand and said his name and the name of the church he pastored somewhere in West Texas. When he spoke, I knew I had never met him. Then he said, "Brother Bill, your sermon last night was such a blessing to me." He thought I was Bill Stafford! I knew if I corrected his error, it would have embarrassed him greatly, but I didn't want to carry the deception too far. Fortunately, some other men told him they needed to be seated and he needed to join them. As he was leaving, I said to him, "Brother, thanks for your encouragement. I'm glad you were blessed!"

I didn't see Brother Bill again before we had to leave Euless, but I couldn't wait to tell him about the encounter. When I called him at his home in Chattanooga a few days later, I had fun giving him my revised version of the meeting: I told him the pastor was from Muleshoe, Texas, and, following the handshake, I'd said, "Thank you brother. I really preached the socks off Charles Stanley, didn't I?" Bill said, "Dr. John, you didn't tell him that, did you?" I said I surely did, and the pastor was so impressed he booked me (Brother Bill) for a four-day revival in Muleshoe! There was a very long pause on the phone while Brother Bill was trying to process what he had just heard. I finally relieved his anxiety by telling him the truth about the conversation, and we both had a good laugh.

In remembering the event I've wondered how much farther I would have allowed the conversation with the preacher to have gone before I had to tell him I was not Brother Bill. Probably not much longer. Besides I never thought I looked like my evangelist friend!

163. A DIVINE APPOINTMENT IN SOUTH AFRICA

God Always Goes Ahead of Us

Luampa Mission Hospital Staff, Zambia, 1982

Dr. Gordon Jones was a well-known missionary surgeon in Zambia for over twenty-five years. I was fortunate to have known and loved him, but I knew about him long before we ever met. He was born and raised in El Dorado but had already left for his graduate and post-graduate work in medicine by the time I got to my teen years. His younger brother Delmas was the same age as my sister Marilyn, and I knew him because he was an excellent football player in high school. Gordon's younger sister Carolyn was married to James Thomas, who was a friend from high school days.

When Cathy and I moved to El Dorado in the early 1970s, James was in the food-service business, and it wasn't long before he opened a restaurant. The Union Station Restaurant was a particular favorite of our family for Sunday lunch. James and Carolyn would tell us interesting and sometimes funny stories about Gordon, his wife Jeanette, and their ministry in Zambia. After hearing about them and their ministry, we made it a top priority to meet them on their next furlough home, which occurred in the late 1970s.

Gordan and I had an immediate connection, because he had received his surgical training in New Orleans where Cathy and I had spent four years while I received my training at Charity Hospital. We had several common friends from those days and were able to reconnect some of those relationships from the past. Over the next fifteen years, we were able to maintain our relationship with Gordon and Jeanette and were part of their support team with AEF (Africa Evangelical Fellowship). We received regular correspondence from them and learned their ministry was at the Luampa Mission Hospital in the village of Luampa. Their home was a full-day's auto trip from Lusaka, the capital of Zambia. According to Gordon, "Luampa is three hundred miles out in the bush and three hundred and fifty miles from the supermarket in Lusaka."

Every four years, Gordon and Jeanette would take a furlough for six months or so and would spend most of the time in El Dorado. He would assist me with many of my surgical cases, and he told me it was invaluable experience for him because he had very little interaction with other surgeons in Luampa. We exchanged lots stories, and, because Gordon was very vocal, it was sometimes difficult to tell mine. We both enjoyed the fellowship we shared. The photo above shows the staff of the hospital in the early 1970s. Dr. Jones is located on the back row next to the end on the right.

The International Congress on Revival is an overseas mission organization which encourages and enables pastors and their wives in many countries of the world. Cathy and I were privileged to have been a part of the ministry for over twenty-five years and traveled together with the team to seven different countries. ICR had a long-standing relationship with the pastors in South Africa, and a conference was held there annually during the month of July. I had a desire to go to South Africa, but Cathy preferred I travel with other men in the organization because far fewer wives made those conferences than the ones in Eastern Europe. I made plans to attend my first conference in South Africa in July of 1999.

Elsewhere, I've written about some of my experiences travelling to that initial conference with John Morgan and Freddie Wilson from El Dorado. On the first day of the conference, I was seated at a table positioned toward the front of the conference room. I had not met any of the attendees of the conference, and only knew they were from South Africa and several adjoining countries. At the first break in the morning session, I turned around and introduced myself to a pastor and his wife from South Africa. I asked how long he had served as a minister, thinking it must have been twenty-five years because he appeared to be in his late fifties. He said he was a civil engineer for the first twenty-five years of his professional life and had only surrendered to vocational ministry in the previous ten years. He asked me how many trips I had made to South Africa, and I told him this was my first. I said, "In fact I have only known one man from Africa, and he was a missionary doctor in Zambia for almost thirty years."

He asked if he was still there, and I told him unfortunately he had died just two years earlier, and I had never taken the opportunity to visit and work with him despite being invited many times. When he asked where he worked, I said it was a little-known mission hospital in Luampa which had been there since the early 1960s. He said, "You may not believe this, but in the early 1960s, I was a civil engineer working in Lusaka and was given the responsibility as project engineer for building that hospital in Luampa. I know every stone and piece of lumber used in that hospital!" He said he had never met Dr. Gordon Jones but had heard stories about what a wonderful man he was and what an impact his life and ministry had been there.

As I turned around in my place to enjoy the remainder of the conference that morning, I thanked God for his amazing grace. The first man I meet in South Africa is the one man responsible for building the only hospital in Zambia I knew anything about and was managed by the only doctor I knew in all of Africa. My what a God!!

164. "NEVER SIGN ANYTHING YOU HAVEN'T READ"

Some Things Are Better Signed than Spoken

Our son is a gifted attorney, and we are very thankful for his accomplishments, not only as a lawyer, but as a Christian, a husband, a father, as well as a son. He has given us wonderful advice on legal matters and in many other areas as well. One particular piece of advice, which I usually try to follow is this: "Never sign anything you haven't read and understood." Excellent advice for a time in our culture in which a simple handshake does not have the significance it once had. I have a special friend who is an evangelist who was prepared on one occasion to sign his name to a document he had not read and certainly didn't understand. God's grace and mercy prevented him from making a grave error.

Brother Bill Stafford lives in Chattanooga, Tennessee and has been a Southern Baptist evangelist for the greater part of his fifty-five year ministry. Cathy and I have grown to love Bill and his wife Sue for more than twenty-five years and have served with them on the board of the International Congress on Revival for almost fifteen years. We have travelled overseas and served in this ministry to pastors and their wives to encourage them, pray for them, and help strengthen their ministries. All of their expenses were paid to come to a central place in Europe and to stay in a nice hotel where the annual conferences were held.

The ministry was a spiritual highlight every year for Cathy and me, and ICR was especially wonderful for us in allowing us to know Brother Bill and Sue on a deep friendship level. Brother Bill trusted my counsel in spiritual matters, and he sought advice and counsel on health issues as well. In several instances, he allowed me to schedule medical tests and evaluations by other specialists who were colleagues in my hometown. Bill's home was at least five hundred miles away, so appointments had to be scheduled well in advance.

For this particular appointment, Brother Bill had been experiencing some gastric problems requiring medications, and I thought it best he have an endoscopic procedure on his stomach. This required preliminary preparations and also the use of strong sedatives during the procedure. The only physician in our town qualified to do the procedure was an excellent doctor with lots of experience, but he wasn't a professing Christian. I made him aware that my friend was a well-known Baptist preacher who had travelled a great distance to have the procedure done.

On the scheduled day for the procedure and after introducing the two men, I decided to remain in the procedure room in case anything unexpected might occur. I was feeling the responsibility for the safety of my friend since I had recommended this colleague to him, and he could have had it done more easily in his own home where there were twenty or more equally qualified specialists. As the intravenous line was quickly inserted and the sedative was being slowly given, I was feeling a little calmer even though I was not receiving any of the sedative.

Before insertion of the scope, the physician began asking routine questions, but I could tell from the inflection in his voice there was also some sarcasm. He asked, "Mr. Stafford, do you drink whiskey, beer, or wine for special occasions?" Brother Bill chuckled a little with his answer, "No sir, I never have." I could tell the sedation was beginning to work, because Bill's words were slower than usual, and his tongue was a little thicker. The doctor then asked, "Well, you probably use tobacco in some form. Do you smoke an occasional cigar or take a chew of tobacco when you go out on a fishing trip?" As more of the medicine entered his vein, Bill very slowly said, "No sir, I never cared for any of it." Seemingly a little frustrated with the answers he was hearing, the doctor then said, "Well, I know when someone really makes you mad, you will use cuss words! You occasionally cuss when you get mad, don't you?" The doctor was certain the amount of sedation Bill had received would act as a truth serum, and he would discover how a preacher really acted and talked in private. I was thinking I might have to put my hand over Bill's mouth just in case he would say something he would not want heard. Then, in Brother Bill's typical manner, he said very slowly and with a tongue so thick it hardly sounded like his voice, "Well sir, if a man makes me mad enough, you could write some of those words on a piece of paper, and I would sign it!!" The skeptical doctor was astonished at Brother Bill's candor, and even laughed at the response. I was greatly relieved I didn't have to cover his mouth, and Brother Bill didn't have to sign anything he had not read. When the procedure was over, he didn't remember a word of the conversation he had with the skeptical doctor. And the best news was that the findings revealed a common problem easily treated with medicines.

165. TEACHING WITH TEARS

Expressing Emotions while Teaching

I first developed the dread of public speaking during my last year at El Dorado Junior High School (now renamed Barton Junior High). I was elected president of the ninth grade, and one of my responsibilities included addressing the entire student body on occasion. I can remember an instance in which I got so nervous the evening before a scheduled address that I developed stomach cramps, and Mom had to call the next morning to report I was unable to be present. I would never have accepted the presidential position in the first place had I known I would be speaking in front of several hundred students and fifteen to twenty faculty members. What was I thinking?

Over the next twenty-five years, I occasionally spoke to an audience, usually in teaching a Sunday school class, but I was not a regular teacher until 1975 at First Baptist Church, El Dorado. Over the next ten years, I gained more experience in teaching, and then, following a spiritual conversion in 1977, I was invited to preach in a number of local area churches.

By the mid-1980s Cathy and I were very active in the teaching and encouragement ministry of our church. I was one of four teachers of the Men's Bible Class, a unique group of senior men whose session was broadcast live over a local radio station from 10:00 to 11:00 every Sunday morning. The other teachers who shared the teaching duties were Judge Oren Harris, a federal judge, Bob Watson, the school superintendent, and Bob Merkle, a retired business executive.

I was not aware of a Sunday school class anywhere which was broadcast on radio each week. The challenges for a teacher in such a format included, among other things, the inability to ask questions of the listeners and have any vocal interactions with class members. The speaker was required to continue speaking with no interruptions; otherwise, listeners at home would think the program was over and turn off their radios. We had no way to judge how many people tuned in to the class, but all week long, I would hear people in the community say, "I listen to your Sunday school class each week."

During this time, I began wearing contact lenses for the only time in my life. I had worn glasses since I was ten and had never considered contact lenses in the intervening years. I was playing tennis one day with my friend Dr. Myron Shofner, an excellent optometrist and outstanding tennis player. He was causing me to sweat profusely with his aggressive play, and, while wiping my glasses between sets, I told him the only times glasses bothered me were while playing tennis and jogging. He said, "Why don't you come to the office tomorrow? I'll fit you with contacts and solve your glasses-fogging problem." The lenses he used were gas-permeable lenses (hard lenses) because of my astigmatism. I was able to immediately wear them and really enjoyed the freedom they offered. The only problem was that occasionally a speck of sand or an irritant would get behind a lens causing tearing and great discomfort until I removed the lens, cleansed it, and replaced it. That particular problem never occurred while teaching or publicly speaking until one particular Sunday morning while teaching on radio.

I don't remember the subject of the lesson, but right in the middle of the thirty-minute teaching time, I developed considerable irritation in my right eye. I assumed it was nothing more serious than an irritant speck, but it was causing excessive tearing down my right cheek. I refrained from rubbing my right eyelid lid too vigorously, because, when I had done that in the past, the contact lens popped out, and I was temporarily blind in one eye. I decided the best course of action was to continue teaching and to tolerate the irritation. My eye, however, continued to water profusely. That's when I looked into the audience and noticed two of the men who were regular attenders shedding real tears. They believed I was being moved to tears by the things in my heart I was trying to say to the class, and they were empathizing with me. I recall those same men who were so moved had trouble in previous weeks remaining awake and alert during my teaching time.

I learned some important teaching principles this tearful Sunday morning. There are certain stresses of teaching which are unavoidable, but if one can prevent continuing eye irritation while teaching, it is much less stressful. Second, teaching the Word with tears from a real broken heart is very impactful to a sensitive audience; but just don't try to manufacture tears, which are not real. If nervousness produced tears, I would have shed a bunch.

Either way, "God's Word will not return void. It will accomplish that which He pleases and will prosper in the thing to which He sent it" (Isa 55:11).

166. "LET'S PRAY FOR A BOOT"

Some Prayers Are Answered before They Are Prayed

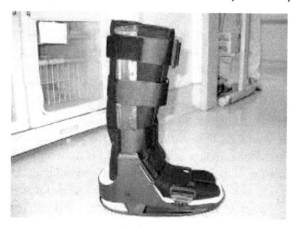

Bledsoe Boot

The privilege of prayer is given as a gift to every believer, but the way prayer is handled is as different as each individual. There are many promises in the Word related to prayer including the necessity of praying, the frequency of prayer needed by every believer, the power of prayer, and the swiftness of God's answers when one prays. I had the privilege of experiencing each one of these four supernatural aspects of prayer one morning in the Wound Care Clinic at Washington Regional Medical Center in Fayetteville, Arkansas, where I was working at the time.

I had served many years as a general surgeon in a private practice, but when Cathy and I moved to Fayetteville to be near our daughter Ginny and her family, I made the transition to a wound-care practice. My working hours were during the day, and I no longer was doing any type of operative surgery. This type of practice suited my personality and ministry very well, because I was able to spend more time with each patient. This gave me the opportunity to learn more of their needs, their fears, and their faith. Because of the nature of wound problems, I would usually see and treat most patients weekly for many months.

A significant number of our patients were diabetic, and ulcerations of the feet and legs were common problems for them. A dreaded complication of diabetes is peripheral neuropathy, which causes a loss of sensation in the feet and sometimes the hands. Most people who are not diabetic do not understand that the sensation of pain is a protective mechanism which can prevent continuing injury to a foot or hand. A diabetic with a neuropathic ulcer on the sole of his foot can continue walking without pain, which causes infection and worsening of the ulcer. In some cases, amputation of toes, the foot, or even the leg becomes necessary. The treatment plan for a diabetic foot ulcer must include "off-loading," which means no pressure on the ulcer site. One excellent method for off-loading is wearing a Bledsoe Boot, with which a person can still walk without having to use crutches or a wheelchair. One major drawback for the boot is the expense. They can cost as much as three hundred and fifty dollars, which will be an out-of-pocket expense if not covered by insurance.

I had been treating Rev. Robert S. for a diabetic ulcer on the sole of his right foot for several months with minimal success. He kept assuring me he was "keeping as much weight as possible" off his right foot, but his responsibilities as pastor of a small church made it very difficult. He was afraid that if he didn't keep going rather than take off work for several months, his church attendance, which was already sparse, would decline to zero. He tried crutches, but just couldn't manage the many stairs in his life, and the option of a wheelchair was not feasible. I had briefly mentioned a Bledsoe Boot early in his treatment, but he had no health insurance, so I didn't talk about a boot until his ulcer became severely infected and a major change in his treatment plan became critical.

I had told him early on that a boot was very expensive but had not told him the approximate price. I explained he could wear the boot and the ulcer could heal while he could continue visiting and preaching, as well as meeting all his other pastoral responsibilities. When I told him the cost, his response was, "Doc, I know I need to have one, and I might not ever heal without one, but right now there is no way I can afford to pay that much." I said, "Brother Robert, let's agree right now in prayer that God knows your need and perhaps he will put in on the hearts of some of your church members to help you buy one." He and I both prayed, but his prayer seemed more impassioned than mine. The nurse bandaged his foot, we shook hands, and I told him I would see him in a week.

I walked down the hall toward the nurse's desk and noticed a well-dressed woman whom I had never met talking with one of our nurses. After introducing myself she said she represented a surgical supply firm in Little Rock, and wanted to know if there was anything from her company we might need. I told her I had a patient who needed a Bledsoe Boot, but he had no way to pay for it. "Do you know how I might get one at a reduced cost?" I asked her. "I sure do," she said. "For some reason, I put one in my car this morning before I left Little Rock, and you may have it." I was stunned our God had answered our prayers so quickly! I wanted to hug her, but just thanked her instead. I also said, "You had no way of knowing this, but your putting the boot in your car this morning is the answer to a specific prayer prayed down in treatment room #1 less than two minutes ago!" Her response was, "That is so nice."

When I walked back to Brother Robert's treatment room, I left the boot just outside the door and asked him, "What was it we just prayed?" "For God to supply a boot," he hesitantly said. When I got the boot and handed it to him, I said, "God just sent you one!" He shouted the loudest shout I think was ever heard in the wound clinic. I didn't mind the noise distraction to the staff and the other patients, because I knew it was coming from a deeply grateful heart. I would have shouted with him, but thought it might not sound too professional.

I was reminded in a very impactful way our God hears all the prayers of his children; he answers all of them according to his will, and a few he answers immediately. Brother Robert and I both were reminded that when we have a need, God will meet the need, and the supply is on the way (from Little Rock) even before we pray (Phil 4:19).

167. "I DON'T HAVE THE RIGHT TO PRAY"

Tragic Experiences Leave Deep Scars

Prayer is the most powerful privilege given to man and unfortunately the least understood biblical mandate given to both believers and non-believers by our sovereign God. It is through the prayer of faith God redeems a lost sinner by his grace. It is through prayer and obedience a believer matures and becomes conformed to the image of the Lord Jesus Christ. It is through believing prayer the windows of heaven are opened according to his will. As children of God, we are commanded by God to "call upon me and I will answer and show you great and mighty things which you do not know" (Jer 33:3). Despite the unbelievable and eternal riches available to everyone, there are those who still refuse the offer. Such was the case of a surgical patient of mine whom I will call Robert, who was approximately sixty-eight years old.

Robert was referred by another physician who had done a colonoscopy with polyp biopsy and had encountered sudden and uncontrolled bleeding of some magnitude. I immediately left my clinic filled with patients and met

Robert in the emergency room. His vital signs were stable, but he was quite anxious because his treating physician had correctly told him he needed an immediate operation. Within the hour, all preliminary testing was completed including typing and cross-matching for two units of blood, and he was taken to the operating room. The operation involved the surgical opening of the distal colon (large intestine), location of the bleeding polyp, removal of the polyp, and suturing the actively bleeding area. The blood loss, although large, did not require transfusion, and his post-operative recovery was free from complications.

During his initial, post-operative office visit, we had a conversation on how quickly his physician recognized the extent of his problem and immediately sent him to the emergency room for surgical care. I said he should be thanking God for his doctor and for his rapid recovery when he said the following, "I don't ever pray." "Do you mind me asking why?" I replied. "I don't believe I have the right to pray because of what I did during World War II. I took things away from men which I was not able to return. I ruthlessly and deliberately killed many men." This was forty-five years earlier, and the shame he still carried as he told his story broke my heart.

He had been selected along with at least a hundred men to be part of a special combat unit which today might be the equivalent of a special-forces unit. They were trained separately under cover from the rest of the combat units, and during this intense training time, they were informed of some of their assignments. They were not to wear uniforms indicating their ranks, and each man would be given specific orders for their assignments going forward. Robert said they would be given photographs and information concerning men in various cities who were enemies of the Allied Forces. They were supposed to locate those men and use whatever methods necessary to kill them. According to Robert most of their targets were civilians rather than military.

I'm not certain how long Robert remained on active duty in the unit, but when the war was declared over, the men remaining alive were placed on a ship in the North Sea where they remained for the next several months. Also on the ship were doctors, psychiatrists, psychologists, and social workers whose responsibilities were to deprogram the men and rehabilitate them back into civilian life. The emotional wounds from their war experiences were very deep. In effect these brave men had been trained as military assassins.

When Robert relived some of those experiences which he had buried long ago, he was visibly moved to tears. He reiterated his belief that he was unworthy to pray and could not pray. My response to him was, "Robert, I want to tell you some wonderful news about our loving God." I emphasized that we are all sinners and because of our sins, none of us is worthy to pray. God sent his only Son to take our sins on himself and die on a cross two thousand years ago. He fully paid our sin debt, and with his resurrection made it possible for us to pray, because we had been pardoned from the penalty of our sins. "Robert, the Lord Jesus not only set you free, but he wants you to pray and invite him into your heart for him to live there forever. Don't you want to accept his invitation?"

I wish I could report that Robert repented and received the free gift of salvation from God, but he did not. I told him I respected his decision but would be praying he would consider what I had said. I gave him a copy of the Gospel of John after showing him several passages where the Bible affirms the things I had told him. He said he would read the tract and "think about it."

There are millions of people living in darkness with their eyes blinded to the wonderful promises of God regarding eternal life. Many of them are like Robert, believing they have no right to pray, or, that if they happened to pray, nothing of consequence would happen. I have no idea what became of Robert, but I believe someone later watered the field of his life where a seed had been planted, and before he departed this life, he became a follower of The Way (1 Cor 3:6).

168. AN AFRICAN ELEPHANT OPENS A DOOR

A Painter Benefits from His Work

One doesn't often think of something as large as an African elephant opening a door unless he crashes through it, but in the case of this particular elephant, God opened the door to a special relationship in a most unusual way.

Cathy and I have had the privilege through the years of knowing and having fellowship with some of the most wonderful people serving the Lord in other countries. One of the couples who impacted us early in our Christian experience were Gordon and Jeanette Jones, who lived and served with their children in Zambia.

Dr. Gordon Jones was a general surgeon from El Dorado who was several years older than I, and I didn't know him in his younger years. His younger brother Delmas was in my sister Marilyn's graduating high school class, and I knew about his skill in playing high school football. Gordon's younger sister Carolyn was married to James Thomas, a friend from Boys Club baseball days, and the two of them opened and operated a downtown restaurant called Union Station. The restaurant was a favorite, where our family dined on most Sundays following church. Through James and Carolyn, we became acquainted with the Gordon Joneses and were introduced to them in the early 1980s when they were home for a six-month furlough.

When Gordon and I discovered that we both had trained in general surgery several years apart at Charity Hospital in New Orleans, our professional bond grew closer. Gordon began coming to the hospitals in El Dorado and operating with me when home on furlough. I was able to pay him an assistant's fee, which helped with their finances, but more importantly, we had the opportunity to spend hours talking about his work and ministry in Zambia. Gordon and I developed a close friendship during those years, and I learned a great deal about life as a medical missionary in Zambia and elsewhere. (I have written two pieces regarding our friendship—"Dr. Jones and the Spitting Cobra" and "A Divine Appointment in South Africa.")

On one of their furloughs during the Christmas holiday season, they brought us some unique gifts from Zambia, which we really appreciated. One was a special drawing (painting) of an African elephant done by a person who lived in central Kenya and was on the staff of the Rift Valley Academy. All we knew of the artist's name was "Lasz," which was in the lower left corner. The academy is well-known as an excellent boarding school for missionary kids throughout all of Africa, and all the Jones kids attended there. The drawing, although beautiful, didn't find a special place in our home because, about the time they gave it to us, we were in the process of moving. We moved the drawing along with all of our other household items.

Fast forward ten years when Cathy and I moved to Fayetteville, Arkansas from Clearwater, Florida. We noted among our paintings and drawings this one of the elephant. It was about this time our son-in-law John Luther, who is an avid hunter, was moving into his new office as the director of Emergency Management for Washington County, Arkansas. Cathy found a very nice frame, and we gave the drawing to John to hang in his office.

John took one look at the signature, "Lasz" on the drawing and said his friend Phil Lasse was the artist of the drawing. I said, "John, do you really know this man who lives in Kenya?" He responded, "Phil and his wife Shirley moved from Kenya to Fayetteville several years ago and are very active members of our church. Yes, I know him." I thought to myself, "What a small world!"

At the time I was co-teaching a Sunday school class at University Baptist Church with Dr. Don Herring, professor and chairman of the department of agriculture at the University of Arkansas. He said he would like for me to join him in visiting a close friend who was dealing with far-advanced cancer; he believed we could encourage him and could pray with him. "Who is the friend?" I asked Don. He said it was Phil Lasse. I said it would be an honor to meet him and pray with him. On three separate occasions over the next month, we went to Phil and Shirley's home and were able to encourage and be encouraged by them. During the first visit, I told Phil the story of the elephant drawing and how I came to be in possession of it. He did not personally know the Gordon Jones family, but remembered there were three missionary kids in the Rift Academy from Zambia.

I am still learning in God's economy of time and events that there are no chance occurrences. It was not a coincidence Gordon and Jeanette happened to choose the drawing of an African elephant as a gift for us. God knew in his sovereignty a door of opportunity would be opened by the drawing years later. As I reflect on these events, it causes me to look more closely for God's mighty hand in everything and especially something as large as an elephant!

169. "WE'RE TRYING TO GET THE BUGS OUT"

Misspoken Words Create Anxiety

The experiences Cathy and I had through the overseas ministry of the International Congress on Revival (ICR) were many and life-changing. That ministry was begun by the evangelist Manley Beasley Sr. in the 1980s as an encouragement to European pastors and their wives who were struggling to preach the gospel in countries which were Communist-controlled.

ICR provided the leadership to host three-to-four-day conferences in a major European cities and supply the funding to pay all the expenses for the invited pastors and wives to attend. The early conferences were held in Switzerland and Austria, and, because funding was initially limited, only twenty to thirty were able to attend. The Americans who traveled overseas to supply the preaching and music paid their own expenses. Because Manley himself had serious personal health issues, the leadership for ICR was eventually passed to Bill Stafford who became the President of ICR in 1989. That was the year Brother Bill invited me to become a member of the board. In the beginning, Cathy and I were reluctant to attend an overseas conference thinking we would not have much to offer in terms of preaching and music. We simply asked that the money we would spend in travelling be used to invite another European pastor and his wife. After facing two years of our resistance, Brother Bill convinced us we would have much to offer in terms of loving and personally encouraging the attendees. We agreed to make our first trip in 1991.

The conference that year was held in Salzburg, Austria in a beautiful downtown hotel. There were approximately twenty Americans including Cathy and me who had flown over together to meet with our European guests. There were approximately sixty attendees from fourteen different countries throughout Western and Eastern Europe. The unique thing about this particular conference was that for the first time we were having simultaneous translation of the preaching. There were to be translators for Romanian, Hungarian, German, and Russian attendees. If needed, each pastor could put on a headset, switch to the proper channel for his particular language, and hear the sermon translated from English into his native tongue.

Before the conference began, all the speakers were encouraged to not employ commonly-used idioms in their preaching because of difficulties for the translators in having the correct words to convey the exact meaning. One example is the phrase, "He sure knocked it out of the park," when describing a preacher delivering an especially impactful sermon. Another might be, "She can sing the stars down!" Pastors with previous experience in overseas ministry were more aware of this type of translation difficulty.

Paul Harper was the program coordinator for this conference and was an experienced leader. He served as executive administrator of Woodland Park Baptist Church in Chattanooga, Tennessee, which was Bill Stafford's home church. The pastor of this large and influential church was Wayne Barber, and he was also in attendance at the conference.

Everyone was excited for the conference to begin, and many who were in attendance had been to previous conferences, so friendship bonds had already been established. The large conference room of the hotel was made ready by the hotel staff, and all the tables and comfortable chairs were positioned to take maximum advantage of the acoustics. The tables, which would seat eight people, had six to eight headsets which could be set to one of the four channels. We tried to position at least two Americans at each table to encourage interaction with our guests.

Paul began the conference by leading us in singing the theme song of the ICR conferences, "Jesus Be Jesus in Me." The words were projected on the large screen so those unfamiliar with the song could join in. After singing this praise chorus several times, everyone had the tune and words correct, and it was a beautiful praise lifted to the Lord from at least fifteen nationalities! Following a prayer of consecration for the meeting given by Brother Bill, Paul began giving instructions to the attendees, and his words were being translated simultaneously. The four translators were each positioned in a booth at the far back of the conference room, and if one stood next to those booths, there was quite a cacophony of voices. The booths were far enough back that the people seated at the back table were not distracted.

As Paul was explaining to everyone the technicalities of simultaneous translation, he said this was our first experience, and we all wanted it to be a good one. He then said, "We ask you to please be patient with us as we are trying to get all the bugs out of the system." All us the Americans nodded our heads in agreement, but immediately many of the Europeans and especially the wives, began taking their headsets off. It looked strange and some even stood up and looked in their seats while shaking their clothing. It took only an instant to realize the translated message they were hearing was that there were literal bugs in the system and we had been trying to get them out as quickly as possible! No one wanted bugs crawling through the headsets and possibly into their ears and down their backs. Paul realized what he had said and began apologizing profusely. He reassured everyone there were not actual bugs in the system, and it was perfectly safe to wear the headsets with confidence.

The remainder of the conference was free from such language glitches which caused fear or discomfort. Bill Stafford frequently would say that when he preached, he wanted to "distress the comfortable and comfort the distressed." I suppose in this case with bugs in the system, both of these goals were accomplished; and it was all to the glory of God!

170. AN ENCOUNTER WITH DUNCAN CAMPBELL

Meeting the Successor to Duncan Campbell

Rev. Duncan Campbell

In 1991, when Cathy and I made our first overseas trip with the International Congress on Revival, we had no idea of the wonderful, godly people we would meet, and with whom we would bond. I have recently written about meeting Mia and Costel Oglice who were our Romanian translators for the conference, and how our friendship resulted in many Romanian and eastern European pastors and their wives coming to El Dorado for some much-needed medical care ("In Need of a Russian Translator").

The conference we attended was held in Salzburg, Austria, and the American team was scheduled to have a few days in Innsbruck to rest and recover from jet lag. We were then to go to Salzburg to begin the meeting, which had attendees coming from eighteen different countries. While in Innsbruck, I was given a copy of Wesley Duewel's book, *Ablaze for God,* and was told there were a number of accounts in the book of great revivals of the past. I was told the accounts would be an encouragement to pray for revival in Salzburg. One of the accounts in the book was in chapter ten, entitled, "God's Power in the Ministry of Duncan Campbell." I had never read anything about Duncan Campbell prior to this.

One of the first of many manifestations of God's power in Duncan Campbell occurred when he was seriously injured in 1918 during World War I. He was taken to a casualty clearing station where he said he felt an unusual presence of God when he prayed aloud Psalm 103 in his native Gaelic tongue of the Scottish Highlands. He said seven wounded Canadian soldiers who understood Gaelic were lying nearby were immediately born again. Several other examples of the unexplainable power of God through Duncan's life were given. Years later while Reverend Campbell was preaching throughout the Scottish Hebrides, a huge movement of God occurred resulting in most of the people on the island chain being converted to faith in Christ. Duncan Campbell spent the last years of his life as Principal of Edinburgh Bible College.

When we arrived in Salzburg two days later, I was enthused about the possibility of God's power being manifested in Cathy's and my life and in all the conference attendees' lives. On the first morning as Cathy and I got on the hotel elevator to go for breakfast, there was an older, well-dressed couple who appeared to also be attending the ICR meeting. I noted that their name tags only stated their names, Colin Peckham and wife Mary Peckham, and their native country Scotland. Following introductions, I told them of the book I had just read, and asked if by chance they had ever met Duncan Campbell. Both smiled and said they knew him very well! Reverend Dr. Peckham said he had followed Duncan Campbell as principal of Edinburg Bible College and had in his possession all of Duncan's papers from the college. Mary said she was a young woman on the Island of Lewis when converted to faith in Christ while Duncan Campbell preached during the Hebrides Revival of 1949! I was speechless, but managed to ask if they would join Cathy and me for breakfast. They gladly accepted our invitation.

They had never attended an ICR conference but had been invited to share the ministry of Christ through them in Scotland. They were excited to have the opportunity to speak to such a diverse American and European group. They asked us to tell them about Christ's ministry through us in South Arkansas, and how we became involved in ICR. They had met the founder of ICR, the late Brother Manley Beasley, years before in Switzerland, but had never met Brother Bill Stafford the current president.

Rev. Dr. Colin Peckham   Mary Peckham

During breakfast I told them of the account I had read of Reverend Campbell, who was critically wounded, praying Psalm 103 in Gaelic and of the conversion of the wounded Canadian soldiers who heard his prayer. I asked if they would mind quoting all or part of that Psalm in Gaelic. I didn't mean to embarrass them, but certainly caught them off guard. Dr. Peckham said he was born and raised in South Africa and was not fluent in the Gaelic tongue of the Scottish Highlands, but Mary certainly was fluent. He said, "What if Mary quoted Psalm 23 in Gaelic, and I quoted that Psalm in Zulu?" I said, "That would be awesome!" Neither Cathy nor I had ever heard those two languages spoken, but we knew what they were saying, and I thought while they were speaking, "What a wonderful way to begin our time and meeting in Austria!" There was certainly a spirit of revival beginning in our hearts that morning.

The time spent over the next five days in Austria was life changing for Cathy and me. We met and had fellowship with Christians from all over the world and heard and shared stories of God's working through all of us. As we returned home, I remember praying, "God set me ablaze for your glory and let it continue until I meet you!"

171. THE FIRST EVANGELISTIC VISIT

Being Taught by an Expert

Christ calls all of His disciples to be his witnesses to the ends of the earth and promises he will go with them (Matt 28:18–20). Despite the importance and the provision of his power, this one imperative strikes more fear into the hearts of Christians than any other command. All Christians are aware of their responsibility in this regard, but sadly very few have led a non-believer to a saving knowledge of Christ.

I love hearing wonderful stories of faith in which a person is brought from spiritual darkness into the light of Jesus's love and is saved. I particularly loved hearing my brother Berry Lee (Bubba) recount stories of his patients' praying to receive Christ as their Savior, either in Bubba's medical office or in the hospital while being treated for serious medical issues. I never saw a physician pray with a patient for the first ten years of my medical practice until I saw Bubba pray with one of his patients. Within a few years of this event, I gave my life to Christ and was mentored by Bubba on how to minister Christ with my own patients.

One of my heroes of the faith is Reverend Anton (Buddy) Uth, who was the father of Dr. David Uth. Brother David, who is now pastor of the First Baptist Church of Orlando, is married to Rachel, Berry Lee and LaNell's middle daughter. Cathy and I have known and loved Rachel since she was born, and after she began dating and finally married David, we have loved him and his family as well. Brother Anton was a Southern Baptist pastor for many years and faithfully served our Lord in numerous churches until his death in 2009 at age eighty. His widow Joan lived in Bryant, Arkansas and was active in her church, Geyer Springs First Baptist, until she departed this life in 2022.

Brother Anton could tell some of the best and funniest stories of his many years of ministry. I'll always remember his account of his first evangelistic visit, which occurred when he was a student at Ouachita Baptist University.

By Anton's admission, his early life was not spent as a believer pursuing God's will. Following his conversion, he decided to begin his education toward a ministerial degree by enrolling at Ouachita Baptist University (OBU) for his undergraduate degree. He was older by almost ten years than most students and was eager to learn as much as he could as quickly as possible.

One of his close friends was Bailey Smith, who was a senior at OBU although he was ten years younger than Anton. Bailey was an enthusiastic soul-winner who, in his ministry as pastor of a megachurch—First Southern Baptist Church of Dell City, OK— was able to lead as many as two thousand people a year to Christ. Anton said he wanted to learn how to witness his faith to others, and there was no one at Ouachita better equipped to teach him than Bailey. He agreed to take Anton out on an evangelistic visit and demonstrate how easy and wonderful it was to lead someone to a saving faith.

On the designated afternoon, Bailey and Anton made their way to a local trailer park which Bailey had visited several other times. He told Anton this particular park was very fertile grounds for lost people, and he had led people there to Christ in the recent past. Anton said he was very excited to learn from such a bold and experienced teacher.

They approached a particularly shabby trailer which Bailey said housed a lost man whom he had visited one other time. Bailey knocked on the door, and, in a few moments according to Anton, it was opened by a large, unkept man with a two-to-three-day growth of beard. He was wearing pants with no shoes and a tight-fitting t-shirt with lots of black chest hair exposed. Bailey said, "Good afternoon, Mr. Johnson. I'm Bailey Smith whom you met before, and I want you to meet my friend Buddy Uth. May we come in?" "Sure, come in and have a seat. I need to go back in the bedroom for a minute," he said. Anton said he and Bailey sat in two chairs in the living area awaiting Mr. Johnson's return.

In less than a minute, Mr. Johnson appeared in the living room with a double-barreled shotgun pointed at the two evangelists and said, "I told you last time you were here I would kill you if you returned!" Anton said he was so stunned at this turn of events he was temporarily frozen in the chair, but the moment Mr. Johnson appeared with the shotgun, Bailey instantly bolted out the door of the trailer without speaking. Within another moment, Anton followed Bailey through the door and started running as fast as he could, noticing Bailey was at least ten paces ahead running, at a faster pace. Mr. Johnson meanwhile was shouting curse words at both men, and Anton said he expected to hear a shotgun blast and feel the pain of the pellets at any moment! When he finally caught up with Bailey, who had stopped to catch his breath, and they were far enough from the trailer to be out of shotgun range, he also stopped. His first words were, "I'm sure glad you brought me out to teach me how to be a soul-winner. I can't imagine what the next lesson will be like!" Anton never gave me a follow-up account, but I suspect they did make other more fruitful visits together without revisiting Mr. Johnson.

Jesus said in Matthew 10:13–14 that when we go to a house to witness and are not received nor heard, just leave and shake the dust off your feet.

I suppose the first lesson Anton learned on his first evangelistic visit with Bailey was the technique of dust shaking!

172. THE EVANGELIST GIVES AN INVITATION

Careful Preparation before Preaching

Evangelistic revivals are fast becoming events of a past generation in the modern church. I am old enough to remember when a scheduled revival meeting would begin on a Sunday morning continuing through the following Saturday evening, and, if the meeting was successful, it might be extended for another week. As time progressed, the usual revival of the 1980s and 1990s was reduced to a Sunday-morning-through-Wednesday-night affair. Fewer and fewer churches after the 1990s even scheduled evangelists to come preach, and now only a very few pastors consider an evangelistic revival a relevant event for their church. I believe the church is missing a very significant tool for outreach evangelism, which for many decades was responsible for tens of thousands of spiritually dead sinners' making lasting professions of faith. I use the term *lasting* because one of the arguments against revivals is that many recorded professions of faith from the past were simply emotional responses to high pressure techniques of over-zealous evangelists.

In a previous post, I related the account of my friend Rev. Anton (Buddy) Uth's first evangelistic visit. He was a college student at Ouachita Baptist University at the time, and, upon graduation, went to seminary to receive his MDiv at Southwestern Baptist Theological Seminary. He pastored many Southern Baptist churches in the South during his years of ministry. I was privileged to know and love him because his son David, who is Senior Pastor of First Baptist Church Orlando, is married to our niece Rachel Moore. Brother David became our pastor at Immanuel Baptist Church in El Dorado for a five-year period in the 1990s. Besides being a wonderful pastor-shepherd, Brother Buddy could tell some of the most interesting and hilarious stories I have ever heard. One of his best stories concerned a visiting evangelist at one of his churches. I don't recall the name of the evangelist, and this account might well have been the first time he had preached in one of his churches.

For the initial service on Sunday morning, prior to his going to the platform, no one noticed that the evangelist had failed to close the zipper of his pants. The visitor, however, recognized his mistake when he sat down in his chair while the choir was singing the opening anthem. This was not the time to close a zipper while all the congregants had their eyes on the choir behind him. The preacher thought he could easily close his zipper when he stood to preach standing behind the pulpit, and the action would not be noticed by even the most observant viewer.

The church sanctuary was an old one without air conditioning, and during the hot summer months, the windows along the sides were kept open. This meeting was being held in the final days of August before Labor Day. With the help of the ceiling fans the circulation was enough on most Sundays to keep the inside temperatures pleasant enough for the duration of the service. The pulpit had been built years before by one of the skilled members, and, to add a little color and formality, a small silk cloth with tassels was covering the top of the pulpit. Those overlays were common in many country churches. The evangelist had no idea this colorful but unob-trusive item was about to become a focal point of his delivery this morning.

At the close of the choir special, the evangelist kept his Bible and notes in front of him as he stood and quickly positioned himself behind the pul-pit. While he was making introductory praise remarks to Pastor Buddy and the congregation, he quickly pulled on the zipper and succeeded in closing it. His preaching style was not typical of many evangelists, because he pri-marily remained behind the pulpit while preaching. It was more common for preachers to move back and forth across the platform while speaking and stopping frequently to emphasize a particular point. His style delayed the discovery of what had just happened.

The evangelist noted during his message that the pulpit overlay seemed to moved slightly when he shifted positions, but he attributed it to the slight breeze coming into the auditorium and thought no more of it. He remained stationed behind the pulpit and re-positioned his preaching notes. Nearing the close of his message, he began making an appeal for anyone desiring to make a public profession of faith or re-commitment of their life to Christ to stand and make their way to the front of the auditorium. He said he and Brother Buddy would be at the front to receive them and pray with them. He asked the pianist to begin softly playing "Just As I Am." With a quick turn and move the evangelist stepped fully out from behind the pulpit, and he discovered what had occurred when he zipped up his zipper!

One of the tassels was trapped in the top of his zipper and the entire overlay with his Bible and preaching notes came flying off the pulpit. He was suddenly, fully-exposed to the congregation with the brightly colored overlay hanging down from his pants. He made several attempts at freeing the tassel, but it was so deeply embedded, it was not to be removed apart from being cut free.

Brother Buddy said he and the entire congregation were so near to breaking out into laughter that the solemnity of the invitation was gone. As the evangelist turned his back to the crowd, he continued in his efforts to free the tassel. Brother Buddy said all he knew to do at the moment was to call on the chairman of deacons seated near the front to close in prayer. At that moment, the deacon seemed less likely to break out in laughter and was, indeed, able to successfully voice a prayer.

As Brother Buddy usually said when recalling this incident, "Don't ever assume what God may do in any church service. He will have his way." God wants us to come to him with a humble and contrite heart knowing anything good we have is from his hand. (Ps 51:16, 17). I can't think of anything which would humble a preacher more than standing in front of his hearers with a brightly colored pulpit overlay hanging from the front of his pants!

173. MORE ABOUT LUAMPA MISSION HOSPITAL IN ZAMBIA

The Worldwide Mission of a Small Hospital

It should be no great surprise the countless ways God interweaves our lives with the lives of others and, in particular, with fellow believers. What we consider as coincidences or chance encounters God had planned all along to encourage us and make us know how highly he values our investment in others. When Cathy and I became acquainted with Gordon and Jeanette Jones in the 1980s, we did not envision how our friendship and association with them would connect us with so many and stretch out to involve a friendship even thirty-five years in the future.

In other pieces ("A Divine Appointment in South Africa," "Dr. Jones and the Spitting Cobra," and "An African Elephant Opens a Door"), I describe a few of the doors God has opened to Cathy and me. Until we met the Joneses when they were on furlough in El Dorado, I could not have told anyone where Zambia was located. I wasn't particularly interested in the country because we knew no one there or anyone going there. Gordon and Jeanette changed all that. They had been medical missionaries with Africa Evangelical Fellowship (AEF) in Zambia for about twenty years when we met them, and we developed an instant connection. In addition to the relationships already established, there was yet another connection to be made to Zambia, Luampa Mission Hospital, and the Joneses right here in Branson, Missouri.

About ten years ago, the Van Haitsma family joined First Baptist of Branson and began attending Sunday and Wednesday night services regularly. Their oldest daughter April, who had been a student at the College of the Ozarks, had begun a dating relationship with and finally married Corey Huddleston, the older son of my best friend, Tim, and his wife Teresa Huddleston. Before we met the Van Haitsmas, Corey and April had celebrated the birth of their first child Palmer, and Cathy and I wanted to take a gift and be introduced to Palmer. They were in the process of building their home on property immediately adjacent to April's parents, and during the interim, they were living with them. We took the gift one afternoon to Scott and Melinda's home. Scott, who is a building contractor, was not at home. Neither was Corey, who was teaching at his school when we visited. Melinda, April, and Palmer were there and welcomed us.

Their beautiful country home is in Reeds Spring, which is a fifteen-minute automobile drive from Branson. Upon arrival, we were warmly greeted and invited for a short visit in their spacious living room. Following brief introductions, Cathy asked Melinda where she and Scott were raised, thinking they might be native Missourians. She said they both were missionary kids and were raised literally "all over the world." She said Scott was raised in Zambia. This caught our attention because of our connection to the Joneses, so I asked her more questions concerning Scott. I told her the only missionaries we knew in Zambia lived and served for over thirty years in a small mission hospital in Luampa. "That's where Scott grew up!" she exclaimed. It was several weeks later when I had a conversation with Scott that I got a few more details of his connections with the Joneses and his life in Zambia.

Scott's parents were also missionaries with AEF (Africa Evangelical Fellowship), which was the sponsoring entity of the Luampa Mission Hospital in Zambia. His dad Roger was in charge of all maintenance at the hospital and served there for five years from 1975 until 1980, when they transitioned to another location. When I initially asked Gordon Jones the location of his hospital he said, "Luampa is three hundred miles out in the bush and three hundred fifty miles from the supermarket in Lusaka!" (capital city of Zambia). During most of the years I knew Gordon and Jeanette, they were with AEF, but in 1998, the organization merged with a larger organization called SIM (Sudan Interior Mission) in order to broaden its scope and outreach.

Scott spent his formative years from age nine to fourteen in Luampa, deepening his love for ministry to people who need to know Christ as Savior and Lord. He related that he enjoyed scrubbing in and assisting "Uncle Gordy" and "Aunt Evie" (Evelyn Hattan) in the operating room on many occasions and frequently went on hunting trips with Uncle Gordy to get fresh meat for the hospital patients and staff.

I am no longer amazed nor surprised when connections of acquaintances and friends are made in our Christian lives. God interweaves us with others in order to encourage and challenge us in our ministries. Cathy and I are so grateful for our friendship with and co-laborer involvement with Gordon and Jeanette Jones during those years in the 1980s and 1990s. Our life in Branson, Missouri, since 2005 has been wonderful and full of ministry. We fully anticipate God showing us many more connections with his saints he knew about all along.

PS: If you turn back to the photograph connected with another piece, "A Divine Appointment in South Africa," you'll see the Luampa Mission hospital staff in the mid-1970s. Evelyn Hattanm who provided the photo, was a registered nurse at the hospital for over twenty years. She's seen on the back row facing toward her left. Dr. Jones is on the back row next to the end on the right side. At the time of my last correspondence with Evelyn over four years ago, she had retired to Spokane, Washington to be near family. It is my understanding she has now departed this life.

174. THE MINISTRY OF FOOT CARE

The Treatment of Foot Problems Can Open Spiritual Doors

When I was a young and enthusiastic general surgeon in our hometown of El Dorado, my medical colleagues gave me several responsibilities reserved for the newest and most eager surgeon on the staff. One of these involved assisting several aging surgeons with their operative cases. One surgeon in particular had been doing major operations for over fifty years in spite of the fact he was a general practitioner and was not certified by the American Board of Surgery. His eyesight was failing, he was quite shaky with his surgical technique, and I considered him a danger to the patients who had trusted him for their surgical care for years. I resolved then I would voluntarily stop doing major surgery at a much younger age than this doctor and certainly before I became shaky and unstable. Consequently, when I was in my late fifties, I began considering a transition out of general surgery yet still maintaining an active practice in a different area.

In 1997, a company responsible for establishing wound care clinics approached me about opening such a clinic in El Dorado. In addition to providing medical treatment for the healing of chronic wounds, the clinic would provide hyperbaric, oxygen treatments to enhance the healing of certain types of wounds. I agreed to be the co-director of the clinic with one of my surgical colleagues, Dr. Moses Menendez. I spent about 10–15 percent of my practice time in wound care with the plan that one day I would transition full-time into wound care and stop providing operative surgical care.

When Cathy and I returned to Arkansas from Florida in 2000 following an eight-month adventure in opening a church-based medical clinic, we moved to Fayetteville to be near our daughter Ginny and her family. It was there I began a full-time wound care practice in the Washington Regional Wound Care Clinic. I was one of four medical directors of the clinic and the only one who didn't have a surgical practice. The nursing director and founder of the clinic was Diane Gallagher, and she was the most knowledgeable wound care nurse I have ever known. I learned a great deal of practical-treatment information from her and appreciated her compassionate care of our patients.

One of the benefits I learned early concerning wound care was that we saw our patients regularly and often. This gave me the opportunity to know each patient on a more personal level than I'd enjoyed with my surgical patients. In addition to their physical problems, patients would often open other problem areas of their lives, such as the emotional and occasionally the spiritual difficulties they had. This gave me the opportunity to witness the healing power of the Lord Jesus and to pray with the majority of them.

I worked in the Washington Regional Wound Care Clinic for five years and was offered the position as director of Skaggs Wound Care Clinic in Branson, Missouri. For Cathy and me, the attraction to Branson was that our daughter Mary Kay, her husband Dave Janke, and their daughters, Rebecca and Sara Beth, lived there. We moved to Branson in November, 2005.

Since I was the sole director of the Skaggs Clinic, I had much more freedom in the management of the clinic. Although it was not a requirement, all of the nurses and personnel of the Skaggs Clinic were committed Christians, and we considered our work a ministry and not just medical employment. Prior to beginning my service, I had asked and received permission from the hospital administrator, Bob Phillips, to pray with those patients who desired prayer. The staff of the clinic began each day with a brief devotion and prayer for our patients and for each other. We asked God to make us the eyes, ears, and hands of Jesus to minister to them. As a result, many doors of witness opportunity opened to us.

It was not unusual to observe patients praying to invite Jesus Christ into their life while being treated in our clinic. One such patient was referred to us with horrendous wounds of his feet as a result of diabetic complications. He was in great emotional distress with a fear of losing both his legs and his life. On his second clinic visit, he opened his heart to the saving power of Christ and prayed for forgiveness of his sins. There was great rejoicing by him, his wife, and our entire staff that day! We treated him twice weekly for over a year, and, although he required partial amputation of his feet, his legs were spared amputation. During each visit we discussed with him how he might grow spiritually, and we regularly prayed with him and for him.

A physician in another town once asked me how I was able to adjust to the transition of having all the responsibilities of being an "important surgeon" to just being assigned to "cutting toenails" in a wound clinic. I told him it was very easy because those toenails were attached to a very important person, and, occasionally while I was cutting the toenails, the person would allow me to witness to him. (Most of my surgical patients were asleep under anesthesia while I was working on them.)

When Jesus was in the Upper Room with his disciples on the night before his crucifixion, he offered an example of how they were to serve others. He washed their dirty, grimy feet, including those of Judas, the one who betrayed him. He told them, "As I have done for you, so should you also do to others." There is something very humbling to have someone sit at your feet and wash them.

My Bubba mentored me for twenty-five years concerning our medical practices and the spiritual skill of foot washing. It was God who gave us the desire and the skills to practice medicine to the best of our abilities, and he also commissioned us to be witnesses for him within the scope of our practice. Whether a person needs his gall bladder removed or his feet washed and his toenails trimmed, he needs the saving and healing power of the Lord Jesus. I was honored for the past forty-eight years to be an agent for the administration of all of the above.

175. THE ETERNAL BENEFITS OF A SERIOUS WOUND

God Uses a Serious Wound to Bring New Life

When one is suffering from the painful and embarrassing consequences of a non-healing wound, it is extremely difficult if not impossible to appreciate any benefits as a result. Such was the case for Alex Johnson when he presented himself for treatment at the Wound Care Center of Washington Regional Medical Center in Fayetteville, Arkansas. I was privileged to serve as one of the medical directors of this clinic during the years 2000–2005, and Mr. Johnson became one of my patients during my tenure.

Mr. Johnson was in his mid-eighties and had been seeking treatment of his lower-extremity wound for several months prior to coming to our clinic. He was brought to the clinic by his daughter, Betty Ann, and son-in-law, Eddie Bradford. When I first met him, we made a connection stronger than the usual doctor-patient relationship. He had a wonderful, sweet countenance and smile, and conversation with him was easy because of his outgoing personality. He was the kind of man whom I felt I had known for years after just one, thirty-minute patient encounter.

In the practice of wound care, it is often necessary to see the patients regularly and frequently in order to facilitate reversal of their wounding processes. Most patients with chronic wounds are middle-aged or older and have other, significant medical issues. Diabetes is a common co-morbidity and peripheral vascular disease, which is usually present and either delays or prevents a normal healing process. Mr. Johnson was dealing with both problems, and because his efforts to heal his wounds were failing, he was becoming very discouraged. Despite the circumstances and frequent medical visits, he had a gentle and cheerful spirit, and I knew whatever plan was initiated, he would be compliant.

I had never met Mr. Johnson or his family but immediately recognized his son-in-law, Eddie Bradford. Any loyal Razorback football fan who is over sixty years old remembers Eddie as an excellent football player from the early 1950s. In 1954, he played for Coach Bowden Wyatt on a team which had only twenty-five players and became known as "The 25 Little Pigs." Eddie was a starter on the offensive line, and the team was so good they won the Southwest Conference championship and played in the Cotton Bowl on January 1, 1955 against Georgia Tech. I wrote about my experience in Dallas on that New Year's Day when I was privileged to go with some friends to see the game ("A Panhandler at the Cotton Bowl").

Eddie and his wife Betty Ann love the Lord Jesus and were perceptive enough in loving Mr. Johnson to know he did not have a personal relationship with Christ. Eddie told me in a private conversation at the clinic during the initial visit that he and Betty Ann had witnessed to him "for years," but something in his belief system had prevented him from receiving and embracing Christ as Savior. Eddie said they would really appreciate any witness I might offer toward their beloved father. I began praying that God would open the door to allow his Spirit to convict Mr. Johnson.

Because of the severe nature of his wound, it was necessary to see Mr. Johnson at least once weekly, and, by the third visit, he and I had developed a strong and trusting relationship. On the second visit, I challenged him to (before I saw him again) strongly consider the truth of God's love for him, how he had created him uniquely and desired more than anything to forgive him, cleanse him, and give him a new and eternal life. I told him the full measure of God's love for him was in the well-known verse John 3:16! Whatever change took place in Alex's mind happened between his second and third visit, because on his next visit to the clinic he was totally open to the gospel. I told Alex that God had been waiting patiently to enter his life because this was the reason he had sacrificed his only Son for sinners like Alex and me. It was a gift from him, freely given to us at the costly price of Jesus Christ's death on the cross.

At this point in our conversation, Alex stopped me to ask, "On what basis do you claim all of this is true?" I said, "Alex, I'm basing everything I have told you on God's written Word, the Bible. I believe every word contained in it is the truth, and I'm staking all of my future on it!" Alex said, "I can buy that." I said, "Alex, why don't you bow your head, ask God to forgive you from your sins, enter your heart, and save you?" He said, "I would like to do that!" Alex prayed a simple prayer of faith, and God answered and entered his life and heart as he promised. The Bible says there was great rejoicing in heaven over Alex Johnson that morning!

I didn't see what took place in heaven, but I sure experienced the joy, the tears, and hugs from the Johnson and Bradford family that morning in the Wound Care Clinic. As a wound-care physician for many years, I know how difficult it is to see any benefit from a severe, life-altering wound, but when I see Alex Johnson again in glory at the feet of Jesus, I will ask him, "Was it worth it?" I can imagine his response will be something like, "Look around here and look at our Savior Jesus Christ! What do you think?"

176. FORGIVEN

A Patient Teaches Me a Life-Changing Lesson

Dr. C. E. Tommey was one of the senior surgeons of the Surgical Clinic of South Arkansas and had been in practice in El Dorado with Dr. David Yocum for almost twenty years when I joined the clinic in 1974. Dr. Bill Scurlock had joined the clinic about four years earlier than me. I learned a great many surgical techniques and practice-management skills from these wonderful men. All three were men of extraordinary character and had faithfully served the people of South Arkansas with their surgical expertise. There were several other trained surgeons in the area who were in solo practices, but their volume of work was nowhere near that of the Surgical Clinic, whose referral area extended approximately seventy miles.

A scrub nurse, while operating with him, once asked Dr. Tommey the question, "How do you keep from making mistakes in the operating room?" to which he immediately answered, "By experience." She continued, "How do you gain experience?" to which he said, "By making mistakes!" I assisted Dr. Tommey, and he assisted me on hundreds of cases over the thirty years of practice together, and I don't remember any surgical mistake he ever made in my presence.

As in life, when some mistakes are made in the operating room, there are no life-endangering consequences. However other mistakes can be extremely costly, and, unfortunately, some can lead to the death of the patient. It is one of the unspoken fears of any conscientious surgeon that they will make a deadly mistake.

Early in my practice life I made a costly surgical error which had the potential of a major law suit, but, through this painful experience, I learned the immense and life-changing lesson of forgiveness.

Andy Jameison (fictitious name) was a prominent El Dorado businessman who developed a serious and life-threatening, intra-abdominal infection. He was referred to me by his primary care physician, and an emergency operation was scheduled. Because Mr. Jameison was a large man, I asked one of my surgical partners to assist in what I knew was going to be a physically and emotionally demanding procedure. Despite being a long procedure, it went well, and Mr. Jameison began the long process of recovery and return to work. Over the following three to four weeks, he was gaining strength but had a persistent area of pain deep in his abdominal cavity. I kept reassuring him it would improve, but it did not. Finally an x-ray was made of the painful area, and it was immediately discovered I had made a serious error in the procedure. Mr. Jameison needed an immediate re-operation. He was admitted to the hospital for an operation the next morning. At this point, he knew the problem and what was required to correct it.

In terms of medical malpractice litigation, the error I made fit into the legal category of *Res ipsa loquitor,* which is interpreted as "The thing speaks for itself." These cases are always settled for the plaintiff against the doctor. It was not so much I was dreading a medical malpractice suit, but I felt badly for Mr. Jameison having to go through another operation to correct an error which I alone had made. I dreaded the pre-op visit I would have to make the evening prior to the operation.

As I entered his hospital room, Andy was alone, sitting up in bed reading a magazine, and when I came into the room, he cheerfully said, "Hi Doc. Come on in and have a seat." I said, "Andy, I am so sorry this happened, and I caused you this problem." Almost his exact words were, "Oh Doc, don't worry about it at all. I'm just glad we found out the cause, and it can be corrected!" I didn't respond, but he continued, "I know you feel badly about this, but I don't want you to give it another thought." He reached over to his night stand and gave me a small book entitled *The Greatest Thing in The World* by Henry Drummond. Andy had written a brief note to me in the fly-leaf of the book. He said, "This book has meant a lot to me in times when I have been in distress, and I think you'll enjoy it." As I reached over to take the book from his hand, I tearfully said, "Andy, you'll never know how much this means to me in your forgiving me for this situation. I will never forget it."

The operation the next morning fully corrected the problem, and Andy healed quickly with no further complications. He was able to return to work within six weeks. His hospital bill and surgical fees for the second procedure were fully forgiven. As a result of this incident, the hospital instituted a new operating room policy which prevented future problems of this nature.

Andy could have significantly altered my future surgical practice had he been vindictive in his attitude toward me. Instead, he chose to forgive me for my error. He taught me, my immediate family, and everyone associated with this event the immense and life-changing value of forgiving those who have harmed you. What I didn't know about Andy's forgiveness until much later was that he told his family the night before the second operation, "If I don't make it through this procedure, I don't want any of you bringing legal action against Dr. Moore. He saved my life with the first operation."

Andy Jameison is in glory now, and his earthly lesson continues to live in my heart. How could I ever fail to forgive anyone who hurt me in any way when I have been forgiven so much? (Matt 18:21–35)

177. THE HIGH COST OF PEACE AND CONTENTMENT

The Greatest Blessings Come at a High Cost

Spiritual lessons are best learned in the crucible of life, and many if not most are painful and difficult. The Apostle Paul in his letter to the Philippian church told them that the contentment and joy he experienced while incarcerated in the Roman prison was learned by having a lot (of stuff) and then having nothing. In a culture which today measures success and happiness by the amount of stuff one has, Paul's formula for contentment is often rejected as foolish (Phil 4:11–13). During the time Cathy and I were dealing with plans for retirement and thoughts related to how much money we might need, I met an unusual person with a serious medical problem. I was about to learn a wonderful lesson on peace and contentment.

A lady who was in her eighties was brought by her daughter to the Wound Care Clinic seeking advice and treatment for problems with her lower extremities. Both ladies were very polite in their demeanor and pleasant in their personalities. They spoke with considerable accents, but their English was excellent. My first question to most people whom I meet in Branson is, "Where did you come from?" Their answer was often, "We moved from California." I didn't doubt their truthfulness but asked, "Are you originally from California?" knowing their accents were not Californian! "No, we lived most of our lives in Zimbabwe." I had never met anyone in the states from Zimbabwe, but I had conversations with a few pastors from that southern African country while on two separate mission trips to South Africa in 1999 and 2003.

My next question to them was, "What caused you to move from Zimbabwe to California?" thinking perhaps they had children living there and wanted to be closer. What they told me shocked and deeply saddened me.

In the early 1980s, the nation of Zimbabwe was undergoing tremendous political upheaval. There was a revolution for control to take back farmland owned and controlled by whites for many years. The leader of the revolution was Robert Mugabe, a fierce guerrilla fighter. When his forces prevailed and he became president, he began a massive land reform by which the beautiful and productive farms owned by whites were nationalized and turned over to native Zimbabweans. In previous years the farms were so bountiful that the country was known as "the breadbasket of Africa."

One fateful morning with no warning, an armed militant group appeared at the door of their farm and also the door of their daughter and son-in-law's adjacent farm. They demanded both families immediately evacuate their homes and farms by order of the new government of Zimbabwe, and each was presented some official-looking papers which seemed to validate their demands. They were told they could take the clothes they were wearing and a few valuable possessions they could individually carry. The shock and horror of such news caused such immediate, emotional reactions the son-in-law of my patient suffered a heart attack and died the same afternoon.

In recounting the events of that painful day, I could tell it was still difficult for them to relive those experiences, so I stopped asking questions. Despite their great losses, I did not discern lingering bitterness or hatred in either of them. They had both seen their lives rebuilt and redirected through God's power. Following their move to California, my patient's husband lived another ten years and died when he was in his late seventies from a chronic medical problem. The daughter had remarried a few years prior to her father's death. Her husband was originally from Southwest Missouri, and the family decided to move here to build a new life. They were both active in a strong, local, evangelical church and were sharing the love of Christ through the church's ministries and in their personal walk.

Since the day I heard their story, I have often wondered how I would handle similar circumstances. None of us is immune to sudden, cataclysmic life changes upon receiving bad news, but no one really knows how they will respond—to the unexpected appearance of a law enforcement officer at your front door at 3:00 a.m. to tell of a fatal car accident, the phone call from the doctor's nurse telling you the doctor needs to see you immediately for your biopsy results, or the early morning appearance of armed, government officials on your farm banging on your front door. While there is still calm weather with clear skies, I must be refreshed and reassured by God's unchanging Word to know he alone is sovereign and nothing catches him by surprise. He has promised that "though I walk through the valley of the shadow of death, He is with me; His rod and staff will comfort me" (Ps 23). He has said that in the midst of any storm, "I will give you beauty for ashes, the oil of joy for mourning and the garment of praise for the spirit of heaviness that you might be called a tree of righteousness, the planting of the Lord that He might be glorified" (Isa 61:3).

That morning in my medical clinic I met two trees of righteousness who witnessed to me the reality of God's promises to them, and, in my hearing and observing, God was greatly glorified.

PS: Tragically for the country of Zimbabwe, many of those lush farms which were nationalized during the 1980s were poorly managed and maintained by inexperienced and ill-trained farmers. A large number are no longer productive and have been abandoned.

178. OBSERVING A BRIS MILA

A Baptist Doctor at a Jewish Ceremony

As a general surgeon with forty-five years' experience of observing and performing thousands of operations, the most interesting by far was as an observer at a Jewish circumcision. While stationed at Moody Air Force Base in Valdosta, Georgia, as the only surgeon on the base from 1969 to 1971, I was responsible for all the surgical procedures done at the base. I was fresh out of surgical training at Charity Hospital in New Orleans and eager to apply my newly acquired skills where needed.

Not long after my arrival, the lone internist (internal medicine specialist) on the base, Dr. Steve Zaron, asked if I would be interested in observing the circumcision of his newborn son. I knew that the spiritual importance of circumcision for the Jews dated back to Abraham, as recorded in the Old Testament in Genesis 17:10–14. He was instructed to be circumcised along with all Jewish men as a covenant sign of their faith in the Lord God Almighty. According to God's commandment, all newborn males were to be circumcised on the eighth day of life.

I readily accepted Dr. Zaron's invitation to be present at the ceremony of his son's circumcision. Any Jewish ceremony requires ten men of Jewish faith to be present, and, since there were not ten Jewish men at Moody AFB, Dr. Zaron said I could stand in as a Jew despite being a Southern Baptist. I had been baptized in a Southern Baptist church as a pre-teen, but in those Air Force days, Cathy and I were only occasional attenders of the First Methodist Church in Valdosta. My only requirement for attendance was to wear the Jewish skullcap, the yarmulke. After he arrived, the rabbi who performed the ceremony joked with me about a Baptist's wearing a skullcap saying, "Don't worry about it Doctor. We only ask for you to give $1,000 to the National Jewish Appeal!" At this time in our life, Cathy and I didn't have even $100 in our savings account, so I was grateful he was only joking!

The Rabbi invited by the Zarons was from the synagogue in Jacksonville, Florida, which was about ninety miles from Valdosta. Because there were only eight to ten Jewish families in Valdosta at the time, most of them traveled to Jacksonville to worship and be present for special Jewish ceremonies. I don't recall the rabbi's name, but he was elderly (approximately seventy-five years old), and I remember he had been in Jacksonville for nearly fifty years. The other things I remember about him were that he was forgetful of names and had a visible tremor in his hands. As I think about his physical signs now, he probably had Parkinson's Disease. I was curious and a little concerned about his skill and ability to perform such a delicate procedure on a tiny, eight-day-old infant. Dr. Zaron obviously knew the rabbi well, because he joked with him saying, "We have Dr. Moore here as a surgical observer to make sure you do the procedure correctly." To which the Rabbi responded to me, "Don't worry yourself Doctor. I have done thousands of these!"

A Rabbi who does circumcisions is called a *mohel* (pronounced "moil"), and the ceremony is called *Bris Mila*, or *Bris*. I was curious about his instruments, and, before he began, he showed me a beautiful, cherrywood box, which was velvet lined. There were two instruments in the box; one was a surgical C-clamp, and the other was a beautiful, ceremonial knife, which appeared to be fourteen to sixteen inches in length and very sharp. Both appeared to be stainless steel and neither was pre-sterilized.

With some preliminary remarks by both Dr. Zaron and then the rabbi, the ten men gathered around the baby. Dr. Zaron sat in a comfortable chair and held his son in his arms. The Rabbi stood while preparing the baby for the procedure by cleansing him with some type of fluid. All the while, he was speaking in Hebrew, which I could not understand, but the other men who were Jewish seemed to know exactly what he was saying. I do know that when he was to speak the baby's Jewish name, he kept forgetting it, and Dr. Zaron had to correct him. The rabbi was not in the least perturbed by his memory lapses as if this was common for him.

As I watched over the next five minutes and observed the rabbi's shakiness and heard his memory lapses, I became more anxious that my surgical services might well be needed before this afternoon was over. The baby had been lightly sedated with a nipple which had a wine-soaked cotton ball inside, and he was perfectly happy with everything taking place. With a deftness of hand, the Rabbi then applied the C-clamp across the foreskin making certain only skin was in the clamp. This was the only time the baby whimpered a little with pain. Several more statements by the rabbi were made in Hebrew as well as several mentions of the baby's name, which had to be corrected. Then the rabbi took the knife and, with a very swift motion, he excised the protruding foreskin without the baby's even making the slightest motion or even crying out in pain. I think I winced more than the baby!

Following a few more remarks by the rabbi, he removed the C-clamp and I leaned over to look at the surgical site. To say I was shocked would be an understatement because the result was the most perfect circumcision I have ever seen! There was not even one drop of blood, and young son Zaron seemed to be as happy as he could be. I was extremely happy my surgical expertise was not needed.

Following the Bris was a celebration which, in addition to the men present, included the baby's mother and the wives of the men present. There was an abundance of delicious food and alcoholic beverages, none of which I drank. Young son Zaron seemed perfectly content to have his baby bottle of milk, which I assumed contained no wine!

In considering why a Bris is done on the eighth day following birth, it is a medical fact that in a newborn, the amount of Vitamin K is the highest on the eighth day and only minimally present at birth. Vitamin K is essential for blood clotting, and, prior to all circumcisions done today (which is the day after birth), the babies are given an injection of Vitamin K. God knew injectable Vitamin K was not available in Abraham's day.

After my experience that afternoon, whenever I did a circumcision, whether on a newborn or an adult, I thought about and longed for the instruments used by the rabbi. For certain the procedure and methods I used were not at all similar to what I observed. I also know for certain I knew the names of my patients.

179. OBSTETRICAL CARE AT FBC DALLAS

Providing Care During the Sermon

After becoming believers in the late 1970s, Cathy and I heard many stories of great faith from First Baptist Church of Dallas under the leadership of Dr. W. A. Criswell. We occasionally visited Dallas for various reasons, but were never in a position to attend a worship service there together. The opportunity to attend worship there opened to me in a very unusual way.

In the mid 1980s, our son John Aaron and I had the opportunity to travel to Dallas with my friend, Gary Hegi, and two sons to attend a Dallas Mavericks basketball game. They were playing the Milwaukee Bucks, and our favorite former Razorback player Sidney Moncrief was the star of the Bucks. Our friend, Gary Braswell, who lived in Dallas, obtained the tickets for us to all go together, and he brought his son with him to the game. One of the things I remember about the game was that our seats were so high in the upper deck I couldn't even make out the numbers on the players' shirts. I had to pick out which one was Sidney by the way he was playing and the fact he was the star and scoring leader of the team. I do remember that the Bucks won the game, but I don't remember anything else about the game statistics. It was just fun to all be together for this father-son outing in Dallas. Our hotel reservations were at the Wyndham Hotel, and this was an added treat because it is such a beautiful property with outstanding amenities.

The game was over late Saturday night, and we all stayed up late into the early morning hours of Sunday. Our plan was to have a late lunch and then travel back to El Dorado in mid-afternoon. As was my usual routine, I awakened by 5:00 a.m. and prepared myself some coffee in the room that John Aaron and I shared. During my quiet-time meditation, I thought it would be fun if all of us would attend worship at First Baptist Dallas, but this had not been a part of our initial plans for this Dallas trip. I discovered there was a 10:00 a.m. worship service which would be perfect for us so we could have lunch at the usual time and still leave Dallas as planned.

At approximately 8:00 a.m., I began making my plans known to everyone, but they fell on very sleepy ears. No one wanted to go to church on this day and especially at such an early hour. I also considered staying at the hotel with everyone, but the more I thought about it, this was an excellent opportunity for me to hear Dr. Criswell preach. I started getting ready and decided it would be easier to get a taxi and be taken directly to the church without having to worry about directions, traffic, and parking.

I left the hotel at approximately 8:45 in order to have plenty of time to look around the church and perhaps get an opportunity to meet Dr. Criswell. When I arrived, there was a worship service in progress, so I had enough wait time to walk around the church campus in a brief and informal tour. The church was extremely impressive in its size and obvious place in Southern Baptist church history.

I decided to sit near the back and close to an exit door so I wouldn't get caught in a traffic jam at service end. Then I'd be able to quickly catch a cab back to the hotel. Dr. Criswell announced that his sermon had twelve points, and he had only been able to get to eight of them during the earlier service. He was determined during this hour to "get to all twelve points!" There were lots of "Amens" when he said it and not too many groans, so I settled in for a long but exciting sermon.

About midway through his message, I noted some unusual activity by several people in a pew to my left and about four rows ahead. Two people were standing and seemingly ministering to another individual. This activity continued for at least a minute when I saw the person to whom they were ministering. It was a woman who was approximately thirty years old, obviously pregnant, and appearing near term. The people assisted her in standing up and, with great effort, helped her walk to the exit door directly behind me. As she passed, I could tell she was in distress and close to fainting, but Dr. Criswell who saw what was happening kept on preaching his twelve-point sermon.

As they exited the door, I decided to offer my assistance, because the people with her had a confused and distraught look. Just as I exited, a man who was a deacon came through the door toward me and, with a wide-eyed look, asked, "Are you a doctor?" When I said I was he said, "She's about to have a baby!" They had her sitting in a chair in the foyer of this side entrance and were holding her up so she wouldn't slide out onto the floor. This deacon was grateful to turn her care over to me since obstetrical care had not been part of his orientation. I have to admit my excitement at this point thinking that I was going to deliver a baby right here in the hall of First Baptist Church, even before Dr. Criswell finished the twelve points of his sermon!

After I asked her a few questions and did a brief abdominal exam, I determined she was in the early stages of labor in her second pregnancy. She acknowledged she thought it would be at least another hour before she delivered, giving us enough time to get an ambulance to the church. The ambulance was called, and I remained with her to calm her until they arrived about ten minutes later. I was relieved in one respect for the lady's safety but disappointed to have not been part of the first delivery at First Baptist Dallas, not the sinful kind but the obstetrical. I couldn't wait to get back to the hotel to tell the guys what they missed while they slept. I really don't think they were impressed, or sorry they had not gone with me.

180. FROM A USED CAR LOT TO HEAVEN

An Unusual Place of Revival and Spiritual Growth

Used car salesmen have not always received the best reviews when ratings of public esteem are assigned to the various professions. Prior to meeting Gerald House, I had no personal experience with either buying or selling used cars, so I could not relate to some of the unkind things or jokes which were said about their profession. My friendship with Gerald changed my attitude about judging someone based on the type of work he does.

Gerald was a natural-born salesman. He never met a stranger and seemed to be comfortable in every environment from an executive board-room to a sale barn. He owned and operated a well-known used car dealership in my hometown, so he was easy to find when I began shopping for an inexpensive, low-mileage vehicle for our teenage son. "Come on in, Doc," he said when I introduced myself and told him my need, "Let's find you just what you need for your boy!" At that point, I knew he would find the right car or at least make me think he had. The one thing which attracted me to Gerald was his ongoing conversation about the things of the Lord. He knew I was a member of a sister Baptist church, but he did not know initially I was passionate in my desire to walk by faith and hungry for Christian fellowship. There was an immediate and eternal bond forged between us, and the bond was Christ.

I learned that Gerald's car lot was his mission field, and everyone who set foot on the lot became a prospect either for salvation or spiritual growth. It didn't matter to Gerald if you were a "dignified physician," which is the way he would teasingly identify me to some of his customers, or if you were unemployed. Most of his customers were plain and simple folk, and Gerald knew how to speak their language. Over the next several weeks while I continued shopping at his lot for the right vehicle, I witnessed his unique techniques for sharing the gospel. I happened to be present one afternoon when a man who "just happened" to stop at the lot came under conviction of his need and prayed to receive Christ's free gift of salvation.

Even after I purchased the vehicle we needed, I spent a few hours of every free Wednesday afternoon at his lot observing and learning the "House" techniques of evangelism. Gerald had a unique way of identifying each of the regular attenders at his lot. After a person had been there two or three times, he was given a nickname or an identifying phrase. Most often when I walked into his office, which was usually filled with four or five men, he would say, "Look, here comes Dr. Moore—all flash and no cash!" I never really knew exactly what he meant but accepted it as his way of saying, "I'm glad to see you. Come on in and take a seat!"

One particular Saturday afternoon while I was at home watching an exciting Razorback football game on TV, the phone rang, and Gerald asked if I "had any more of those pocket Bibles in the glove compartment of your car?" He said he was witnessing to a man and had run out and needed one. I told him I did, but could I wait until half-time of the game to bring it? He said, "I guess that'll be all right." Over the next few minutes, the Spirit convicted me to leave the football game and do something much more important. With some grumbling and complaining in my spirit, I drove the seven or eight minutes to his lot to deliver the Bible.

Upon arrival and prior to parking, I heard the sounds of shouting and laughter inside the office and was not prepared for my next "House experience." As I opened the door to the office, a very large black man had picked Gerald up off the floor and was twirling him around while shouting and chanting, "Thank you, Jesus, thank you Jesus, thank you Jesus!" Gerald seemed to be crying and laughing at the same time but had the presence of mind to say to James, "There's Dr. Moore. Grab him!"

James immediately loosed Gerald, lifted me, and began twirling me with his brawny arms while continuing his shouting to Jesus. When Gerald could control himself, he said James had just prayed to receive Christ as his Savior and was rejoicing since "he was now sure he was going to heaven one day." I had learned not to be shocked by anything which occurred at Gerald's used car lot. My grumbling and complaining had quickly vanished and was replaced with a spirit of thanksgiving, even before James put me down!

It was perhaps a year later I received a phone call from Nell, Gerald's wife of thirty-five years. The call was late in the evening on another Saturday, and Nell said these words: "Gerald just died." Certain she was in on another of his pranks, I said, "Come on Nell, what's the old boy up to now?" She said, "No, I'm serious, Gerald just drove down to the lot, and when he got there, he slumped over the wheel and his heart must have stopped." I was in total shock just like Nell.

We buried his remains a few days later, but his funeral was not a concession of defeat but rather a celebration of victory. Whenever I drive past the used car lot now my mind is flooded with many wonderful remembrances of spiritual battles which were fought and won there. In the process of learning, witnessing, laughing, and crying at that place, I know my spiritual life enlarged while having the time of my life. I don't know the current spiritual atmosphere of the lot, but I can attest to the fact there was once a time when the Spirit of Christ embodied in my pal Gerald House walked and worked at that used car lot. Many souls received Christ as Savior and heaven as their reward right there. It is only fitting on Gerald's last trip to his lot that Saturday evening, he stopped his car, bowed his head, and stepped into the physical presence of his Lord and Savior Jesus Christ.

181. SEEING AND EXPERIENCING GOD'S PROVISION

Seeing God Through Eyes of Faith

For the past twelve years of operation of the Free Medical Clinic of the Ozarks (FMCO), I have been continually thankful for God's provision and the many ways he has demonstrated he is always on time with just the right resource!

In the beginning when the founders and board members of the clinic were considering the extent of the monthly expenditures, we were praying for God's direction in supplying our needs. Because all who served the clinic were volunteers, including the doctors and nurses, our overhead costs were nowhere near those of a private clinic. Nevertheless, there were expenses for monthly rent, utilities, insurance, equipment needs, and office supplies in addition to the cost of the medications, which were to be at no cost to the patients. Initially we had no idea whether we might be involved in fundraising efforts, which all of the non-profit organizations in Branson found needful. Several local churches pledged monthly support, and a few individuals who understood the magnitude of the ministry gave sacrificially.

In previous posts I have testified to God's on-time provisions. These have included Skaggs Community Hospital's providing us with our present beautiful clinic in 2012 at no cost and the ongoing use of the Patient Assistance Program (PAP), which provides medicines at no cost for most of our patients. The company which provides our weekly maintenance is Brokate Janitorial from Springfield, Missouri, and the owner Jeremy Brokate came to me in mid-2013 with the offer they would love to provide their services at no cost! There have been other instances in which God sent just the right person at just the right time to supply just what we needed.

One regular individual financial contributor from Sacramento, California has been sending a generous monthly check in honor of her father who died in 2012. He had been an integral part of the start-up of the clinic, and she has been contributing since 2013 without missing a month in her support of FMCO.

About four years ago, a local optometrist, Dr. Kevin Umbright, was in my office discussing the possibility of his volunteering his time and skills to the ministry of FMCO. We talked about how we might secure the much-needed but costly equipment for eye exams. There was discussion also about the provision of eyeglasses for those needing them and where we might obtain good but low-cost eyewear. He said the cost for used eye-exam equipment might be in the range of five to ten thousand dollars. I told him that I was not anxious about such a high cost, because we had learned though experience that God has always provided for our needs, and his provision arrived about the time we knew of the need. He nodded his head in agreement, and we both prayed right then that God would make it clear how we should proceed.

As we were talking and praying, the monthly envelope from our Sacramento donor containing what I assumed to be her regular monthly contribution was lying in my desk drawer unopened. It had arrived the day before, and I intended to deposit it later in the day after our visit. When Dr. Umbright left, I removed the envelope from my desk, and, upon opening it, noticed there was also an accompanying letter. There had never been a letter with any of her previous checks. I thought she might be notifying us she was no longer able to continue the support, so I took it out to read before looking at the check.

The typed letter had some introductory salutations which were personal, and then she stated she had recently sold some family property in Arkansas and wanted to donate part of the proceeds of the sale in honor of her father. There was this statement in her letter, "I think Mom and Dad would be pleased." The check was for $10,000, which was the largest single contribution ever given to FMCO!

I bowed my head in gratitude and, through tears, thanked our Heavenly Father who had once again demonstrated his on-time provision for the ministry he had begun nine years previously. I immediately called Dr. Umbright, who was still driving home, to report that our prayer for the equipment had been answered, and the provision had been sent even before we ever prayed.

182. "DR. JOHN, THIS IS LILLIAN"

A Former Caregiver Becomes a Beloved Patient and Friend

Lillian Thompson

Over the thirty years I practiced medicine and surgery in El Dorado, I had the privilege of serving thousands of people in the town and the surrounding communities. God opened doors of opportunity which extended far beyond the technical aspect of performing countless thousands of surgical procedures. My brother, Berry Lee (Bubba), encouraged me in the ministry Christ had given me within the medical practice and helped me better understand some of the reasons God had placed me there.

When Cathy and I had the spiritual change in our lives which occurred six years after beginning the practice, I began viewing each patient encounter as a divine appointment. Those appointments included people who needed not only physical healing, but also prayer, encouragement, counsel, challenge, and, in some cases, rebuke. There were some who were dead in their sins and needed a Savior. Some of the patients whom God appointed to my surgical care I am certain he sent for encouragement and as a challenge to me. One of those blessed saints he sent many years ago is a lady named Lillian Thompson.

When I first met Lillian as a patient, she was in her mid-sixties and had a problem she feared was malignant. A relatively minor surgical procedure proved the problem was not malignant, and this greatly relieved her anxiety. Because Lillian was forthright in her personality and not intimidated by white coats, I got to know her quickly and immediately in connection with her outgoing Christian witness. She had a distinctive phone voice, and, when she called, she would say, "Dr. John, this is Lill'-ian!" I was never in doubt over which Lillian I was speaking to. I looked forward to her calls, because they were usually about someone else's problem or a particular need for her church.

Lillian moved to El Dorado in 1940 and was married the same year to her husband, L. G. He was a hard-working man who provided well for his family. He worked faithfully for Andrews Funeral Home for many years assisting in the preparation and burial of people who entrusted their final arrangements to their care. L. G. and Lillian had no children of their own, but they took a nephew of Lillian into their home when he was five years old and raised him into adulthood as if he were their son. Lillian poured her life and energy into numerous nephews and nieces through the years and provided needed clothes, food, and money as she was able. L. G. lived until 1999 and departed this life one year prior to their fiftieth wedding anniversary.

Early in our friendship, I learned Lillian was very loyal to St. John's Missionary Baptist Church, in which she was a charter member. She was one of the primary fund raisers for improvements in the building and the ongoing ministries of the church. She was never shy about asking her friends and acquaintances to help with the financial obligations of her church, because everyone knew how much she gave of herself for the welfare of the church. She was continually visiting needy church members either in their homes or in the hospital, and her ministry to the church was not unlike one of a deacon. I greatly admired this quality in her.

In a recent conversation, Lillian told me years ago when I was a small boy she assisted Lillian Singleton in cleaning our home and working for Pop ("Kisses From Lillian"). I have previously written about the impact Lillian Singleton had on our family during the years of adjustment in our lives when Mimi, my birth mother, died of breast cancer. The two Lillians lived within a few blocks of each other. I was not aware of any these facts, and, in the same conversation, Lillian said, "I have loved you, your brother, and sister since then."

When Bubba was in his final illness, Lillian included him in the large number of people to whom she was ministering. He had been providing total home care for his wife, LaNell, for the ten years of her struggle with progressive dementia and was doing the majority of cooking for the two of them. When I would visit with him by phone, he would tell me he had lost his appetite by eating his own cooking. His comment was, "If you want to lose weight, just start cooking for yourself. Everything will taste like cardboard." Over the course of a year or so, Bubba must have lost twenty-five pounds. Lillian would tell me when she called, "Your brother is not looking good, so I cooked him some greens and cornbread which he loves." I told her how much I appreciated her doing this for him, and her response would usually be, "I just love your brother; he is a good man; he is a Christian. Did you hear what I said? He is a Christian!" Several times I asked her how many other people for whom she was cooking, and she would never answer. I always suspected she had five or six others for whom she regularly cooked greens and cornbread.

Lillian recently celebrated her ninety-sixth birthday and, by her account, had a "house-full of company" (nieces and nephews from out of town)) who stayed for more than a week. Lillian probably cooked the majority of meals while they were there. The photo above was taken recently, and it is not difficult to see that usual twinkle in her eyes. When I called to congratulate her on making ninety-six years, I asked how she was feeling, to which she quickly responded, "I'm doin' pretty good, Dr. John. How you feelin'? Are you taking care of yourself and are you eating right?" Her responses like this one usually made me ask myself if I was concerned as Lillian about the welfare of others.

I have been studying Jesus's account of the final judgment concerning the sheep and the goats recorded in Matthew 25:31–46. He told the sheep on his right hand to come into his Kingdom because they had fed him, given him drink, taken him into their homes, clothed him, visited him when he was sick, and ministered to him in prison. They asked when they had done that for him and he said, "When you have done it to the least of my brethren, you have done it to Me." Lillian has spent most of her life doing for the least of his brethren, and she will be greatly rewarded.

PS: Since writing this account of my friend Lillian, she departed this life on December 9, 2020, while living with her niece in San Antonio, Texas. She had moved there a year earlier because of progressive deterioration in her health. I called and spoke with her by telephone on a number of occasions before her death, and she was always cheerful and upbeat. She always asked me, "How you feelin' Dr. John? And how's your beautiful wife?" She was three months shy of her hundred and third birthday when she departed. When she came into the presence of her Savior and Lord Jesus Christ she heard Him say, "Well done my good and faithful servant. Enter now into your rest with Me!"

183. THE PRAIRIE GROVE REVIVAL

My Brother and I Are Invited to Conduct a Revival

REVIVAL

NOVEMBER 16-19

7:00 p.m. NIGHTLY

SUNDAY 11:00 a.m.

BERRY LEE MOORE, JR.
General Practitioner
Deacon

JOHN HENRY MOORE
Surgeon
Deacon

Prairie Grove Revival Poster

Brother Tommy Freeman has been a wonderful friend and Christian brother since the late 1970s. We had known about each other as kids playing baseball in the summers at the El Dorado Boys Club, but because he was two years older, we never played on the same team. Our current friendship began on the evening I gave the commencement address to the graduating nurses of Warner Brown School of Nursing in 1978. Brother Tommy's sister Ann, whom I didn't know at the time, was a member of the class, and Brother Tommy and wife Joyce were there. Joyce (Hawkins) Freeman was in my high school graduating class of 1957, so, at the time, I knew her much better than her husband.

As part of my talk, I exhorted the nurses to use their new profession as a means to share the gospel with their patients and not be intimidated, afraid, or ashamed. I firmly believe the Lord Jesus has commanded us to be witnesses for him in whatever position or profession we find ourselves. Patients who are seriously ill and may be facing long-term disability or even death need to know they have a Savior who loves them, and he is able to heal them of all their diseases (Ps 103).

After the ceremony, Brother Tommy and Joyce spoke with me, saying he was so glad to know a medical doctor who would witness to his patients and encourage those working with him to do the same. He asked if I ever spoke in churches, and I said I had spoken in a few in the El Dorado area. He said he was pastor of the First Baptist Church of Keo, which is in Southeast Arkansas between Pine Bluff and Little Rock, and he would like to arrange a convenient date for me to preach in his church. The date was set for the following month.

The weekend Cathy and I spent with Brother Tommy and Joyce in Keo began a lifelong friendship between our family and the Freemans. He invited me to preach and teach Bible studies in every subsequent church he pastored. We attended Bible conferences together and worked together during Christian Focus Week at Ouachita Baptist University in Arkadelphia. For a number of years, we spoke by phone every few weeks, and he would ask questions about my teachings in the Sunday school class and what new churches had invited me to speak. Without fail he would ask, "How many people have you led to the Lord since we last talked?" During this period, Brother Tommy was one of my greatest spiritual encouragers apart from Cathy. Among men he rivaled my brother Berry Lee and was certainly more of a mentor than my own pastor at the time.

In 1980, Brother Tommy was called to pastor the First Baptist Church in Prairie Grove, Arkansas. This town, though larger than Keo, was a small municipality in Northwest Arkansas, about ten miles from Fayetteville. All of this part of the state was in the midst of a population growth and economic boom due to the three industrial giants headquartered there—Walmart, Tyson Foods, and J B Hunt Trucking Company.

In mid-summer he called and said he had a ministry proposal for Berry Lee and me and wanted our opinions. He wanted to schedule a lay revival in the fall with both Berry Lee and me preaching and leading. The revival would begin on Sunday morning and extend through Wednesday evening. There would be two services on Sunday, one in the morning and one in the evening. Then there would be evening services on Monday through Wednesday. Berry Lee (Bubba) and I had never done anything like this, but, after committing it to prayer, we believed this was God's will for us. We agreed that Bubba would preach the Sunday noon service, and I would preach the evening services from Sunday through Wednesday. We called Brother Tommy and the date was set for November 16–19, 1980.

For the Sunday noon service, the church was full, and I remember Bubba's preaching a particularly excellent salvation message followed by an invitation for salvation and church membership. There were two people, a teenager and a middle-aged man, who repented, asked for forgiveness, and invited Jesus to save them. There was great rejoicing in the church as these men had been the recipients of witnessing both by Brother Tommy and their families. Brother Tommy, Bubba, and I agreed that had this been the only visible fruit of the revival, our meager efforts had been well spent.

Following a delicious meal with Brother Tommy and Joyce in their home, Bubba left Prairie Grove and returned home. I began my series of evening messages that Sunday night on the subject, "What is a Church in Revival."

Early Monday morning following breakfast, Brother Tommy had scheduled us to begin visitation, and did we ever visit! Typical of his entire ministry, Brother Tommy's goal was always to meet and know everyone in his community. For this revival, I believe his goal was that I meet and shake hands with every citizen in Prairie Grove, and I'm convinced that before the revival ended on Wednesday evening, we had accomplished his goal. We even visited the lone physician in town at his office.

He was a young family doctor with a very active practice but had some unusual personal beliefs. First, his dress was unusual for this time period because he wore bib overalls under his white coat. I was accustomed to the dress culture of the doctors in El Dorado, who wore coats and ties in their practice. More significantly, he said he was raised by a preacher father, but while he was in college, he rejected the teachings of the church and embraced Daoism. I had no idea what he was talking about, so I couldn't discuss with any intelligence his new-found religion. Later I discovered this was an ancient Chinese philosophical belief system in which believers were to live at peace and in love with everyone. Heaven was achieved for each person by living a loving life. The doctor respectfully declined our invitation to the revival, stating there would be nothing offered or said which he had not heard before.

Throughout the experience of this laymen's revival, I gained a new perspective on the hard but rewarding work of pastors of small country churches. Brother Tommy in my opinion epitomized what a pastor should be and how he should love and shepherd the flock given to him by God. Because he was poured out to all for the sake of the gospel, he was greatly loved in the churches and communities he served. I love him as a brother, a mentor, and one of my best encouragers. He not only tolerated my attempts at preaching, but, regardless of the quality of the content and the style of my delivery, he would always say at the close of a service, "Good job, John Henry!"

184. SPIRITUALITY AND HEALING

The Spiritual Ministry of Healing

In May 2000, Cathy and I joyfully packed our belongings in Clearwater, Florida and moved to Fayetteville, Arkansas. We had been in Florida for eight months, having accepted a position as director of the Indian Rocks

Medical Clinic, which was a ministry of First Baptist Church of Indian Rocks. I soon discovered the clinic position was the wrong fit for my skill set, so we decided to move back to Arkansas.

On arrival in Fayetteville, I interviewed for and accepted the offer to become one of four medical directors of the Wound Care Clinic of Washington Regional Medical Center. This was to be my first experience in full-time wound care having been a general surgeon for thirty-five years, doing wound care and hyperbaric medicine only as a secondary profession. The other three directors were actively practicing general surgeons.

The nursing director of the clinic was Diana Gallagher RN, who was very knowledgeable in the field and well-respected by her peers in the nursing and wound care field. I learned the general protocol of the hospital from her and others while learning specific wound care principles and the multitude of wound-dressing usages from her experience. She was a very able teacher while managing the clinic in a firm but caring manner.

The hospital administration had given me permission to continue praying with patients when appropriate and did not object to my engaging patients in spiritual conversations. To my knowledge, no other physician had interacted in this manner with patients in this clinic. My impression after about six months was that most of the nurses encouraged and appreciated what I was doing while a very few were skeptical and perhaps even a little turned off. However, no one was openly critical towards me.

In my second year as director, I was invited by Mrs. Gallagher to speak in a conference for which she was the leader. It was to be held in Tulsa, Oklahoma. The conference was sponsored by the South-Central Region of the Wound, Ostomy, and Continence Nurses, and she asked me to speak on "Spirituality and Healing." I prepared for several months utilizing information from scientific journals, anecdotal stories concerning specific miraculous healings, and personal experiences from my lengthy surgical career.

Several days prior to the conference, I began having symptoms of an upper-respiratory-tract infection, and I developed chills and fever. I knew Diana was counting on me for the presentation, and I was not going to cancel unless I was unable to speak. Cathy drove the two hours to Tulsa allowing me to rest as much as possible. My part on the program was in the early afternoon. Despite having fever and a very hoarse voice, I was able to deliver the forty-five minute speech, but I don't remember much about the details of the event.

In my speech, I attempted to answer four general questions regarding faith and healing: 1) Is God actively involved in healing today or is healing a natural process which was activated in the beginning? 2) What role does faith play in healing? 3) How is personal faith mobilized to activate healing?

and 4) What should be my role as a health care provider in the process? I tried to interweave examples of healing from both the Old and New Testaments with contemporary examples of healings I had eye-witnessed.

In my research, I discovered that the New Testament contained more than seventy-five references of the healing work of Jesus. The four Gospels record some but not all of the instances of healings by Christ and comprise a major part of his ministry on earth. In many examples of healing, Jesus said to the one healed, "Your faith has made you well." A great deal of data published in current scientific journals shows that people of faith have fewer illnesses and recover faster from serious illnesses with fewer complications than people who profess no religious affiliations.

It was interesting for me to find a journal article from Johns Hopkins University concerning church attendance and health. In a study involving over ninety thousand people in Washington County, Maryland, we learn that if people attend church one or more times per week, they have a lower death rate from coronary artery disease, emphysema, cirrhosis, and suicide. Another study from Dartmouth Medical School concluded the survival rate in elderly people undergoing open-heart surgery is three times greater in regular church attenders than non-church attenders.

Modern science has only recently acknowledged the therapeutic benefits of prayer in healing. One of the first articles published on the matter in a recognized medical periodical was in 1988 in the Southern Medical Journal. In it, Dr. Randolph Byrd concluded that three hundred ninety-three heart patients in an ICU who had intercessory prayer over them had fewer complications, required less medication, and had fewer deaths. Skeptics of his study and similar papers maintained there was no way to gauge the extent of prayer offered and the same results could have been achieved by chance. Those who are opposed to any positive effects of faith in healing will never be convinced otherwise. The Bible says, "Their eyes have been blinded by the God of this world" (2 Cor 4:3, 4).

In concluding the presentation, I challenged the attendees to consider their own beliefs in the Lord Jesus Christ and his claims regarding faith and physical health. I further asked that they might begin praying with patients and open the door to discussion with patients on the correlation between spiritual and physical health.

By the time I finished the presentation, my throat was so swollen I could barely speak, and my voice so hoarse I was surprised they could understand what I was saying. The audience was so moved by my feeble efforts to finish they gave me a standing ovation, for which I was shocked. In retrospect it was foolish for me to be there, because I certainly must have contaminated the entire conference with an influenza virus. At least I knew

Cathy was praying for me, and within a few days I had recovered. I have no way of knowing how many attendees at the meeting developed the flu, but if anyone became sick, perhaps they applied some of the principles I tried to teach.